Th

The BBC microcomputer in science teaching

R. A. Sparkes

Hutchinson

London Melbourne Sydney Auckland Johannesburg

Hutchinson & Co. (Publishers) Ltd

An imprint of the Hutchinson Publishing Group

17-21 Conway Street, London W1P 6JD

Hutchinson Group (Australia) Pty Ltd
30-32 Cremorne Street, Richmond South, Victoria 3121
PO Box 151, Broadway, New South Wales 2007

Hutchinson Group (NZ) Ltd
32-34 View Road, PO Box 40-086, Glenfield, Auckland 10

Hutchinson Group (SA)(Pty) Ltd PO Box 337, Bergvlei 2012, South Africa

First published 1984

Printed and bound in Great Britain by
Anchor Brendon Ltd, Tiptree, Essex

British Library Cataloguing in Publication Data

Sparkes, R. A.
The BBC microcomputer in science teaching
1. Science — Computer assisted instruction
2. Science — Study and teaching
3. BBC microcomputer
I. Title
507'.8 Q181.A2

ISBN 0 09 154571 4

For Margaret

Acknowledgements

The BBC microcomputer, on which the programs in this book were written, belongs to my wife and I am grateful for the use of it (not to mention the television set too). Once again I thank Miss A. Hynes for producing the art work and I also acknowledge the support given by the publishers, especially Bob Osborne. My ideas changed radically (and often), yet they were always patient and able to supply advice and encouragement. I am especially grateful to teachers who attended in-service courses at St Andrew's College and were willing to try out my ideas and offer further suggestions.

However, none of these can share any blame for the errors and omissions that occur in this book, and I take full responsibility for them. I look forward to receiving comments from readers on how this book and the use of the BBC microcomputer in the areas I have discussed might be improved.

Once again most thanks are due to my wife, Margaret, for her encouragements and criticisms and for her patience and understanding. The development of this book and the ideas in it has been at the expense of both Margaret and the children. I can only hope that their sacrifice is found to be worthwhile.

The University of
Stirling.

Contents

Listed programs

The programs listed in the Appendix are given below. To allow them to be stored on disk each has also been given a shortened name to fulfil disk-name requirements.

Program 1	LOGIC GATES	(LGCGATE)	These three programs teach (or test practically) the principles of Boolean logic and show the use of a microcomputer in solving logic problems. They require a logic board connected to the user port, details of which are given in the text.
Program 1A	LOGIC TEST	(LGCTEST)	
Program 2	LOGIC TUTOR	(LGCTUT)	
Program 3	LOGIC MAKER	(LGCMKR)	
Program 4	6502 SIMULATION	(MICSIM)	teaches the instruction set and mnemonic codes of the 6502 microprocessor.
Program 5	STOPCLOCK	(STPCLK)	measures time intervals with a visual display of the elapsed time in large digits
Program 6	REACTION TIMER	(REACT)	measures reaction times.

The next four programs require a digital input connected to bits 0 or 1 of the user port.

Program 7	FAST TIMER	(FASTTMR)	measures time intervals in ten microsecond units.
Program 8	TSA METER	(TSA)	measures time, speed and acceleration.
Program 9	CONSERVATION OF MOMENTUM	(CONSMOM)	measures the speeds of two colliding trolleys, simultaneously if necessary.
Program 10	SPEED-TIME PLOTTER	(SPTPLOT)	plots a speed-time or distance-time graph.

The next two programs demonstrate the use of separate gates to control timing.

Program 11	PULSE TIMER	(PLSTMR)	measures the length of a square pulse.
Program 12	FREQUENCY METER	(FREQMTR)	measures pulse frequency.

Program 13	PROGRAMMABLE OSCILLATOR (PROGOSC)	provides alternating voltages with changeable waveforms and frequencies. This program needs a digital to analogue converter connected to the user port.
Program 14	CAPACITOR DISCHARGE (CAPDIS)	measures the voltage across a large capacitor as it discharges.
Program 15	FAST ADC (FASTADC)	takes rapid readings of input voltages using a special converter.
Program 16	DIGITAL MULTIMETER (DIGMULT)	displays voltage, current, power and resistance.
Program 17	CURRENT-VOLTAGE PLOTTER (IVPLOT)	automatically plots I-V characteristics.
Program 18	FOUR-CHANNEL CHART RECORDER (CHRTREC)	displays four channels of voltage input and scrolls horizontally.

The remaining programs do not need interfaces. Their use is described in Chapter 1 and they are referred to throughout the text as examples.

Program 19	MECHANICS DRILL	(MECHDRL)
Program 20	INTEGRATED SCIENCE TEST	(INSCTST)
Program 21	RADIOACTIVE DECAY	(RANDECY)
Program 22	SUM OF TWO DICE	(SUMDICE)
Program 23	STANDING WAVES	(STWAVES)
Program 24	WAVE SUPERPOSITION	(WAVESUP)
Program 25	WAVE REFLECTION	(WAVREFL)
Program 26	MOLECULAR MOTION	(MOLMOT)
Program 27	BROWNIAN MOTION	(BRWNMOT)
Program 28	GRAVITY	(GRAVITY)
Program 29	RESONANCE	(RSNANCE)
Program 30	PROJECTILES	(PROJECT)
Program 31	NEWTON	(NEWTON)
Program 32	RUTHERFORD	(RUTHFRD)
Program 33	MASTERMIND	(MSTRMND)
Program 34	ELEMENTS	(ELMENTS)

Introduction

This book is a BBC microcomputer version of my previous book *Microcomputers in Science Teaching,* which was written mainly for PET and Apple users. The differences between these machines and the BBC microcomputer are such that a major rewrite has been necessary. That previous book was also not helpful to those who wished to develop their own interfaces for using the microcomputer in the laboratory, so I have tried to remedy this. These chapters assume some knowledge of basic electronics such as that found in *Microelectronics* (Hutchinson, 1984). To allow this book to be self-contained, some of the relevant ideas in *Microelectronics* have been repeated here.

To some extent this book is also a sequel to *Microelectronics.* That book concluded that the most sensible way to introduce students to microelectronics is through programming a microcomputer to control the environment. Accordingly a large part of this book considers the use of the BBC microcomputer in analogue and digital measurement and control.

To reduce the overall amount of material, I have tried to exclude things that are described in the BBC microcomputer user guide and I assume that readers are well acquainted with that manual. Throughout that book the author has drawn attention to areas where 'Space simply does not permit an adequate explanation...'. While not claiming that my explanations are adequate, I have attempted to fill in the gaps in the user guide to allow BBC microcomputer owners to get even more out of their machines.

I have concentrated mostly on those applications of the BBC microcomputer that are particularly relevant to science teachers. I have interpreted this term pretty widely and there is a great deal to interest teachers of engineering science, CDT and mathematics too. Most examples are taken from physics, but the principles they demonstrate apply to all subjects. This area is one of very rapid development and new ways of doing things are constantly being found. For this reason I have emphasized the principles involved as well as providing specific examples. Thirty-eight programs are listed in the Appendix and these are referred to in the text as examples of the points being made. In addition many other listings are included in the text to illustrate particular ideas. Note that these examples (which are also available on disk for readers who wish to save time) are not 'idiot-proof', that is they have not been tested and protected against pressing the wrong keys or entering the wrong information etc.

My programs are mainly intended to help BBC microcomputer users to write their own programs. The listings are utilities that can be developed by teachers for their own purposes. There are those who decry this attitude saying that we can't expect teachers to become program writers. Unfortunately there is never enough money in education to pay for the programs that teachers want, which results in teachers having to write their own (or steal them from someone else). In any case program writing is well within the capabilities of the average science teacher (like learning to drive a car).

I often use the analogy of the motor car in this context. If you occasionally need to travel from one part of the country to another in reasonable comfort, you may take a taxi. This will be very expensive. Alternatively you may learn to drive the car yourself. This will take time initially and is only worthwhile if you expect to do a lot of travelling. Likewise, if you only expect to use the microcomputer on a few rare occasions, or if you want pupils to use it without supervision, then by all means pay the extra and get crash-proof programs. But if you intend to make considerable use of the microcomputer, it is better to learn programming for yourself. Then you will be able to take control. You will not be afraid if a program crashes because you will know how to recover it, you will be able to adapt an unsatisfactory program to your own specification and you will pay very much less for programs.

The effort in writing programs is less in getting them to work than in making them absolutely idiot-proof. I appreciate that programs designed for use by novices must have this protection built into them. If this is an important criterion for you, then you will be quite happy to pay for someone to create the program for you. But if you have the ability to write your own programs and therefore the ability to recover from a crash, you will not be so happy at having to pay extra for someone else's lack of competence. Also you will want the ability to stop programs, list them and alter them to your own requirements and commercial programs generally prevent this. One way of overcoming this 'protection' racket is by writing your own programs and making them available to others.

In support of this precept my programs are presented so that you will be able to modify them for your own applications. If they were locked up on a no-copy disk, the benefit that they could give would be more limited. I hope that anyone else making use of these programs will have the same attitude and will acknowledge authorship in the traditional way.

1 The new resource

'Where shall I begin, please your Majesty?'
(Lewis Carroll, *Alice's Adventures in Wonderland)*

One of the unfortunate results of the history of computing is that most people still regard it as a branch of mathematics. A common response to the call to learn programming is, 'I'm no good at maths'. This is a mistake, since there is no longer much relationship between mathematics and computing. For science teachers, the microcomputer is much more a new piece of educational technology than a super calculating machine. Its use is not confined to the mathematics department nor to a computing department. This chapter explores the possible applications of the microcomputer in science teaching.

To emphasize the difference between the traditional computer and its modern counterpart the new phrase 'information technology' has been invented. The modern microcomputer is mainly concerned with collecting, processing and presenting information. The machine should therefore appeal instantly to the teacher, whose task it is to disseminate information in its widest sense.

There are several aspects of such 'presentation'. First of all the microcomputer can be used to display a page of text on its television screen (or VDU). The information could also include a set of figures or a list of names in columns. Alternatively the information could be presented graphically (i.e. as a diagram or picture or graph) or by an animation or moving picture. This is where the video screen has an immediate advantage over the blackboard or OHP, since animation is not available on the latter. The microcomputer is thus a textbook, blackboard, slide projector and film loop all together in one instrument. It is not restricted to use by individuals, there are several ways in which it can be used with quite large groups. In this case the display is unlikely to be just text, because this cannot be read from a distance (although there are ways of displaying a few words at a time in large letters). More likely it is a picture or an animation that is being presented for all to see, but with the added advantage of interaction. At any stage during a demonstration the students can be asked to suggest how the parameters should be changed. A discussion can then take place as to the likely effects of this change upon the phenomenon being investigated. The changes may then be made to check on the predictions. The general name for this application is **electronic blackboard,** where the microcomputer is used by the teacher in front of the whole class.

The microcomputer is also a powerful tool for helping small groups of pupils. Until class sets of microcomputers become available, it is envisaged that this application will be confined to use by students in a stations laboratory (where there are a number of work-stations and the students move from one to the other). The microcomputer can thus be used by small groups for short periods of time within a lesson. Alternatively students might use the computer in a library or resource centre. I use the generic term **computer assisted learning** or **CAL** for this application.

At the other end of this spectrum the microcomputer can be used by one individual pupil working alone. The program being used might be simple drill and practice or a tutorial or the microcomputer might be controlling a complete programme of work, adjusting the level of presentation to the particular abilities of each individual pupil. One reason why microcomputers have suddenly become important is because they make the dream of individualized learning a reality. The difficulties of managing the workcards and the tests etc. that are needed in the self-paced learning situation are overcome if they are presented by the microcomputer. New material can be written on the screen for the student to read and answer questions about. If the student is correct, then some other material can be presented, but a wrong answer causes the microcomputer to behave differently, either by presenting the question again or by branching to a remedial teaching loop. It is this ability to react differently to different situations that makes the microcomputer more powerful than any other resource we have had before.

The interaction between the user and the microcomputer creates possibilities for monitoring the teaching process much more efficiently than hitherto. The process of instruction can be halted frequently to check that the student is still following. This is something that every teacher tries to do but cannot achieve in the conventional way for each individual student. Given these facilities, the microcomputer's role in programmed learning is obvious.

Scientists have an application of microcomputers that is peculiar to their discipline –its use as a powerful laboratory instrument. We have already reached the stage, where no physics laboratory is complete without a microcomputer and I think that this situation will soon apply in other areas. With suitable transducers and interfaces the computer is fast becoming the only equipment in some industrial laboratories. I do not think that this will happen in schools, but they do need to mirror the real world to some extent. The BBC microcomputer may be used to measure almost any physical quantity desired. At a rough estimate its use in this way can save up to a thousand pounds worth of alternative apparatus, as well as enabling some hitherto unmeasurable quantities (like acceleration) to be displayed. This is my own favourite use of the microcomputer and much of this book is devoted to it.

Inside every microcomputer is an incredibly powerful device called a **microprocessor.** By talking to this device, new horizons can be opened up, especially for animated diagrams and for using the microcomputer as a laboratory instrument. Because this is a new idea for most teachers it is presented in Chapter 6 as a microcomputer simulation and tutorial, providing a step by step approach to the principles of assembly language programming. This is intended not only to explain microprocessor instructions, but also to demonstrate the advantages of a computer simulation. Readers who follow this through might care to reflect on how this way of visually presenting a new topic could be transferred to teaching in other areas, for example, the operation of a nuclear power station or the electrics of a motor car.

Outside the classroom the microcomputer could take over the role of keeping records, in the same way that bigger computers have been doing in commerce for some time. As might be expected, a great deal of research and development has already been done in this area, and there is little point in any individual teacher doing it all again. There are several projects under way on the development of administration packages for schools and, before very long, these will become generally available. These will not only include student records, timetabling, equipment records, library loans, etc., but also there will be complete packages for marks processing and assessment. Even if no other part of the school is affected by microcomputers, the school office certainly will be.

Under this heading too I consider the use of a microcomputer as a wordprocessor or texteditor to be very exciting. Readers of my previous book *Microcomputers in Science Teaching* will note how parts of it have been used in this book too. It was a simple matter to call up the text of that book onto the screen, to select the parts required, alter them and save them once more on disk. There are several such wordprocessors available for the BBC microcomputer and their use more than repays their cost. Teachers who prepare their own worksheets will find that their productivity increases by a factor of three or four at least. There is an even bigger saving of time for one-fingered typists like me.

Let us now explore some of these ideas in more detail with particular examples to illustrate the principles discussed. Note that these examples (which are listed in the Appendix and are also available on disk for readers who wish to save time) are not thoroughly tested programmes, guaranteed to work with even the most stupid of users. They are examples only of the sort of things that can be done with microcomputers. Nevertheless they have been tried and they do work and provided the user has a moderate understanding of programming, they will produce no problems.

Specific examples

Testing

A common use of microcomputers in schools is testing. This means not so much the end-of-term examination as the routine question-and-answer sessions, with which teachers attempt to reinforce learning. Because time does not permit the conventional method to be used on an individual basis, not all children benefit from it. Indeed, the public nature of the responses often causes pupils to adopt strategies for avoiding an answer. If a child remains dumb for long enough, most teachers will direct the question elsewhere. The microcomputer can be viewed as a resource for handling question-and-answer sessions.

At the simplest level are numerical tests; the microcomputer is perfectly capable of setting its own arithmetic questions and working out the answers for itself. MECHANICS DRILL (program 19) illustrates this application. It would be relatively easy to adjust the number range and the difficulty of programs like this to suit the user. For practical purposes this program needs to be improved in several ways. Where is the power of the microcomputer being used? There are no diagrams or pictures or animations. INTEGRATED SCIENCE TEST (20) shows what can be done in this area. In this program the number of correct and wrong answers may be counted, so that a final score can be given. It is also useful to note which questions the student gets wrong, in case this reveals the source of the ignorance. A properly structured test would be written for

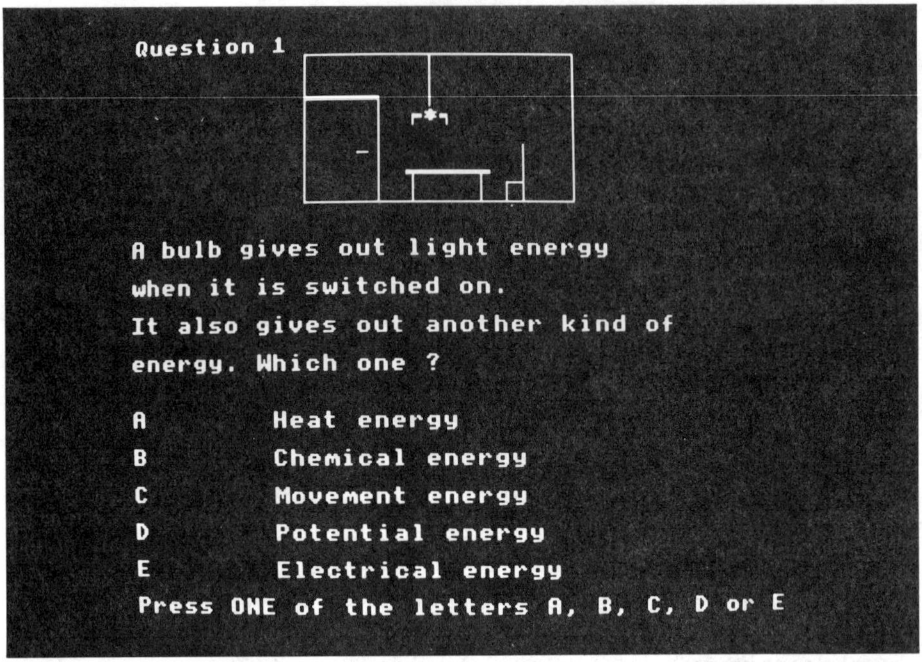

Plate 1 Integrated science test

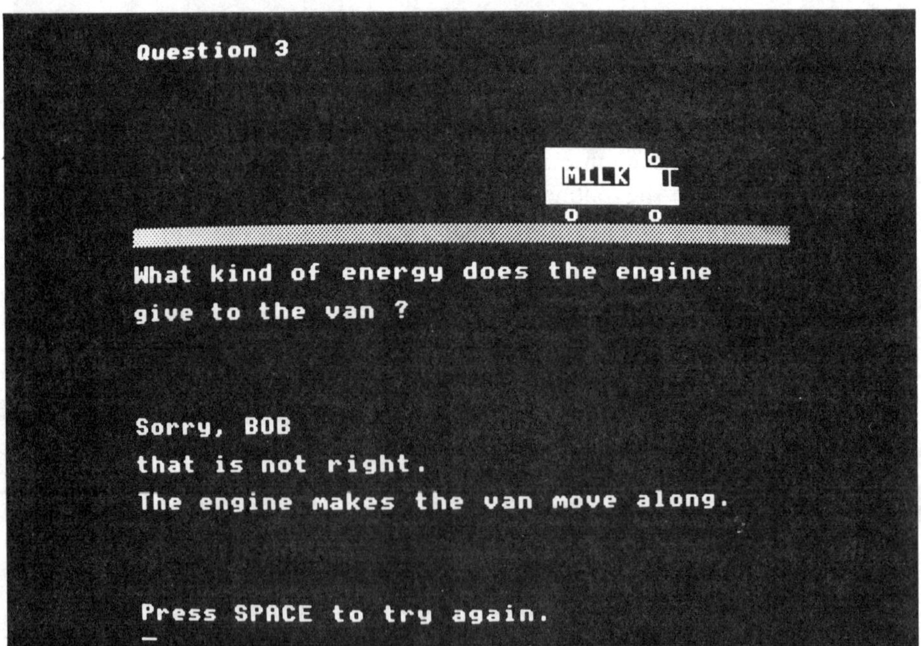

Plate 2 Remedial response for a wrong answer

this purpose anyway. A way of doing this can be seen in the score routines of INTEGRATED SCIENCE TEST.

A particularly powerful use of the microcomputer is to allow the student to ask for help, if the offered problem proves too difficult. This could be automatically given after, say, three attempts, or it could be available upon pressing key H. After the first few questions, it is a little wearisome to a student to be given exactly the same 'Well done!' response each time. No teacher would do this, so why should we accept a lower standard from the microcomputer? It is not difficult to create a whole range of responses in an array, and to pick one out at random. Also, thought should be given to more dramatic ways of responding. Arcade invaders leap about with delight, when they score a hit on the defenders, why can't the same graphics be used in education? As a suggestion FAST SCREEN TRANSFER (program 36) illustrates how this might be done by flashing words onto the screen in rapid succession. This could be incorporated into a test program to indicate whether the student has got the right or wrong answer. The most exciting thing about test examples presented via the microcomputer is that children tend to treat them more as a game. They aim to 'beat the computer' or to 'do better than last time'.

INTEGRATED SCIENCE TEST illustrates several of the basic principles of using multiple choice items. This program can be used as the framework for any other multiple choice test. The items are kept separate from the main program, which handles all keyboard inputs and scores etc. The question numbers, clues and correct responses are passed to procedures as parameters. Scoring is a separate procedure and the final

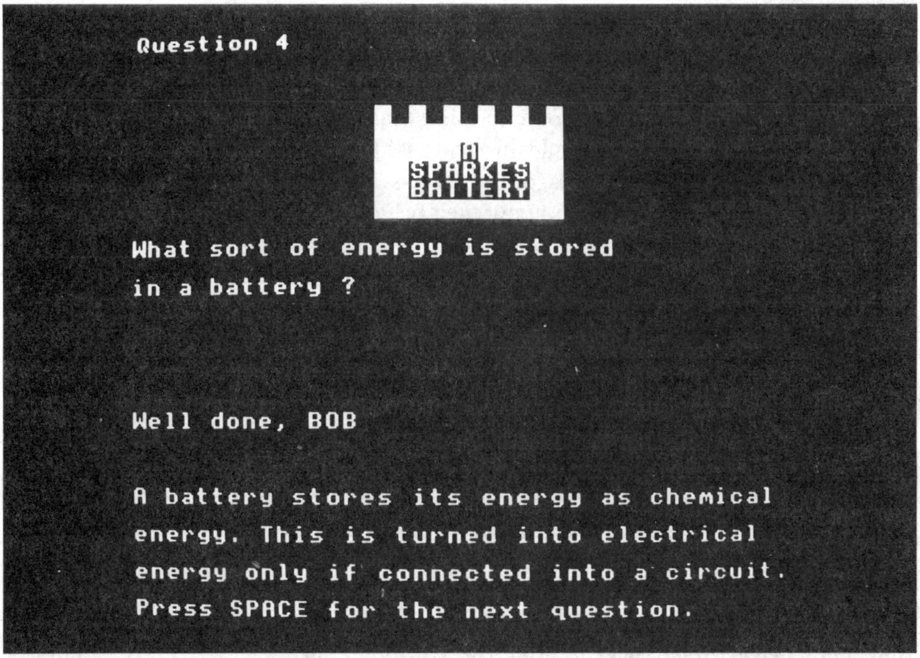

Plate 3 Reinforcement of correct response

presentation of the results is also self-contained. Note the way that graphics have been included with each item. These are not essential in all cases, but they do increase motivation. The longer test, from which these items were taken, was the one that made me realize the power of the microcomputer. Some children ran the test again and again to see if they could get full marks. I have never noticed this in a traditional school test.

This area is also known as drill-and-practice. The microcomputer is programmed to ask the questions and to monitor the responses. To do this there has to be some way for the user and the microcomputer to interact with the user, an aspect which is covered in the next chapter.

Simulations

Almost any phenomenon, model or experiment can be imitated or simulated by the computer. Some programs of this type give tables of numbers as results, while others give graphs or animations. GRAVITY (program 28) is an example of the former and the remaining simulations show the use of graphics.

Computer simulations are most useful where the real experiment is impossible (negative gravity?) or very difficult to perform satisfactorily (Millikan's experiment?) or not accessible (behaviour of an atomic pile?). I do not think that students should carry out computer simulations of experiments, where the practical experiment itself could be performed. A microcomputer could be used to demonstrate, for example, how to titrate an acid against an alkali. One could press keys to allow the acid to drip in and, with high resolution colour graphics, could produce a superb effect of the indicator changing colour. A meter could be displayed also to indicate the current pH as the acid is added. As an introduction only, this could be very useful for showing the student what steps were involved. The only objection to this would be if it replaced the actual experiment.

There is also another danger in simulation experiments, of implying that one is actually observing nature. Students may come to think that the characters moving around the screen are behaving just like molecules in a real gas. This cannot be true, because we have no notion of what the molecules of a real gas are actually doing. We can make observations and draw conclusions about their behaviour and then produce simulations that appear to produce the same behaviour. But that does not mean that the gas molecules are like the particles on the screen. The students are really being encouraged to 'discover' our model of the behaviour of the molecules, which is the reason why the simulation experiments must be integrated with experiments on the real world, so that our theories about its behaviour can be tested.

Programs 21 to 32 are straightforward simulations of physical events, some of which make use of machine code graphics to achieve the necessary speed. The calculations needed to keep 256 particles continuously moving at once are quite beyond the capabilities of BASIC. RADIOACTIVE DECAY (21), is a simulation of the decay of radioactive particles using the RND function of the BBC microcomputer. A graph of the number of nuclei remaining after each time interval is displayed. Each nucleus that decays emits a click, thus giving an audible record of the rate of decay at any instant. The aim of the simulation might be for students to discover about half-life from a series of runs, but a teacher might wish to use it for a different purpose instead. For example it could be used in comparison with CAPACITOR DISCHARGE (14) and students asked why the results are so similar from such different physical starting points. Alternatively it could be incorporated into a CAL package and the student instructed to make certain observations.

SUM OF TWO DICE (22) is another example of the use of the random number generator to simulate the shaking of two dice. The program adds the dice together and displays the number produced each time. This program illustrates the graphics capabilities of the BBC microcomputer in displaying a bar chart, while at the same time continuously updating it.

The next programs are simulations designed to get across ideas of the behaviour of waves. STANDING WAVES (23) shows what happens when two waves travelling in opposite directions interfere to produce standing waves. WAVE SUPERPOSITION (24) is designed to explain the relationships between speed, frequency and wavelength and also to demonstrate the nature of a transverse wave. The amplitude, frequency and relative phase between two waves may be altered and the production of beats between two waves of different frequency demonstrated. Classical interference between two waves that only differ in phase may also be shown.

The way that the microcomputer is used to obtain these effects is discussed in detail in Chapter 7. Basically they use machine code plotting or scrolling routines. Another application of the same technique is to keep a record of the positions of dots on the screen and so to move them around under the control of certain laws. In WAVE REFLECTION (25) this method is used to simulate the behaviour of water waves in a ripple tank, where the water waves are themselves imitating the behaviour of light waves as they meet a reflecting barrier.

The next program also uses this directed motion technique. Graphics characters are directed across the screen in straight lines, and they bounce off the walls simulating the behaviour of molecules. MOLECULAR MOTION (26) demonstrates what happens to gas molecules at different temperatures. Here a sound routine is used to demonstrate how the number of collisions with the walls of the container is dependent both upon the number of molecules and the temperature of the gas.

Similar routines in a high resolution mode enable the behaviour of smoke particles to be simulated. Pupils look at a Whitley Bay smoke cell through a microscope, but have no idea what they are supposed to see. BROWNIAN MOTION (27) directs their attention to the essentials so that they may then observe properly. No one is suggesting that the simulation should replace the practical experiment, it is only another weapon in the teacher's armoury.

Computer assisted learning

This area has many names depending upon whether it is emphasizing what the program is doing (instruction) or what the student is supposed to be doing (learning). I shall ignore the fine distinctions involved, while still using the general term or CAL, for short. The above discussion of drill-and-practice inevitably leads onto the use of the microcomputer for CAL. INTEGRATED SCIENCE TEST moves some way towards it, since that program replies to each response with a statement about why the chosen answer is correct or wrong. It is clearly possible to integrate such testing with the teaching of new material in the same way. The idea is to present the topic and then ask questions to establish whether the student understands. Then, if it becomes clear that the student does not understand, remedial action can be undertaken.

A program that does this is termed a **tutorial** and there are many in circulation. The most common are self-instructional tutorials in BASIC programming. Most students, particularly of those subjects which lend themselves to linear progression, such as mathematics and computing, find such tutorials useful. They may even prefer them to traditional classroom methods, because of the immediacy of the feedback and the fact that they can learn at their own pace. Programs like this are not difficult to write, but they should use the full range of interaction, reinforcement and, of course, graphics that is available. Several author languages, like PILOT, exist to aid writers of CAL programs, but these can be too restrictive. They were not developed with microcomputers in mind and may need special adaptation to allow an author to incorporate graphics or other special techniques.

There is, though, a great deal more to CAL than is implied above. To begin with, there is a clear distinction between teaching and telling. Too many of the self-teaching packages that have been published so far, fall into the latter category. What is involved in producing a good CAL package?

There are two broad categories of CAL programs, one of which favours a structured approach to learning and the other a more open-ended approach. The former is based on programmed learning theory, which may be summarized as follows:

1 The main objectives of the topic to be learned are specified, in terms of observable outcomes, as precisely as possible. Not 'the student should understand something about molecular weight', but specific, like 'given a list of chemical compounds and a table of the atomic masses of the elements, the student should be able to calculate the corresponding molecular masses for at least seven out of ten of them'.
2 The objectives should then be listed in hierarchical order, in the sense that each objective earlier in the list should not be dependent upon objectives that come later. For example, the following objective should be attained before the one stated above: 'given a list of chemical compounds, the student should be able to write out the corresponding chemical formulae for at least eight out of ten of them'.
3 The next step is to arrange the objectives into a learning sequence. Teachers tend to do this automatically, so they usually find no difficulty here. The difference with programmed learning is the attempt to ensure mastery of the earlier objectives before the later ones are tackled. One of the difficulties of traditional classroom teaching has been the insistence that all pupils should progress at the same rate. Thus pupils who had a particular learning difficulty, might never acquire later objectives, not because they were unable to, but because they had never quite mastered the earlier ones. This is why the objectives above are criterion referenced. Students do not just have to get higher marks than average, they actually have to attain the external standard set by the objectives.
4 The learning sequence is then turned into a series of lessons, using appropriate

teaching strategies for each objective. At certain stages throughout the sequence, tests have to be devised to see whether a student is ready to proceed to the next objective. These diagnostic tests are not stored up for the students' end-of-term grades, their purpose is to inform the student of his or her mastery of each particular objective.

5 Finally the package needs to be tested on a sample of students similar to those who will ultimately use it. Any or all of the preceding stages may have to be modified in the light of this experience.

A CAL package is thus not just something that any knowledgeable person can write down in an evening. Estimates vary as to the length of time needed, but a good average figure is that 100 hours of development time must be devoted to produce material to keep a student occupied for one hour. So an expert programmer could put a year's full-time work into a CAL package to keep a class occupied for one week! The failure of programmed learning in the past has not necessarily been that it doesn't work, but that there were not enough people around to write the packages. This position has not changed with the introduction of microcomputers. It requires a massive effort to produce good software.

Even then there are hardware problems to be overcome. With graphics and animations, a complete teaching package which could adapt its teaching to the individual needs of its students could not be run with a cassette system for program loading. A disk system is essential.

Should teachers, therefore, give up the whole idea of CAL? I do not think so, because it can never come unless there is a substantial number of teachers who have experience of it. But I think that this is a task for a properly funded team of writers, not individuals. Unfortunately the ease with which software can be copied is likely to deter commercial organizations from being interested.

Teachers, or better still a group of teachers, could begin by taking some topic that is particularly suited to a programmed learning approach; one that is linear in structure, will fit into the video text method of presentation and where it is easy to write the objectives. The commonest fault is to attempt too much, so that insufficient time is spent in ensuring the mastery of each component part. After writing it, several trial runs with students (and not just the school's computer addicts) should be made with the teacher in attendance. They should be challenged to 'crash the program' if they can. All problems discovered by them should be noted and rectified. Only then should it be placed on the market; it should not be the end users who have to debug the programs!

There is one powerful reason for not spending a great deal of effort at the moment on CAL (apart from the fact that few schools possess a class-full of microcomputers) and that is the technology is changing fast. Within a few years the video disk will be used to present the graphics, text, tests and other items that currently have to be put into a CAL program. In future the microcomputer will become much more of a manager, calling up from the disk the current lesson and also having previous lessons available for remedial review. With a single video disk holding the equivalent of several hundred floppy disks of information, CAL will no longer be a dream.

Discovery learning

The other way of using the microcomputer to teach is, in my opinion, much more exciting than CAL anyway. It is also less likely to be superceded when the video disk arrives. This is its use in open-ended investigation. Instead of the computer asking the student, the student interrogates the computer. Already several data-base programs exist (e.g. MICROQUERY) to allow students to obtain information by typing certain keywords into the computer. In biology this promises to be very useful since a student can then carry out a search without being forced into a particular direction by a CAL program. At a simpler level many programs can be developed that allow the student to determine what he or she would like to know.

Imagine that you wanted to teach a student about the properties of waves using a Nuffield-type ripple tank. This could be done by direct instruction, with the teacher pointing out the essential details. Or it could be left to the student to discover the principles for himself or herself. My experience is, however, that pupils cannot see the waves because they do not know what to look at. WAVE REFLECTION (25) strips away the inessentials and allows the pupil to concentrate on the features that are important. The student may alter the angle at which the waves strike the barrier and then see if the same results occur with the real waves. This approach does not teach directly, but it does point the student along a particular path. There is no guarantee that learning will take place. But all our experience indicates that if it does, then the student will not just have

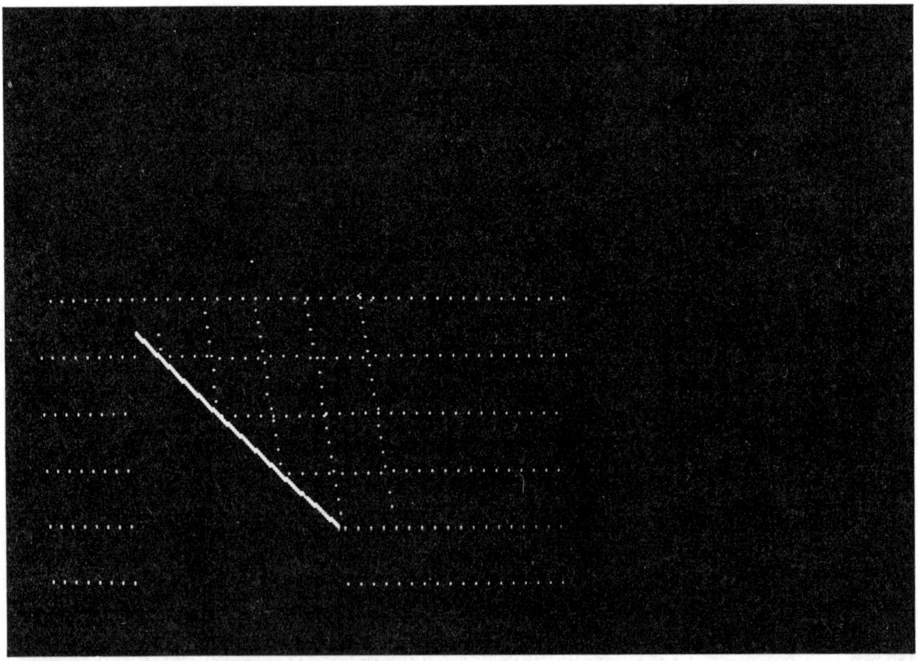

Plate 4 Plane wave reflection from a barrier

learned the facts, he or she will also have gained an insight that could transfer to other properties of waves too.

Most of the simulation programs listed were originally devised for this purpose. They illustrate the principles of discovery learning quite clearly, but their use is not restricted to it. The versatility of the microcomputer ensures that a program can be used for many different purposes, only a few minutes of adaptation being required.

Number-crunching

A glance at a list of available software reveals programs on Fourier transforms, least squares fit, linear circuit analysis, linear programming, numerical methods, integration by Simpson's rule and so on. The microcomputer is being used as a programmable calculator, with all the advantages of screen display and editing, error detection and program storage.

There are occasions in teaching when an equation needs to be solved many times and where the result is more important than the solution itself. One example is typing experimental data into a microcomputer to obtain an automatic straight-line plot. In this case the important aspect is the interpretation of the data, not the long process of plotting it out by hand. GRAVITY (28) gives another instance, calculating the height of a ball thrown vertically against gravity. It is the nature of the motion that is being investigated, not the solution of algebraic equations. Even here though a graph of the results would be even more meaningful.

Modelling

The equation of motion used in GRAVITY (28) is a mathematical model of the behaviour of a real stone falling. It is inaccurate because it ignores certain features such as friction, but it does give some insight into the nature of the motion. In Chapter 3 we shall discuss ways of making the model more real by using iterative methods. Physics and chemistry abound with such models and most students can understand an equation much better if they can see what happens to it when different parameters are changed. For example RESONANCE (29) uses a simple technique to plot the resonance curve for an LCR circuit. The student may observe the effect of altering the capacitance or the resistance of the circuit.

Usually in science we eliminate some of the variables in order to make the mathematical analysis of the phenomenon easier. The microcomputer allows some of these other variables to be considered. GRAVITY ignores the effects of friction, but this is not too difficult to incorporate provided the traditional technique of analysis is abandoned in favour of the iterative method. PROJECTILES (30) uses this technique to provide a more accurate picture of the motion of real stones being thrown through the air. The iterative method, which is discussed in detail in Chapter 3, is particularly powerful when dealing with central forces since the motion of satellites is obtained without recourse to integral calculus (a solution that Newton would himself have liked). In addition, the motion is not confined to the circular case, elliptical motion is no more difficult for the microcomputer than is the imaginary circular case. NEWTON (31) is a mathematical simulation of Newton's thought experiment on why the moon doesn't (or rather does) fall towards the earth. RUTHERFORD (32) is a variation of this program, that replaces the attractive force with a repulsive one to simulate the scattering of alpha particles by gold nuclei.

Games

If the recent fury that has developed over video games does not obscure the issue, there may be very little distinction between this section and discovery learning. It may be possible to distinguish between educational and recreational games, but I doubt if even that could be maintained. There are reports of slow learners who have been very greatly helped by 'space invaders', which, it is claimed, has increased their span of attention at other, more academic activities. Nevertheless, I do think that some games exercise the intellect more than others, and it is in these that I am interested.

A standard favourite amongst beginners to computing is learning to program MASTERMIND (33) or one of its forerunners like Bulls-and-Cows, which is easier because it uses numbers. This game requires a strategy for getting the answer and I should like to improve on it by encouraging the user to develop the correct strategy. I have seen even older children adopting a trial and error method rather than using the information in previous guesses as a basis for the next. If strategy training could be done here, would a

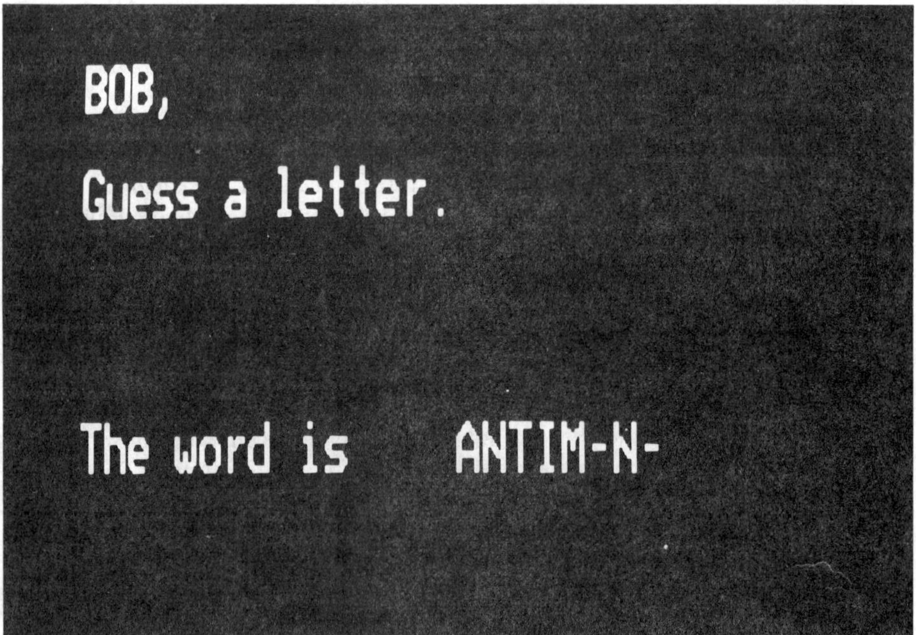

Plate 5 Guessing game – elements

similar system be possible to teach students a strategy for, say, solving equations? It is clearly an important potential development.

Guessing games are among the most popular and I have included my own quiz ELEMENTS (34). I am not sure that I agree with the traditional version of this game (HANGMAN) on educational grounds. Doesn't learning theory require us to reward success rather than punish failure? I have included my version to illustrate the technical ways of handling guessed inputs. The game is easily adaptable to other topics by changing the nature of the words (this one is based upon the elements) – this is easily done because they are all contained in data statements at the end. The program chooses the next word at random and, to avoid repetition, contains a routine to pick each word once only. Therefore, if you intend to adapt it to your own use, you will need to alter the maximum number of words available (103 in this case) wherever it appears in the program.

My favourite guessing game is called ANIMALS and several versions are available for the BBC microcomputer. The computer 'learns' the names of different animals and guesses the one that you are thinking about, by asking a series of yes/no questions.

```
Does your animal live in the sea?
Does your animal fly?
Does your animal have horns?
```

When the computer gets to the end of its branching search without success, it gives up and asks the user to say what the animal is and to suggest a suitable question for distinguishing it from the previously named animal. Thus the computer 'learns' a new animal. The form of the game usually given needs alteration, since it asks whether the animal in question has long ears before even discovering whether it is insect, bird, fish or mammal. As a strategy for guessing, it is therefore very poor. In the hands of a competent biologist the program could be invaluable for teaching about classification. In chemistry too, it could be used to develop an understanding of the periodic table.

Finally, I add another game that is designed solely to promote thinking; PILES (35). The user is provided with five piles each of four blocks, which may be yellow or blue. The aim is to build four piles of five blocks with the colours in any one pile being the same. Bricks are moved from the top of one pile to another by hitting the keys 1, 2, 3, 4 or 5 only. The number of attempts is recorded and revealed to the user as the game progresses. The program also illustrates the use of sound to reinforce the user's responses. The program was developed for use in primary schools from a version written by A. Wiltshire; I find it very good as a means of encouraging logical thinking in secondary schools too.

The new curriculum

I suppose it is inevitable that teachers first use microcomputers to enhance the current curriculum. At the drill-and-practice level it is even reinforcing current syllabuses. The discussion under Discovery learning above, though, does imply that the microcomputer will eventually alter both *how* and *what* we teach. The way forward has been shown by Papert and the LOGO language. With this, pupils can explore the world of space, shape, size and angle and discover the properties of language at the same time. Would it be possible in the same way to use a microcomputer as a context-free method of developing process skills in science?

It might be possible to invent different worlds with particular properties to be investigated. Gamov's *Mr Tompkins in Wonderland* describes worlds where the speed of light is reduced to ten m.p.h. and where Planck's constant is unity. The purpose of this is not just to provide entertaining science fiction, it is rather to explain the real world by exploring the properties of an imaginary one. I should like to see this done with a microcomputer. At a simple level GRAVITY and some of the simulation programs in Chapter 3 allow the acceleration due to gravity to be altered from its normal value of 9.81. Could this be extended to exploring situations where an inverse cube law of force existed? What would be the properties of visible light if our eyes could see into the X-ray or microwave regions? This exploratory use of microcomputers cuts across traditional subject boundaries, so that science, mathematics and art become united.

At the moment few schools possess teletext facilities allowing them access to the vast data-banks of information that exist. When these do arrive they will raise important questions regarding the content of school syllabuses. In particular we shall have to question the current emphasis upon knowledge. The 'Brain of Britain 1983' is the one who can remember the most information. What will be the value of this skill when we each have access to any desired information via a home computer terminal? A good memory will be as out-moded as the ability to extract square roots by pencil and paper (which I was taught). The skills we shall come to prize will be the processes of handling information. 'Brain of Britain 1999' will be the one who can solve problems.

Despite a generation or more of protagonists for process skills, most school science (and nearly all university physics) is still heavily content based. Students have little chance to apply their minds to new situations, they are too busy learning about old ones. Given the opportunity the microcomputer could be used to put us back on the right track. This is why I call this section 'The new curriculum'. I believe that the introduction of microcomputers will be far more revolutionary than any of us expect.

2 Programming techniques

> 'I'm afraid I don't quite understand,' said Alice.
> 'It gets easier farther on,' Humpty Dumpty replied.
>
> (Lewis Carroll, *Through the Looking Glass*)

This chapter is *not* an introduction to BASIC programming, I assume you can do that already. Instead, it attempts to explain some of the things that the BBC microcomputer user guide omits (because they are of specialist interest). It also looks at ways of improving tutorial programs with the use of graphics, proper display of text and methods of collecting and processing responses from the keyboard. Finally it looks at the whole process of developing an educational program.

Programming

Introduction

The heart (or perhaps it should be brain) of any computer is its **central processing unit (CPU).** A microcomputer like the BBC microcomputer is no exception, its CPU is the Rockwell 6502 microprocessor. Note that this word 'microprocessor' refers only to the CPU. People who use it in place of the word 'microcomputer' are fundamentally incorrect. The microprocessor is only one of many chips inside the microcomputer, even if it is the one which does all the work. Figure 2.1 shows a simple picture of the way that a microcomputer works.

For most purposes the **INPUT** to the microcomputer is via its keyboard. The **OUTPUT** is via the television screen or monitor (in computer jargon this is a VDU or visual display unit). One purpose of this book is to show you how to make use of other forms of INPUT and OUTPUT.

The microprocessor is a programmable device. There are two kinds of program that control the microprocessor, the **resident** program and the **user** program. The same 6502 microprocessor is used in the Apple, the PET, the VIC and the Atom as well as in the BBC microcomputer. These machines all behave in different ways because they have different operating systems which tell the microprocessor how to read the keyboard, where to print characters on the screen and so forth.

A programmer can write different application programs for the microcomputer to execute. For example, one program can be written to draw pictures on the video screen, another can search through a list of numbers for the smallest value. This user program will not remain in the machine after it has been switched off (it is said to be **volatile**). Every time that the microcomputer is switched on, a new user program must be placed in its program memory. This can, of course, be entered from the keyboard or loaded from disk

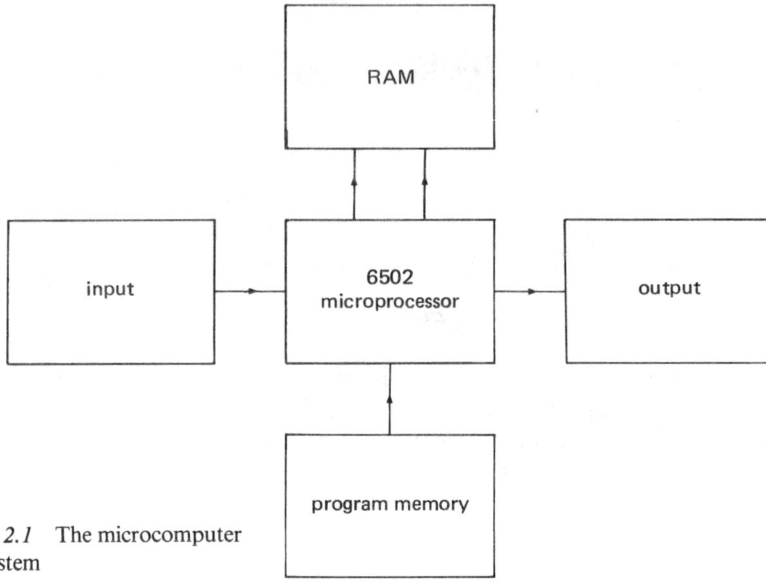

Figure 2.1 The microcomputer as a system

or cassette tape. To allow the microcomputer to store different programs, the memory for user programs is alterable. It is called **RAM** (which stands for **random access memory**).

To make it easier to produce such programs, they are often written in the language called BASIC. The microprocessor does not understand BASIC, it is a digital device and only 'understands' digital signals.

Information can only be sent to the microprocessor as a set of HIGH and LOW voltage levels. The 6502 microprocessor has eight lines for this information and it reads all eight lines at once. From our point of view these eight lines can be considered to be a binary number. (Note, however, that the microprocessor does not understand binary any more than it understands BASIC.) With eight lines there are 256 possible binary numbers (in the range 0000 0000 to 1111 1111) and any information received by the microprocessor must be one of these numbers. Each digit of this binary number (called a **bit**) is either a 0 or a 1. To make it easier for us, we usually convert these binary numbers into decimals using the following values for each bit position:

Binary	Decimal
0000 0000	0
0000 0001	1
0000 0010	2
0000 0100	4
0000 1000	8
0001 0000	16
0010 0000	32
0100 0000	64
1000 0000	128

The binary number 0110 0011 is equivalent to

0 + 64 + 32 + 0 + 0 + 0 + 2 + 1, or 99 in decimal

The whole set of eight bits is called a **byte.** One measure of the power of a computer is the number of bytes of information that it can store. The BBC microcomputer model A can store about 16 000 bytes and the model B about 32 000. It might seem that having only eight bits to a byte is very limiting, if we can only give the microprocessor 256 different pieces of information. However there are only seventy keys on a typewriter keyboard, yet how many different books can be written? It is clearly the sequence of the instructions given to the microprocessor that is important.

Machine language

One way of programming the microprocessor would be to give it sequences of binary numbers via eight switches. A separate switch could be used to tell the microprocessor when the next coded instruction was ready. This is obviously very slow and many mistakes might be made. (It was the way that the early computers were programmed.)

A better way would be to write all the binary numbers into the memory beforehand. The microprocessor could then fetch each one in turn and execute it. It would be better still if we could type in these numbers from the keyboard. This is the purpose of a **machine language monitor.** (The word 'monitor' here has no connection with the television monitor.) The BBC microcomputer does not possess a machine language monitor, since it has an even better method of entering instructions. Older microcomputers, like the PET and the Apple have machine language monitors as part of their resident program.

Assembly language

Using a machine language monitor is still slow, laborious and very prone to mistakes. The BBC microcomputer allows the programmer to type in instructions for the microprocessor in a special **assembly** language. For example, the instruction to the microprocessor to return from a subroutine is 0110 0000 in binary and RTS in assembly language. The latter is obviously easier to remember.

The BBC microcomputer's resident program contains an **assembler** which takes each line of an assembly language program and turns it into the correct binary number for the microprocessor to execute. It is a very powerful tool for a programmer especially when the BBC microcomputer is being used for measurement or control. Assembly language programming is the subject of Chapter 7 of this book.

BASIC

Even assembly language is not simple, so **high-level** languages have been developed. BASIC is one of these. The BASIC instruction to return from a subroutine is RETURN, which is even easier to remember. The microcomputer needs a special program, called the BASIC **interpreter,** to turn BASIC statements into the binary numbers needed by the microprocessor. This interpreter also contains error checking, so that errors in programming give the message 'mistake' to the programmer. BASIC is so very easy (by comparison with the other methods) that only a fanatic would use assembly language unnecessarily. BASIC programs are used wherever possible throughout this book. For certain purposes, however, like rapid measurements, assembly language programs are necessary and Chapter 8 of this book is devoted to this topic.

The resident program

The operating system, the assembler and the BASIC interpreter are all part of the resident program in the BBC microcomputer. Since this must always be there when the machine is switched on, it is **non-volatile,** and is written in **ROM (read-only memory).** ROM cannot be changed, but it has the advantage of not disappearing when the machine is switched off. Because it has to do so much, there is quite a lot of it in the BBC microcomputer, over 30 000 bytes. Some of this is useful to us even when we are not using BASIC. Also, as we shall see later, it is quite possible to write machine language programs to make the BBC microcomputer behave in different ways. You could even write your own operating system (and make the BBC microcomputer behave like a PET!). The advantage of machine language is the extra power it gives to the user.

Hexadecimal notation

In BASIC most users are unaware of binary, but when we start to talk to the microprocessor it is not possible to avoid it altogether. But what are we to make of a binary number like 1110 0110 1010 0111? Even copying it down might produce errors. We use a shorthand system called hexadecimal coding. Each set of four bits (half a byte is called a nybble) is represented by a code according to the following table:

Decimal	Binary	Hexadecimal
0	0000	0
1	0001	1
2	0010	2
3	0011	3
4	0100	4
5	0101	5
6	0110	6
7	0111	7
8	1000	8
9	1001	9
10	1010	A
11	1011	B
12	1100	C
13	1101	D
14	1110	E
15	1111	F

The sixteen-bit number 1111 1100 0000 0001 is thus written as FC01. To show that it is a hexadecimal number, BBC BASIC uses the & sign, so the number becomes &FC01. The addresses used in the BBC microcomputer have sixteen bits giving a total of 65 536 different locations (from &0000 to &FFFF). The contents or data in any location are eight-bit bytes with 256 possible different values (from &00 to &FF). Converting such numbers to and from decimal is easily accomplished.

PRINT &FC01 produces the decimal number 64513

PRINT ~ 32768 produces the hexadecimal number 8000

Talking directly to the memory

BASIC allows the user to be unaware of how the microcomputer works. This is usually advantageous, but occasionally better results are obtained if the peculiar characteristics of the machine are exploited to the full. Usually this prevents a program from being transportable to a different microcomputer, but this is not in itself a sufficient excuse for avoiding it. After all, each new microcomputer soon has its own specific version of 'Invaders' written for it and these are totally machine specific. Graphics are a particular example of the advantages of machine dependent programming, so a little time will be devoted to looking at BBC graphics from the microcomputer's viewpoint.

The BBC microcomputer memory contains 65 536 locations each with its own address. The contents of any address (for example 65535) can be seen with the BASIC statement PRINT ?65535. The same can be done by writing the address in hexadecimal PRINT ?&FFFF.

New data can be sent to a particular memory location with the statement:

LET ?65535 = 0 (or ?65535 = 0, since 'LET' is optional).

In hexadecimal notation this becomes LET ?&FFFF = 0.

With this particular address there will be no effect, &FFFF is in ROM and its contents cannot be changed like this. Only RAM can be altered in this way. However, if you start changing RAM indiscriminately, you may upset the operating system of the microcomputer. Certain parts of RAM are reserved by the machine for its own use. If you change these the BBC microcomputer may get lost inside itself. The screen may 'freeze' or go blank and the microcomputer may refuse to respond to the keyboard. Even the BREAK key may produce the situation where everything appears normal, but unexplained error messages appear. On listing your program you find that it is now a 'bad program' or that someone has written rubbish over parts of it.

None of this causes any permanent damage to the microcomputer. In computer jargon you have caused a **crash.** The remedy is very simple. Switch off the microcomputer, wait a few seconds and then switch on again. The proper operating system will be restored and all will be well. The only casualty will be that your program has disappeared. This is your own fault for not obeying the maxim:

ALWAYS SAVE A PROGRAM BEFORE YOU RUN IT

This is particularly sound advice when running machine code programs, when writing directly to the memory or when external devices are connected to the microcomputer.

One very useful place to write is the screen memory. Certain parts of the memory hold the information that is displayed on the screen. This RAM can be read and written to without any fear of disaster. It also has the advantage that you can see what happens to the location. Let us try this now.

This investigation is designed for MODE 4, hence type MODE 4 and press RETURN. The screen will go blank. Each dot on the screen is now the visible representation of a particular bit in the screen memory and can be turned on or off directly. For example, type

```
LET ?30000=1
```

A single dot should appear approximately in the middle of the screen, because bit 0 of memory location 30000 has been turned on. Try

```
LET ?30000=16
```

to get a different dot. A good investigation now is to discover the positions of the dots corresponding to each bit. Try this program:

```
10 FOR i = 0 TO 255
20 LET ?30000=i
30 FOR t=1 TO 1000:NEXT t
40 NEXT i
```

Line 30 is a delay to slow everything down. You should observe that combinations of the numbers 1, 2, 4, 8, 16, 32, 64 and 128 give different combinations of dots. In particular, 255 switches on all the bits and produces a line.

Now try different addresses, such as

```
LET ?30001=255 or
LET ?30010=255
```

To find out where the different memory addresses are located on the screen, run this program:

```
10 FOR i = 32767 TO 22528 STEP -1
20 LET ?i=255
30 FOR T=1 TO 50:NEXT T
40 NEXT i
```

You will soon discover one fact: the screen positions are not contiguous. That is, the end of one line is not followed immediately by the start of the next. Each block of eight contiguous bytes is stacked vertically and is next to the following set of eight bytes. This makes it more difficult to address the screen directly, but still far easier than with the APPLE or most other microcomputers.

BBC health warning!

The BBC microcomputer user guide is full of dire warnings about the evil effects of writing directly to the memory. There is good reason for this: The BBC machine is expandable – a number of second processors and other accessories is to be made available in the future. The manufacturers clearly wish to preserve this expandability and programs that write directly to the memory do not allow this to happen. The user guide explains quite clearly (to those with the background knowledge) how programs should be written, using the special OS calls that are provided. Some use of these is made in Chapter 7.

I have only one objection to this advice; when written in this way my programs do not work! Using the OS calls slows down machine code graphics by a factor of a hundred and makes fast data acquisition impossible. In the future when all the extras for the BBC microcomputer are available, I may be able to revise this view (and re-write this book) but for the moment there is still no other way to do many of the things I describe. The consequences of this position are that some programs will need to be re-written in the future. I regard this as a small price to pay for having access to these programs now. In any case I do not think that much re-writing will be necessary. I believe it will be quite feasible to place a machine code routing in the memory of the main processor, which can be called by a program in the second processor, and which can pass parameters back to that program using the proper OS calls. In this way we shall get the best of both worlds.

It is gratifying to know that I am not alone in this view. The games programs published by Acornsoft rely heavily upon direct addressing for their sophisticated graphics. If theirs is the standard that science programs have to compete against for pupils' attention, then we had all better learn machine code programming!

BBC microcomputer graphics

There are two different ways of producing pictures on the video screen, which are exemplified by MODE 4 and MODE 7 (the teletext mode). MODE 4 has a high resolution screen, meaning that any of its 81 920 dots (called **pixels**) can be individually switched on or off. We saw above how this can be done. The method is identical to that which will be used in Chapter 4 to switch LEDs on and off. You can imagine the TV screen as a matrix of pixels each connected to a different memory location. Each bit at each address controls a single pixel. Any combination of dots can be produced anywhere on the screen by turning on the appropriate bits. You could theoretically paint a complete picture by specifying each individual dot but in practice this is time consuming and impracticable.

The normal graphics commands of BBC BASIC are sufficiently fast for most purposes, indeed they are its most valuable asset for creating pictures and animations. Although graphics characters are not available, they can be created by the programmer. It is possible to define any desired shape by specifying which pixels of an eight by eight matrix should be on and which should be off. For example, a diamond shape could be defined as follows:

```
VDU23,250,24,60,126,255,255,126,60,24
```

It is given an identifying number (250 in this example) so that diamonds can be placed on the screen at the point (x,y) with the statement PRINT TAB(x,y);CHR$250. By varying the x and y values the character can be made to move around the screen at will. By creating two or three different versions of the same character, for example a man in different walking positions, very lifelike animations are possible. The techniques of drawing pictures with user-defined graphics are well described in the user guide and INTEGRATED SCIENCE TEST has been specifically designed to illustrate the different methods that can be used. Briefly, these are as follows. Once a graphics character has been defined (or is already defined in MODE 7) it can be placed on the screen with PRINT CHR$250 or whatever. If the picture to be drawn is at all large though, this technique consumes far too much memory (four bytes per character since CHR$ is stored as a single token). Some saving can be made by defining string variables thus, LET A$ = CHR$240 or LET fly$ = CHR$250 + CHR$8 + CHR$240. For large pictures it may be easier to store all the picture codes in a set of DATA statements, calling up each one in turn and placing it on the screen. This usually involves putting blank characters in too wherever they are needed, so there is rarely any saving of memory with this technique. All these methods are illustrated in INTEGRATED SCIENCE TEST.

Another technique is to redefine certain rarely-used symbols like 'q' and '+'. Once done, this allows a picture to be drawn with the actual graphics characters themselves so that it is easier to see which ones to use and where to put them. Listing the program on a printer produces the original symbol rather than the new graphics character and this makes it easier for someone reading thc program to type it into his or her machine. Inspect the listings for LOGIC TUTOR (3) or 6502 SIMULATION (4) to see how this is done in practice. In MODE 7 the following technique is recommended. Each numeric code normally represents an alphanumeric symbol, for example CHR$170 is the *-character. If this is preceded by a graphics conversion code, say CHR$151, then CHR$170 becomes a particular graphics character instead. So a whole picture can be drawn with the 'normal' symbol, which becomes the corresponding graphics character when the program is run. Look at the way that the V, I and W symbols are made in DIGITAL MULTIMETER (16) to see this technique in operation.

Another use of the high resolution screen is for drawing graphs with the MOVE, DRAW and PLOT functions. This is described in detail in the next chapter. These commands are sufficiently fast for most purposes, except for making waves. For this it is necessary to create a machine code routine (as described in Chapter 7), but this is complicated and not easy to understand.

Teletext graphics

The other method of producing pictures (called chunky graphics) is used in the teletext mode. Some of the possible characters that can be printed on the screen are shapes, called the graphics characters. A picture can be made up from different combinations of these shapes. The simplest way to use these is to treat them like letters in the PRINT statement, so building pictures rather than words. Chapter 28 of the user guide describes the process very well.

Another possible way of using chunky graphics characters is to write them individually onto the screen by number. The teletext screen is memory mapped as follows:

	column no. 0.	39
Row 0	address 31744	31783
Row 24	address 32704	32743

which is 1000 positions on a 40 by 25 grid. Note that this is only true immediately after a CLS or MODE 7 has been executed. After the screen has 'scrolled' the memory locations are in different places on the screen.

Each position occupies 64 pixels arranged in an eight by eight block. The character displayed at any position is defined by the contents of a single byte that controls each position. This is why the teletext screen needs only an eighth of the memory requirements of MODE 4. Since each byte can have any of 256 values, there ought to be 256 different characters that can be displayed at any one position (one of which is the 'blank' character, number 32). In practice some of the codes are repeated for the same character and some are control codes to change the colour or format of the succeeding characters. Reference should be made to the user guide for details of what each code does. What the guide does not say, is that these codes can be written directly onto the screen. There is no advantage of this in BASIC, but in machine code this technique produces very good animations. To try this, type

```
MODE 7
?32000=42
```

which, will place the *-character somewhere near the middle of the screen. Investigate this by writing other characters to different parts of the screen.

The teletext method is good for animations, because it is then quite easy to remove the *-character by overprinting it with a blank (?32000=32) and to place it in the adjacent position (?32001=42). Carried out at speed, this gives the appearance of continuous motion and is of great use for simulating objects in motion. Unfortunately, if there are more than just a few objects, BASIC cannot perform this process fast enough and machine language becomes essential.

Motion

To make the *-character move across the top of the screen, it must be written into each successive memory location in turn, and then erased again after a short delay to give it time to be observed. The *-character has the value 42 and the blank has the value 32.

```
 5 MODE 7
10 FOR X = 31744 TO 31783
20 ?X=42:REM PLACE * ON SCREEN
30 FOR T = 1 TO 100:NEXT:REM DELAY
40 ?X=32:REM ERASE *
50 NEXT X
```

To move the character vertically 40 must be added to or subtracted from the current position.

```
 5 MODE 7
10 FOR X = 31744 TO 32704 STEP 40
20 ?X=42:REM PLACE * ON SCREEN
30 FOR T = 1 TO 100:NEXT:REM DELAY
40 ?X=32:REM ERASE *
```

```
 50  NEXT X
 60  FOR X = 32704 TO 31744 STEP -40
 70  ?X=42:REM PLACE * ON SCREEN
 80  FOR T = 1 TO 100:NEXT:REM DELAY
 90  ?X=32:REM ERASE *
100  NEXT X
```

General motion is achieved with the following numbers.

Value	Direction
1	east
41	south-east
40	south
39	south-west
-1	west
-41	north-west
-40	north
-39	north-east

```
  5  MODE 7
 10  FOR X = 31744 TO 32728 STEP 41
 20  ?X=42:REM PLACE * ON SCREEN
 30  FOR T = 1 TO 100:NEXT:REM DELAY
 40  ?X=32:REM ERASE *
 50  NEXT X
 60  FOR X = 32728 TO 31744 STEP -41
 70  ?X=42:REM PLACE * ON SCREEN
 80  FOR T = 1 TO 100:NEXT:REM DELAY
 90  ?X=32:REM ERASE *
100  NEXT X
```

More usually it is small pictures that are moved around the screen in this way (for example the piston in the cylinder of a motor car). Low resolution pictures can be moved about in the same way as defined characters on the high resolution screen. The direct method of screen addressing can also be used, although it has no advantages in BASIC. The technique is to use two tables, one to hold the character and the other to hold the relative place for that character. This will be illustrated with a moving engine. This program also shows how the teletext screen achieves its graphics characters with a set of CHR$(151) characters down the left of the screen. The real advantage of this technique will become apparent later.

Engine

```
10  MODE7
20  REM SET UP SCREEN FOR GRAPHICS
30  CLS
40  FOR i=31744 TO 32703 STEP 40
```

```
50  ?i=151
60  NEXT i
90  REM MOVE ENGINE
100 FOR offset = &7CC9 TO &7CE9
110 RESTORE
120 FOR i=1 TO 35
130 READ position
150 READ character
160 ?(position+offset) = character
170 NEXT i
180 NEXT offset
190 END
200 DATA 0,32,1,252,2,252,3,32,4,32,5,32,6,32
210 DATA 40,32,41,234,42,255,43,240,44,240,45,240,46,244
220 DATA 80,32,81,234,82,255,83,255,84,255,85,255,86,255
230 DATA 120,32,121,250,122,255,123,255,124,255,125,255,126,255
240 DATA 160,32,161,32,162,79,163,32,164,32,165,79,166,32
```

The position of each character is specified relative to its top left corner. This top left corner is moved across the screen with the variable offset. To avoid leaving parts of the engine behind, its trailing edge is filled with blank characters (32). The picture can be moved in any direction, for example upwards, by adding –40 to the next offset each time, although in this case it might be necessary to surround the whole picture with blanks. The result is most unsatisfactory in BASIC. The point of doing it at all is to demonstrate the principle. When we return to do the same thing in machine code, we shall obtain a much more pleasing result.

Interaction

The most usual means of communication from the microcomputer to the user is the display. In this there are numerous pitfalls for those writing their own programs, which will now be described.

The display of text

The statement PRINT 'PARIS IS THE CAPITAL OF FRANCE'. is probably the most easily understood of all BASIC statements. The sentence is just written out on the video screen of the microcomputer. It is so easy to use, that some programmers fail to give any attention to the result.

The use of capitals (upper case) makes for difficult reading at the best of times, and if the programmer does not use double-spacing either, it is doubly difficult to read. With lower case letters and the use of double-spacing the result is more pleasant. The amount of text presented also needs to be adjusted to the level of the user: secondary pupils particularly merely scan the text without reading it properly. Later they complain that they 'don't know what to do!'.

VERTICAL HEIGHT

Acceleration	Speed	Height	Time
-10.00	100.00	0.00	0.00
-10.00	90.00	95.00	1.00
-10.00	80.00	180.00	2.00
-10.00	70.00	255.00	3.00
-10.00	60.00	320.00	4.00
-10.00	50.00	375.00	5.00
-10.00	40.00	420.00	6.00
-10.00	30.00	455.00	7.00
-10.00	20.00	480.00	8.00
-10.00	10.00	495.00	9.00
-10.00	0.00	500.00	10.00
-10.00	-10.00	495.00	11.00
-10.00	-20.00	480.00	12.00
-10.00	-30.00	455.00	13.00
-10.00	-40.00	420.00	14.00
-10.00	-50.00	375.00	15.00
-10.00	-60.00	320.00	16.00
-10.00	-70.00	255.00	17.00
-10.00	-80.00	180.00	18.00
-10.00	-90.00	95.00	19.00
-10.00	-100.00	0.00	20.00

>_

Plate 6 Motion against gravity showing tabulation

An automatic line-feed occurs when there are forty characters in a line. The forty-first character appears on the next line and the crime of wrap-around is committed. There is no excuse for this, it simply requires the programmer to read what the program prints with a critical eye and not accept inferior presentation. If the same things were done on paper, they would be glaringly obvious. BBC BASIC has the ability to display figures in neat columns, so there is no excuse for not doing so (Plate 6). This is described in the user guide.

In the days of tele-typewriter output there was no way to prevent text from scrolling up from the bottom. Part-sentences remained at the top of the screen, and these were most distracting. There is no need to continue with this practice today. The programmer should clear the screen before each new page of text. Also less text should be displayed at one time, in which case the student will need to indicate when a new page of text is to be displayed. This is described later.

Input from the keyboard

Some published programs limit interaction to 'press SPACE' at the foot of each page of video text. This is a misuse of a powerful machine, especially if the opportunity to return to a previous page is denied. The microcomputer is more than an electronic page-turner and its facility for interaction should be fully utilized. At the highest level an interactive program could determine the level of understanding attained by its users and adjust the presentation to suit. At the lower levels the interaction will probably be confined to responding to questions.

There are several ways of managing the response situation. The simplest is via the INPUT statement. This needs careful handling, since the pupil can easily enter the wrong information by pressing the wrong keys or sit in vain while the microcomputer waits for the RETURN key to be pressed. Full instructions need to be given, especially to first time users. The first INPUT in a program might be to get the student to enter his or her own name, so that the microcomputer can appear more personal. Some instructions such as the following need to be displayed, not only on the screen itself, but also on any accompanying documentation.

> Hello!
>
> I want to learn your name.
>
> Please type your first name on the keyboard.
>
> If you make a mistake, you can rub it out with the DELETE key.
>
> This key is near the bottom-right corner of the keyboard.
>
> When you have typed in your name correctly, press the key marked RETURN.
>
> Then I will know you have finished.
>
> Begin typing now....

Note the double-spacing between paragraphs, the use of lower case text and the use of capitals for emphasis. Also as mentioned above, the text should be preceded by CLS (screen clear).

The BASIC program to PRINT this text would be followed by the INPUT statement. Since a string response is required, this must be INPUT A$. The student, who presses RETURN before entering anything, returns the empty string, which could be detected if it is important. (Often experienced users will be too impatient to type their name and will wish merely to press RETURN anyway; they should be allowed to do so.)

A$ = GET$ retrieves a single key entry, which may be any character on the keyboard. Whole words can be entered with GET$, one letter at a time, and the word can be assembled from these letters. This avoids the problems of having to use the RETURN key, but the possibility of erasing an error is then removed also. This facility can be restored with yet more lines of programming and MASTERMIND illustrates the technique for doing this.

A$ = GET$ causes the program to halt until something on the keyboard is pressed. Keyboard entries are, however, stored in a buffer and there may be entries in this buffer from previous keypresses. Novice users particularly, press keys very firmly and the BBC microcomputer then uses its auto-repeat facility. Spurious responses get stored and produce peculiar results later. There are ways round this problem. First, the buffer can be cleared immediately before the A$ = GET$ statement with *FX15,1. Secondly, the auto-repeat facility can be turned off completely with *FX11,0. It is recommended that both of these techniques be adopted. A$ = GET$ is most useful for accepting single letter inputs, such as A, B, C or D in response to a multiple choice item, or the inevitable 'press SPACE' at the end of a page.

```
L$ = INKEY$(800)
```

produces a delay of several seconds and may be used to pause to give a user time to read the text. While this is adequate for single words or sentences, readers differ so markedly in their speed that no common time can be fixed for them all. The alternative technique requests the student to 'Hit a key' or better to 'Press SPACE to continue'. The SPACE can be detected with the BASIC statements

```
100 IF INKEY$(0)<>" " THEN 100
```

or

```
100 REPEAT UNTIL GET$=" "
```

This has the advantage that pressing a different key has no effect. Consecutive pages of text can be turned by alternating between 'Press SPACE' and 'Press RETURN', this latter being detected by

```
100 REPEAT UNTIL GET$=CHR$(13)
```

There is then no danger that a ham-fisted pupil will rest a finger on a key for so long that pages flash on and off the screen in rapid succession. A conscious action is required every time.

A common use of A$ = GET$ is to select from a menu. The user is offered several alternatives and invited to choose one. A typical menu in a tutorial might look like this:

```
You are correct, the shutter speed must be as fast as possible, i.e.
1/1000th of a second.
What would you like to do now?
1  Try another problem on shutter speeds?
2  Try a problem on apertures?
3  Go on to study film speeds?
4  Finish the lesson for now?
Press one of these numbers to make your choice.
```

```
2540 LET A$=GET$
```

waits for a keypress and returns with its key 'face value'. The desired response can then be inspected with

```
2550  IF A$="1" THEN 5000:REM Next problem
2560  IF A$="2" THEN 6000:REM New problem set
2570  IF A$="3" THEN 8000:REM Next lesson
2580  IF A$="4" THEN 9000:REM Finish
2590  GOTO 2540 :REM Incorrect response
```

If the user has accidently pressed SHIFT-LOCK, then pressing keys 1 to 4 apparently has no effect, since A$ will return with the shifted character. It may be necessary then to convert the characters to ASCII code (X = ASC(A$)) or use X = GET and manipulate the result.

```
2545  IF ASC(A$)<48 THEN A$=CHR$(ASC(A$)+16)
```

converts the shifted symbols of the top row to their corresponding numeric character.

Similar problems occur if the CAPS-LOCK or SHIFT-LOCK conditions are (or are not) in operation and the program expects an alphabetic key:

```
100 REPEAT
110          A$ = GET$
120 UNTIL INSTR ("ABCD abcd", A$<>0
```

Possible upper case entries can also be converted to lower case with

```
IF ASC(A$)<97 THEN A$=CHR$(ASC(A$)+32)
```

It may sometimes be necessary to impose a time limit on a pupil. If the pupil has failed to answer within say thirty seconds, the program could jump to a remedial loop. A$ = INKEY$(n) will wait for n centiseconds (maximum 327 seconds) before continuing automatically if no key is pressed.

Other techniques

Novices take ages to find a particular key on the keyboard. One way to overcome this is to use alternative methods of INPUT. These also remove the need for disabling keys and all the other problems encountered above. The best of these devices is a light pen which can be pointed at a particular part of the screen. These are available commercially and plug directly into the analogue port at the back of the microcomputer.

For some responses switches can be connected to the user port and detected with fairly simple routines. One scheme is described in Chapter 4 to allow up to eight pupils to respond independently. The first one to respond is recorded and the others are locked out after the first response. This is ideal for competitive quiz programs.

An alternative for the future is the soft or concept keyboard, which plugs into the microcomputer, and where the number and function of the keys can be changed by the program itself. The keys can thus become letters, numbers, pictures or special symbolic characters as in BLISS. This is a far better way of communication with younger pupils, avoiding all the above pitfalls and giving more freedom to the programmer. The discussion of how to connect one of these to the BBC microcomputer is taken up in Chapter 4.

Crash protection

Ideally it should be impossible for a novice user to crash a program by indiscriminately pressing the wrong keys. This can be such an effort (as the above discussion shows) that it may take too much time. The best way is to put key entry checks into a separate PROCEDURE, which already contains the protection (see INTEGRATED SCIENCE TEST). This can then be called whenever it is needed. Even then a determined pupil can crash by pressing the ESCAPE of BREAK keys.

ESCAPE is relatively easy to handle. Begin each program with

```
ON ERROR GOTO 9000 (or wherever)
```

and at line 9000 put a routine to deal with the situation of the pupil having pressed the ESCAPE key.

BREAK is dealt with by redefining that key so that the program restarts (page 143 of the user guide). This is far from ideal, since it re-runs the program from the start, not from the place where the BREAK key was pressed. Neither of these suggestions thus solves the problem by returning the pupil to his last exit point. My solution is to teach pupils to be careful and not to press all the keys in sight. The display should tell them exactly which keys to press and if they press others, then they can jolly well find out how to recover from the crash themselves. (Actually it is quite amazing how quickly even young children can learn to use the machines properly; there is such a thing as over-protection.)

Processing the response

Once the response of the student has been collected, the microcomputer has to process it. If the entry is the student's name, presumably this is so that a personal touch can be added to requests:

```
'Now, Bob,
can you tell me....'
```

This is achieved by printing out the string variable that was used for the original input. That variable name must not be used again, or the microcomputer will later change the student's name to PHOTOSYNTHESIS or whatever. Note also the need to leave a long space after the student's name. If this is not done, you will find the computer responding to a long name with:

```
'Now, Stephanovanovitci, can you te
ll me....'
```

Wrap-around is unforgiveable in video text.

The response PHOTOSYNTHESIS might be the answer to a question set by the microcomputer. Once this response has been collected, the program has to decide if PHOTOSYNTHESIS is the correct answer. A sequential list of questions can retain the correct response in a DATA statement, which is then collected by READ. If responses have to be accessed at random, then a better way is to keep the correct responses in a string array, thus:

```
100  R$(1)="PHOTOSYNTHESIS"
110  R$(2)="RESPIRATION"
120  R$(3)=...etc.
500  PRINT "What name is given to ....
510  INPUT A$
520  IF A$ = R$(1) THEN PRINT "CORRECT"
530  etc.
```

The unfortunate thing about checking responses by the method shown in line 520 above, is that misspelled inputs or even things like PHOTO-SYNTHESIS are considered incorrect. The program could contain a selection of possible responses and check each one separately, but the range of possible correct responses could be enormous.

One solution is to use the LEFT$, RIGHT$ and MID$ functions to check that the majority of a word is correct, but every word tends to behave differently and about the best that can be achieved is to disregard leading spaces and hyphens. The problem mentioned above, about the use of upper and lower case letters, can be overcome by the use of the ASC and CHR$ functions.

One desirable feature of tutorials is to give clues if the student has no idea. In the case above, after the first wrong response, the microcomputer could prompt with

```
CLUE: PHOTO---------
```

LEFT$(word$(1),5) is used to extract the initial letters, and this can be printed out on top of

```
FOR I=1 TO LEN(word$(1)):PRINT"-";:NEXT I
```

ELEMENTS (34) demonstrates the way that this is achieved in practice.

Techniques like these are learned by studying the user guide, the programs of others and books specifically about BASIC and the BBC microcomputer. A list of such books is given in the Appendix.

Writing a program

This topic is a subject in its own right and at least one book has been entirely devoted to it. Thus it is not possible to do more than indicate the overall principles. The whole process can be subdivided into three parts:

Design
Coding
Debugging

Of these the most important, and the one most often neglected, is the design stage. There is always a great urge to begin coding, that is to write BASIC statements into the microcomputer. This should be resisted as long as possible, because the faster one begins coding, the poorer the program will be.

An example of this is MICSIM (4) which was never planned at all. This program began on the PET as a diagram to illustrate the various registers in the 6502 microprocessor. While it was being written, the thought occurred to me that it would be useful to load different numbers into the registers and see their effect. First the mnemonic instructions LDA, LDX and LDY were added and then STA, STX and STY. Then it was decided to include the main 6502 instructions too and illustrate the different addressing modes. At this point it was discovered that some addressing modes could not be implemented; the program was beginning to creak.

After a great deal of effort it finally worked to my satisfaction, but it was becoming difficult to deal with new problems as they arose during the evaluation. At one stage a

RENUMBER was implemented to create more space and this destroyed any vestige of sensible numbering that had originally been incorporated. When the program was transferred to the BBC microcomputer, it was merely translated into BBC BASIC, although some of the advantages of the latter were utilized. Further patches removed a few more problems and at this point I decided to make the simulation a dynamic one. As well as just illustrating the instructions, I made it execute sequences of instructions too. This addition showed serious faults in the original idea and ad hoc solutions were introduced to solve each problem as it arose. I finally abandoned the whole project and decided to leave the program as it now is. It is full of errors, it is impossible even for me to interpret, it is probably incapable of improvement, but it works after a fashion and gives a satisfactory introduction to machine code programming.

The purpose of this tale is to warn of what can happen if the planning stage is neglected. What I have just described is called **bottom up programming** – starting from a simple idea and adding refinements to it. A computer scientist would argue that I should have designed the whole program from the start and anticipated the problems that might arise. This is called **top down programming** and is what the rest of this chapter is about. I do, however, want to give a note of caution.

It often happens that programs are developed by chance. For example, my first (PET) programs on wave motion were the result of an accident. I had spent some time trying to make waves that moved across the screen, but BASIC was much too slow. Then, while working on a routine to paint a picture on the screen in machine code, I assumed that the end of the screen was in position 40 (in fact it runs from 0 to 39). The routine painted the picture quite happily but then scrolled it across the screen. I realized that a sine curve would become a travelling wave and the solution to one of my problems had been overcome. I was able to use this accidental discovery to write several wave programs for the PET.

The point of this story is that planning by itself does not always provide a solution. There nearly always has to be interaction between experimentation and program development. In the commercial world program designers must specify accurately what they want to do. Poorly constructed programs cost money, so top down programming is an economic necessity. The educational world is not quite the same as this. Teachers are almost certainly writing programs in their own time, which is never costed. Also they do not have all the necessary programming skills at their fingertips beforehand. For them strict top down programming is not possible until they become more expert.

I shall therefore describe a technique that can be used by non-experts. To aid the discussion we shall look closely at one particular program RESONANCE IN A TUBE, which is listed at the end of this chapter. This is not a program merely developed to illustrate the principles, it is a genuine one. Thus it gives a better insight into the whole process of program development than any artificial example can provide. It also utilizes animated graphics and sound and illustrates most of the techniques so far discussed in this chapter.

I wanted a program to simulate the resonance tube experiment. In this experiment a tuning fork is held over the mouth of a long tube, whose other end is closed by a movable piston. As the piston is moved, so the tube reaches its optimum length for the frequency of the tuning fork and a loud sound results. This is called resonance and the length of the tube is a quarter of a wavelength at this point. From a knowledge of this length and the frequency of the tuning fork it is then possible to determine the speed of sound in the tube. The experiment itself is difficult to perform, since students do not know what to look for. The purpose of the simulation is to isolate the principles from the mass of conflicting details. Once students know what they are expected to do, they can carry out the real experiment for themselves. I cannot emphasize too strongly that this simulation was never intended to replace the actual experiment, although I realize that some will misuse it in that way. It will be a sad day if computers take over from laboratory work – they simulate mathematics, not science.

Design

There must be a diagram of a tube and a tuning fork with a movable piston that can be moved in and out with the left and right cursor movement keys. These are the best keys to use since their arrow heads point in the correct directions. As the piston is moved, so the loudness of the sound changes, becoming a maximum at resonance. Then the user measures the length of the tube and plots the graph. This specification immediately threw up problems.

Should the user measure the length of the tube with a real ruler? Considering the different sizes of screen that might be encountered, this idea might be difficult to implement. The values obtained would be unlike the real situation, since 300 mm tube lengths are used in practice. The program would need to use fairly high frequencies to fit the limited width of some screens and the frequencies chosen would be different in each case too. It was decided therefore, to use an artificial ruler measuring up to 330 mm, which allows tuning forks in the range 256 Hz to 512 Hz to be selected.

Should it be possible to obtain the higher harmonics? This was considered to be one of the distracting details that I was trying to eliminate. By restricting the tube length and choosing the frequency range as I did above, these harmonics do not exist.

Should the user plot real values or those chosen by the computer? The latter would make graph-plotting much easier but might hide the purpose of the simulation. I knew how to do the graph anyway so I was not afraid of this. I decided to allow pupils to enter their own results, which could be wrong (within limits), but which could be altered later if necessary. One of the purposes of the simulation was the development of good experimental technique. I therefore decided to plot the graph as soon as two readings had been taken. The plotting of subsequent points then shows if any of them are in error. I always tell students to 'plot the graph as you go along'; hopefully this simulation will encourage the habit.

Should longitudinal waves be shown moving down the tube? They would indicate clearly how resonance is produced. However, this is not the purpose of the experiment and its inclusion in the simulation would be a distraction. It is the same trap that teachers are always falling into, trying to make experimental work verify theory instead of existing in its own right.

Now that we have decided what we want to achieve, it is time to start top down programming. We do not go straight to the computer and start programming, that state is still some way off. We begin by writing the program on paper in **pseudo code** – meaningful statements that can later be turned into BASIC statements (or indeed any other language). For this code we recognize three distinct processes:

Sequence

Repetition

Choice

A sequence is a set of instructions that follow one another in strict order. TRAFFIC LIGHTS in Chapter 4 is a good example of this.

Turn on red traffic light
Long delay
Turn on red and amber traffic lights
Short delay
Turn on green traffic light
Long delay
Turn on amber traffic light
Short delay

Choice is achieved by IF..THEN..ELSE and readers will be very familiar with it (after all it is standard scientific jargon). The sequence branches into two or more separate routes depending upon the conditions encountered initially.

Repetition is similarly obvious, but here there are different kinds. The traffic lights sequence may need to be repeated forever. This can be achieved by a GOTO back to the beginning. A pelican crossing has the green traffic light on until a pedestrian requests the traffic to stop. This can be achieved by a WHILE..DO structure:

WHILE the pedestrian is not requesting traffic to stop,
DO keep the green traffic light on.

A pedestrian crossing at crossroads may be incorporated into the traffic lights sequence itself, but this is wasteful since it makes traffic wait when there are no pedestrians. It is better if the pedestrian request switch interrupts the normal sequence to make it behave differently. The normal sequence is repeated until an event occurs to change it; the REPEAT..UNTIL structure. Finally, it may be necessary to repeat some sequence a given number of times. This uses the well-known FOR..NEXT structure.

In none of these processes are we concerned with BASIC – exactly how we implement this pseudo code is irrelevant. BBC BASIC recognizes all of them except 'WHILE condition DO loop', which is carried out by 'IF condition THEN GOTO start of loop'. Similarly, Apple BASIC does not have REPEAT..UNTIL but all pseudo codes can be implemented in some way on all machines. For example FOR..NEXT can be carried out by incrementing a counter (IF count = maxcount THEN finish ELSE carry on counting). For our purposes at the moment it is the process that is important, not how it is later turned into BASIC.

One way of designing a program (long taught in schools) is flowcharting. This has sequences (rectangular boxes), choices (diamond boxes) and repetitions (returning lines and junction boxes). To introduce the ideas of design flowcharting is a good method, but it is not popular with serious programmers. Programs of any size spill over onto several sheets of paper and are difficult to follow. Also it is very difficult to plan a flowchart until all its limbs are known. This results in the same chart being endlessly redrawn to accommodate extra requirements. Most programmers draw the flowchart after the program has been written!

Top down programming allows the program to be developed from the general plan right down to the level of coding in BASIC by a process known as **stepwise refinement.** This cuts out a great deal of the redrawing (or rewriting in this case) of those elements that are already known. It also allows each step to be checked for error before it is turned into code. In this way any bugs in the final program will only require simple patches, not wholesale rewriting. Now that we have an overall strategy for our program, let us begin this process.

```
RESONANCE IN A TUBE
A     Initialize mode, variables etc.
B     Give instructions
C     Draw tuning fork, tube, piston and ruler
D     REPEAT
D1    Select tuning fork frequency
D2    REPEAT Compute sound intensity
D3              REPEAT Make sound
D4              UNTIL piston is moved
D5    UNTIL tube length has been measured
D6    Process the measured length
UNTIL ESC key is pressed.
```

The structure of the program is becoming obvious. A, B and C are sequential and are executed once each time the program is run. D is executed repetitively until the program is halted by pressing the ESC key. This is not very elegant and for younger users would be wrong but, considering our target users, this is acceptable. Within this REPEAT..UNTIL loop are other nested loops, each of which is terminated by a different condition. Thus the sound is maintained until a cursor key is pressed to move the piston. The sound is switched off when the new length has been measured. Then the graph-plotting routine (D6) runs sequentially after which control returns to D1. To make the pattern more obvious each of the nested loops is indented to show where it begins and ends.

The question raised now is where to go next. As a rule one should stick to the order of execution unless there are some processes that are not yet clearly defined. These should be tackled first, because they may throw up problems that cause the original design to be modified. The earlier such modification takes place, the better. In our case we have to ask about D4, D5 and D6.

D4 tests whether the user wants to move the piston. As stated above this is to be done with the left and right cursor movement keys. It should be possible to detect these with INKEY$(0). But alternatively, the user might want to enter the measured length of the tube (D5) and this requires INPUT. The two can be combined by using INKEY$(0) for both types of information. The RETURN key could be used to confirm the entered measurement or the DEL key could be used to delete some or all of it. So D4 and D5 are further refined thus:

```
    Note which key pressed
D4  IF key is cursor shift left
    THEN move piston left
    IF key is cursor shift right
    THEN move piston right
D5  IF key is numeric
    THEN keep it as a number
    IF key is DEL
    THEN remove last numeral entered
    IF key is RETURN
D6  THEN process the result
```

We must still ask what is meant by 'keep it as a number'. If the user wishes to enter the number 345, say, the first numeral entered will be 3. This needs to be printed on the screen to let the user see it. Then the user presses 4, so the first numeral must be multiplied by ten and added to the second. Finally the numeral 5 is added and the process is repeated. We want to stop the user entering numbers greater than, say, 329 and numbers equal to 0, since these are clearly wrong. Shall we tell the user they are wrong or just ignore them? Bearing in mind our target users, I adopted the latter strategy. When RETURN is pressed the number entered is accepted as the measured length and D6 begins. If DEL is pressed the last numeral entered is deleted by removing the last digit from the assembled number. Each of the simple choices in D4/5 is mutually exclusive, since a single key can only be one character. If this had not been the case, a series of nested IF..THEN..ELSE processes would have been used. Simple IF..THEN processes are always to be preferred for readability. This produces the further refinement:

```
    Set measurement to zero
    Note which key pressed
D5  IF key is numeric
    THEN measurement = 10*measurement + numeral
    IF key is DEL
    THEN measurement = measurement DIV 10
    PRINT measurement
```

The whole structure can be searched and refined further until it all ends up as simple statements, each of which can be converted into code without problems. If there are things that are not known, (and non-experts will find plenty of these) then the top down technique has to be modified as I shall show shortly.

Before coding begins it is necessary to check that all the likely problems have been foreseen and allowed for. The programmer should make a dry run through the program with imaginary data to see what happens (as we did with 345 above). In this dry run we should notice that 345 should not be acceptable since it exceeds 329. However, if a user enters 34 we cannot tell if another numeral is intended to follow, so we have to accept this. We can, however, reject any further numerals if the existing value of measurement exceeds 32. Dry runs of this type usually lead to modifications in the program.

The user knows when too large a number has been entered, because it is printed on the screen. Do we want to print the initial value of zero? Clearly this is a distraction and, in any case, we do not accept zero as a measurement. So unless the measurement is zero, we print it. If the user has entered 34 and meant to enter 240, he or she will delete back to zero and start again. How will the program know whether the user has deleted back to zero or has not yet started? If the latter, the program prints nothing, if the former, the program must delete what was there previously. So 'nothing' will have to be a blank to delete any previously printed value. Likewise, when a measurement is reduced from three digits to two, or two digits to one, the previous end digit must be erased. This can be done by following the printed 'measurement' with a blank character. What do we do if the user presses non-numeric keys? I decided to ignore these, without telling the user why; programs for younger users might well include such messages. There are also other pitfalls, like pressing RETURN or DEL when there is no measurement. We shall have to allow for all these.

Such a dry run through the program reveals several problems to be overcome. Having discovered them, we build their solutions into the program at the planning stage.

```
      Set measurement to zero
      Note which key is pressed
D5    IF key is numeric AND measurement < 33
      THEN measurement = 10*measurement + numeral
      IF key is DEL AND measurement <> 0
      THEN measurement = measurement DIV 10
      IF measurement <> 0
      THEN PRINT measurement + blank
      ELSE PRINT blank
      IF key is RETURN AND measurement <> 0
      THEN process the measurement
```

To determine when the RETURN key has been legitimately pressed, we set a **flag,** which is initially FALSE, but is set to TRUE at the right point. This flag is called 'measured'. In this way almost the whole program can be written and tested in pseudo code before going near the computer itself.

This is the theory! In practice the strict pattern of top down programming breaks down whenever a problem is encountered for which the programmer can see no solution. For example I need to know how to move the piston under the control of the cursor keys. This is where the advice of computer scientists has to be ignored – no amount of stepwise refinement will tell me how to do this, only experimentation, that is bottom up programming. I used to feel guilty at ignoring the advice of expert computer scientists, until I realized that they are dealing with different problems. They already know how to handle their machines so they do not need to break off to find out. I have not yet reached this stage and I am sure that few other science teachers have either. The problem with bottom up programming is the restrictions it might impose on later top down refinements. It is advisable to discard any code created during the experiment, its retention might force the programmer into a predetermined mould and lead to later problems.

It is difficult to follow this advice because of lack of time. Having developed some code that works we tend to want to keep it. If it is a procedure then that is fairly easily incorporated at a later stage, but if it is part of the main program it may be necessary to RENUMBER it and merge it with the rest of the program later. For example, I knew that the piston would have to be moved inside the tube, so the graphics for the latter had to be constructed too. I developed lines 3020 to 3480 to draw the tuning fork, tube, piston and ruler. Originally this was done in MODE 2, giving four colours. Logical colour 3 was made into flashing black and white and the repetition rate was speeded up to make it appear to vibrate. Later it was found that the program had exceeded the memory available in this mode, so the program was changed to MODE 4. The reason for choosing a high resolution mode was to make use of the VDU5 statement to move the piston smoothly in and out in the manner described earlier in this chapter. The routine to move the piston was developed as the procedure PROCpiston(position) with the position of the piston in the tube passed as the parameter 'position'. This is converted into an x coordinate and drawn as a line. Prior to this the previous line is erased by drawing over it in black ink (GCOL0,0).

Coding

Having refined each process until I was sure how to do it, I was then in a position to begin turning it into a BASIC program. I did this linearly from the beginning. With the fundamental structure developed this was quite an easy job. Some problems were encountered and needed ad hoc solutions (see later), but the structure remained intact throughout. Even so, a structure alone does not necessarily lead to a readable program. There are some ground rules for structured programming that should be borne in mind.

One oft-quoted rule is 'avoid GOTO and GOSUB'. I agree with this up to a point. Some programs are such a mass of convoluted GOSUBs and GOTOs that it is impossible to see what different conditions are doing. MICSIM is a particularly notorious example. But this advice can be carried to ridiculous extremes. Where a routine is only called once (for example in setting up arrays or graphics characters) then GOSUB is no less meaningful than a procedure. Which of these conveys the most sense?

```
GOSUB 20000:REM define graphics characters
```

or

```
PROCgraphics
```

Given that it is much easier to find line 20000 in the listing than to find a procedure definition, GOSUB is clearly better. Similarly, to repeat a process indefinitely (as in D of our program), which of these is more meaningful?

```
3000 REM Start of main program
etc.........
etc.........
etc.........
9000 GOTO 3000:REM Restart main program
```

or

```
3000 REM Start of main program
3010 finished = FALSE
3020 REPEAT
etc.........
etc.........
etc.........
9000 UNTIL finished:REM Restart main program
```

Whether a progam uses procedures or subroutines, these should be located in high line numbers at the end of the program (unless speed is at a premium, in which case GOSUBs are faster and the closer they are to the current line the better). In RESONANCE IN A TUBE, I kept procedures in lines 30000 upwards and subroutines in 20000 upwards.

Apart from moving the piston, speed of execution was not important in this program. I was therefore able to be very liberal with REM statements, using them to mark off the different sections and to explain what each was doing. Another help in this respect is the facility for using long variable names. Where these were used for holding integers, then integer variables were used to increase speed. A further aid to readability was to declare constants at the beginning of the program, rather than just use numbers. For example,

```
IF INKEY(-26) THEN .......
```

is less meaningful than

```
IF INKEY(cursor left) THEN ......
```

Debugging

As mentioned above, correcting any errors in the program is not something that can be left until last. Each step should be checked with dummy data to ensure that nothing has been overlooked. Even so there will be errors in the program once it has been coded. Simplest to eliminate are syntax errors (or mistakes) since BASIC contains error detection routines and obligingly tells the programmer where the error has occurred. More difficult to determine are errors in the logic. Hopefully these should not exist, but that is a counsel of perfection. In my case several such problems arose, which were detected with dummy data as soon as the code had been written.

For example, I wanted to move the piston with the cursor movement keys and, during the design phase, I assumed that these could be detected with INKEY$(0). I thus carried on with stepwise refinement in the proper way. When checking the coding stage I found that the method I had chosen did not work, INKEY$(0) returned the null value whichever cursor key was pressed. I then tried GET$, GET and INKEY(0) in vain and even resorted to reading the keyboard directly from memory (see Chapter 7). The latter was rejected as breaking the rules; I wanted to make the final program usable with the second processor added. In the end I used a combination of INKEY$(0) for RETURN, DEL and the numeric keys and INKEY(−26) or INKEY(−122) for the cursor keys. This is inelegant and I am still hoping for a better solution. By the time I had discovered this I had gone too far to change the structure (I could have separated off the piston movement with separate statements to INPUT the measured length). Bottom up programming at this point would have saved trouble later. The fault lay in not being an expert in BBC BASIC beforehand.

The problem with producing the sound was how to keep it going indefinitely until the piston was moved. Again no difficulty was anticipated until the relevant part of the program was tested. Eventually, the solution was found in the user guide with a technique for turning off the previous sound when a new one is reached (SOUND &11 instead of SOUND 1).

The graph plotting routines were also developed by trial and error. I used the VDU5:MOVEx,y:PRINT"+" method to plot crosses on the screen, but found that the centre of the cross did not coincide with the point x,y. Some adjustment of x and y was necessary to overcome this. Drawing the line was a linear regression technique already known to me. But after writing this section (line 5000 onwards) I spent some time entering dummy data to see its effect. I hope this will be rewarded by having no crashes in future. One problem was that the linear regression routine can only work with at least two points, so I had to develop a method of counting how many points the user had measured so far, and to distinguish this from one point measured twice. The variable 'numreadings' was used for this and the ensuing code is clumsy. All measurements of the tube length for each tuning fork are set to zero initially. Each time a new measurement is entered, all thirteen measurements are checked and only the non-zero ones are counted. This produces an undesirable GOTO in line 5490. I have yet to find a more elegant way of tackling this.

After the program had been debugged by me, I gave it to teachers for evaluation. Almost immediately one had caused a crash. As stated before in this chapter the auto-repeat facility is a nuisance and is one reason for avoiding the INPUT statement. The only INPUT left in the program is to determine which tuning fork is to be used. One user entered F blank and found that this was not acceptable. She could not see why, since all she could see on the screen was the 'F'. Lines 12092 and 12094 were thus added to eliminate leading and trailing blanks from the input string.

The full listing of the program now follows. Doubtless there are further bugs, but in the time-honoured method of all lecturers, I leave them as an exercise for the student.

```
     RESONANCE IN A TUBE - PROGRAMMING EXAMPLE
LIST
    1 REM RESONANCE IN A TUBE
    2 REM  BY R.A.SPARKES
    3
    4 REM 30/3/83
    5
 1000 MODE 4
 1010 LET cursorleft=-26
 1011 LET cursorright=-122
 1012 LET returnkey$=CHR$13
 1013 LET deletekey$=CHR$127
 1014 LET space$=CHR$32
 1030 LET endcorrection=20
 1040 LET top=860:bottom=704:REM top and bottom walls of tube
 1050 LET place=1000:REM x-coordinate of piston
 1060 LET length=280:REM INITIAL LENGTH OF TUBE
 1070 LET forever=255:REM LENGTH OF NOTE
 1080 GOSUB 21000:REM SET UP ARRAYS FOR TUNING FORK
 1090 GOSUB 20000:REM DEFINE GRAPHICS
 1200
 1500 REM***************************
 1510 REM
 1520 REM   INSTRUCTIONS
 1530 REM
 1540 REM***************************
 2000 CLS:PRINT TAB(8,0);"RESONANCE IN A TUBE"
 2010 PRINT TAB(0,5);"This program simulates the resonance"
 2020 PRINT TAB(0,7);"tube experiment."
 2030 PRINT TAB(0,9);"A tuning fork held at the mouth of"
 2040 PRINT TAB(0,11);"the tube causes the air to vibrate."
 2050 PRINT TAB(0,13);"The sound produced is loudest when the"
 2060 PRINT TAB(0,15);"length of the tube is closest to the"
 2070 PRINT TAB(0,17);"resonant length."
 2080 PRINT TAB(0,20);"First choose your tuning fork."
 2090 PRINT :PRINT"Enter one of the following values:-"
 2100
 2500 REM***************************
 2510 REM
 2520 REM  REPEAT UNTIL ESC KEY
 2530 REM
 2540 REM***************************
 2550
 2560 PROCchoose
 2600 LET measurement%=0
 2700 REM***************************
 2800 REM
 3000 REM    DRAW PICTURES
 3005 REM
 3006 REM***************************
 3010 CLS
 3020 PRINT TAB(8,0);"RESONANCE IN A TUBE"
 3024 REM***************************
 3025 REM
 3026 REM    DRAW TUNING FORK
 3027 REM
 3028 REM***************************
 3040 PRINT TAB(0,5) CHR$243;SPC(2);CHR$248
 3050 PRINT TAB(0,6) CHR$243;SPC(2);CHR$248
 3060 PRINT TAB(0,7) CHR$243;SPC(2);CHR$248
```

```
3070 PRINT TAB(0,8) CHR$243;SPC(2);CHR$248
3090 PRINT TAB(0,9) CHR$244;CHR$245;CHR$246;CHR$247
3100 PRINT TAB(1,10) CHR$249;CHR$250
3110 PRINT TAB(1,11) CHR$249;CHR$250
3120 PRINT TAB(1,12) CHR$249;CHR$250
3130 PRINT TAB(1,13) CHR$249;CHR$250
3140 PRINT TAB(1,3);tone$(tuningfork%)
3150
3200 REM****************************
3210 REM
3220 REM     DRAW TUBE
3230 REM
3240 REM****************************
3250 FOR X=5 TO 39:PRINT TAB(X,4) CHR$240:NEXT X
3260 FOR X=5 TO 39:PRINT TAB(X,10) CHR$242:NEXT X
3270 REM****************************
3280 REM
3290 REM     DRAW PISTON
3300 REM
3310 REM****************************
3315 PROCpiston(length)
3320 REM****************************
3330 REM
3340 REM     DRAW RULER
3350 REM
3360 REM****************************
3370 MOVE 130,684
3380 DRAW 1279,684
3390 DRAW 1279,620
3400 DRAW 130,620
3410 DRAW 130,684
3420 VDU5
3430 FOR value= 0 TO 33
3440 LET x=129+value*32:MOVE x,684
3450 IF value MOD 5<>0 THEN PRINT CHR$251
3460 IF value MOD 5=0 THEN PRINT CHR$252
3470 IF value MOD 5=0 THEN MOVE x+4,660:PRINT;value*10
3480 NEXT value
3490 VDU4
3500 PRINT TAB(0,15)"Use the left-right cursor keys"
3510 PRINT TAB(0,17)"to move the piston in and out."
3520 PRINT TAB(0,19)"When you have found the resonance"
3530 PRINT TAB(0,21)"position, measure the length of the"
3540 PRINT TAB(0,23)"tube up to the piston in millimetres."
3550 PRINT TAB(0,25)"Enter this length as a whole number and"
3560 PRINT TAB(0,27)"confirm this value with RETURN"
3570 PRINT TAB(0,29)"(the DELETE key works normally)."
3580 PRINT TAB(0,31)"Press ESCAPE to finish.";
3590
3600 REPEAT
3605       VDU 23,1,0;0;0;0;:REM TURN CURSOR OFF
3610      REM************************
3620      REM
3630      REM       MAKE SOUND
3640      REM
3650      REM************************
3660      LET resonantlength%=80000 DIV freq%(tuningfork%)
3670      LET comparison%=ABS(resonantlength%-length-endcorrection) DIV 3
3680      LET loudness=-2
3690      IF comparison%<12 THEN LET loudness=comparison%-15
```

```
3700       SOUND &11,loudness,note%(tuningfork%),forever
3710
4000       REM*********************
4010       REM
4020       REM GET KEY FROM KEYBOARD
4030       REM
4040       REM*********************
4050
4060       measured = FALSE
4070       REPEAT:LET key$=INKEY$(0)
4080       UNTIL key$<>"" OR INKEY(cursorleft) OR INKEY(cursorright)
4090       IF INKEY(cursorleft) THEN PROCmoveleft
4100       IF INKEY(cursorright) THEN PROCmoveright
4105       IF key$=deletekey$ AND measurement%<>0 THEN measurement%=
measurement% DIV 10
4110       IF key$=returnkey$ AND measurement%<>0 THEN measured =TRUE
4120       IF key$<="9" AND key$>="0" AND measurement%<33 THEN LET
measurement%=10*measurement%+VAL(key$)
4130       IF measurement%<>0 THEN PRINT TAB(31,31);measurement%;space$;
4140       IF measurement%=0 THEN PRINT TAB(31,31);space$;
4150 UNTIL measured
4160 REM*************************
4170 REM
4180 REM PROCESS MEASUREMENT
4190 REM
4200 REM*************************
4240 REM
4250 LET measurement%(tuningfork%)=measurement%
4260 SOUND&11,0,0,0:REM TURN OFF SOUND
4500 VDU 23,1,1;0;0;0;:REM TURN CORSOR BACK ON
4800
4900
5000 REM***************************
5010 REM
5020 REM    PLOT GRAPH
5030 REM
5040 REM***************************
5050 CLS
5060 MOVE 128,256:DRAW 128,960
5070 MOVE 96,256:DRAW 1279,256
5080 PRINT TAB(12,0)"RESONANCE IN A TUBE"
5090 PRINT TAB(0,1)"length/mm"
5100 VDU5
5110 FOR y=0 TO 3.5 STEP 0.5
5120 MOVE 0,(268+192*y):PRINT;100*y
5130 MOVE 116,(268+192*y):PRINT;"-"
5140 NEXT y
5150 MOVE 100,256
5160 PRINTCHR$251;SPC(3);CHR$251;SPC(3);CHR$251;SPC(3);CHR$251;SPC(3);CHR$251;
SPC(3);CHR$251;SPC(3);CHR$251;SPC(3);CHR$251;SPC(3);CHR$251
5170 MOVE 112,230
5180 PRINT"0  0.5 1.0 1.5 2.0 2.5 3.0 3.5 4.0"
5190 MOVE 300,192
5200 PRINT TAB(10,26)"1/frequency    /ms"
5210
5220 REM**********************
5230 REM
5240 REM   LINEAR REGRESSION
5250 REM
5260 REM**********************
```

```
5270 LET xtotal=0
5280 LET ytotal=0
5290 LET sumxsquares=0
5300 LET numreadings=0
5310 LET sumxyproduct=0
5320 FOR tuningfork%=0 TO 12
5330 LET x%=111+1024*256/freq%(tuningfork%)
5340 LET y%=268+1.92*measurement%(tuningfork%)
5350 IF measurement%(tuningfork%)=0 THEN 5420:REM next tuningfork%
5360 LET xtotal=xtotal + x%
5370 LET ytotal=ytotal + y%
5380 LET sumxsquares=sumxsquares + x%^2
5390 LET sumxyproduct=sumxyproduct + x% * y%
5400 MOVE x%,y%:PRINT;"+"
5410 LET numreadings=numreadings + 1
5420 NEXT tuningfork%
5430 REM***************************
5440 REM
5450 REM CALCULATE SLOPE AND INTERCEPT
5460 REM
5470 REM***************************
5480 REM
5490 IF numreadings<2 THEN 9000:REM IGNORE PLOT ROUTINE FOR A SINGLE READING
5500  LET slope=(numreadings * sumxyproduct - xtotal * ytotal) / (numreadings
* sumxsquares - xtotal^2)
5510  LET intercept = (ytotal - slope * xtotal) / numreadings
5520 REM***************************
5530 REM
5540 REM   PLOT LINE
5550 REM
5560 REM***************************
5570 REM
5580 REM plot minimum x-value
5590 LET x%=111:y%=intercept + slope*x%
5600 MOVE x%+12,y%-12
5610 REM plot maximum x-value
5620 LET x%=1135:y%=intercept + slope*x%
5630 DRAW x%+12,y%-12
5640 VDU4
5650 REM***************************
5660 REM
5670 REM  DISPLAY SPEED OF SOUND
5680 REM
5690 REM***************************
5700 LET speed = slope*1024*256*4/1000/1.92
5710 @%=&20105:REM ONE DECIMAL PLACE
5720 PRINT TAB(6,3);"Speed of sound = ";speed;" m/s"
5730 @%=&A0A:REM NORMAL PRINT FORMAT
5750
9000 VDU4:PRINT TAB(0,26):REM RESTORE TEXT MODE
9010 GOTO 2500:REM REPEAT FOREVER
9999
10000 REM***************************
10010 REM
10020 REM     PROCEDURES
10030 REM
10040 REM***************************
10050 REM
10060 DEF PROCmoveleft
10070 IF length>0 THEN length=length-2
```

```
10080 PROCpiston(length)
10090 ENDPROC
10100 DEF PROCmoveright
10110 IF length<330 THEN length=length+2
10120 PROCpiston(length)
10130 ENDPROC
10140 DEF PROCpiston(position)
10150 REM This procedure draws the pistion in the place specified by 'position'
10160 REM Delete old piston
10170 GCOL0,0:MOVE place,bottom:MOVE place+16,bottom:PLOT85,place,top:PLOT85,
place+16,top
10180 LET place=159+position*3.2
10190 REM Put piston in new position
10200 GCOL0,1:MOVE place,bottom:MOVE place+16,bottom:PLOT85,place,top:PLOT85,
place+16,top
10210 ENDPROC
12000 DEF PROCchoose
12010 REM****************************
12020 REM
12030 REM   CHOOSE TUNING FORK
12040 REM
12050 REM****************************
12060 PRINT:PRINT"C  C#  D  D#  E  F  F#  G  G#  A  A#  B"
12070 PRINT:PRINT"or UC (which means upper C)     ";
12080 REPEAT:tuningfork%=13
12090 INPUT tuningfork$
12092 IF LEFT$(tuningfork$,1)=CHR$32 THEN LET tuningfork$=RIGHT$(tuningfork$,
LEN(tuningfork$)-1):GOTO 12092
12094 IF RIGHT$(tuningfork$,1)=CHR$32 THEN LET tuningfork$=LEFT$(tuningfork$,
LEN(tuningfork$)-1):GOTO 12094
12100 IF tuningfork$="C" THEN tuningfork%=0
12110 IF tuningfork$="C#" THEN tuningfork%=1
12120 IF tuningfork$="D" THEN tuningfork%=2
12130 IF tuningfork$="D#" THEN tuningfork%=3
12140 IF tuningfork$="E" THEN tuningfork%=4
12150 IF tuningfork$="F" THEN tuningfork%=5
12160 IF tuningfork$="F#" THEN tuningfork%=6
12170 IF tuningfork$="G" THEN tuningfork%=7
12180 IF tuningfork$="G#" THEN tuningfork%=8
12190 IF tuningfork$="A" THEN tuningfork%=9
12200 IF tuningfork$="A#" THEN tuningfork%=10
12210 IF tuningfork$="B" THEN tuningfork%=11
12220 IF tuningfork$="UC" THEN tuningfork%=12
12230 IF tuningfork%=13 THEN PRINT:PRINT"This value is not listed. Try again."
12240 UNTIL tuningfork%<>13
12250 ENDPROC
20000 REM DEFINE GRAPHICS CHARACTERS
20010 VDU23,240,0,0,0,0,0,255,255,255
20020 VDU23,242,255,255,255,0,0,0,0,0
20030 VDU23,243,7,7,7,7,7,7,7,7
20040 VDU23,244,7,7,3,1,0,0,0,0
20050 VDU23,245,0,128,192,240,124,63,15,3
20060 VDU23,246,0,1,3,15,62,252,240,192
20070 VDU23,247,224,224,192,128,0,0,0,0
20080 VDU23,248,224,224,224,224,224,224,224,224
20090 VDU23,249,3,3,3,3,3,3,3,3
20100 VDU23,250,192,192,192,192,192,192,192,192
20110 VDU23,251,1,1,1,1,0,0,0,0
20120 VDU23,252,1,1,1,1,1,1,1,0
20200 RETURN
```

```
20300
21000 REM SET UP FREQUENCIES FOR TUNING FORKS
21004 DIM measurement%(12)
21005 DIM tone$(12)
21010 DIM freq%(12)
21020 DIM note%(12)
21030 FOR tuningfork% = 0 TO 12
21040 READ tonsolfa$, frequency%, soundvalue%
21045 LET tone$(tuningfork%)=tonsolfa$
21050 LET freq%(tuningfork%)=frequency%
21060 LET note%(tuningfork%)=soundvalue%
21065 LET measurement%(tuningfork%)=0
21070 NEXT tuningfork%
21080 RETURN
21100 DATA C,256,53
21110 DATA C#,271,57
21120 DATA D,288,61
21130 DATA D#,304,65
21140 DATA E,320,69
21150 DATA F,341,73
21160 DATA F#,362,77
21170 DATA G,384,81
21180 DATA G#,406,85
21190 DATA A,427,89
21200 DATA A#,456,93
21210 DATA B,480,97
21220 DATA UC,512,101
```

3 Computation and mathematical modelling

'She can't do sums a bit!' the Queens said together, with great emphasis.
(Lewis Carroll, *Through the Looking Glass*)

This chapter explores the uses of the BBC microcomputer as a mathematical tool, including calculations, graphical display of functions, plotting experimental data, simulations using the random number generator and problem solving by iterative methods.

The super calculator

Calculation is the traditional domain of the computer (as its name implies). There are many books that deal exhaustively with this aspect of computing, with many illustrative examples. In fact, there may even be too many! Why do so many books of programs include one on the solution of quadratic equations? It is not because there are many problems that require its solution, in fact, hardly anyone uses it after leaving school. I suspect the real reason is that it has become a standard example upon which mathematical programmers cut their teeth (while physicists do radioactive decay and the rest write programs on sorting). The real value of writing such programs is the insight they give the programmer into the nature of the problem. Try writing your own quadratic equations program and you will see what I mean. How do you interpret 'too big' or 'syntax error'? Perhaps you forgot about equal or imaginary roots. If this is true, then one way to teach students about LCR circuits might be to get them to write their own LCR circuit analysis program.

There is no point in just using a computer to carry out the often meaningless exercises set in school physics and chemistry examinations. For example, we would not want a student to enter a set of data into some previously prepared program on, say, Newton's rings, that then automatically calculates the wavelength of sodium light. In this case the process is more important than the product – we are trying to get the student to appreciate the properties of the equations being used.

The microcomputer can aid this understanding of equations and concepts in two ways. One of these, the iterative method, is left till last. The other is the sledge-hammer technique of getting the computer to solve an equation many times over while varying one of the parameters. As an example, consider the motion of a stone being thrown vertically against gravity (GRAVITY, program 28). By entering different starting speeds a pupil should be able to discover the relation between the vertical height reached and the initial speed. This technique may be used with almost any other standard equation in science. It would be much better though if the graphics capabilities of the microcomputer were used as well.

Producing a table of results used to be a nightmare but the excellent tabulation facilities of the BBC microcomputer have changed that (Plate 6). Practice changing the parameters of the @% variable until you appreciate how it works and you will have no more problems (page 70 of the user guide).

Graph plotting

The high resolution screen is particularly useful for sketching functions. MOVE and DRAW are easily used and some very sophisticated graphs can be drawn. The process is a little slow for complex functions, but this is not necessarily a disadvantage. One can ask the students to predict 'What will happen next?'. For those whose coordinate geometry is a little rusty, the following discussion may be of assistance.

The most useful screen of the BBC Model B microcomputer is MODE 1. This gives a normal 40 columns of text, sufficiently high resolution for most purposes and three colours at any one time (plus a background colour). This mode is similar to MODE 4, which is the alternative for Model A users. VDU19 and GCOL0 should be used to select the different colours of the lines and the backround as described in the guide. If you do not have access to a colour monitor, then use MODE 4 to get the extra memory.

The statement to plot a single dot is

```
PLOT69,0,512
```

You may just be able to see the small dot on the left of the screen and half-way up, which is the point you have just plotted. Now type

```
PLOT69,10,512
```

which gives a point nearer to the right, but at the same height as the other point. The first number in the PLOT69 command tells how far the point is from the left edge. Type

```
PLOT69,10,200
```

to get a point below the ones plotted before. This shows that the second number in the PLOT69 command gives the vertical position of the point. The smaller the number, the nearer it is to the bottom. The largest value for the horizontal position is 1279 (extreme right) and the smallest is 0 (extreme left). The largest value for the vertical position is 1023 (top) and the smallest is 0 (bottom). Any attempt to plot points outside these limits will be ignored.

Clear the screen with CLS and prove for yourself the positions of the extreme corners of the screen as follows:

```
TOP-LEFT      : PLOT69,0,1023
TOP-RIGHT     : PLOT69,1279,1023
BOTTOM-LEFT   : PLOT69,0,0
BOTTOM-RIGHT  : PLOT69,1279,0
```

Occasionally it is necessary to visit a point without plotting a dot; the MOVE statement can be used for this purpose. MOVE x,y refers to the same point as PLOT69,x,y except that the dot is not plotted.

Lines

We get lines by drawing a set of dots close together using the DRAW statement. This draws a line from the previous point visited (PLOT69 or MOVE or a previous DRAW) to the new point specified in the DRAW statement. For example:

```
MOVE0,0
DRAW1000,512
DRAW0,1023
DRAW0,0
```

The points on the screen have the coordinates x,y (as in coordinate geometry). To plot graphs there must be some relationship between x and y, which must be included in the program. Here is a simple example:

```
100  MODE 1
110  GCOL0,3
120  FOR x = 0 TO 1279
130  LET y = x/2
140  PLOT69,x,y
150  NEXT x
```

Note how the program plots the equation given in line 130. Any equation connecting x and y can be used, provided the equation is of the form y = function of x only. Try this for yourself, with different equations in line 130. For example:

```
130 y = 800 - x/2
130 y = x*x/1000
130 y = 500 - x + x*x/1000
```

You will see that only values of y within the range 0 to 1023 are plotted. To fill in any gaps between the different points the DRAW statement may be used instead of PLOT69. Unfortunately this causes problems because the program also draws a line from the origin to the first point plotted. Ideally we want to PLOT the first point and only DRAW thereafter. This can be done by noting that PLOT4 is exactly equivalent to MOVE and PLOT5 is exactly equivalent to DRAW. The program thus becomes

```
100  MODE 1
110  GCOL0,3
115  LET n = 4
120  FOR x = 0 TO 1280
130  LET y = 800-x/2
140  PLOTn,x,y
145  LET n = 5
150  NEXT x
```

The first time that the PLOTn statement is reached, n has the value of 4, so it is the equivalent of MOVE. Subsequently n is 5, so all the remaining PLOTn statements are equivalent to DRAW.

Different origins

The methods used so far only allow us to plot graphs in one quadrant, for positive values of x and y. Some graphs, particularly sines and cosines produce negative values too. To plot these requires us to move the axes with the VDU29 command. To keep the origin of the x axis at the left of the screen (x = 0) and put the y axis in the middle (y = 512) we write

```
VDU29,0;512;      (Note the semi-colons!)
```

The graph will now show points in the range 0 to 1279 (x coordinate) as before, but −512 to +511 (y coordinate). For some purposes it is better not to redefine the screen in this way, but to add the required displacement to the x or the y value with statements like

```
PLOT69,x,(y+512)
```

The range of plottable values for y will now be from −512 to +511 as above. In both methods axes are drawn with MOVE and DRAW statements.

Another problem with sine and cosine graphs is that they are functions of angles in radians. To get at least two cycles on the screen, the range for the angle must be from 0 to 4*PI radians (0 to 12.566). The range for x is 0 to 1279, so a conversion factor has to be included to make 1279 equivalent to 12.566. It is better to define a conversion factor **(confac)** to carry out this operation at the start of the program and to do this in such a way that it is obvious what is happening.

```
LET cycles = 2
LET confac = 2 * PI * cycles / 1280
```

The value of any sine function goes from −1 to +1, so it must be multiplied by an amplitude (maximum of 511 to get the full range on the vertical axis). Here is the program for the sine function (Plate 7):

```
100  MODE 1
110  VDU29,0;512;
120  GCOL0,3
130  MOVE 0,0
140  DRAW 1279,0
150  MOVE 0,−512
160  DRAW 0,511
200  LET cycles = 2
210  LET confac = 2 * PI * cycles / 1280
220  LET amplitude = 300
230  LET n = 4
240  FOR x = 0 TO 1280
250  LET y = amplitude * SIN(x * confac)
260  PLOTn,x,y
270  LET n = 5
280  NEXT x
```

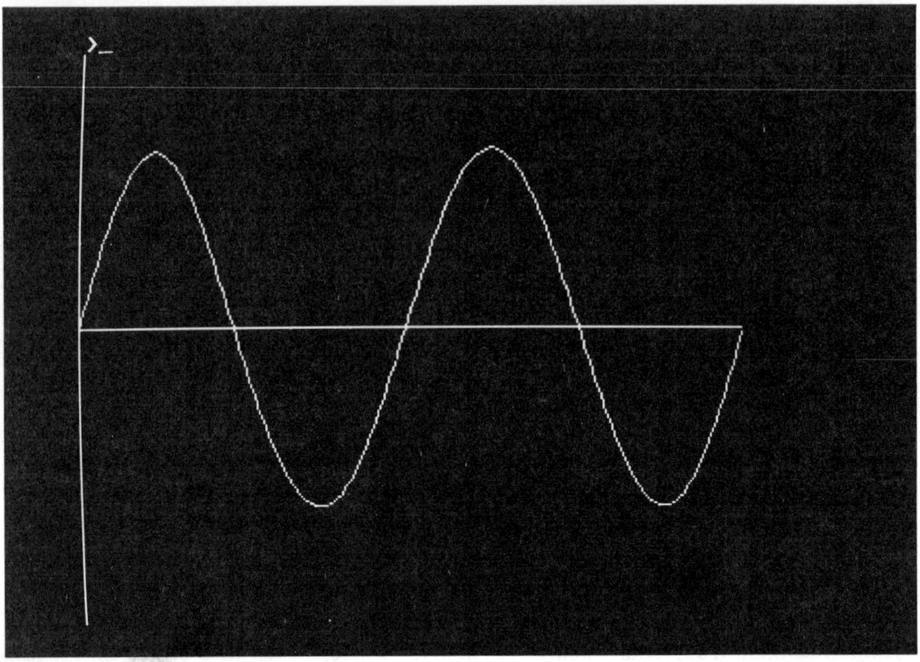

Plate 7 Sine curve

The speed of plotting can be dramatically increased by plotting every tenth point thus:

```
240 FOR x = 0 TO 1280 STEP 10
```

This makes little difference to the appearance of the final graph. Note that this can only be done with the DRAW statement.

A program to plot the cosine function involves changing line 250 to

```
250 y = amplitude * COS(x*confac)
```

A program to plot two functions at the same time requires two FOR-NEXT loops. Let us plot three cycles of the sine function and two of the cosine function at the same time. The use of DRAW now becomes awkward and it is better to revert to PLOT69 again. This allows the two graphs to be drawn in different colours.

```
100  MODE 1
110  VDU29,0;512;
120  GCOL0,3
130  MOVE 0,0
140  DRAW 1279,0
150  MOVE 0,-512
160  DRAW 0,511
```

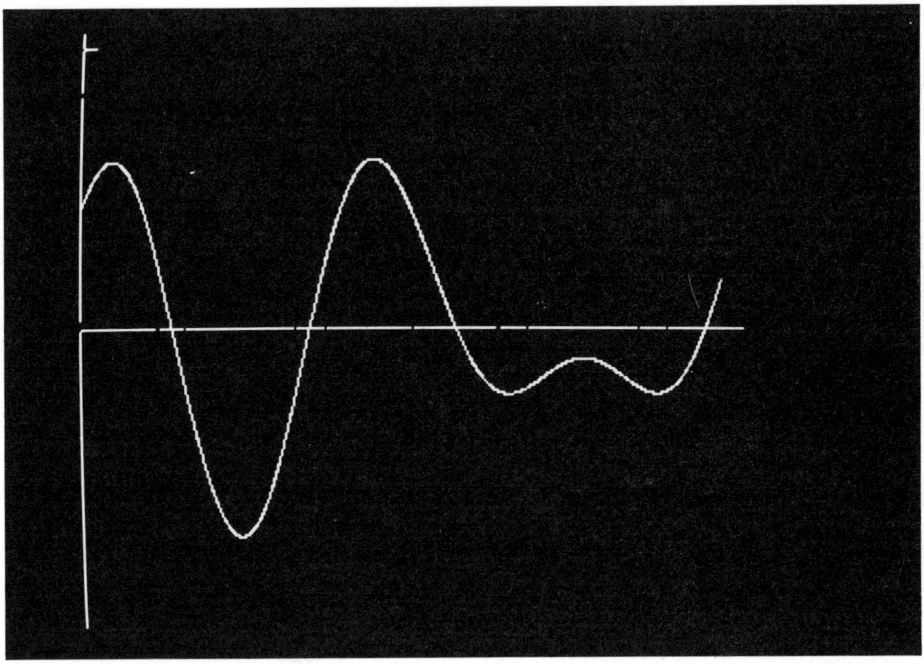

Plate 8 Sum of two waves

```
200 LET sincolour = 1
210 LET coscolour = 2
220 LET sincycles = 3
230 LET coscycles = 2
240 LET sinconfac = 2 * PI * sincycles / 1280
250 LET cosconfac = 2 * PI * coscycles / 1280
260 LET sinamplitude = 300
270 LET cosamplitude = 400
280 FOR x = 0 TO 1280
290 LET siny = sinamplitude * SIN(x * sinconfac)
300 GCOL0,sincolour
310 PLOT69,x,siny
320 LET cosy = cosamplitude * COS(x * cosconfac)
330 GCOL0,coscolour
340 PLOT69,x,cosy
380 NEXT x
```

With other trigonometrical functions although it does not cause an error message if the plotted point is not within the range of the screen, it is useful to ensure that the graph can be seen. The function plotted should be checked for its maximum and minimum values and the amplitude adjusted. An example is the function 300sin(3A) + 400cos(2A), which can have a value of 700, so the amplitude should be reduced accordingly. To plot this function as well as the functions that go to produce it, add these lines to the previous program:

```
350 GCOL0,3
360 LET sumy = (siny + cosy)/2
370 PLOT69,x,sumy
```

Sometimes, however, the use of a range check is unavoidable. For example, the function tan(A) goes to infinity when A is ninety degrees producing an error. ON ERROR GOTO will detect this condition and avoid crashing the program. This program plots tan(A) for two cycles and to get as much of the function as possible on the screen the amplitude is made quite low (Plate 9).

```
100 MODE 1
110 VDU29,0;512;
120 GCOL0,3
130 MOVE 0,0
140 DRAW 1279,0
150 MOVE 0,-512
160 DRAW 0,511
200 GCOL0,3
210 LET cycles = 2
220 LET confac = 2 * PI * cycles / 1280
230 LET amplitude = 10
240 LET n = 4
250 FOR x = 0 TO 1280
260 ON ERROR LET x=x+1:GOTO 270
270 LET y = amplitude * TAN(x * confac)
275 IF y>1000 OR y<-500 THEN LET n = 4
280 PLOTn,x,y
290 Let n = 5
300 NEXT x
```

This use of ON ERROR prevents the normal function of the ESCAPE key to exit the program. To do this, perform a BREAK (followed by OLD <RETURN> to recover the program). Line 275 is a 'bug-fix' to prevent +infinity being joined up to –infinity. Try removing it to see its effect.

Some functions still cause problems. Consider the equation of the circle

$$x^2 + y^2 = radius^2$$

where the maximum value for the radius is 511. BASIC cannot handle the equation as it is, it must be transformed to get a single value of y (or x) on the left of the equation.

```
y = SQR(radius*radius - x*x)
```

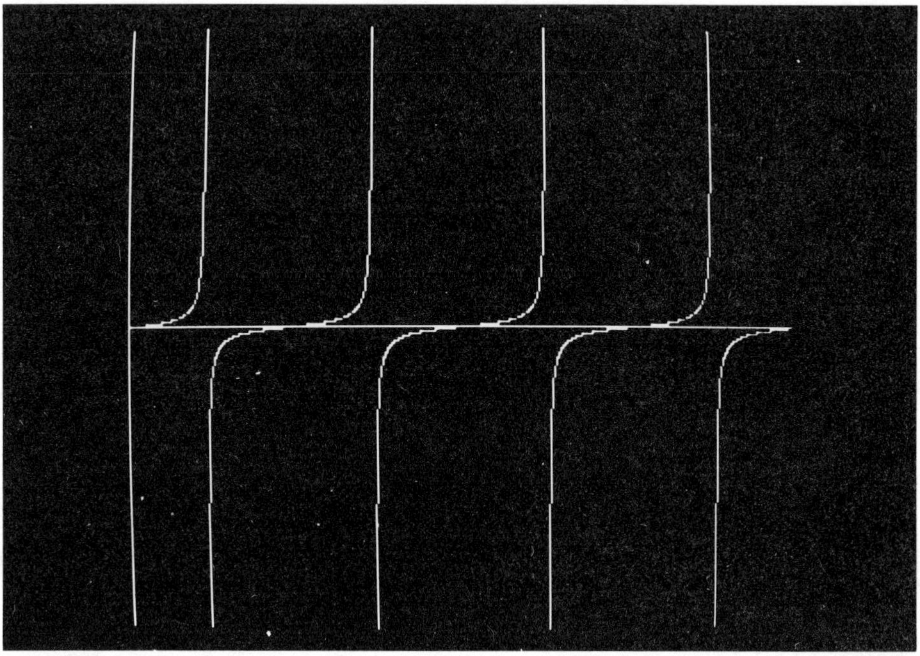

Plate 9 Tangent curve

Care must now be taken to prevent the absolute value of x from exceeding the radius, otherwise y becomes imaginary. Also the square root is automatically positive, so we shall only get the whole circle by separately including the negative value.

```
100 MODE 1
110 VDU29,640;512;
120 LET radius=400
130 FOR x = -radius TO radius
140 y = SQR(radius*radius - x*x)
150 PLOT69,x,y
160 PLOT69,x,-y
170 NEXT x
```

This gives uneven spacing between the plotted points and a more satisfactory way, which makes use of a separate parameter is preferred. For circular functions angle is the most useful parameter.

```
100 MODE 1
110 VDU29,640;512;
120 LET amplitude = 300
200 FOR angle = 0 TO 360
210 LET x = 1.1 * amplitude * COS(RAD(angle))
```

```
220  LET y = amplitude * SIN (RAD(angle))
230  PLOT69,x,y
240  NEXT angle
```

Here the x amplitude is made larger than the y amplitude to make the circle more circular in the display. The factor 1.1 in line 210 will need to be changed for different monitors.

The parametric method is widely applicable to most conic sections. The ellipse is given by

```
100  MODE 1
110  VDU29,640;512;
120  LET xamplitude = 400
130  LET yamplitude = 200
200  FOR angle = 0 TO 360
210  LET x = xamplitude * COS (RAD(angle))
220  LET y = yamplitude * SIN (RAD(angle))
230  PLOT69,x,y
240  NEXT angle
```

The parabola is given by

```
x=2*a*t
y=a*t*t
```

For example,

```
100  MODE 1
110  VDU29,640;512;
200  FOR t = -500 TO 500
210  LET x = 20 * t
220  LET y = t * t
230  PLOT69,x,y
240  NEXT t
```

The hyperbola has an awkward parametric equation

```
x=a/COS(RAD(angle))
y=b*TAN(RAD(angle))
```

This can produce infinite values, so the ON ERROR technique is used here too.

```
100  MODE1
110  VDU29,640;512;
120  GCOL0,3
130  ON ERROR LET angle=angle + 1:GOTO 210
200  FOR angle = 0 TO 360
210  x = 100/COS(RAD(angle))
220  y = 200*TAN(RAD(angle))
230  PLOT69,x,y
240  NEXT angle
```

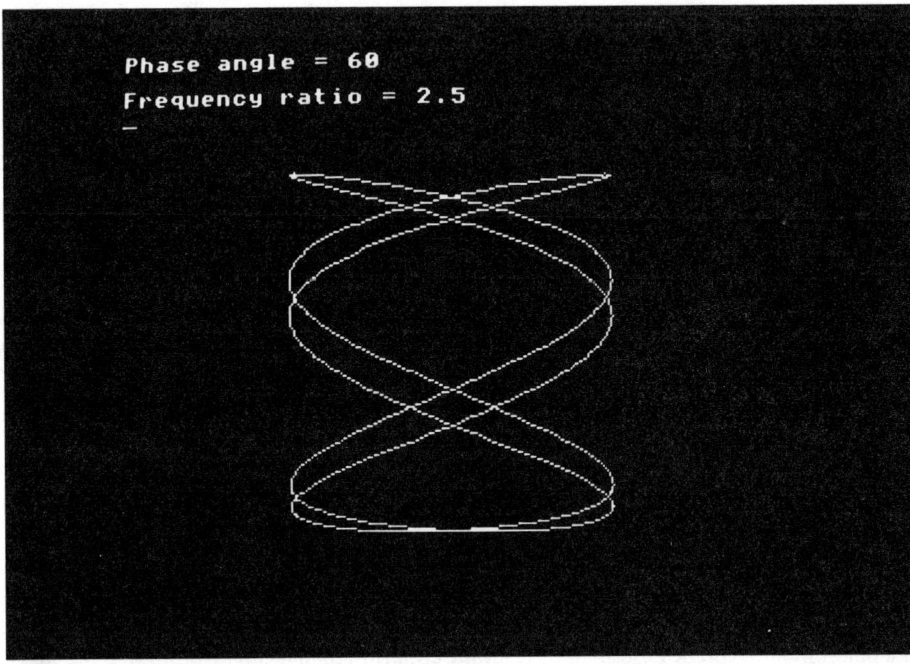

Plate 10 Lissajous figures

Particularly pleasing to the physics teacher is the production of Lissajous figures using sine equations with different frequencies and phase angles (Plate 10).

```
100 MODE1
110 VDU29,640;512;
120 GCOL0,3
130 INPUT TAB(0,0) "Phase Angle = " phase
140 INPUT TAB(0,1) "Frequency Ratio = " freqratio
150 LET amplitude = 300
160 LET n = 4
200 FOR angle = 0 to 100000
210 LET x = amplitude * SIN(RAD(angle*freqratio + phase))
220 LET y = amplitude * SIN(RAD(angle))
230 PLOTn,x,y
240 LET n = 5
250 NEXT angle
```

If non-integral values of the frequency ratio are desired, it can be many cycles before the pattern repeats itself, hence the need for the large number of cycles in line 200.

EVAL

The BBC BASIC function EVAL allows equations to be entered from the keyboard instead of the user having to stop the program to try out a different function. In some cases this is useful and you can see one application of it in PROGRAMMABLE OSCILLATOR (13). Usually, however, the necessity to enter the function with BASIC syntax means that the user has to have some familiarity with programming anyway. In this case it is no more difficult to halt the program and alter the line numbers. Program 3 (LOGIC MAKER) uses this technique since a particular Boolean function may spread over several lines of programming.

Applications

These ideas can be turned to practical classroom use in a number of ways. Once the principles are appreciated, a few hours at the keyboard will tell students more about the behaviour of functions than a whole series of lectures.

Simple functions

If a phenomenon can be described by a simple equation then it can be plotted in the ways just described. For example the distance-time graph of a body that falls from rest can be plotted with the equation

```
s = g * t * t / 2
```

This translates into a program as follows:

```
100 MODE 1
110 VDU29,0;900;
120 GCOL0,3
150 PRINT TAB(0,0);"Enter the acceleration due to gravity"
160 INPUT g
170 LET acc = -g
180 LET n=4
200 FOR t = 0 TO 1280
210 LET s = acc * t * t / 2
220 PLOTn,t,s/1000
230 LET n=5
240 NEXT t
250 GOTO 150
```

Different values for gravity may be entered and their effects noted. In this program values between 0 and 10 give the best results.

Wherever there are more than two variables, the others can be held constant during each scan of the screen and altered later by entering new values in precisely the same way as this. This process fits most equations experienced in O-level physics and chemistry.

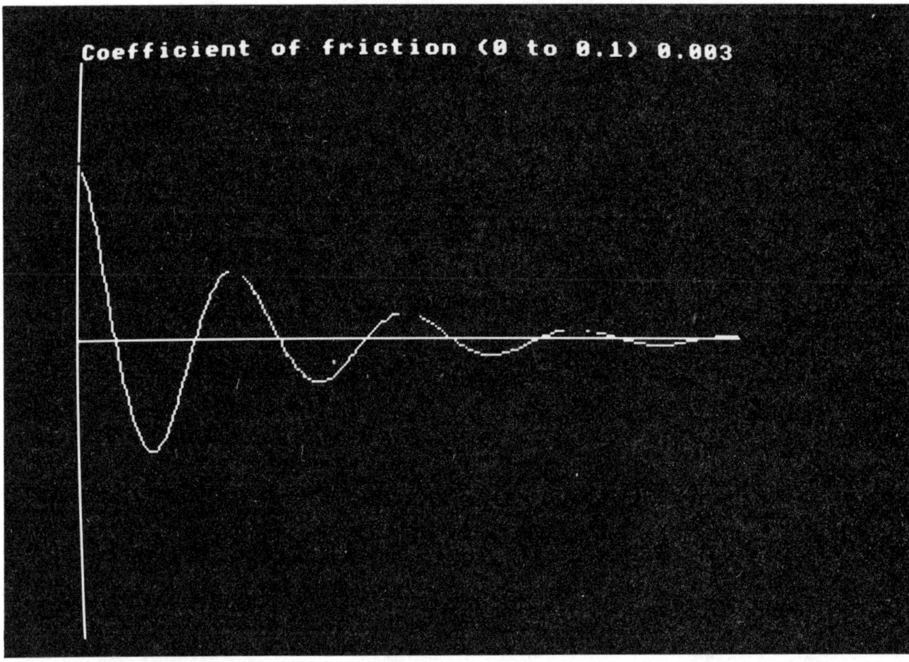

Plate 11 Damped oscillations – via mathematics

Typical examples are as follows:

```
V = I * R
W = I * I * R
P * V = const
1/v + 1/u = 1/f
F = k * m * M / (r * r)
```

Trigonometrical functions allow some of the properties of vibrations and waves to be investigated. The superposition of two waves to give interference, beats and modulated waves was demonstrated above. Here is another example: a program for an object executing damped oscillations. This includes a plot of the wave envelope too, so that the student can appreciate which part of the equation causes the different shapes of the graph (Plate 11). This program is actually an oversimplification, since no account has been taken of the effect of damping on the frequency of the oscillations. A much better way of doing the whole thing is discussed later in this chapter.

```
10 REM DAMPED OSCILLATIONS
100 MODE 1
110 VDU29,0;512;
120 GCOL0,3
130 MOVE 0,0
```

```
140 DRAW 1279,0
150 MOVE 0,-512
160 DRAW 0,511
190 INPUT TAB(0,0) "Coefficient of friction (0 to 0.1) " friction
200 LET cycles = 4
210 LET confac = 2 * PI * cycles/1280
220 LET amplitude = 300
230 MOVE 0,amplitude
240 FOR t = 0 TO 1280 STEP 5
250 LET angle = t * confac
260 LET displacement = amplitude * EXP(-t * friction) * COS(angle)
270 GCOL0,3
300 DRAW t,displacement
310 NEXT t
320 REM DRAW PEAK ENVELOPE
350 MOVE 0,amplitude
360 GCOL0,1
370 FOR t = 0 TO 1280 STEP 5
380 LET envelope = amplitude * EXP(-t * friction)
390 DRAW t,envelope
400 NEXT t
410 GOTO 190
```

A particularly satisfactory demonstration of the Fourier synthesis of a square wave is obtained with the following program:

```
 10 REM FOURIER SYNTHESIS
100 MODE 1
110 VDU29,0;512;
120 GCOL0,3
130 MOVE 0,0
140 DRAW 1279,0
150 MOVE 0,-512
160 DRAW 0,511
200 LET cycles = 2
210 LET confac = 2 * PI * cycles / 1280
220 LET amplitude = 300
230 LET n = 4
240 FOR x = 0 TO 1280
250 LET angle = x * confac
260 LET y1 = amplitude * SIN(angle)
270 LET y2 = amplitude / 3 * SIN(3 * angle)
280 LET y3 = amplitude / 5 * SIN(5 * angle)
290 LET y4 = amplitude / 7 * SIN(7 * angle)
300 LET y5 = amplitude / 9 * SIN(9 * angle)
```

```
310  LET y = y1 + y2 + y3 + y4 + y5
320  PLOTn,x,y
330  LET n = 5
340  NEXT x
```

Provided you are prepared to wait this process may be continued for as many harmonics as you wish.

Complicated functions

Many functions cannot easily be rearranged to make one variable into the subject of the equation. There is usually no necessity for this in any case as the microcomputer is quite capable of carrying out the calculation in parts. A good example of this is the voltage across a capacitor in an LCR circuit (Figure 3.1). If this is plotted against frequency a resonance curve is produced. The input voltage is assumed to be constant (E) and this produces a current in the circuit (I).

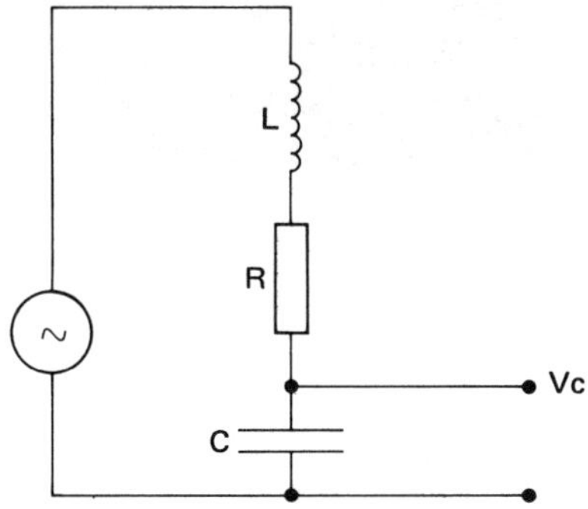

Figure 3.1 LCR circuit

I is given by E/Z, where Z is the impedance of the circuit at the given frequency (f). The voltage across the capacitor (C) is thus $I/2\pi fC$. The value for Z is obtained from the formula

$$Z^2 = R^2 + (2\pi fL - 1/2\pi fC)^2$$

RESONANCE (29) plots the desired curve (Plate 12). The values of L and C should be chosen to make the resonant frequency come near the middle of the screen (frequency = 500). Assuming inductances in millihenries and capacitors in microfarads, this gives L = 100 mH and C = 250 μF. (Strictly, this frequency is the angular frequency, but this is not apparent in the final plot, so it is ignored here. If required it is simple enough to allow for it.) Here is the essential part of the program.

```
INPUT "Inductance = " L
INPUT "Capacitance = " C
INPUT "Resistance = " R
```

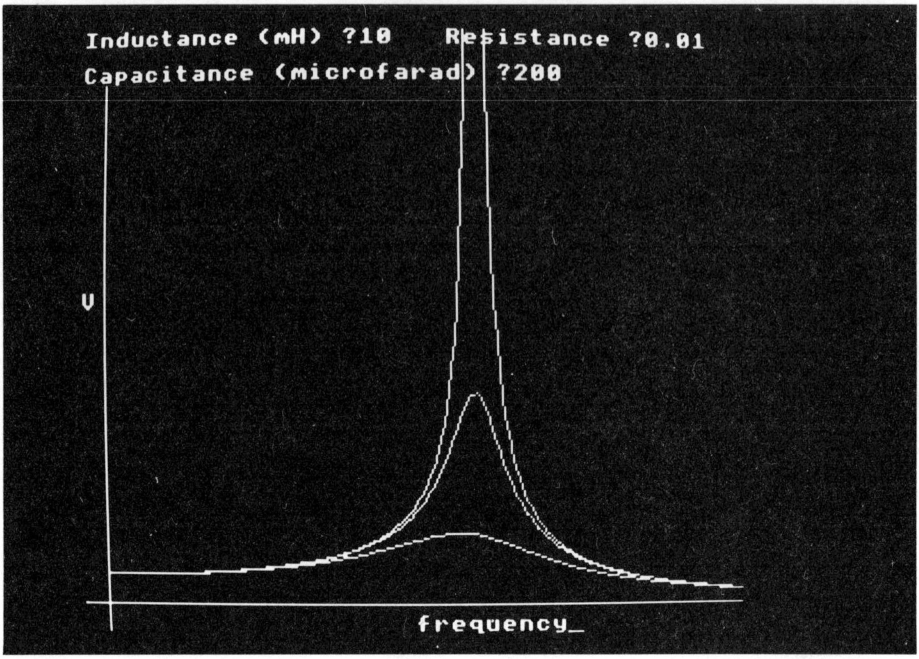

Plate 12 LCR resonance curves

```
LET E = 50 :REM APPLIED VOLTAGE
FOR frequency = 1 TO 1280
LET XL = frequency * L
LET XC = 1/(frequency * C)
LET X = XL - XC
LET Z = SQR(R*R + X*X)
LET I = E/Z
LET VC = I * XC
PLOT frequency,VC
NEXT frequency
```

It can be seen how the final capacitor voltage is obtained after several separate calculations, each of which should be familiar to the student. By showing each step of the calculation like this, it is easier to keep sight of the physics. The value of this kind of program is that students can vary one parameter at a time and observe the effects. PROJECTILES (30) also shows this technique.

Graph plotting with experimental data

Probably the most useful application of graphs in science is the plotting of experimental data. This is usually carried out to obtain the slope or intercept of a straight line graph, where the best line is obtained from the data by guesswork. The computer can be a great help in teaching students to do this, since the 'best' line can then be obtained by the method of least squares. The technique was used in Chapter 2 to draw the best line for RESONANCE IN A TUBE. This program also demonstrates one method of plotting crosses, by printing them in the position of the graphics cursor.

```
VDU5
MOVE x-12,y+12
PRINT"+"
```

This plots a cross at the point x,y. It is necessary to reduce the x coordinate and increase the y coordinate as shown in order to get the centre of the cross as near to the point x,y as possible. The + sign is far from ideal for this purpose, since its vertical part is actually two lines wide. A better way is to use a user-defined cross as follows:

```
VDU23,255,16,16,16,254,16,16,16,0
VDU5
MOVE x-12,y+12
PRINT CHR$255
```

Better still is a procedure (PROCplot(x,y)) that draws a cross exactly at the point x,y without the hassle of changing these values first. The procedure is defined by:

```
DEF PROCplot(x,y)
MOVE x-16,y
DRAW x+16,y
MOVE x,y-16
DRAW x,y+16
ENDPROC
```

A complete program to accept students' data and to process it is not easy if the data can have all possible values. The following program works within limits and may easily be adapted to suit any particular application. RESONANCE IN A TUBE demonstrated one such adaptation.

```
LEAST SQUARES FIT
 100  MODE 4
 200  @%=&A0A:REM Restore normal format
 300  VDU23,250,8,8,8,8,8,8,0,0
1000  REM****************************
1010  REM
1020  REM        COLLECT DATA
1030  REM
1040  REM****************************
1050  CLS
1060  PRINT:PRINT"Enter the number of data pairs."
1070  PRINT:INPUT numreadings
```

```
1080 DIM x(numreadings),y(numreadings)
1090 PRINT:PRINT "Enter each pair of readings"
1100 PRINT:PRINT "in the order x-coord.,y-coord."
1110 PRINT:PRINT "for example 56.3,89.75"
1120 FOR n=1 TO numreadings
1130 PRINT
1140 INPUT x(n),y(n)
1150 PRINT x(n),y(n)
1160 NEXT n
1170 CLS:PROClist
1180 PRINT:PRINT "Do you wish to change any readings?"
1190 PRINT:PRINT "Answer Y or N."
1200 PRINT:INPUT answer$
1210 IF answer$<>"Y" AND answer$<>"N" THEN 1180
1220 IF answer$="N" THEN 2000
1230 PRINT:PRINT "Enter the reference number for the"
1240 PRINT:PRINT "data pair you wish to change."
1250 PRINT:INPUT m%
1260 IF m%>numreadings THEN PRINT:PRINT"You did not enter this
     reading.":GOTO 1170
1270 PRINT:PRINT"Enter the new pair of readings"
1280 PRINT:INPUT x(m),y(m)
1290 PRINT
1300 PROClist
1310 GOTO 1170
1320
2000 REM*****************************
2010 REM
2020 REM        DETERMINE AXES
2030 REM
2040 REM*****************************
2050 CLS
2060 PRINT:PRINT"Enter the maximum x-coordinate"
2070 PRINT:INPUT xmax
2080 PRINT:PRINT"Enter the maximum y-coordinate"
2090 PRINT:INPUT ymax
2100 LET xscale=xmax/1000
2110 LET yscale=ymax/1000
2120
5000 REM*****************************
5010 REM
5020 REM          DRAW AXES
5030 REM
5040 REM*****************************
```

```
5050 CLS
5060 REM Move origin
5070 VDU29,128;64;
5080 MOVE 0,-32:DRAW 0,1000
5090 MOVE -32,0:DRAW 1200,0
5095 @% = &202:REM short format
5100 VDU5
5110 FOR y=0 TO 10
5120 MOVE -128,12+100*y:PRINT;100*y*yscale
5130 MOVE -28,12+100*y:PRINT;"-"
5140 NEXT y
5150
5160 FOR x=0 TO 10
5170 MOVE -16+100*x,0:PRINT CHR$250
5180 MOVE -48+100*x,-32:PRINT;100*x*xscale
5190 NEXT x
5200
5210 REM****************************
5220 REM
5230 REM      LINEAR REGRESSION
5240 REM
5250 REM****************************
5260
5270 LET xtotal=0
5280 LET ytotal=0
5290 LET sumxsquares=0
5300 LET sumxyproduct=0
5320 FOR n=1 TO numreadings
5330 LET x=x(n)/xscale
5340 LET y=y(n)/yscale
5360 LET xtotal=xtotal + x
5370 LET ytotal=ytotal + y
5380 LET sumxsquares=sumxsquares + x*x
5390 LET sumxyproduct=sumxyproduct + x*y
5400 PROCplot(x,y)
5410 NEXT n
5420
5430 REM****************************
5440 REM
5450 REM   CALCULATE SLOPE AND INTERCEPT
5460 REM
5470 REM****************************
5480
5490
```

```
5500  LET slope = (numreadings * sumxyproduct - xtotal *
      ytotal)/(numreadings * sumxsquares - xtotal * xtotal)
5510  LET intercept = (ytotal - slope * xtotal) / numreadings
5520  REM****************************
5530  REM
5540  REM           PLOT LINE
5550  REM
5560  REM****************************
5570
5580  REM Plot minimum x-value
5590  LET x%=0:y%=intercept + slope * x%
5600  MOVE x%,y%
5610  REM Plot maximum x-value
5620  LET x%=1200:y%=intercept + slope * x%
5630  DRAW x%,y%
5640  VDU4
5650  END
5660
10000 DEF PROClist
10010 PRINT TAB(19,2);"x , y"
10020 PRINT
10030 FOR n=1 TO numreadings
10040 PRINT n,x(n),y(n)
10050 NEXT n
10060 ENDPROC
10070
11000 DEF PROCplot(X,Y)
11010 MOVE X-16,Y
11020 DRAW X+16,Y
11030 MOVE X,Y-16
11040 DRAW X,Y+16
11050 ENDPROC
```

For statistical data a bar chart is preferred. In this case the x coordinate is probably discontinuous, but whether it increases in steps of one, two or five, etc. is a matter of choice in each case. Hence again a single program will not suffice for all occasions and one like the following will need to be adapted for each particular case. The procedure to plot a bar of length y at the position x is:

```
DEF PROCvbar(x,y)
MOVE x,0
MOVE x+48,0
PLOT85,x,y
PLOT85,x+48,y
ENDPROC
```

One program to handle the data input for bar charts is as follows:

```
BAR CHART
 100 MODE 4
 200 @% = &A0A:REM Restore normal format
 300 VDU23,250,8,8,8,8,8,8,0,0
1000 REM***************************
1010 REM
1020 REM        COLLECT DATA
1030 REM
1040 REM***************************
1050 CLS
1060 PRINT:PRINT"Enter the number of data readings."
1070 PRINT:INPUT numreadings
1080 DIM y(numreadings)
1090 PRINT:PRINT "Enter each reading in ascending order"
1100 PRINT:PR!NT "of the x-coordinate."
1120 FOR n=1 TO numreadings
1130 PRINT TAB(5);n;" ";:INPUT y(n)
1160 NEXT n
1170 CLS:PROClist
1180 PRINT:PRINT "Do you wish to change any readings?"
1190 PRINT:PRINT "Answer Y or N."
1200 PRINT:INPUT answer$
1210 IF answer$<>"Y" AND answer$<>"N" THEN 1180
1220 IF answer$ = "N" THEN 2000
1230 PRINT:PRINT "Enter the reference number for the"
1240 PRINT:PRINT "data you wish to change."
1250 PRINT:INPUT m%
1260 IF m%>numreadings THEN PRINT:PRINT"You did not enter this
     reading.":GOTO 1170
1270 PRINT:PRINT"Enter the data."
1280 PRINT:INPUT y(m)
1290 PRINT
1300 PROClist
1310 GOTO 1170
1320
2000 REM***************************
2010 REM
2020 REM        DETERMINE AXES
2030 REM
2040 REM***************************
2050 CLS
2080 PRINT:PRINT"Enter the maximum y-coordinate"
```

```
2090  PRINT:INPUT ymax
2100  LET xscale=numreadings/1000
2110  LET yscale=ymax/1000
2120
5000  REM****************************
5010  REM
5020  REM            DRAW AXES
5030  REM
5040  REM****************************
5050  CLS
5060  REM Move origin
5070  VDU29,128;64;
5080  MOVE 0,-32:DRAW 0,1000
5090  MOVE -32,0:DRAW 1200,0
5095  @% = &202:REM short format
5100  VDU5
5110  FOR y=0 TO 10
5120  MOVE -128,12+100*y:PRINT;100*y*yscale
5130  MOVE -28,12+100*y:PRINT;"-"
5140  NEXT y
5150
5160  FOR x=0 TO 10
5170  MOVE -16+100*x,0:PRINT CHR$250
5180  MOVE -48+100*x,-32:PRINT;100*x*xscale
5190  NEXT x
5200
5210  REM****************************
5220  REM
5230  REM            BAR CHART
5240  REM
5250  REM****************************
5260
5320  FOR n=1 TO numreadings
5330  LET x=n/xscale
5340  LET y=y(n)/yscale
5400  PROCvbar(x,y)
5410  NEXT n
5500
5640  VDU4
5650  END
5660
10000 DEF PROClist
10010 PRINT TAB(9,2);"x , y"
10020 PRINT
```

```
10030  FOR n=1 TO numreadings
10040  PRINT n,y(n)
10050  NEXT n
10060  ENDPROC
10070
11000  DEF PROCvbar(X,Y)
11010  MOVE X,0
11020  MOVE X+48,0
11030  PLOT85,X,Y
11040  PLOT85,X+48,Y
11050  ENDPROC
```

Another example of the plotting of bar charts is given in SUM OF TWO DICE (22).

Horizontal bar charts are just as easy to achieve thus:

```
11000  DEF PROChbar(X,Y)
11010  MOVE 0,Y
11020  MOVE 0,Y,48
11030  PLOT85,X,Y
11040  PLOT85,X,Y+48
11050  ENDPROC
11000  DEF PROCvbar(X,Y)
11010  MOVE X,0
11020  MOVE X+48,0
11030  PLOT85,X,Y
11040  PLOT85,X+48,Y
11050  ENDPROC
```

Pie charts are obtained with the circle drawing technique already shown. The filled circle uses the triangle-filling PLOT85 instruction too. To ensure that the pie is closed each amount is converted to its nearest whole number of degrees (line 1320). Each sector is added onto the previous one and hopefully the total angle reaches exactly 360 degrees. MODE 2 allows the seven colours to be used (line 1370), but if there are exactly eight sectors this will need to be modified or two adjacent colours will be the same.

```
PIE CHART
 100  MODE 7
 200  DIM amount(100)
1000  REM*****************************
1010  REM
1020  REM           COLLECT DATA
1030  REM
1040  REM*****************************
1050  CLS
1060  PRINT:PRINT"Enter the amounts for each sector"
1070  PRINT:PRINT "of the pie chart."
```

```
1080 PRINT:PRINT "Enter 0 to obtain the pie chart."
1090 LET n=0:total=0
1100 REPEAT
1110 LET n=n+1
1120 PRINT:INPUT amount(n)
1130 LET total=total + amount(n)
1140 UNTIL amount(n)=0
1150 LET numreadings=n-1
1160
1200 REM*****************************
1210 REM
1220 REM        DETERMINE AXES
1230 REM
1240 REM*****************************
1250
1260 MODE2
1270 REM Move origin
1280 VDU29,600;500;
1290 LET totalangle%=1
1300 MOVE 400,0
1310 FOR n=1 TO numreadings
1320 LET angle% = 360 * amount(n)/total + 0.5
1330 FOR totalangle%=(totalangle%-1) TO (totalangle% + angle%)
1340 LET X=400*COS(RAD(totalangle%))
1350 LET Y=400*SIN(RAD(totalangle%))
1360 MOVE 0,0
1370 GCOL0,(n MOD 7)+1
1380 PLOT85,X,Y
1390 NEXT totalangle%
1400 NEXT n
```

The use of RND

The random number function of BASIC is not provided only for computer games! It is invaluable for carrying out statistical experiments, particularly where the results can be displayed graphically. RADIOACTIVE DECAY (21) illustrates the use of this function to decide which nucleus should decay next. Since the position of this next nucleus is decided at random, the chance of choosing a position with an undecayed nucleus depends upon the number of such nuclei remaining. This therefore simulates radioactive decay quite well (Plate 13). The use of SOUND to simulate a Geiger counter is an idea suggested by W.Jeffries at a conference in Jordanhill College of Education in June 1982.

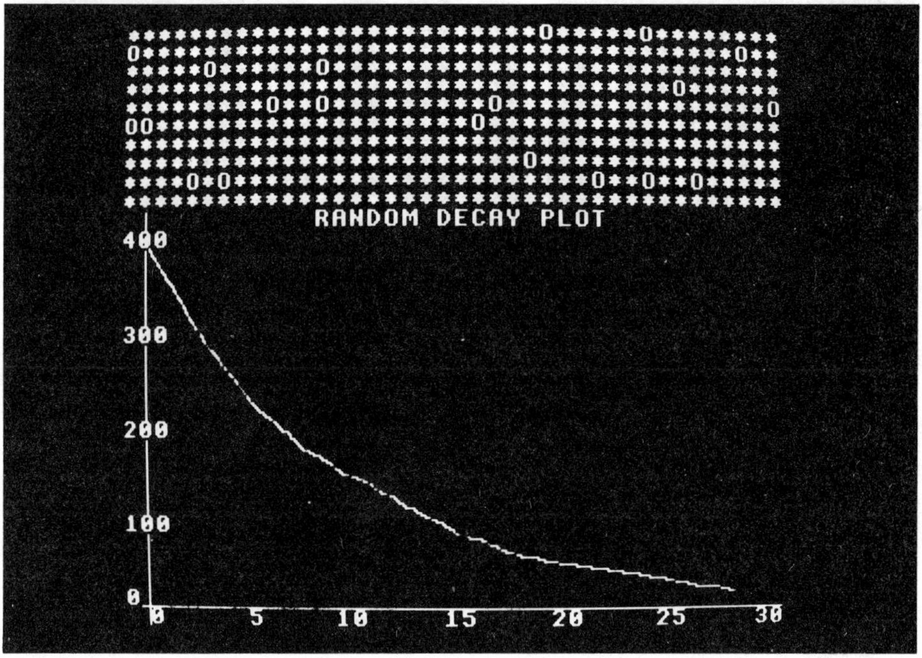

Plate 13 Radioactive decay

If one of the variables is discontinuous, then the bar chart is an obvious means of display as SUM OF TWO DICE (22) illustrates. This is a standard experiment, but few students could do it more than a few times as a practical exercise, so the microcomputer can help to make the pattern more obvious. In the space of a few minutes the experiment is performed hundreds of times (Plate 14).

The use of RND is particularly valuable in biology for simulating genetic linkage and there are very many programs available for this. It is also used in the simulation of Geiger and Marsden's experiment discussed later (RUTHERFORD, 32).

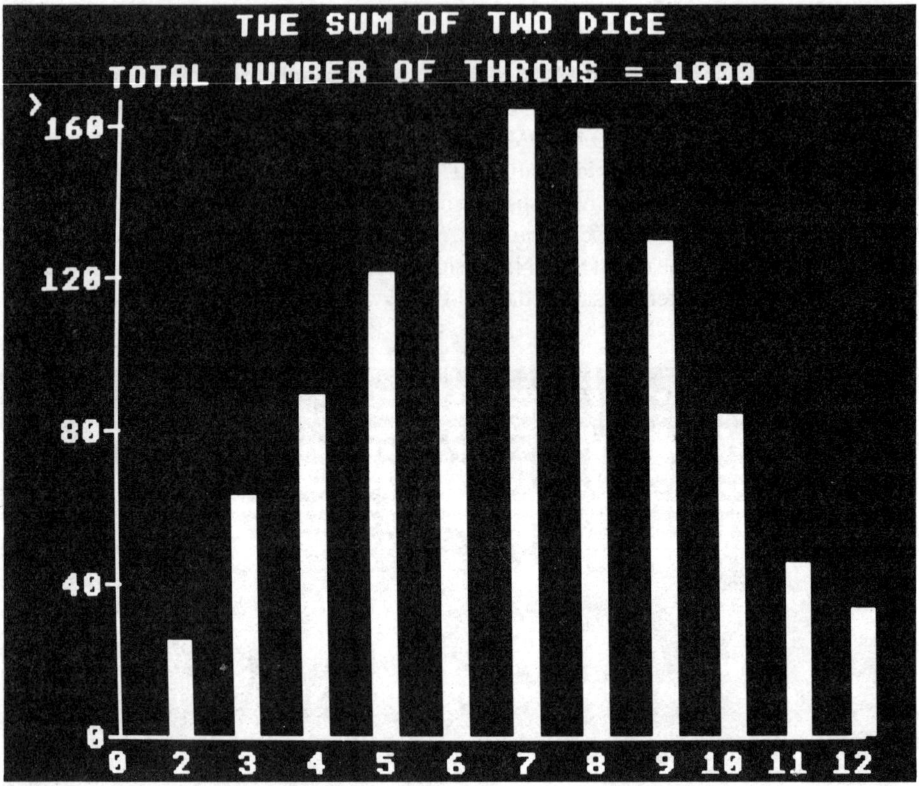

Plate 14 Probability distribution – the sum of two dice

Iterative Methods

The *Nuffield Advanced Physics* originators were far-sighted in noting probable trends towards more and cheaper calculators. They describe several experiments which run very nicely on a microcomputer. Basically they suggest that as well as the traditional algebraic (usually integral calculus) analysis of physical phenomena, teachers should explore numerical solutions. A good example is the discharge of a capacitor through a resistor. This can be solved algebraically by noting that the current flowing through the resistor is the differential of the charge on and hence the voltage across the capacitor. Since this current is directly proportional to voltage, all that has to be done is integrate a reciprocal and end up with an exponential logarithm. The mathematics so obscures the physics that it is better to seek a step-by-step solution to the problem.

The voltage (V) across the capacitor is related to the charge (Q) in the capacitor by

$$Q = V * C \qquad \text{(Eq. 1)}$$

This voltage causes a current (I) to flow through the resistor according to the well-known formula

$$V = I * R \qquad \text{(Eq. 2)}$$

If a current of one ampere flows for one second, the capacitor will lose one coulomb of charge, so in one millisecond, say, it will lose one millicoulomb of charge. Thus the remaining voltage on the capacitor after one millisecond is a bit less than it was before, and we can use Eq. 1 to calculate exactly how much less. This gives us a new value for V, with which to begin the next millisecond. By hand it could take some time to see how the capacitor voltage is falling, but the microcomputer makes very short work of the calculations. The exponential curve is obtained with only the three fundamental equations. The actual program is listed below, but any student, particularly one able to comprehend the calculus approach, could write such a program.

The main difficulty is ensuring that the chosen values give results that fit the screen. The time axis (x axis) goes from 50 to 1279 units. If these are seconds, then a time constant of about 300 seconds is needed for the R-C circuit. This is somewhat unrealistic, so we pretend that our time scale is in microseconds instead. The value for R can thus be a few thousand ohms and the value for C between 1 and 10 microfarads. The increment of time between each successive calculation (timeinc) is fixed at 5 units in this program. It can be changed to give a finer line (which is slower) or a more chunky line which is faster. Since

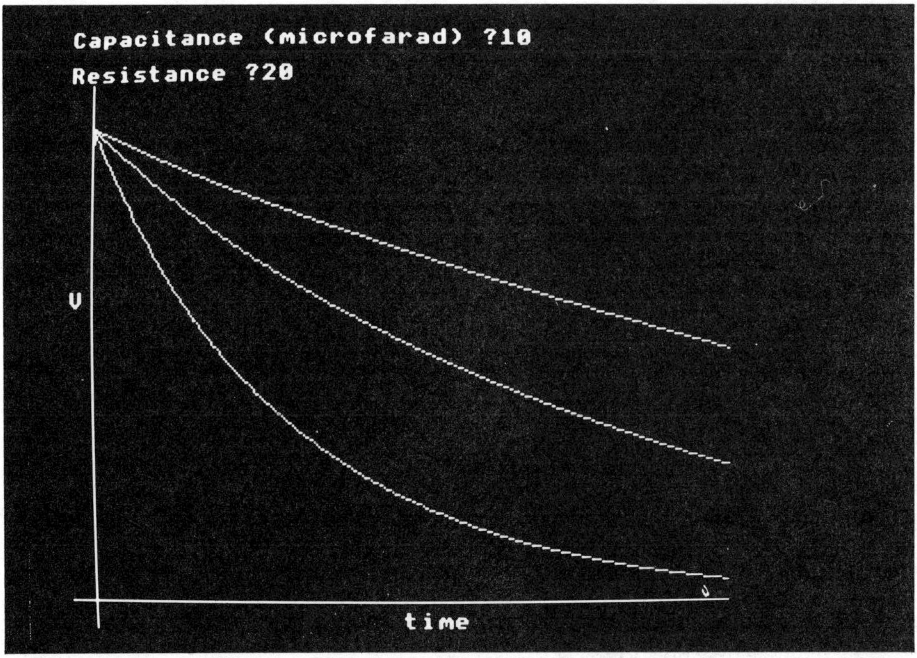

Plate 15 Capacitor discharge by formula

different values for R and C can be entered, students can be asked to discover how the rate of decay depends upon R and C (Plate 15). In so doing, they learn a great deal about the decay curve, which should transfer to their understanding of, say, radioactive decay too.

```
100 MODE 1
110 GCOL0,3
120 MOVE 0,50:DRAW 1279,50
130 MOVE 50,0:DRAW 50,1023
140 PRINTTAB(0,0);"                                        "
150 PRINTTAB(0,1);"                                        "
160 PRINT TAB(0,0);"Capacitance (microfarads) ";:INPUT capacitance
165 PRINT TAB(0,1);"Resistance (ohms) ";:INPUT resistance
170 PRINT TAB(0,14);"V"
180 PRINT TAB(20,31);"time"
185 IF R=0 THEN R=0.0001
190 REM INITIAL VALUES
200 LET E = 800:REM INITIAL VOLTAGE
210 MOVE 50,E
220 LET time = 50
230 LET charge = E * capacitance:REM microcoulombs
240 LET voltage = E
250 LET timeinc = 5
260
300 REPEAT
310 LET current = voltage/resistance
320 LET charge = charge - current * timeinc
330 LET voltage = charge/capacitance
340 LET time = time + timeinc
350 DRAW time,voltage+50
360 UNTIL time>1279 OR voltage<5
370 GOTO 140
```

This approach to the analysis of phenomena is called the **iterative method.** It is applicable in very many areas (and not just physics). Programs 30 to 32 show how it may also be applied to motion. Plate 16 shows the sort of results obtained with PROJECTILES (30). The basic algorithm is as follows:

1 Assume initial position, velocity and acceleration.
2 Assume a small increment of time.
3 Determine the new velocity after this time interval.
4 Determine the distance travelled at this velocity during this time interval.
5 Calculate the new position.
6 Return to step 1, with new values of velocity and acceleration.

This gives a delightful way of tackling simple (and damped) harmonic motion, without recourse to differential equations.

```
 10 REM DAMPED OSCILLATIONS
 20 REM BY THE ITERATIVE METHOD
100 MODE 1
110 VDU29,0;512;
120 GCOL0,3
125 MOVE 0,0
130 DRAW 1279,0
140 MOVE 0,-512
150 DRAW 0,511
160 INPUT TAB(0,0) "Damping coefficient (0 to 0.1) " friction
170 INPUT TAB(0,1) "Spring constant (0 to 10) " springconstant
180 INPUT TAB(0,2) "Mass of object (0 to 10) " mass
190 LET amplitude = 300
200 LET displacement = amplitude
210 LET speed = 0:REM INITIAL SPEED
220 MOVE 0,amplitude
230 LET time = 0
240 LET timeinc = 5
250 REPEAT
260 LET restoringforce = -springconstant * displacement/10000
270 LET frictionalforce = -friction * speed
280 LET totalforce = totalforce + frictionalforce
290 LET acceleration = totalforce/mass
300 LET speed = speed + acceleration * timeinc
310 LET displacement = displacement + speed * timeinc
320 LET time = time + timeinc
330 DRAW t,displacement
340 UNTIL time > 1279
```

On each run different values can be entered to discover the role that each variable plays in the overall motion. If this is coupled with actual experimental work with masses on the end of a spring, I believe the approach to be much more truly physics than the traditional mathematical approach.

For projectiles there are two directions (x and y) to consider. However, these can be considered entirely independently, so the only complication is that there are twice as many calculations in each cycle. PROJECTILES (30) illustrates this: the motion in the x direction is constant velocity, while that in the y direction is constant acceleration (Plate 16). This program also shows how easy it now is to include more difficult ideas. The usual treatment of projectiles ignores friction and leads to the ideal case of 45 degrees as the angle for maximum range. PROJECTILES incorporates a frictional drag, proportional to the speed, which reduces the speed and leads to the idea of terminal velocity. The resulting motion is not unlike that predicted by Bacon's impetus theory. The acceleration

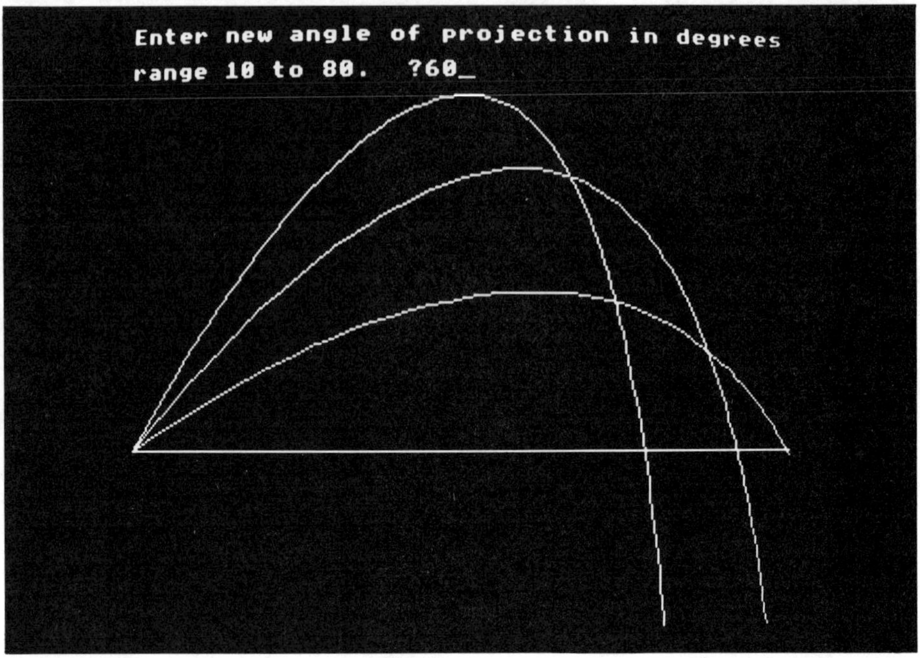

Plate 16 Projectiles

due to gravity and the friction (dragcoeff) can be altered for different effects (projectiles in treacle?).

Motion under a central force is rarely understood. NEWTON (31) is a game that any student should be able to solve, but it often fools physics graduates. The objective is to put a rocket into moon orbit from outside. Try it and see if you understand Newton's laws yourself (Plate 17). The program first calculates the distance between the rocket and the centre of the moon. This is converted into two forces, one which affects the acceleration in the x direction, the other the y direction. This in turn leads to predictions of where the rocket will be after the next unit of time (timeinc) and the process reiterates until the rocket crashes on the moon's surface or disappears off the screen. The value of 'timeinc' can be altered as before to achieve smoother if slower motion.

Alpha particle scattering by a gold nucleus provides a classic derivation for university undergraduates. I understand that the mathematics of this was too difficult for Rutherford and was handed over to a mathematician. I imagine that Rutherford would have loved the iterative method. The essential part of RUTHERFORD (32) is very similar to its equivalent in NEWTON, except that the force acting is reversed to produce repulsion instead of attraction. The motion is also speeded up (with a loss in resolution) to allow a large number of particles to be observed. These are fired at random at the gold nucleus and only a few pass close enough to be deflected (Plate 18).

So the mathematics is reduced to the level where any sixth former can understand it. I

Plate 17 Satellite motion

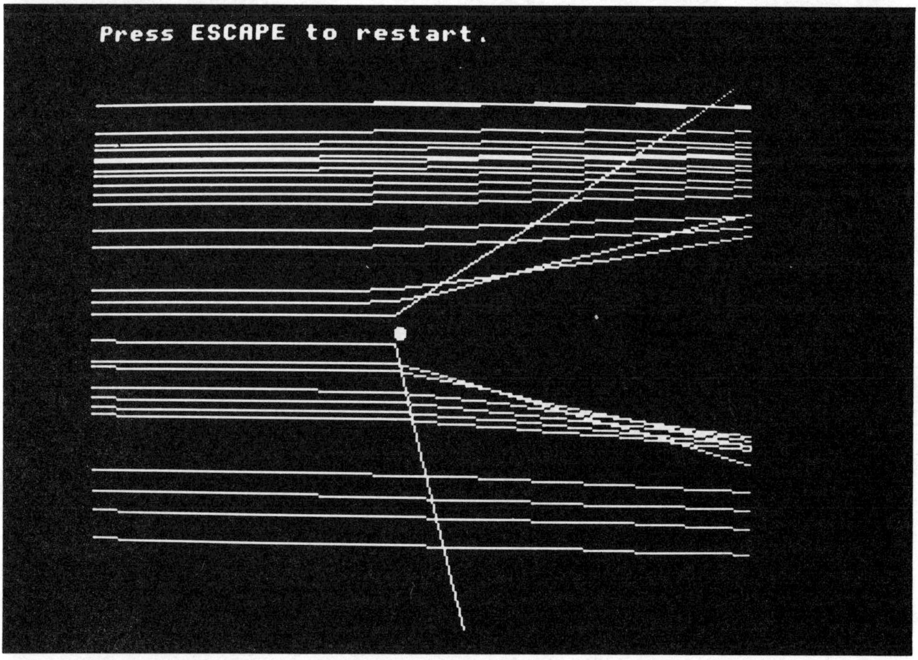

Plate 18 Rutherford alpha particle scattering simulation

am not sure that many teachers, particularly of physics, have yet realized the implications of this. If, as I suspect it will, computer programming becomes the fourth R, the traditional dependence of advanced science subjects upon mathematics could be allowed to decline, thus opening them up to more students than hitherto.

Modelling the environment

The iterative process has wider applications than those above and it was used by the Huntingdon Project, which produced the well-known simulations in biology and chemistry. One of these, POLLUT, analyses the effect of certain types of pollutant upon water life and another, HABER, looks at the effects of changing the temperature and pressure etc. of the reactants in an industrial process. Practically anything that can be quantified, can be mathematically modelled, although the accuracy of the predicted outcomes is not necessarily reliable. It depends upon whether all the important factors have been taken into account.

To illustrate the principles, fox and rabbit populations can be modelled to predict how they change with time. It is assumed that the rabbits' food is infinite so that they can reproduce without restriction. Although the increment of time is assumed to be one week, it is possible to enter an arbitrary rate of growth for the rabbit population between 0 and 5 per cent.

The growth in the fox population is dependent upon the supply of rabbits. If foxes only

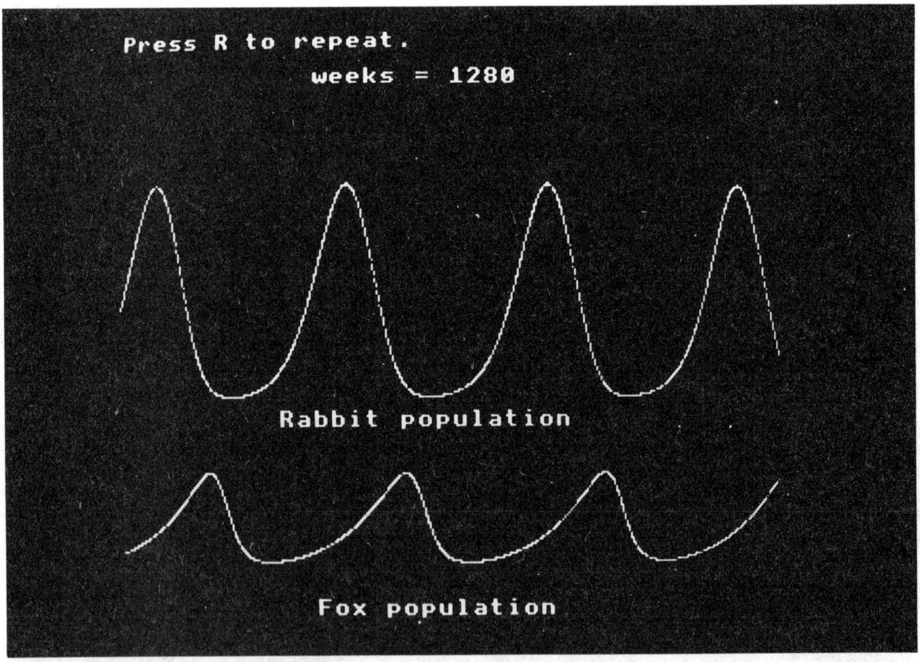

Plate 19 Fox and rabbit population simulation

eat rabbits, then they will begin to die if their population exceeds some factor of the rabbit population. Foxes with abundant food reproduce at a constant rate, which is also chosen before the start of the iteration. It is assumed that the starvation rate of foxes depends upon the ratio of foxes to rabbits, which seems reasonable. It is further assumed that the death rate of rabbits is proportional to the product of rabbits and foxes. This assumes that one fox with 1000 rabbits will still eat twice as much as the same fox with 500 rabbits. (I greatly suspect the model at this point.) The number of rabbits that are eaten depends upon the number of foxes and the number of foxes depends upon the number of rabbits. This classic problem can only be solved by an iterative process, since the equations generated have no analytical solution (Plate 19).

```
  10 REM FOX AND RABBIT SIMULATION
 100 MODE 4
 110 ON ERROR GO TO 500
 200 CLS
 300 INPUT "FOX GROWTH RATE (range 0 to 5%) " foxgrowthrate
 310 INPUT "RABBIT GROWTH RATE (range 0 to 5%) " rabbitgrowthrate
 320 PROCpopulation
 500 PRINT TAB(0,0);"Press R to repeat"
 510 IF INKEY$(255)<>"R" THEN 510
 520 GOTO 200
1000
2000 DEF PROCpopulation
2010 CLS
2020 LET weeks = 0
2022 LET rabbitgrowthrate=rabbitgrowthrate/100
2024 LET foxgrowthrate=foxgrowthrate/100
2030 PRINT TAB(0,0);"Press ESCAPE to stop"
2040 PRINT TAB(12,2);"weeks = "
2050 LET rabbits = 3000
2060 LET foxes = 20
2070 PRINT TAB(12,30);"Fox population"
2080 PRINT TAB(10,20);"Rabbit population"
2100 REPEAT
2200 LET babyrabbits = rabbits * rabbitgrowthrate
2210 LET deadrabbits = foxes * rabbits / 1000
2220 LET rabbits = rabbits + babyrabbits - deadrabbits
2230 LET babyfoxes = foxes * foxgrowthrate
2240 LET deadfoxes = 5 * foxes / rabbits
2250 LET foxes = foxes + babyfoxes - deadfoxes
2260 LET weeks = weeks + 1
2270 PRINT TAB(20,0);weeks
2280 GCOL0,1:PLOT69,weeks,2*foxes + 100
2290 GCOL0,3:PLOT69,weeks,rabbits/20 + 400
```

```
2300 UNTIL weeks>1279 OR rabbits>25000
2400 ENDPROC
```

As a physicist I find this much less satisfying than the same approach applied to physics, because I can justify some of the values entered into the equations of motion. I am not at all sure about the constants entered into the fox and rabbits program. (I chose them to get the right result!) However, I am sure that biologists will be able to do it properly once the essential idea has been appreciated.

4 Microcomputer timing and control

'The question is,' said Humpty Dumpty, 'which is to be Master – that's all.'
(Lewis Carroll, *Through the Looking Glass*)

Interfacing a microcomputer

Most control applications use **two-state** devices. An electric light switch can be up or down. An electromagnetic relay can be on or off. A valve can be open or closed. Digital electronic systems are used to switch such devices on or off. Although quite complex, a microcomputer is still only another digital system, so it is possible to use a microcomputer to control the above devices. It can switch lamps, relays, motors and valves on or off.

This is not a normal function of a microcomputer and it has not been designed specifically to do this. Consequently the current needed to switch on these devices may be larger than that provided by the microcomputer output. There has to be some **interface** between the microcomputer and the device being switched, to boost the switching current to the correct levels.

A microcomputer can also be used to detect whether any particular two-state device is in its on or its off state. Here, the switching voltages involved may be different for each device, so some interface must be used to change the voltage levels of the device to the levels acceptable to the microcomputer.

In digital electronics we are only concerned with two-state devices, ones that can be switched on or off. Generally, to switch a device on, we send a HIGH voltage to its input. To turn it off, we send a LOW voltage. HIGH and LOW are obviously not the same for different devices, here are a few examples:

Device	On	Off
light emitting diode	1.2 V	0.5 V
torch bulb	3.0 V	1.5 V
electromagnetic relay	5.0 V	2.0 V
silicon transistor	0.7 V	0.5 V
TTL integrated circuit	2.4 V	0.4 V

To remove this uncertainty about what is 'HIGH' and what is 'LOW', engineers use **TTL** logic levels. TTL stands for **transistor transistor logic;** it is a particular standard used in the electronics industry. A TTL HIGH voltage is between 2.4 and 5.5 V, which, as you can see, will switch on all the above devices. A TTL LOW voltage is between 0.4 and 0 V, which will switch all these devices off. A HIGH voltage is also called **logic level 1** and a LOW voltage is called **logic level 0.**

Connections to the BBC microcomputer are made through its user port. This is described in detail later in this chapter, but to begin with we shall just use it without explaining how it works. A logic board or a two-input board may be connected to this user port and all investigations in this chapter will be done with these. The design of these boards and the method of connecting them to the user port are described at the end of this chapter. The power supply for these logic boards comes from the microcomputer itself.

The two-input board (Figure 4.1) consists of two input sockets and a transistor driven LED to indicate the logic state of the output. It can be used by the microcomputer to

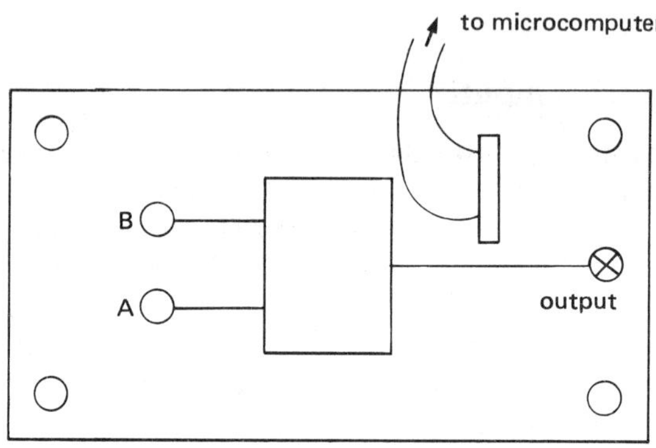

Figure 4.1 The two-input board

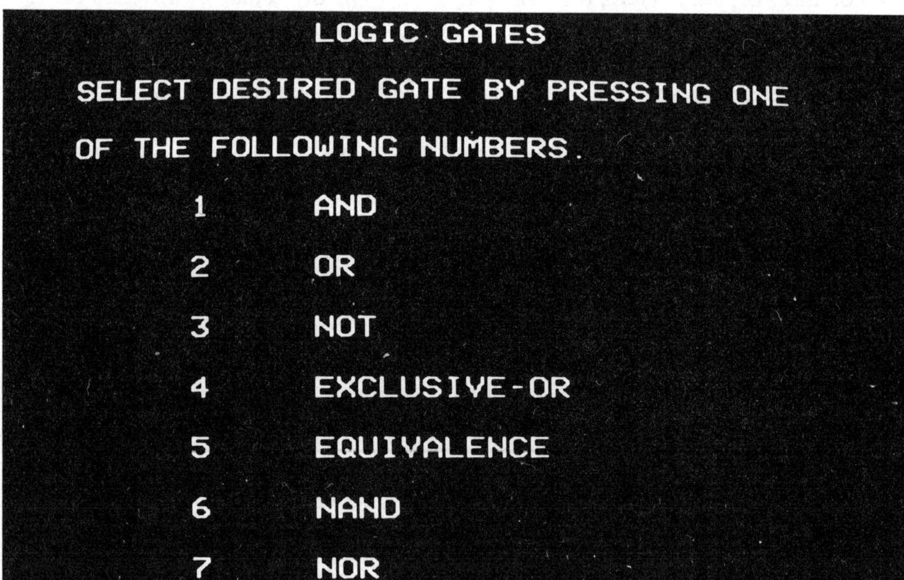

Plate 20 LOGIC GATES

simulate each of the standard logic gates. Once the board has been connected to the microcomputer in the manner discussed in the Appendix, LOGIC GATES (1) should be loaded and run. It works in the following way.

The two-input board has two inputs labelled A and B. When the program is run it asks which logic gate is to be simulated (the choice is AND, OR, NOT, NAND, NOR, EXCLUSIVE-OR or EQUIVALENCE) (Plate 20). After the selection is made (by pressing one of the keys 1 to 7) the screen displays a diagram of the board (Plate 21), indicates the current logic states of the inputs and the output, displays the appropriate truth table and highlights the particular line of this truth table which is currently being implemented.

The input logic levels can be changed by connecting them to the 5 V terminals (red), which makes them go HIGH, or they may be connected to the black 0 V terminals, which makes them go LOW. Unconnected inputs float HIGH; the normal condition for TTL devices. When the logic level of either input is changed, the display also changes accordingly.

This program has been found to give a good introduction to the principles of logic gates. It also illustrates the way that a programmable device, like a microcomputer, can be used to produce different Boolean functions under the control of a program.

Program 1A is a variation on the above called LOGIC TEST. This illustrates the capability of the microcomputer to assess practical ability as well as just knowledge (admittedly in a specialized area). This program uses the same two-input logic board, but this time it is the program that selects the type of gate being implemented. The student has

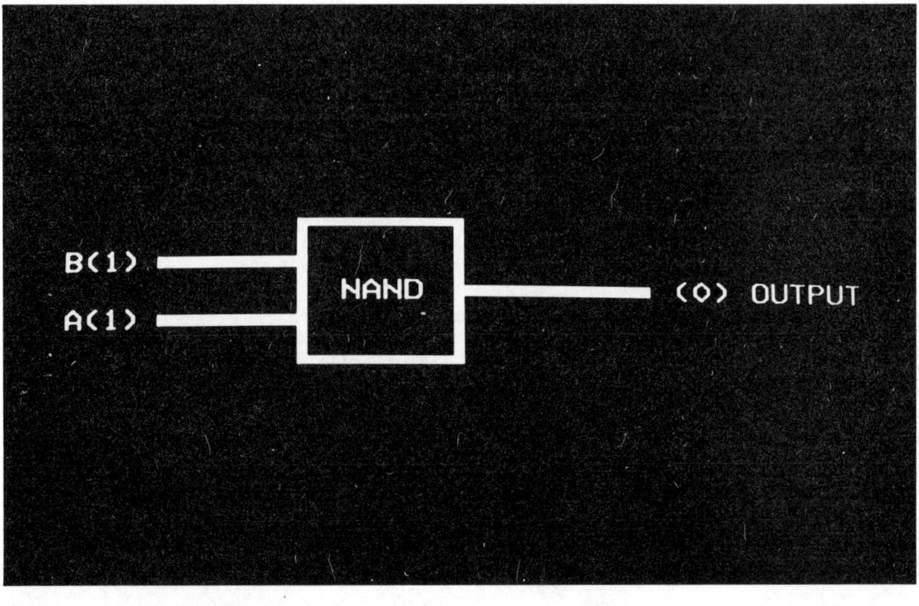

Plate 21 Simulation of logic gates

to send the inputs HIGH or LOW and look at the output logic level each time. From this the truth table is constructed and the student guesses which of ten possible gates is being produced. After three guesses the student is informed of the correct answer and its truth table is displayed. The student may verify this before proceeding with another gate.

Four-bit logic

The logic board (Figure 4.2) has four input terminals labelled A, B, C and D and four output terminals labelled W, X, Y and Z. All terminals are connected to LED indicators to show their logic state. When a terminal is HIGH, its LED is on, when a terminal is

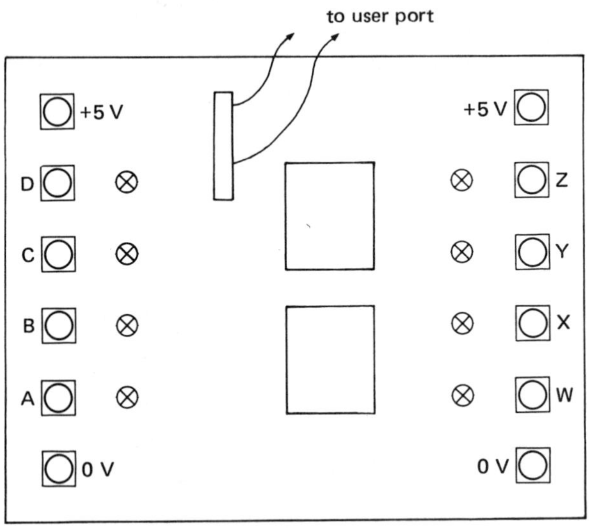

Figure 4.2 The logic board

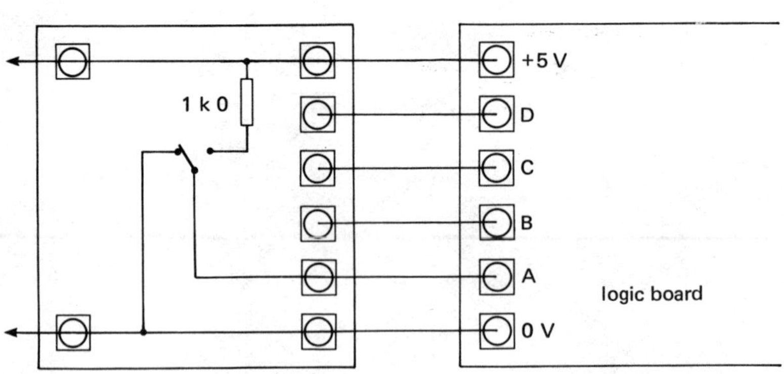

Figure 4.3 Switch inputs

LOW, its LED is off. The LEDs connected to A, B, C and D indicate the state of the inputs. These states are determined by the voltages at the input terminals, usually from some external device like a switch. The LEDs connected to W, X, Y and Z show the output logic levels. These are the levels chosen by the microcomputer. They do not depend upon the devices connected to the output terminals.

Logic inputs
The easiest way to create HIGH and LOW logic inputs is with switches. When a switch is to the left, its output is connected to the 0 V line (also called **ground**), so it will be LOW, or at logic 0. When the switch is to the right, the output is connected to the 5 volt line through the 1 kilohm resistor, so it will be HIGH, or at logic 1. Connect the outputs from the four-switch unit to the logic board inputs as in Figure 4.3. Make sure that the 5 V and 0 V lines of each board are connected too. When the switches are operated, the LEDs should go on and off.

Logic gates

With integrated circuits different Boolean functions can be made by connecting NAND gates together. Each function is made by combining the gates in a different way, as described in Chapter 2 of *Microelectronics.* The advantage of a programmable system is that the same circuit can be used to produce these different functions, under the control of the program. This can be demonstrated with LOGIC GATES, but the more powerful version of this program, called LOGIC TUTOR (2) enables several different gates to be simulated at the same time. This program uses the logic board and makes each of the four outputs into different Boolean functions of the inputs. For example, in Figure 4.4, output W has been set up as the AND combination of inputs A and B. The program allows you to set up any output as a particular logical combination of any inputs. The best way of explaining it is to do this example.

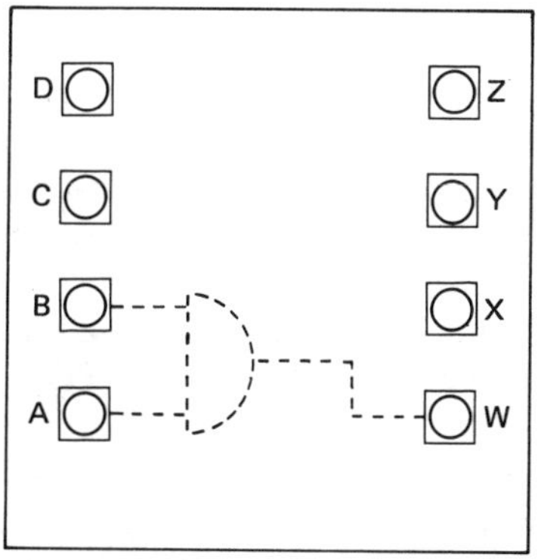

Figure 4.4 Simulating an AND gate

When the program is run, it asks which Boolean function is required, thus:

BOOLEAN FUNCTIONS
SELECT ONE OF THESE FUNCTIONS BY TYPING ITS NUMBER THEN PRESS <RETURN>

1 AND
2 OR
3 NOT
4 EXCLUSIVE-OR
5 EQUIVALENCE
6 NAND
7 NOR

Select the AND function by pressing key 1 followed by the RETURN key. The program will then ask which output you want to provide this function:

WHICH OUTPUT ?
ENTER ONE OF W, X, Y OR Z
THEN PRESS <RETURN>

Select output W by pressing key W followed by the RETURN key. The program now asks

HOW MANY INPUTS ?
ENTER 1, 2, 3 OR 4 AND THEN PRESS <RETURN>

Select two inputs by pressing key 2 followed by RETURN. Finally the program asks

WHICH INPUTS ?
ENTER TWO OF A, B, C OR D
THEN PRESS <RETURN>

Select inputs A and B, by typing A followed by RETURN and then B followed by RETURN.

The screen clears to display a symbol for the AND gate, indicating your chosen inputs and outputs. At the same time the logic board is set up to behave in the same way. Output W will become the AND combination of inputs A and B. The display will show the logic state of the inputs and the outputs as a 1 or as a 0.

Connect the logic board to the switches as in Figure 4.3 and then investigate this AND combination by switching inputs A and B HIGH and LOW. Note what happens to the LEDs associated with W and with A and B. First make both inputs LOW and check on the W output. Then make input B HIGH and input A LOW. Then make input A HIGH and input B LOW. Finally make both inputs HIGH. Note that the screen display also shows the logic state of these inputs and outputs (although there is a short delay after they are changed, because the program is in BASIC and is rather slow).

It is possible to summarize all the information about the AND gate with its truth table:

Input A	Input B	Output
LOW	LOW	LOW
LOW	HIGH	LOW
HIGH	LOW	LOW
HIGH	HIGH	HIGH

The 'HIGH' and 'LOW' in this table are voltages. Note that the output from the AND gate is only HIGH if both of its inputs are HIGH. If only one or neither inputs are HIGH, then the output is LOW. The reason for calling this an AND gate is now clear. The output is HIGH only if both input A *AND* input B are HIGH.

This program allows all the standard gates to be investigated as before, but with the advantage of being able to compare different gates. For example it is easy to show that the EQUIVALENCE gate is the inverse of the EXCLUSIVE-OR gate by giving them the same inputs and two adjacent outputs.

For later reference, the truth tables that can be investigated with these two programs will now be discussed. First, note that there are two other ways of writing truth tables, as follows:

A	B	Output
0	0	0
0	1	0
1	0	0
1	1	1

A	B	Output
L	L	L
L	H	L
H	L	L
H	H	H

The 'H' and 'L' stand for HIGH and LOW voltages as before, and the '1' and '0' have the same meaning: they are called logic 1 and logic 0 to avoid confusion with the integers 0 and 1.

The NOT gate

Select the NOT function by entering key 3 when the menu is displayed. Make W the output for this function in the way described above. A NOT gate only has one input, so make this input A, by entering A as the required input.

A switch can be used to make this input HIGH or LOW and the LED can be used to see if the output is HIGH or LOW. The NOT gate produces this truth table.

Input	Output
LOW	HIGH
HIGH	LOW

You will notice that the output is always the exact opposite or inverse of the input, which gives this function its other name: the INVERTER.

The NAND gate

Create the NAND function by selecting 6 on the menu. Set up W as the output and A and B as the inputs, exactly as for the AND function above. Two switches are needed to provide the inputs to this NAND gate, called input A and input B. The LED indicators show the logic level of these inputs and of the NAND gate output. Try different combinations of inputs A and B and note the effect on the output each time.

Input A	Input B	Output
LOW	LOW	HIGH
LOW	HIGH	HIGH
HIGH	LOW	HIGH
HIGH	HIGH	LOW

The OR gate

The OR function can be investigated after being selected with key 2.

Input A	Input B	Output
LOW	LOW	LOW
LOW	HIGH	HIGH
HIGH	LOW	HIGH
HIGH	HIGH	HIGH

The NOR gate

Select and investigate the NOR function with key 7.

Input A	Input B	Output
LOW	LOW	HIGH
LOW	HIGH	LOW
HIGH	LOW	LOW
HIGH	HIGH	LOW

The EXCLUSIVE-OR gate

Select the EXCLUSIVE-OR gate by entering key 4 from the menu.

Input A	Input B	Output
LOW	LOW	LOW
LOW	HIGH	HIGH
HIGH	LOW	HIGH
HIGH	HIGH	LOW

The EQUIVALENCE gate

Select the EQUIVALENCE gate with key 5 and continue as before.

Input A	Input B	Output
LOW	LOW	HIGH
LOW	HIGH	LOW
HIGH	LOW	LOW
HIGH	HIGH	HIGH

Boolean algebra

The language of Boolean algebra is used to describe the functions produced by different logic gates. In this algebra only three relationships are used: AND, OR and NOT. 'NOT' refers to the INVERTER. If the input to an INVERTER is called A then its output is NOT A. The words AND, OR and NOT have particular meanings not to be confused with their normal English usage. Let us therefore digress for a moment to study the meaning of these terms as used by BBC BASIC. This will help to explain how AND, OR and NOT may be used for controlling and monitoring external equipment.

From the point of view of the microprocessor, data is processed as eight-bit bytes. Each byte has eight separate logic levels giving 2 x 2 x 2 x 2 x 2 x 2 x 2 x 2 or 256 possible combinations of 1s and 0s. Every piece of information, whether instructions like add or AND or numbers like 99, are sent to the microprocessor as different combinations of bytes. We have already seen how eight bits can be used to represent numbers in the binary code or different alphabetic and graphics characters in the ASCII code. Interpreted as a decimal, each byte can represent any one of the 256 integers from 0 to 255.

When using Boolean expressions BBC BASIC interprets these bytes in yet another different way. A number in a BASIC Boolean expression is regarded as a twos complement integer, with a value between −128 and 127, according to the following table:

Binary	Twos complement	Decimal
0000 0000	0	0
0000 0001	1	1
0000 0010	2	2
0000 0011	3	3
0000 0100	4	4
....	...	...
....	...	...
0111 1100	124	124
0111 1101	125	125
0111 1110	126	126
0111 1111	127	127
1000 0000	−128	128
1000 0001	−127	129
1000 0010	−126	130
1000 0011	−125	131
1000 0100	−124	132
....	...	...
....	...	...
1111 1100	−4	252
1111 1101	−3	253
1111 1110	−2	254
1111 1111	−1	255

It can be seen that adding 1 to any of these representations increases it by 1. When 1 is added to −1, the binary number becomes 1 0000 0000 as its decimal equivalent goes from −1 to 0, but the register can only hold eight bits, so this ninth bit is lost and the result is zero.

The only exception for twos complement coding is when 127 is increased by 1 to become −128. This representation is often used at machine code level to represent negative integers. For example, in Chapter 2, to make a *-character move backwards across the screen, we subtracted 1 from its current screen address. In the equivalent machine code program in Chapter 8, we achieve the same end by adding 255.

Just to complicate matters, BBC BASIC uses four bytes to store integers, so that it actually interprets the binary number

```
11111111 11111111 11111111 11111111
```

as −1. However, since we only deal with eight-bit input and output devices, I shall ignore this and pretend that the table above is the valid one. It makes no difference to the discussion at all.

BASIC and the logic board

The logic operations of BBC BASIC follow straightforward rules, which seem to be nonsense until these rules are understood. The BASIC statement Z = A AND B, performs the AND operation between each bit of the number A and the number B. The corresponding bits of Z are set or cleared accordingly. If A is 6 and B is 5, then the AND combination of the two binary numbers is 4, thus:

```
A is 0 0 0 0 0 1 1 0
B is 0 0 0 0 0 1 0 1
Z is 0 0 0 0 0 1 0 0
```

The AND truth table is applied to each corresponding pair of bits in A and B. There is a 1 in Z wherever there is a 1 in the same bit position of both A and B. Thus the BASIC command PRINT 6 AND 5, gives the result 4.

AND is a very useful expression for turning a logic board output off without altering other outputs. The logic board outputs share the same output address. Output Z is connected to bit 7 of the output port and has the decimal value of 128. Similarly, output Y is 64, output X is 32 and output W is 16. The statement ?outputs = 240 switches all outputs on and the statement ?outputs = 0 switches them all off. To switch one particular output off, we AND all the other outputs with logic 1 and the chosen output with logic 0. For example, to turn off output Z, use

```
?outputs=(?outputs AND 112).
```

112 in binary is 0111 0000, so if output Z is already on (1), it will go off (1 AND 0). If Z is already off, it will stay off (0 AND 0). Output X will be unaffected since it is ANDed with 1. If X is on, it stays on (1 AND 1). If X is off, it stays off (0 AND 1).

The BASIC statement OR behaves in a similar way. A 1 is placed in the result for each 1 in either A OR B at that bit position:

A is	0	0	0	0	0	1	1	0
B is	0	0	0	0	0	1	0	1
Result	0	0	0	0	0	1	1	1

Thus the BASIC command PRINT 6 OR 5, gives the result 7.

OR is useful for turning a logic board output on, without altering the other outputs.

```
?outputs = (?outputs OR 128)
```

will turn output Z on, irrespective of whether it is already on or off, yet the other output bits are being ORed with 0, so they are unaffected.

The NOT operation is the most difficult to understand, since it is here that negative values occur. Decimal zero is actually 0000 0000 in binary, so NOT 0 is the bit-wise complement of this, which is 1111 1111. BASIC interprets this as –1. This also explains why the BBC microcomputer gives such funny results when asked to do comparisons between numbers:

PRINT (1>0) which is TRUE and gives the result –1
PRINT (0>1) which is FALSE and gives the result 0
PRINT (X=X) which is TRUE and gives the result –1

Oddest of all is the following:
PRINT 1 AND –1 which gives the value 1.

The Boolean constants TRUE and FALSE can be converted to single bits by using the AND operation above. This is because TRUE is 1111 1111 ....1111 1111, which it printed as –1. To get TRUE = 1 it (or the result of any logical expression) should either be ANDed with 1 or alternatively the ABSOLUTE value can be taken.

PRINT ABS(1>0) gives the value 1
PRINT (0<1) AND 1 gives the value 1

If A is 1 then NOT A will have the value –2.

A is	0	0	0	0	0	0	0	1
NOT A is	1	1	1	1	1	1	1	0

It can be seen that the twos complement code interprets this as –2, which is the result that is printed.

To overcome such problems when using BASIC with inputs and outputs, it is necessary to ensure that all input variables are single bits to begin with. The BASIC operations AND, OR and NOT can then be used as required. Then, before the final result is printed, it should again be ANDed with 1, to remove all the other bits. An inspection of the listing for LOGIC TUTOR will show how this is actually achieved.

The BASIC statement EOR behaves in the same way as EXCLUSIVE-OR discussed above; a 0 is placed in the result for each corresponding bit position where A and B are the same. A 1 is placed in the result if the A and B bits are different.

A is	0	0	0	0	0	1	1	0
B is	0	0	0	0	0	1	0	1
	same	same	same	same	same	same	diff.	diff.
Result	0	0	0	0	0	0	1	1

Thus the BASIC command PRINT 6 EOR 5, gives the result 3.

This operation is also useful for manipulating an output. EORing it with logic 1 will make it change state, since 1 EOR 1 is 0 and 0 EOR 1 is 1. So the statement ?output = (?output EOR 128) will turn output Z on if it is off and off if it is on. The four outputs of the logic board could thus be toggled in this way by EORing each of them with their corresponding bit value.

Before the invention of the microprocessor, in order to make a new electronic system an engineer would have to design a new circuit. It was most unlikely that new components could just be added on to a previous circuit, so the whole system would have to be re-made from the beginning. This is how digital systems were built in the 1960s and 70s, from combinations of separate integrated circuits. They were all wired together in the correct way to produce the desired function. Even if the system was sold in large numbers, each one had still to be built up separately on a printed circuit board, so that the different gates could be correctly wired together.

The microprocessor changes this, because the same hardware can be made to do different things merely by changing its program. The same microprocessor can thus be made to do many different things, from shearing sheep to controlling a power station, making a teddy bear speak or running a microcomputer or even space invaders. Because it is the same microprocessor in each case, a very large number of them can be produced very cheaply.

Program 3 (called LOGIC MAKER) shows this flexibility, allowing you to create your own Boolean functions. In order to do this the required function must be entered as part of the program. Begin by connecting the logic board to the BBC microcomputer user port and then load LOGIC MAKER. This can be run, to produce the logic function A AND B, which will appear at gate Z. On the screen the inputs and outputs of the logic board will be displayed.

To change the function, press key E, which will end the program, leaving lines 5000 to 5100 of the program displayed on the screen. You may now create any function of your own, provided it conforms to the syntax rules of BASIC and the ways we have already described for writing out Boolean functions.

Change the function in line 5010 to any other function (and remember to press <RETURN> to enter the new function). Then re-run the program and it will now execute with your new function. For example,

```
   5010  Z = (NOT A OR B)
or 5010  Z = NOT(NOT A AND NOT B)
or 5010  Z = A EOR B
```

The variables should be A, B, C or D but you will not have to declare beforehand which you have used. The final outputs should be W, X, Y or Z. It is possible to use other variables, although you will not be able to find out what values they take. For example,

```
5010  T = NOT A AND B
5020  S = NOT B AND A
5030  Z = T OR S
```

This example also shows that it is possible to put in more than one line for the function, provided it does not have to work backwards. That is, you cannot put

```
5010  Z = NOT T
5020  T = NOT B OR A
```

because T does not have its correct value in line 5010 until after line 5020 has been executed. This causes a 'no such variable' message to appear. A few more examples are given below, but the fun in this program is to create your own functions and then see what you have produced. Do this by stepping through the truth table with the switches and noting the outputs in each case.

```
5010  Z = NOT (A OR B)
5010  Z = NOT (NOT A AND NOT B)
5010  Z = NOT (A AND B)
5010  Z = NOT (A EOR B)
5010  Z = (NOT A AND B) OR (A AND NOT B)
5010  Z = (A AND B) OR (NOT A AND NOT B)
```

The BBC microcomputer user port

The microcomputer communicates to humans in the outside world through its keyboard and TV display. It communicates with electronic control systems through its user port. This consists of eight lines through which digital signals can pass in either direction. These signals are voltage levels on each of the eight lines, that are either HIGH or LOW. These lines are connected to a **VIA (versatile interface adapter),** which is a special input/output chip inside each BBC Model B microcomputer. The eight lines can be set up so that they are all outputs, or so that they are all inputs or any combination of the two. The VIA is told which lines are inputs and which are outputs through its **data direction register (DDR).** This is an eight-bit register with each bit corresponding to one of the user port lines. If a bit of the DDR is turned on (logic 1), then the corresponding line of the user port becomes an output. If that bit is turned off, then the same corresponding line of the user port becomes an input. The decimal values of each bit are as follows:

Line number	Bit	Decimal value
7	1000 0000	128
6	0100 0000	64
5	0010 0000	32
4	0001 0000	16
3	0000 1000	8
2	0000 0100	4
1	0000 0010	2
0	0000 0001	1

The individual bits of the DDR are changed from BASIC by writing to its memory location with the decimal equivalent of the bits. The addresses used are as follows:

DDR = 65122 (DATA DIRECTION REGISTER)
PRT = 65120 (USER PORT)

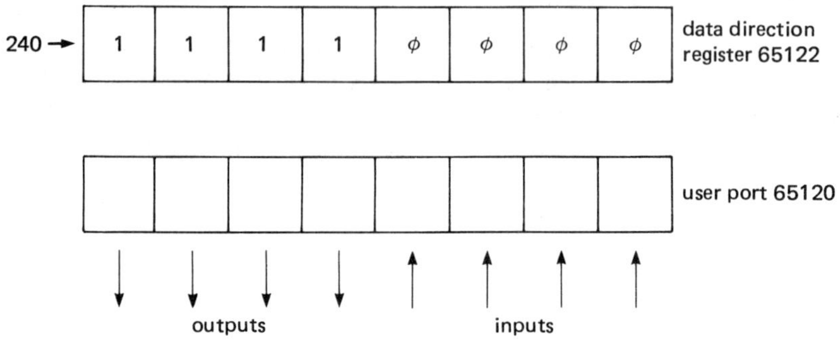

Figure 4.5 Configuring the VIA

?DDR = 4 will turn bit 2 of the DDR on and all other bits off. So the user port will turn line 2 into an output, whereas the other seven lines become inputs. By adding these decimal values together different combinations of input and output lines can be achieved (Figure 4.5). Thus ?DDR = 240 (which is 128 + 64 + 32 + 16) will make the lines corresponding to bits 7, 6, 5 and 4 into outputs and the lines corresponding to bits 3, 2, 1 and 0 into inputs.

Outputs

After being **configured** in the required way, the user port can then be used. Data can only be sent out from a line if it has previously been configured for output. Since ?DDR = 255 will set up all eight lines for output, let us assume that this has been done. Now the user port can be told which of its output lines are to be on (or HIGH) and which are to be off (or LOW). A line goes HIGH if the corresponding bit of the user port (PRT) is a 1; the line is LOW if the corresponding bit is a 0. Thus ?PRT = 1 will switch on line 0 and will switch all other lines off. The decimal values of each line are as in the table above. Combinations of lines may thus be made by adding these decimal values together, for example,

?PRT = 0 (in binary: 0000 0000) sends all lines LOW.
?PRT = 63 (0011 1111) sends lines 0 to 5 HIGH and 6 and 7 LOW.
?PRT = 127 (0111 1111) sends lines 0 to 6 HIGH and line 7 LOW.
?PRT = 255 (1111 1111) sends all lines HIGH.

Inputs
If lines have been configured for input (by executing ?DDR = 0), then their voltage levels can be read from the PRT address with

```
LET X=?PRT or X=?PRT
```

If any line to the user port is connected to a voltage between 2.4 and 5.5 volts, the user port interprets this as a HIGH (or logic 1) level. If the voltage applied to the line is between 0.4 and 0 volts, the interface interprets this as a LOW (or logic 0) level. This range, 0 to 5.5 volts represents the maximum and minimum voltages that can be applied to the user port. Voltages outside this range can damage it, so care must be taken to keep input voltages below 6 V and above 0 V. This implies that alternating voltages should **not** be input to the user port without protective buffering circuits.

Sensing and controlling the environment
Increasingly in industry, the solution of problems in electronics is becoming one of adapting a general purpose circuit to a specific application, rather than designing a special circuit each time. Traditional control technology in schools has laid emphasis upon the second of these approaches: the hardware solution. The user port of the microcomputer can be used to demonstrate the more modern software approach. The first programs described below demonstrate how the unit can be used to control the LEDs of the logic board. Note that in each case, the electronic circuit remains the same, it is only the programs that are changed.

Switching outputs
This investigation enables you to switch the outputs on or off in any sequence. The first example shows how any outputs can be switched on in any order. For this program it is assumed that the top three LEDs on the right side of the logic board (Z, Y and X) represent the red, amber and green traffic lights. The program shows how these lights can be controlled by writing the numbers 128, 64 and 32 (and combinations of them) into the correct address for the logic board. The data direction register in line 100 is used to set up the lines of the user port (bits 4, 5, 6 and 7) as outputs.

```
  1  REM CONTROL EXAMPLE 1 — TRAFFIC LIGHTS
 10  DDR = 65122:REM DATA DIRECTION REGISTER
 20  PRT = 65120 : REM USER PORT
100  ?DDR=240:REM SET UP INPUTS AND OUTPUTS
110  ?PRT=128:REM SWITCH ON RED
120  FOR T=1 TO 8000:NEXT T:REM LONG DELAY
130  ?PRT=128+64:REM SWITCH ON RED AND AMBER
140  FOR T=1 TO 1500:NEXT T:REM SHORT DELAY
150  ?PRT=32:REM SWITCH ON GREEN
160  FOR T=1 TO 8000:NEXT T:REM LONG DELAY
170  ?PRT=64 :REM SWITCH ON AMBER
180  FOR T=1 TO 1500:NEXT T:REM SHORT DELAY
200  GOTO 110:REM REPEAT SEQUENCE
```

Now try switching on the output LEDs in a different sequence with different delays.

To satisfy those critics of example 1, who say that they can do traffic lights just as well without a microcomputer, example 2 is almost impossible to emulate with traditional hardware; switching the LEDs on and off in random sequence. For this purpose a random number between 0 and 255 is sent to the user port address. You may observe that this also switches the bits corresponding to the input lines too, but that the input LEDs are not affected. A line configured for input will not respond to outputs from the microcomputer.

```
  1 REM CONTROL EXAMPLE 2 – RANDOM LIGHTS
 10 DDR = 65122:REM DATA DIRECTION REGISTER
 20 PRT = 65120 : REM USER PORT
100 ?DDR=240:REM SET UP INPUTS AND OUTPUTS
110 R=RND(256)-1
120 ?PRT=R:REM SWITCH LIGHTS AT RANDOM
130 FOR T=1 TO 500:NEXT T:REM SHORT DELAY
140 GOTO 110
```

The next program switches on the LEDs in a more orderly way, by adding sixteen to the number written to the user port address each time. The LEDs thus count up in binary.

```
  1 REM CONTROL EXAMPLE 3 – BINARY COUNTER
 10 DDR = 65122:REM DATA DIRECTION REGISTER
 20 PRT = 65120 : REM USER PORT
100 ?DDR=240:REM SET UP INPUTS AND OUTPUTS
110 FOR R = 0 TO 240 STEP 16
120 ?PRT=R
130 FOR T=1 TO 1000:NEXT T:REM SHORT DELAY
140 NEXT R
150 GOTO 110
```

Can you discover how to make the LEDs count down in binary instead?

A common chip used in microelectronics is the shift register, which is simulated by this example. It is particularly useful for converting **serial** data, where the eight bits are sent one after the other along a single pair of lines, into **parallel** data, where all eight bits are sent simultaneously along a set of eight separate lines (or vice versa).

```
  1 REM CONTROL EXAMPLE 4 – SHIFT REGISTER
 10 DDR = 65122:REM DATA DIRECTION REGISTER
 20 PRT = 65120 : REM USER PORT
100 ?DDR=240:REM SET UP INPUTS AND OUTPUTS
110 R% = 4
120 R% = R% + R%
130 ?PRT=R%
140 FOR T=1 TO 1000:NEXT T:REM SHORT DELAY
150 IF R% < 200 THEN 120
160 GOTO 110
```

Pulse output

The simplest way of producing output pulses is by switching lines of the user port alternately off and on, relying on delay loops to control the timing. In BASIC, the maximum rate at which an output can be switched on and off is about 50 Hz. This is sufficient for a metronome but not for much else. The program used is relatively simple as follows. It produces pulses on bit 7 of the logic board (output Z), which may be connected to an amplifier and loudspeaker if required. The sound could, more sensibly, be produced by the BBC microcomputer's own SOUND statements. Here we are demonstrating the use of the user port:

```
  1  REM CONTROL EXAMPLE 5 – METRONOME
 10  DDR = 65122:REM DATA DIRECTION REGISTER
 20  PRT = 65120 : REM USER PORT 50 CLS
100  INPUT "NUMBER OF BEATS PER MINUTE" N
110  LET limit = 6000/N
120  ?DDR=128:REM BIT 7 AS OUTPUT
130  TIME = 0
140  ?PRT=128:REM BIT 7 HIGH
150  FOR T = 1 TO 10:NEXT T
160  ?PRT=0:REM BIT 7 LOW
170  REPEAT UNTIL TIME>limit
180  GOTO 130
```

Using these principles you should now be able to control any system you wish. For example, the logic board outputs could be connected via relays to a mobile crane to shift a load. One output might be connected to switch a motor in the forward direction to lower an electromagnet. Another output could switch the power to the motor in reverse to raise it again. Another might drive the crane forwards and the fourth could drive it backwards. The distances travelled could be controlled by the length of time that the motor is switched on.

If such a system is tried out, you will discover one problem. A motor switched on for, say ten seconds, in the forward direction might cause the crane to travel say fifty centimetres. Ten seconds in the reverse direction produces a movement of say forty-five centimetres. So each sequence results in the crane ending up in a different place. What is missing is **feedback.** The microcomputer needs to know exactly where the crane has got to at any instant. This is one reason for providing the microcomputer with inputs.

Using the inputs

The state of the user port is read from its address with the LET X = ?PRT statement. Only bits 0 to 3 of the logic board can be inputs. The number read will, however, include the states of the outputs too. It must be decoded to determine which particular inputs are HIGH and which are LOW. If more than one line is HIGH, the value returned in X will be a combination of the corresponding numbers above. Thus if the X value is 12, this means that inputs C and D are HIGH and the others are LOW. Similarly if X = ?PRT yields the value 3, this means that inputs A and B are HIGH and the others are LOW.

Individual inputs can be monitored with the AND statement.

```
LET X = ?PRT AND 1
```

will look at input A only. If A is HIGH then X will become 1, otherwise it will be 0. Similarly

```
LET X = ?PRT AND 2 monitors input B,
LET X = ?PRT AND 4 monitors input C
```

and

```
LET X = ?PRT AND 8 monitors input D.
```

The inputs can be connected to different devices, such as photocells, trip switches, water level indicators, temperature switches and the like. The outputs can be connected to lamp indicators, heaters, water valves and pumps. It is thus possible to operate an automatic washing machine with the logic board, given the necessary 'buffers' to obtain sufficient power. For present purposes though, the different input devices can be simulated with switches and the output devices represented by LEDs.

The next example shows how the state of each input can be echoed to the output LEDs. When this program is run, the input and output LEDs will always show the same state, depending on the setting of the switches.

```
  1 REM CONTROL EXAMPLE 6 – INPUT PORT INDICATOR
 10 DDR = 65122:REM DATA DIRECTION REGISTER
 20 PRT = 65120 : REM USER PORT
100 ?DDR=240:REM LAST FOUR LINES AS OUTPUTS,
    FIRST FOUR AS INPUTS
110 X = (?PRT AND 15) * 16
120 ?PRT=X
130 GOTO 110
```

Burglar alarm

A traditional electronic circuit is the burglar alarm. This can now be made far more versatile. The simple hard-wired version of this does not allow the owner to get out of the house without setting off the alarm. This program introduces a delay, during which the alarm will not operate. The owner has about ten seconds between switching on the system (i.e. starting the program) and the system's being active. The presence of a burglar can be simulated with a switch. The switch will have no effect for about ten seconds after the program is started.

```
  1 REM CONTROL EXAMPLE 7 – BURGLAR ALARM
 10 DDR = 65122 : REM DATA DIRECTION REGISTER
 20 PRT = 65120 : REM USER PORT
100 ?DDR=240:REM LAST FOUR LINES AS OUTPUTS,
    FIRST FOUR AS INPUTS
105 ?PRT=0:REM ALL LEDS OFF
110 FOR T=1 TO 10000:NEXT T:REM DELAY
```

```
120  N = ?PRT
130  IF N = ?PRT THEN130:REM WAIT FOR BURGLAR
140  FOR I = 1 TO 20
150  ?PRT=240:REM ALL ALARM LIGHTS ON
160  FOR T=1 TO 200:NEXT T :REM DELAY
170  ?PRT=0:REM ALL LIGHTS OFF
180  FOR T=1 TO 200:NEXT T
190  NEXT I
```

Time measurement

The principle of measuring time intervals is as follows. The user port is read and stored in a memory location called status. The current state of the user port is then monitored continuously and compared with status. Normally it will be the same, but when it is different, this is because an input has been activated. The microcomputer's internal clock is then started and the new status of the user port is saved in status. When the user port again changes its status, the current contents of the clock are noted. The time interval involved can then be calculated and displayed. The BBC microcomputer has a centisecond timer, which is available from BASIC with the variable called TIME.

Time intervals exceeding a few tenths of a second are measured quite satisfactorily in this way. This simple timer can replace the centisecond timers used in school laboratories in most instances. The usual problems over 'make to start', 'break to stop', are avoided, since the routine detects any change at the input. Accurate timing of short intervals must be achieved by other means, since BASIC is too slow.

```
  1  REM CONTROL EXAMPLE 8 – A SIMPLE TIMER
 10  DDR = 65122 : REM DATA DIRECTION REGISTER
 20  PRT = 65120 : REM USER PORT
100  ?DDR=240:REM LAST FOUR LINES AS OUTPUTS,
     FIRST FOUR AS INPUTS
110  LET status = ?PRT
120  IF status = ?PRT THEN 120
130  LET status = ?PRT:REM INPUT HAS CHANGED
140  TIME = 0:REM START CLOCK
150  IF status = ?PRT THEN 150
160  REM INPUT HAS CHANGED AGAIN
170  PRINT "ELAPSED TIME = "; TIME/100;" SECONDS"
```

Counting

The next example shows how the microcomputer can be used to count closures of a switch connected to input A. It is possible to use hardware to prevent contact bounce, but in this case we shall overcome such problems with a software solution. The program senses a switch closure, waits for a while, and then checks to make sure that the switch is still closed. If not, then no count is made. If the switch is still closed, the program records the count and then waits until the switch is released again.

```
1   REM CONTROL EXAMPLE 9 – AN INPUT COUNTER
10  DDR = 65122 : REM DATA DIRECTION REGISTER
20  PRT = 65120 : REM USER PORT
50  CLS
60  PRINT TAB(5,5) "CURRENT COUNT = 0"
100 ?DDR=240:REM LAST FOUR LINES AS OUTPUTS,
    FIRST FOUR AS INPUTS
110 LET status = ?PRT:REM INITIALIZE SWITCH STATUS
120 LET count = 0 : REM INITIALIZE COUNTER
130 IF status = ?PRT THEN 130
140 REM INPUT HAS CHANGED
150 FOR T = 1 TO 100:NEXT T:REM DELAY TO DEBOUNCE SWITCH
160 IF status = ?PRT THEN 130:REM CHANGE IS NOT VALID
170 LET count = count + 1:REM CHANGE IS GENUINE
180 PRINT TAB(5,5) "CURRENT COUNT = ";count
190 IF status <> ?PRT THEN 190:REM WAIT FOR
    SWITCH TO BE RELEASED
200 GOTO 130
```

Interfacing the user port

So far we have not considered how different external devices can be switched off and on. Certainly this cannot be done just by connecting the user port to the external device. The output current from the user port is very small, just a few milliamps, so it cannot even drive a lamp directly. It will drive the electronic units of the *Nuffield Advanced Physics* 'Electronics and reactive circuits', because these contain the necessary power amplification. We shall now consider the methods of driving other devices also.

User port interfaces are readily available. Some manufacturers make equipment which connects directly into the user port and input and output lines are then accessed via sockets on the front panel. Griffin and George Ltd have produced a digital interface unit, which has been specifically designed for use in the school environment. It is fully isolated, so that even if you inadvertently connect 250 V to the input terminals, the VIA should not be damaged. Most of the programs given as examples in this book will run with the Griffin digital interface directly. Other interfaces may need a few program changes, it just depends which lines are configured as inputs and which as outputs.

Another interface specially designed for use with the BBC microcomputer is the Unilab interface. This has relay outputs, so it is capable of switching quite large currents on and off, for example to small heaters and motors. More details of available interfaces for the BBC microcomputer are given in the Appendix.

DIY interfaces

To make your own interfacing equipment there are several ways of buffering the outputs of the VIA for driving external devices. In Figure 4.6 each output buffer consists of a pair of SN7404 INVERTERS, one of which drives the LED indicator The output from this is sufficient to sink up to 16 mA, although it will source less than 1 mA.

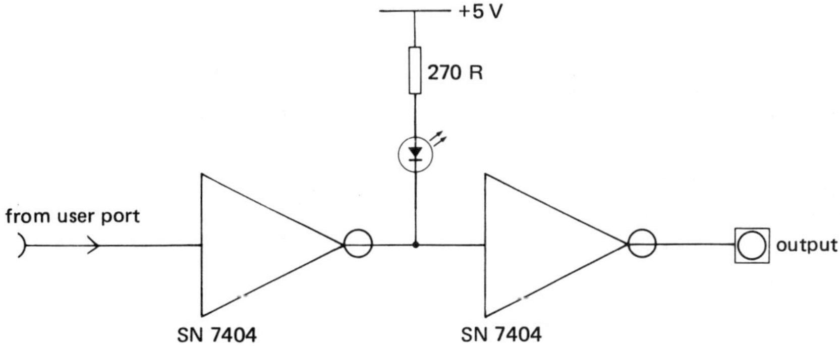

Figure 4.6 7404 buffers

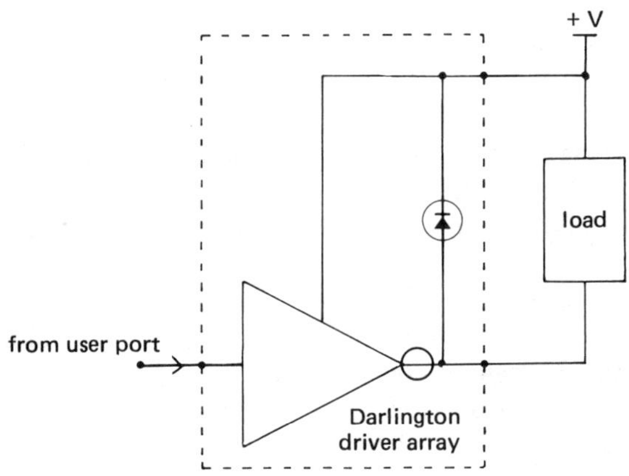

Figure 4.7 Darlington driver

Figure 4.7 shows a Darlington driver, which is ideal for sinking the currents from LEDs, relays, lamps and small motors. The integrated circuit version contains seven (RS 307-109) or eight (RS 307-422) drivers and is thus an ideal buffer for the user port. The power supply for some motors and relays may have to be more than the 5 V indicated but this Darlington driver device will handle voltages up to 50 V, provided the power handling capacity of the whole chip (1W) is not exceeded. Note that this device contains diodes, which protect it when inductive loads (relays and motors) are being switched on and off. A suitable relay is the RS Components sub-miniature device (RS Components 348-526) which can operate from the 5 V supply of the user port.

A suitable amplifier circuit for large currents can be made from a power transistor, itself driven by a smaller transistor in voltage follower mode (Figure 4.8). This may be used with any output from the user port including the CB2 output, which is described later. An 8 ohm speaker may be connected as the amplifier load if sound output is required.

Similar problems occur with inputs; different devices switch between different levels,

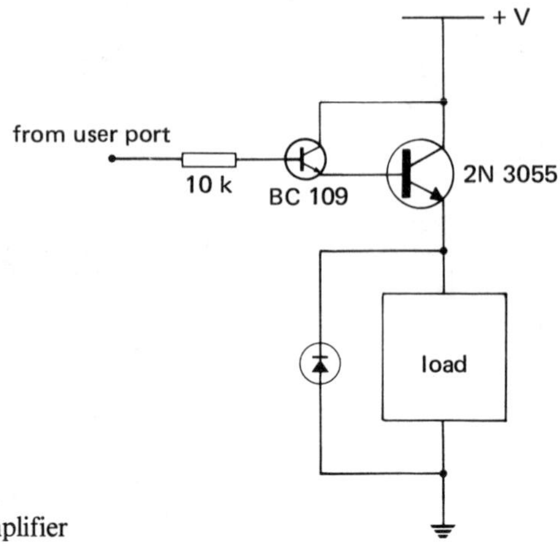

Figure 4.8 Power amplifier

so there has to be some buffer between the user port and the external device to adjust its inputs to TTL levels. Ideally such an input buffer would also protect the user port from voltages outwith its allowable range, for example, negative voltages, which can easily destroy the VIA.

Input buffers are easily provided. The most useful are those that respond to either a voltage change or to a change in resistance such as the LM324 op.amp. circuit of Figure 4.9. One of the problems with inputs is that the voltage might rise rather slowly. For example, the input might be a sine wave voltage, whose frequency is being measured. This could put a logic gate into its indeterminate state where it is neither HIGH nor LOW and (since it is then in its amplifying region) this could result in unwanted oscillations. The op.amp. circuit allows for this by having a feedback resistor that forces the input either HIGH or LOW.

This means that the external input voltage has to push a little harder to overcome this feedback voltage and cause the op.amp. to switch over. The voltage at which it switches on will therefore be slightly higher than the voltage at which it switches off. This effect is called **hysteresis.** In some cases too much hysteresis is a disadvantage. For example when using a photocell to make measurements of the speed and acceleration of trolleys, a card is fixed to the trolley which then passes in front of the photocell. If the light level needed to switch the photocell on is too different from that needed to switch it off, then the apparent length of the card will be different from its actual length. This will cause serious errors in the measuremnets. The larger the feedback resistor in the op.amp. circuit, the less hysteresis there is and the less serious is this error.

An alternative transistor circuit is shown in Figure 4.10. The transistor drives an LED indicator and is followed by a Schmidt trigger, part of an SN7414 integrated circuit. This is an INVERTER, which also provides the necessary hysteresis for slowly changing inputs.

With either of these circuits, if the input terminal is grounded through a resistance of less than about 2000 ohms or if a voltage below about 2 V is applied to it, then the output

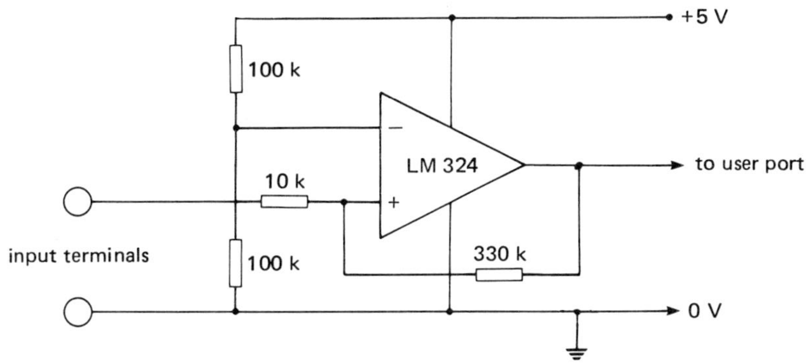

Figure 4.9 Op.amp. input buffer

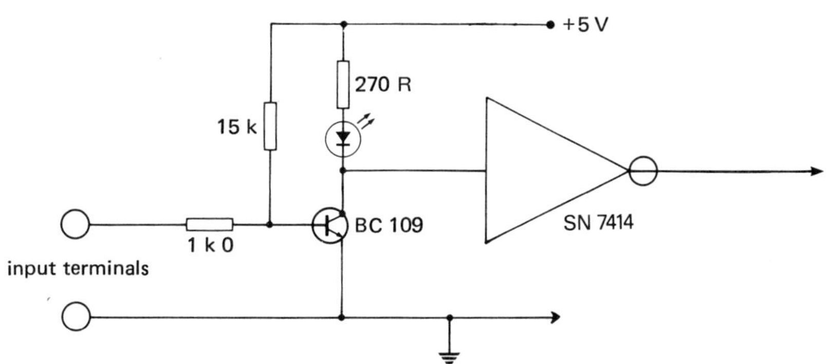

Figure 4.10 Transistor input buffer

output goes LOW. If the input is left unconnected or if a voltage above about 2 V is connected to it, then the line becomes HIGH. The state of the input is shown by the associated LED indicator. The connection between the ground and the input can be a light sensitive resistor, a photodiode, a thermistor, a temperature sensitive switch or a foot switch, etc.

Switch inputs

One problem with simple switches like that of Figure 4.3, is the contact bounce produced when the switch is closed. This can create several pulses which cause problems in counting circuits. Earlier we showed a way of debouncing the switch by adding a few lines of BASIC to the program. The hardware solution to this problem is to use a two-way switch and a bistable, made either from two NAND gates or from a J-K bistable (Figure 4.11).

A particularly useful device is the DM8833 line transceiver, which is used in the logic board. In Figure 4.12 just one of these is shown connected to bit 7 of the user port. Each

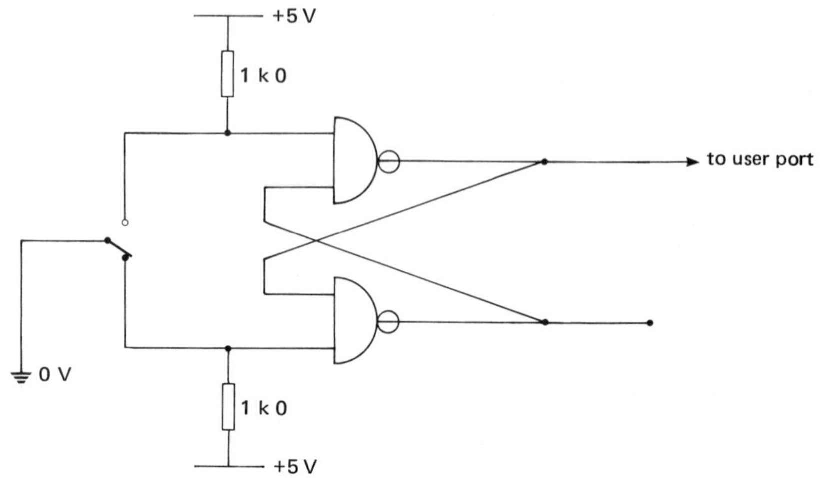

Figure 4.11 A debounced switch

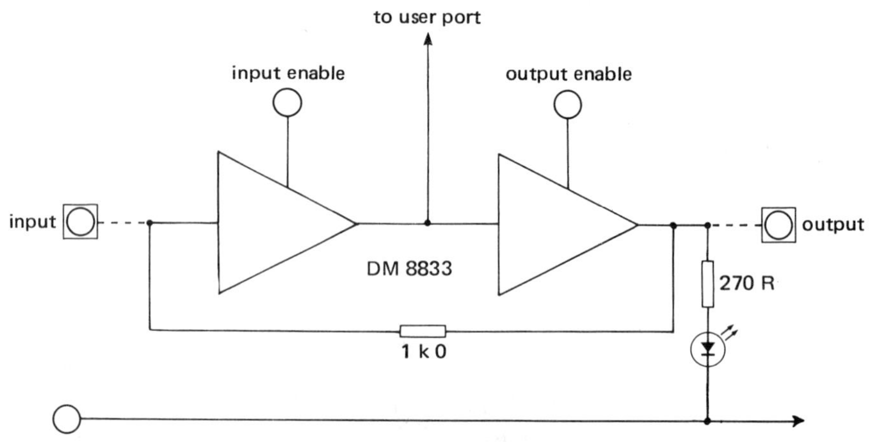

Figure 4.12 Transceiver buffer

chip contains four of these with common disable and power supply lines. Each output can sink or source up to ten milliamps, so it can drive LEDs directly. Either the input buffer or the output driver can be disabled by taking their disable lines HIGH. In our use of this circuit both the input buffers and the output drivers of chip 1 are permanently enabled by tying the disable inputs to the 0 V line. The input buffers of chip 2 are not needed so they are disabled by tying the disable input to the 5 V line. An alternative arrangement with the enable lines connected to switches would allow all eight lines to be inputs or outputs as well as allowing four of each. A point to point diagram for the logic board is given at the end of this chapter (Figure 4.26).

Isolation

Sometimes it is necessary to accept inputs from devices that run at voltages greater than 5 V. To protect the microcomputer and its user port it is a common practice to isolate the input by using an optical communication link (RS Components 307-064). The high voltage device is connected to an LED (through a suitable series resistor to limit the current). When the device goes HIGH the LED comes on. Next to the LED (inside the same chip) is a phototransistor, which can be used to provide correct TTL levels for the user port (Figure 4.13). When the LED comes on, it causes this phototransistor to conduct, so that a LOW output is produced for the user port. Since there is no electrical connection between the LED and the phototransistor, even several hundred volts applied to the input will not damage the user port.

The same device can be used to isolate the user port from devices connected to its output. The user port will not drive the LED directly, so one of the output buffers mentioned above should be used too. Isolation of this type should be used whenever large voltages are being sensed or switched. For switching alternating voltages, particularly the mains voltage, an optically coupled triac (RS Components 308-196) is more useful. This can be connected directly to the device being switched provided this does not need too much current. For larger currents the triac itself can be used to switch on a power **SCR (silicon controlled rectifier)** (RS Components 308-001) (Figure 4.14).

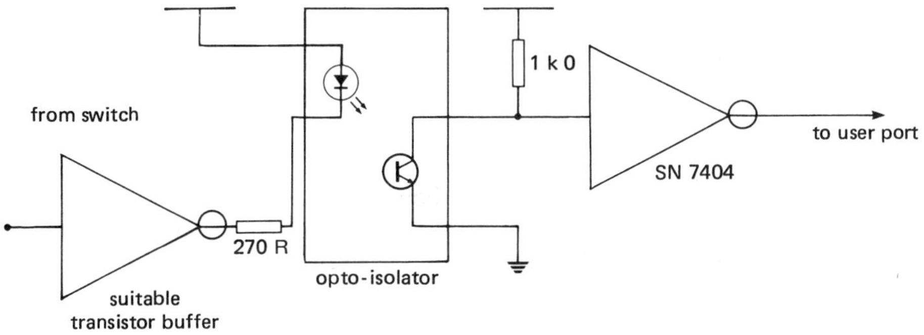

Figure 4.13 Optical isolation

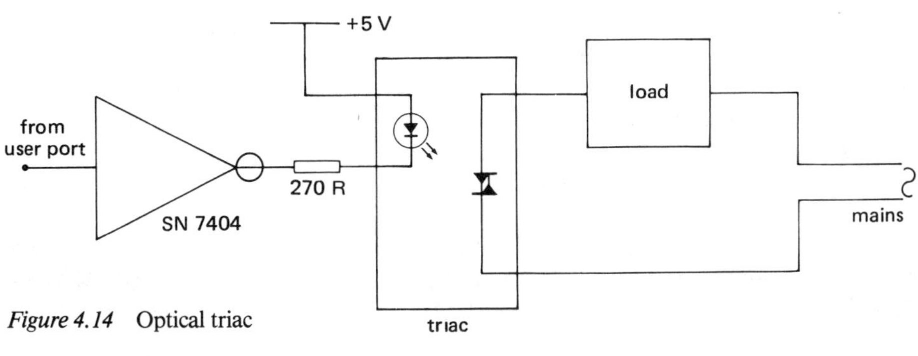

Figure 4.14 Optical triac

Sensors

So far we have only looked at photocells and thermistors as input sensing devices, but there is much more that can be done. Mechanical switches include push button switches, float switches for determining a liquid level, foot switches, tilt switches for determining if something is being moved (useful for an anti-theft system), rotary and edge switches (for choosing one of several options), pressure pads (for automatic door opening) and, of course, keyboards. Electronic switches are even more numerous. The most useful are proximity detectors that react to the presence of metals, non-metals, liquids and animals (human or otherwise). An interesting device is the Hall effect switch which detects the nearness of a magnet. The magnet could be fixed to a model train so that its presence could be determined whenever it passed the switch mounted on the track. For temperature sensing the thermistor needs some sort of buffering, but complete temperature switches are available for direct connection to the user port.

For school purposes the most useful input device is a photocell. This is a photodiode (RS Components 304-346) or **LDR (light dependent resistor)** (RS Components 305-620), which may be connected to the op.amp. or transistor input buffers. When light falls upon the photocell, its resistance is low, so the input is at logic 0 and the LED indicator will be off. If the light is interrupted, the photocell resistance rises and the input goes to logic 1. The LED indicator on the input should be used to check that this does happen. If not, then one or more of the following may be true:

i) The light source is not powerful enough, move it closer or increase its intensity.
ii) The photocell is polarized the wrong way, swap over its connections to the input and ground.
iii) The photocell is unsuitable for this application.

Note that the light dependent resistor (LDR) will do the job of a photocell quite well unless it is required to respond quickly. LDRs should not be used for time intervals of less than a few milliseconds. Faster switching is obtained with photodiodes connected to high speed op.amps. (RS Components 304-346, data sheet R/2135 Dec 81).

The 6522 versatile interface adapter

The BBC microcomputer user port is connected to a most remarkable device, the Rockwell 6522 **versatile interface adapter** or **VIA** for short. At the end of this chapter we will look at a way of connecting another VIA to the 1 MHz bus of the BBC microcomputer. The present description applies equally well to either VIA, but the emphasis is upon the one in the user port. Those wishing to use the programs in this book for a VIA connected otherwise, will need to rewrite them for the different addresses of the new VIA.

The 6522 VIA contains sixteen eight-bit registers, each with an address: two input/output **ports** (the A-port and the B-port), two **data direction registers (DDRA** and **DDRB)** to control the flow of data in these I/O ports, two sixteen-bit timers, timer 1 and timer 2 and the **peripheral control register (PCR)** and the **auxiliary control register (ACR)** for selecting the VIA modes of operation.

In the BBC microcomputer the A-port of the VIA is used for the printer interface, and the B-port goes to the user port connector (together with + 5 V and 0 V lines). Connection to the user port is best made with a ribbon connector cable and an RS Components speedbloc PCB 20-way plug (Stock no. 467-970). The timers and the B-port control lines are all accessible. The VIA is memory-mapped meaning that it can be read and written to just like any other memory location. Its addresses in the BBC microcomputer are as follows:

Name	Function	Decimal	Hexadecimal
BPRT	B-port	65120	&FE60
APRT	A-port (+ handshake)	65121	&FE61
DDRB	Data direction reg B	65122	&FE62
DDRA	Data direction reg A	65123	&FE63
T1LLO	Low-byte Timer1-latch	65124	&FE64
T1LHI	High-byte Timer1-latch	65125	&FE65
T1CLO	Low-byte Timer1-count	65126	&FE66
T1CHI	High-byte Timer1-count	65127	&FE67
T2LO	Low-byte Timer2-latch	65128	&FE68
T2HI	High-byte Timer2-latch	65129	&FE69
SR	Serial register	65130	&FE6A
ACR	Auxiliary control reg	65131	&FE6B
PCR	Peripheral control reg	65132	&FE6C
FLAG	Interrupt flag reg	65133	&FE6D
IER	Interrupt enable reg	65134	&FE6E
APRT	A-port (no-handshake)	65135	&FE6F

Both the A-port and the B-port registers may be configured for input or for output. The number written into the corresponding data direction register determines this (as described earlier). However, the A-port is connected to output drivers (for use as a printer output) so there is little point in configuring it as an input. If necessary, it may be used as an output, with the advantage of already being buffered by an SN74LS244 device. This is capable of sinking 8 mA and sourcing 0.4 mA, enough for transistors or Darlington drivers.

To read the user port after it has been configured for input is simply a matter of loading the contents of the correct address, exactly the equivalent of the 'X = ?PRT' used earlier.

Control lines

There are four control lines available, two for each port of the VIA, a CA1, CA2, CB1 and a CB2 line. They are provided for a variety of functions, which are chosen by two other VIA registers, the peripheral control register (PCR) and the auxiliary control register (ACR). On the BBC microcomputer user port only the CB1 and CB2 control lines are available. One of their functions is like that of the linesman at a football match, to wave a flag to catch the attention of the referee. Of course this could be done by simply having the microcomputer watch one of the user port lines until it changes. For example,

```
100 IF (?PRT AND 4)=0 THEN 100
```

will cause the microcomputer to wait until line 2 of the B-port goes HIGH. But even in machine code it takes several microseconds for the microprocessor to loop round and read the B-port again and a quickly changing input signal could come and go in the meantime and so be missed.

This problem is solved by getting the VIA to set a particular bit in its **flag** register to catch the attention of the microprocessor when it notices a change at its CA1 or CB1 input. There are seven such bits (flags) in this flag register. Bit 1 is affected by changes to CA1 and bit 4 is affected by changes to CB1. Changes to the CA1 or CB1 logic levels can be produced by an external device to tell the microcomputer that it is ready for something. A printer connected to the BBC microcomputer printer port, has one of its output lines connected to the CA1 input. When it changes this line from HIGH to LOW, the VIA interprets this as a request for attention, so it flags the microprocessor accordingly. This is necessary because the printer only prints about ten characters per second and the microcomputer is capable of sending characters very much faster than this. The printer therefore tells the microcomputer when it is ready for the next character by sending an appropriate signal along the CA1 line, called the **acknowledge input (ACK).**

A signal from an external device is often called a **strobe** and it may be a HIGH to LOW transition **(negative strobe)** or a LOW to HIGH transition **(positive strobe).** The PCR, at the address 65132, has one bit for controlling CA1 and one bit for CB1. Either control line can be used in two ways, chosen by the setting of its corresponding bit in the PCR. If this bit is HIGH, the control line will set its flag whenever it receives a positive strobe. If the PCR bit is LOW, the control line will set its flag for a negative strobe.

```
?65132=0 or ?&FE6C=0 will select HIGH to LOW transitions
?65132=16 or ?&FE6C=16 will select LOW to HIGH transitions
```

After being configured, the flag in the flag register (bit 4 for the CB1 flag, bit 1 for the CA1 flag) can be cleared by reading or writing the corresponding A-port or B-port. Thus ?BPRT=0 or LET X = ?BPRT will clear the CB1 flag, and ?APRT=0 or LET X = ?APRT will clear the CA1 flag.

These flags remain LOW until the CA1 or CB1 lines receive their correct transition, upon which the corresponding flag will be raised. Like the football referee the microprocessor does not immediately heed the flag but may wait for a more opportune moment. Nevertheless the flag remains up until some attention is paid to it, even when the strobe has gone. This explains the advantage of this system over the simpler one of just watching the user port until it changes.

Consider one particular application of this idea, the classic problem of which contestant in a quiz was the first to press his or her switch. It is no good just getting the microcomputer to look occasionally at the individual switches, the time interval between two different people pressing their switch might be too short to be discriminated. To solve this problem we use the latching facility of the VIA to capture data into the user port as soon as it is received. This mode is selected by the auxiliary control register (ACR) at address 65131. When bit 1 of this register is LOW, there is no latching of the input data to the B-port, but when bit 1 is HIGH, the latching facility is enabled. When the B-port is latched, any data on its lines is captured so that even if the original input signals are removed, their logic levels will remain. The same is true for the A-port, except that it is bit 0 of the ACR that has to be set HIGH. This is no use for the VIA in the BBC microcomputer, since the A-port cannot be made into an input anyway.

The latching of the data at the user port occurs when the corresponding CA1 or CB1 line gets its expected HIGH-LOW or LOW-HIGH transition (as determined by the PCR). Figure 4.15 gives the circuit diagram for solving the quiz problem. The eight push button switches are normally HIGH. They are connected to the lines of the user port and also to an eight-input NAND gate (SN7430). The output from the NAND gate is thus LOW and is connected to the CB1 line.

```
10  REM INPUT DATA LATCHING
20  BPRT=65120:REM USER PORT
30  DDRB=65122:REM DATA DIRECTION REGISTER
40  ACR=65131:REM AUXILIARY CONTROL REGISTER
50  PCR=65132:REM PERIPHERAL CONTROL REGISTER
60  FLAG=65133:REM FLAG REGISTER
100 ?DDRB=0:REM B-PORT IS INPUT
110 ?ACR=2:REM ACR SET TO ENABLE B-PORT LATCH
120 ?PCR=16:REM PCR SET TO LATCH ON LOW-HIGH TRANSITION
130 IF (?FLAG AND 16)=0 THEN 130
140 X = ?BPRT:REM READ B-PORT AND RESET LATCH
```

Now, whenever any of the switches is pressed, it goes momentarily LOW, so the output from the NAND gate will go HIGH, thus activating the CB1 line. The state of all switches will then be latched into the user port and held there indefinitely. The microcomputer can read them at its own convenience, thus discovering which one was activated first (unless,

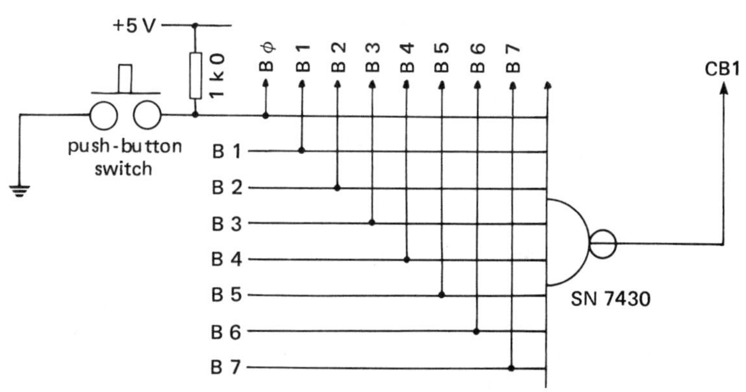

Figure 4.15 Input latching

of course, there were simultaneous switch closures). On reading the user port, the flag is again lowered and the CB1 latching facility is reset ready for the next time. Alternatively, the flag can be deliberately lowered by writing its decimal value to the flag register.

Another application of this latching facility is the connection of a concept keyboard to a microcomputer. This keyboard has pressure sensitive pads, the function of which can be changed with suitable overlays. When pressed each keypad places a seven-bit byte of data on its parallel port and signals this by sending a negative strobe to the CB1 line of the microcomputer user port. The VIA has to be set up so that when the CB1 line goes LOW (indicating a key press), the number on the data lines is latched into the user port. This can then be read at leisure by the microcomputer, upon which the latch is automatically reset, ready for the next key closure. If the CB1 line is pulled LOW, bit 4 of the flag register in the VIA is set, so the program simply waits for this flag to go HIGH and then it reads the contents of the user port.

Interrupts

In several instances so far we have been content to let the microcomputer sit around watching the user port or the flag register waiting for something to happen. In the past, computers cost so much that nobody could afford to waste computer time in this way and the special technique of the **interrupt** was developed. This is similar to when I am reading a book and the telephone rings. I immediately place a marker into the book and attend to the call. When I have finished I return to the task I was doing when interrupted, using the bookmark to find out which page I was on.

The microprocessor has a similar facility. When it receives an interrupt signal, it finishes its current instruction and **services** the interrupt. Afterwards it returns to its original task from where it left off. An interrupt request can be sent to the microprocessor when a CA1 or CB1 line gets its correct strobe. There are also five other ways in which an interrupt can be generated by the VIA; by the CA2 or CB2 control lines, time-outs by either of the timers and shift-outs by the shift register, each controlled by a flag in the flag register. If any flag goes up, an interrupt request could be sent to the microprocessor along its IRQ line. We do not always want this to happen, so it is possible to prevent it. The interrupt facility is only enabled if one of the bits in the **interrupt enable register (IER)** is HIGH, the bit corresponding to the flag concerned.

Bit	6	5	4	3	2	1	0
Flag	T1	T2	CB1	CB2	SR	CA1	CA2
IER	T1	T2	CB1	CB2	SR	CA1	CA2

In the BBC microcomputer the interrupt facility is used a great deal by the microprocessor, for example, to deal with inputs from the keyboard, which occur at very irregular intervals. It is not, therefore, possible in BASIC for the user to make use of it too, nor is it actually necessary in machine code routines. The main reason for mentioning it is so that you will be aware of what can happen during timing routines, etc. You may carefully calculate that a timing loop should last one hundred microseconds only to find that it is some five per cent longer than this. The reason is that the microprocessor is being interrupted by a timer every hundredth of a second to update the clock in the microcomputer. There is a simple solution; to switch off the interrupt facility completely before starting the machine code timing loop. This is done with the instruction **SEI (set the interrupt mask).** The interrupt facility is restored with the instruction **CLI (clear the interrupt mask).** These instructions occur quite often in succeeding programs.

To prevent individual interrupts from occurring without disabling the whole facility, the requisite bits of the IER can be cleared.

CA2 and CB2 control lines

The CA2 and CB2 lines can be used as inputs just like the CA1 and CB1 lines by configuring the PCR and ACR correctly. They can therefore also be used for sending interrupt requests to the microprocessor. They have many more functions than CA1 and CB1 and are more versatile. Their particular advantage is that they can also be turned into output lines. They are switched HIGH or LOW by setting the correct bits of the PCR. Bits 1, 2 and 3 control CA2 and if bits 2 and 3 are both set, this selects the direct output mode. Thereafter if bit 1 is set, CA2 will be HIGH and if bit 1 is cleared then CA2 will be LOW. CB2 is controlled in the same way by bits 5, 6 and 7 of the PCR.

```
?PCR=12:REM SET CA2 LOW
?PCR=14:REM SET CA2 HIGH
?PCR=192:REM SET CB2 LOW
?PCR=224:REM SET CB2 HIGH
```

This facility effectively increases the number of available output lines, although those already there are usually enough. The CA2 line is available as a strobe at the printer connector.

The 'concept' keyboard

This soft keyboard can be used for inputting data without using the standard QWERTY keyboard and all its attendant problems. As described in Chapter 1 a soft keyboard can have its keys altered (or disabled) to suit each particular application. The concept keyboard (available from Star Microsystems) is one particular board that is easily fitted to the BBC microcomputer (Figure 4.16).

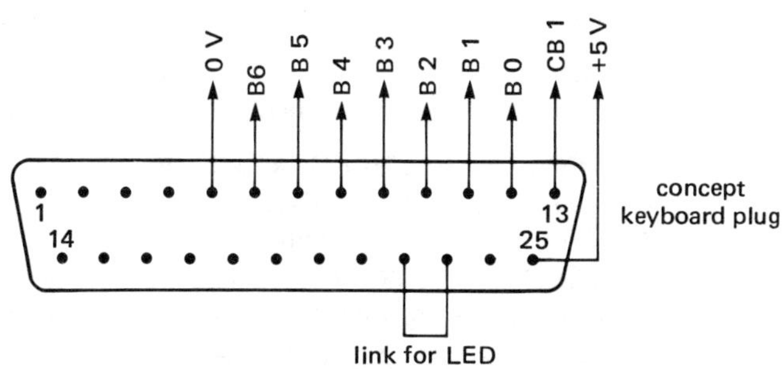

Figure 4.16 Connecting the concept keyboard

0	1	2	3	…	13	14	15
16	17	18	19	…	29	30	31
32	33	34	35	…			47
48	49	50	51	…			63
64	65	66	67	…			79
80	81	82	83	…			95
96	97	98	99	…			111
112	113	114	115	…			127

Figure 4.17 'Concept' key arrangement

The keyboard consists of a washable surface beneath which are 128 pressure sensitive keys (Figure 4.17). When pressed, each key sends a number along seven parallel lines, which can be connected to bits 0 to 6 of the user port. A separate 'strobe' line is connected to the CB1 line and configured inside the connecting cable such that it goes LOW, when a key is pressed. The data on the lines is then latched into the B-Port and the flag set in the flag register. It is necessary to use the latching facility since, if no key is being pressed, the data lines are open circuit and present a random number. Finally bit 7 is grounded for convenience, the keys thus providing data numbers from 0 to 127. The keys are ASCII coded but this is only for ease of reference.

The procedure for reading the keyboard waits for the flag to go HIGH, whereupon the data is read, thus resetting the flag ready for the next keypress.

```
1000 DEF PROCreadconceptkeyboard
1010 REPEAT
1020 UNTIL ?FLAG<>0
1030 LET Q% = ?BPRT
1040 ENDPROC
```

Q% returns with the data for the key pressed since the last time PROCreadconceptkeyboard was called. Initially the VIA must be configured as follows:

```
1 REM CONCEPT KEYBOARD CONFIGURATION
2 BPRT=65120:REM USER PORT
3 DDRB=65122:REM DATA DIRECTION REGISTER
4 ACR=65131:REM AUXILIARY CONTROL REGISTER
5 PCR=65132:REM PERIPHERAL CONTROL REGISTER
6 FLAG=65133:REM FLAG REGISTER
7 IER=65134:REM INTERRUPT REGISTER
```

```
10  ?DDRB=0:REM B-PORT IS INPUT
11  ?ACR=2:REM ACR SET TO ENABLE B-PORT LATCH
12  ?PCR=0:REM PCR SET TO LATCH ON HIGH-LOW TRANSITION
13  ?FLAG=24:REM RESET CB1 and CB2 FLAGS
14  ?IER=24:REM DISABLE INTERRUPTS FROM CB1 and CB2
15  LET Q% = BPRT:REM CLEAR FLAG INITIALLY
```

The way that the keyboard routine is used within the body of the program depends upon the requirements of the program. For example, suppose the program was training a child to recognize colours. The board could be divided into four parts, each differently coloured. The program would proceed as follows:

```
560  PROCreadconceptkeyboard
570  LET N = 1 + (Q% AND 8) + 2*(Q% AND 64)
580  ON N GOTO w, x, y, z
```

N will end up with the values 1, 2, 3 or 4 depending on which quadrant of the board is being pressed. Alternatively, for finer discrimination, adjacent keys could be distinguished by checking on bit 0 of the value in Q%. Individual keys may, of course, simply be checked by number directly.

Handshaking

One useful purpose of the C1 and C2 lines is for handshaking. When data is sent from one machine to another, the sender needs to tell the receiver when the data is available. Similarly the receiver needs to signal the sender to indicate that the data has been received. As an example of this procedure a technique for transferring data from one BBC microcomputer to another is now described. The two machines are connected as shown in Figure 4.18.

After configuring the registers the receiver toggles its CB2 line to send a negative pulse to the CB1 line of the sender. The CB1 line sets its flag, telling the sender that the receiver is now **ready for data (RFD).** The sender responds by collecting the byte of data to be sent and writing it into the user port. The sender then signals **data available (DAV)** by toggling its CB2 line, sending a negative strobe to the CB1 line of the receiver. Upon receiving this strobe (or more accurately the negative transition of the strobe) the CB1 line sets its flag and at the same time latches the data into the user port. The receiver notes that the flag is

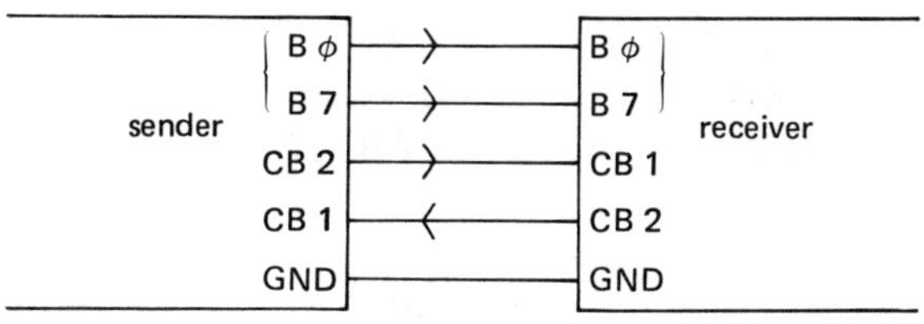

Figure 4.18 Parallel data transfer

raised and reads the data, thus resetting the flag and re-enabling the latch for the next byte.

In this program the byte to be sent is merely input to the sender from the keyboard and is displayed on the receiver's screen. This allows the user to type on one machine and have the characters appear on the other at the same time. The end of a line of text is signalled by sending a carriage return (character 13) and this is sensed in line 230 of the sender's program. It is, however, necessary to precede this with a line feed (character 10), which is the purpose of the subroutine at line 500. These ideas can be extended to any communication between the two microcomputers. Clearly one very important application is the transfer of program and data files from one microcomputer to another. I used a routine like this to transfer programs from a PET to the BBC microcomputer. Unfortunately, the process was not particularly valuable in most instances. For example, MASTERMIND prints everything in upper case letters (as in the original PET program) so it would have been better to have rewritten the program from the beginning on the BBC microcomputer.

```
  1 REM PARALLEL TRANSFER-SENDER ROUTINE
 10 BPRT = &FE60
 20 DDRB = &FE62
 30 ACR = &FE6B
 40 PCR = &FE6C
 50 FLAG = &FE6D
 60 IER = &FE6E
 70
100 REM INITIALIZE REGISTERS
110 ?IER = 16:REM DISABLE CB1 INTERRUPT
120 ?DDRB=255:REM USER PORT AS OUTPUT
130 ?ACR = 0:REM DISABLE LATCH 140 ?PCR =236:REM
    SET CB2 HIGH
150 X = ?BPRT:REM RESET CB1 FLAG
160
200 REM SEND BYTE
210 IF (?FLAG AND 16) = 0 THEN 210:REM WAIT FOR RFD
220 A$=GET$:REM GET BYTE TO SEND
230 IF A$=CHR$(13) THEN 500:REM SEND LINE FEED
240 ?BPRT=ASC(A$):REM SEND ASCII VALUE OF CHARACTER
250 ?PCR = 192:REM SET CB2 LOW
260 ?PCR = 224:REM SET CB2 HIGH AGAIN
270 GOTO 200:REM DO NEXT CHARACTER
280
500 REM SEND CARRIAGE RETURN
510 ?BPRT = 13:REM SEND ASCII VALUE OF CARRIAGE RETURN
520 ?PCR = 192:REM SET CB2 LOW
530 ?PCR = 224:REM SET CB2 HIGH AGAIN
```

```
540 IF (?FLAG AND 16) = 0 THEN 540:REM WAIT FOR RFD
550 ?BPRT = 10:REM NOW SEND LINE FEED
560 GOTO 250
```

```
  1 REM PARALLEL TRANSFER-RECEIVER ROUTINE
 10 BPRT = &FE60
 20 DDRB = &FE62
 30 ACR = &FE6B
 40 PCR = &FE6C
 50 FLAG = &FE6D
 60 IER = &FE6E
 70
100 REM INITIALIZE REGISTERS
110 ?IER = 16:REM DISABLE CB1 INTERRUPT
120 ?DDRB = 0:REM USER PORT AS INPUT
130 ?ACR = 2:REM ENABLE LATCHING FACILITY
140 ?PCR = 224:REM SET CB2 HIGH,
    HIGH-LOW TRANSITION ON CB1
200 REM RECEIVE BYTE
210 ?PCR = 192:REM SET CB2 LOW FOR 'READY TO RECEIVE'
220 IF (?FLAG AND 16) = 0 THEN 220:REM WAIT FOR FLAG
230 X = ?BPRT:REM GET BYTE AND RESET LATCH AND FLAG
240 PRINT CHR$(X);:REM DISPLAY RECEIVED CHARACTER
250 ?PCR = 224:REM SET CB2 HIGH AGAIN
260 GOTO 200:REM GET NEXT BYTE
```

Timer 1

The VIA possesses two sixteen-bit counter/timers with a variety of modes. These provide a great facility for measuring time intervals and for counting pulses. Note that, although the clock rate of the BBC microcomputer is 2 MHz, the VIA timers run at 1 MHz. The different modes of the timers are selected by sending a particular bit-pattern to the ACR.

Bit	7	6	5	4	3	2	1	0
	Timer 1		Timer 2	Shift register			B-latch	A-latch

Auxiliary control register functions

Bits 6 and 7 control timer 1 and bit 5 controls timer 2, but the modes available for each timer are very different. Not all modes are equally useful either, so only a few will be described.

As a sixteen-bit counter each is capable of counting to 65 536, or rather counting *down* from 65 535 to zero, which is the way they work. Upon reaching zero a time-out signal is sent to the flag register (FLAG) in the VIA. Time-outs on timer 1 affect bit 6 of FLAG and time-outs on timer 2 affect bit 5. These bits can be inspected and if one is set, then a time-out has occurred. Alternatively, the interrupt enable bits can be set, thus generating an interrupt request upon time-out.

There are two parts to each timer, the counter itself and its input latches. These are necessary because in some modes the counters automatically restart upon reaching zero. Thus timer 1 can be set to count down from, say, 1000 to zero and on reaching zero the number 1000 is reloaded into the timer from the latches and the countdown repeats. This produces a series of time-outs, at intervals of about one millisecond.

In addition to the time-outs a digital signal can be made to appear at bit 7 of the B-Port (irrespective of the setting of DDRB). The logic level of this line (PB7) changes from HIGH to LOW or from LOW to HIGH, whenever a time-out occurs from timer 1. The selection of this mode is made through bit 7 of the ACR. If ACR7 is set, then the digital signals will be output through PB7. If ACR7 is cleared, then no signals appear at PB7.

ACR bit 6 controls whether timer 1 generates a single time-out signal or continuous signals as follows:

i) ACR6 LOW: the one shot mode
After timer 1 has been loaded with some number, it is decremented at the 1 MHz clock-pulse rate. When it reaches zero, the time-out occurs and a signal is sent to bit 6 of the flag register to say so. If ACR7 is also HIGH, then the logic level of PB7 is changed. PB7 will go LOW as soon as the high byte is loaded into timer 1. Countdown begins at the same instant and, on the time-out signal, PB7 will go HIGH again.

ii) ACR6 HIGH: free running mode
After timer 1 has been loaded, it is decremented at the clock pulse rate until it reaches zero, exactly as before. A time-out signal is sent to bit 6 of the flag register also as before. But the number originally loaded into the latch of timer 1 is then automatically reloaded and the countdown begins again. If, at the same time, ACR7 is HIGH, then the logic level of PB7 changes, as described above. In this mode the PB7 line goes alternately HIGH and LOW with every time-out signal. The countdown of timer 1 begins as soon as its latch is loaded with its starting number. Since it is a sixteen-bit register, it must be loaded in two halves. The low byte is written into T1LLO (address = 65124) and the high byte into T1LHI (address = 65125). The countdown begins when the high byte is loaded, so the low byte must be loaded first. For a particular time interval (t in microseconds) the required numbers are loaded into T1LHI and T1LLO by

```
?T1LLO = (t-2) MOD 256
?T1LHI = (t-2) DIV 256
```

Applications of timer 1

i) Generate output pulses on PB7
In free running mode the PB7 logic level changes once every time-out. Thus, if it is desired to make PB7 generate a frequency of 1 kHz, time-outs must occur every 500 microseconds. Timer 1 thus needs to be loaded with 500. However, this number must be reduced by 1.75 to allow for the reloading time etc. of the system.The pulses cannot therefore be quite as accurate a one might hope. This gives 498 to be loaded into the T1 latches, a low byte of 242 into T1LLO and 1 into T1LHI.

Note that it is not necessary to set up PB7 as an output beforehand – this present function overrides its configuration by DDRB. The pulses can be stopped by loading 0 into the ACR (?ACR = 0). Since this is a sixteen-bit timer, pulse frequencies between 250 kHz and and a few hertz can be produced with this method. This includes the audio range and so is a possible method of producing audio-frequency square wave pulses. This idea is also used in PULSE TIMER (11) to determine the length of a square pulse (Plate 23).

ii) Generate a single (negative) pulse on PB7

To generate a single time-out requires ACR6 to be LOW. Timer 1 should be loaded with the length of the time interval required (less 1.5 machine cycles), so for an output pulse of 1 millisecond duration, timer 1 should be loaded with 998, a high byte of 3 and a low byte of 230. This idea is used in FREQUENCY METER (12) to open a gate for a specified length of time (Plate 22).

```
100 ?ACR=128:REM SET ACR7 HIGH and ACR6 LOW
110 ?T1LLO=230:REM LOAD LOW BYTE
120 ?T1LHI=3:REM LOAD HIGH BYTE AND BEGIN PULSE
```

iii) Provide an internal clock

The BBC microcomputer clock is only a centisecond timer. Timer 1 may be used to provide accurate time-outs at shorter intervals. Rather than use the interrupt system of the microcomputer, it is usually quite easy to inspect bit 6 of the flag register to see if it is set. If so a time-out has occurred and T1LHI can be reloaded to start a new countdown.

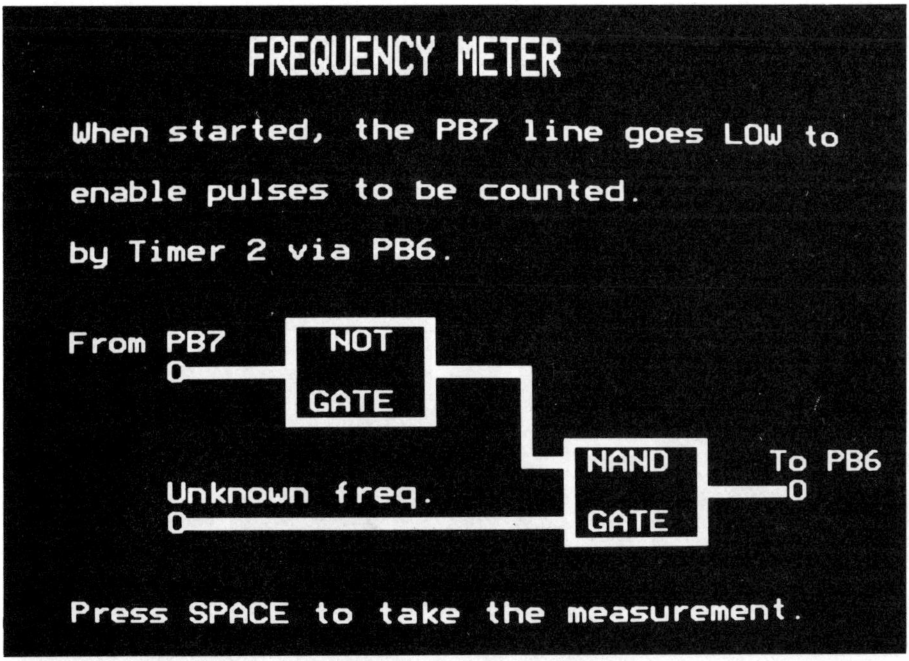

Plate 22 FREQUENCY METER instructions

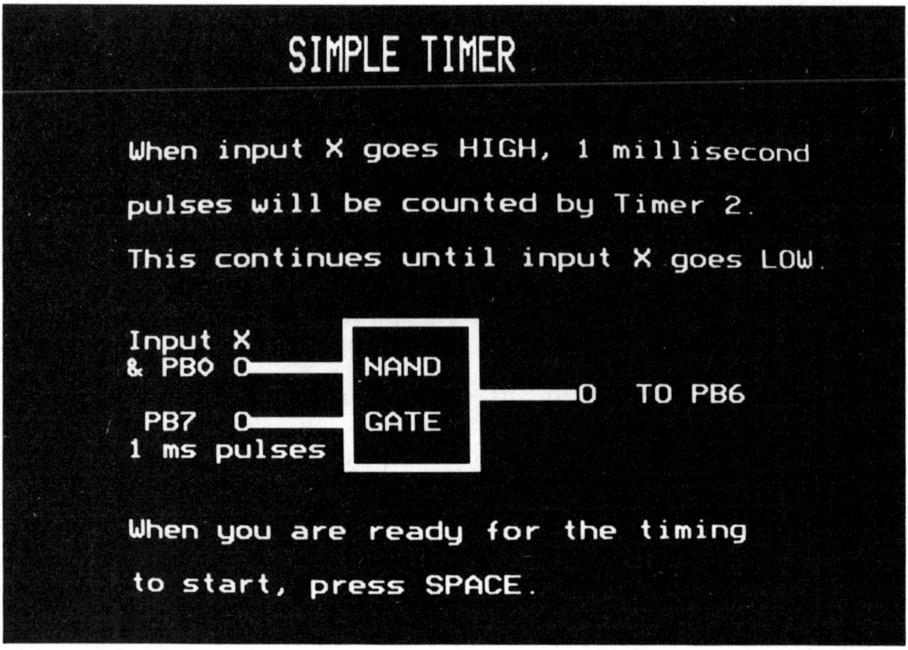

Plate 23 Timing of short intervals

Plate 24 Centisecond timer – STOPCLOCK

This use of timer 1 is illustrated by STOPCLOCK (5)(Plate 24). This is a centisecond clock that is started by an event (a change in logic level) at either bit 0 or bit 1 of the User Port. The current time is displayed in minutes, seconds and centiseconds in large digits on the screen, using the machine code subroutine developed in Chapter 7. Another event stops the clock, which then displays the elapsed time. The whole program illustrates the freedom given by using the timer instead of microprocessor delay loops to do the timing. The latter can then get on with other tasks, like sorting out where the digits have to go and displaying them.

When the countdown in timer 1 reaches zero, it sets a flag in the flag register, reloads itself from the latch and carries on counting down. Thus if the latch contains the number 10000, timer 1 gives out a steady stream of one centisecond signals. STOPCLOCK actually reads the centisecond clock provided by the operating system at address 662 (OS 1.0 and above) or 594 (OS 0.1). This works in the way just described except that it uses the 'other' VIA.

Timer 2

Timer 2 modes are controlled by bit 5 of the ACR and thus it only has two modes. When ACR5 is LOW, timer 2 acts rather like timer 1 in its one shot mode. Since no output pulses are produced, this mode is of no special interest to us. The other mode is a pulse counting mode and is more valuable. It is selected when ACR5 is HIGH. Timer 2 is then loaded with the number to be counted. Every time that line 6 of the B-port (PB6) goes LOW, timer 2 is decremented. When it reaches zero, it has counted the required number of pulses and a time-out occurs. Bit 5 of the flag register is set HIGH to show this time-out.

Applications of timer 2

i) A clock

By getting timer 1 to generate continuous output pulses on PB7 at, say, 10 millisecond intervals and subsequently counting these pulses by timer 2, then quite long time intervals can be produced. To do this PB6 and PB7 should be connected together.

Then, after selecting the pulse counting mode, timer 2 is loaded with the required number of centiseconds to be counted. Upon time-out timer 2 sets bit 5 of the flag register. A BASIC program simply sets up the ACR and the timers and then waits until this flag has been set, thus indicating that the required time has elapsed. By altering the numbers loaded into the timers initially, time intervals as low as one millisecond may be produced, which is about as low as BASIC can handle. Timer 1 set to produce tenth-second pulses and timer 2 set to count 60 000 of these, gives a 100 minute interval.

The following example generates an interval of one second. It measures this time interval by counting a thousand one millisecond pulses. PB7 and PB6 should be connected together for this application.

```
100  ?ACR=224:REM SET ACR5, 6 AND 7 HIGH
110  ?T2LO=232:REM SET TIMER 2 LOW
120  ?T2HI=3:REM SET TIMER 2 HIGH
130  ?T1LLO=230:REM LOAD TIMER 1 LOW
140  ?T1LHI=1:REM START TIMER AND RESET FLAG
```

```
150  X = ?FLAG:REM INSPECT FLAG REGISTER
160  X=X−192
170  IF X<32 THEN 150
180  RETURN
```

Since we are using timer 1 too, bits 6 and 7 of the flag register will also be set, hence line 160.

ii) A frequency meter

Timer 1 is set to produce a single negative pulse on PB7. This is inverted and opens a gate to allow pulses from an alternating voltage of unknown frequency to reach PB6 to be counted by timer 2. Upon observing time-out on timer 1, the microprocessor reads timer 2 to see how many pulses had been received (Figure 4.19)(Plate 22). This number is then converted into a frequency and displayed.

```
100   REM FAST FREQUENCY METER
320   ?IER=127:REM DISABLE INTERRUPTS
330   ?ACR=160:REM PB6 TO COUNT PULSES,
      PB7 TO PROVIDE ONE-SHOT PULSE
340   ?PCR=0:REM TURN OFF LATCHES AND SERIAL REGISTER
350   ?T2LO=255:?T2HI=255:REM INITIALIZE COUNTER
360   ?DDRB=128:REM BIT 7 AS OUTPUT
      (THIS INSTRUCTION UNNECESSARY)
380   ?FLAG=127:REM CLEAR FLAGS
390
500   GOSUB 1000:REM OPEN GATE FOR 50 MILLISECONDS
510   freq=(256 * (255 − ?T2HI) + (255 − ?T2LO)) * 20
530   PRINT freq
540
1000  REM OPEN GATE FOR 50 MILLISECONDS
1010  ?T1LLO=79
1020  ?T1LHI=195:REM OPEN GATE AND RESET LATCH
1030  IF (?FLAG AND 64)=0 THEN 1030:REM WAIT FOR
      TIMEOUT ON TIMER 1
1040  RETURN
```

A frequency below 2 kHz will provide less than a hundred counts in timer 2 and is thus inaccurately measured. For these low frequencies the internal clock is used just to provide a time interval of one second, during which time the gate is opened to allow the input frequency to be measured.

```
800  REM LOW FREQUENCY OPTION
810  ?ACR=32:REM DISABLE OUTPUTS ON PB7
820  ?DDRB=128:REM PB7 AS OUTPUT
830  ?PRT=128:REM SET PB7 HIGH
840  ?T2LO=255:?T2HI=255:REM INITIALIZE COUNTER
```

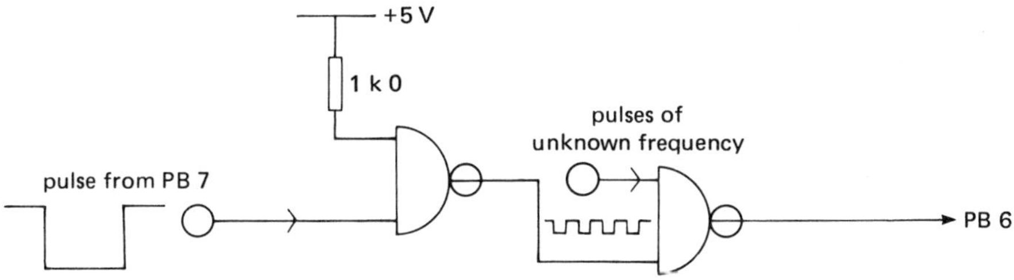

Figure 4.19 Gating input pulses to PB6

```
850 ?PRT=0:REM OPEN GATE
860 TIME=0:REM START CLOCK
870 REPEAT
870 UNTIL TIME = 100
890 ?PRT=128:REM CLOSE GATE
900 freq= 256 * (255 - ?T2HI) + (255 - ?T2LO)
910 PRINT freq
```

The following line can be added to the above program, so that it automatically runs this low frequency section if the frequency is too low for the first method.

```
520 IF freq<2000 THEN 800
```

The full listing of this program is given in FREQUENCY METER (12).

iii) A pulse timer

The same technique can be used in reverse to measure the length of a pulse. In this case the unknown pulse is used to open the gate to allow through millisecond pulses from PB7 to be counted via PB6 (Plate 23).

One difficulty about the automatic nature of this program is to determine when the pulse has finished. For this reason it is also connected to PB1, which can then be monitored (Figure 4.20). Timer 1 should be loaded with 500-2 to provide one millisecond pulses through PB7 (the number is reduced by two to allow for the reloading time described above).

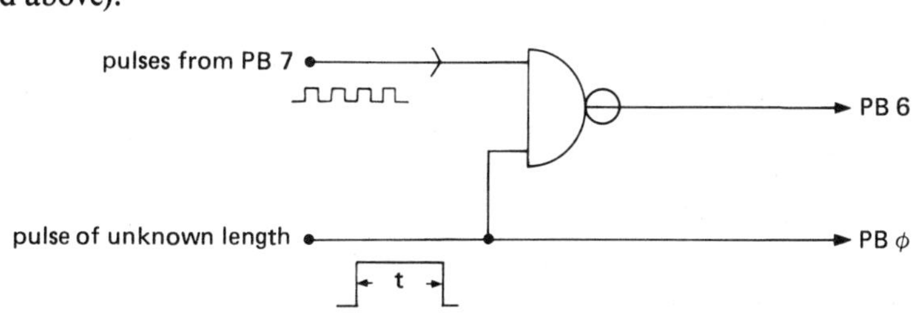

Figure 4.20 Pulse measuring circuit

```
100  REM PULSE TIMER
110  ?IER=127:REM DISABLE INTERRUPTS
120  ?ACR=224:REM PB6 TO COUNT,
     PB7 TO PROVIDE CONTINUOUS PULSES
130  ?PCR=0:REM TURN OFF LATCHES AND SERIAL REGISTER
140  ?T2LO=255:?T2HI=255:REM INITIALIZE COUNTER
150  ?FLAG=127:REM CLEAR FLAGS
155  ?DDRB=128:REM BIT 0 AS INPUT
160  ?T1LLO=242:REM LOAD TIMER 1 WITH 500
170  ?T1LHI=1:REM AND START CLOCK AND CLEAR FLAG
180  IF (?PRT AND 1)=0 THEN 180:REM PULSE HAS NOT
     YET STARTED
190  IF (?PRT AND 1) THEN 190:REM PULSE HAS NOT YET FINISHED
200  time = 256 * (255 - ?T2HI) + (255 - ?T2LO)
210  PRINT time;" milliseconds"
```

The full listing is given in PULSE TIMER (11).

The serial register

This register, **SR,** (at address 65130) outputs its contents to the CB2 line, one bit at a time. There are eight modes for this, determined by bits 2, 3 and 4 of the ACR. If ACR4 is cleared then the bits are shifted into the SR and if ACR4 is set they are shifted out. The advantage of the system is that, once initiated, the bits are output automatically, thus freeing the microprocessor for other tasks.

The main use of the SR is for serial data transfer. Parallel transfer requires all eight bits to be sent at once along eight separate lines but only one is needed for serial transfer (in both cases another line for ground return and two more for control signals are also needed). Thus it is possible to send data from one computer to another, with only four lines instead of the eleven needed for parallel data transfer (Figure 4.21). To illustrate the principles the following BASIC program transfers bytes from one BBC microcomputer to another.

The contents of the serial register can be shifted out in four different ways:

1 Mode 100 – free running, which is discussed later.
2 Mode 101 – under the control of timer 2. This is the mode we shall actually use for data transfer. The contents of the shift register are shifted out bit by bit on the CB2

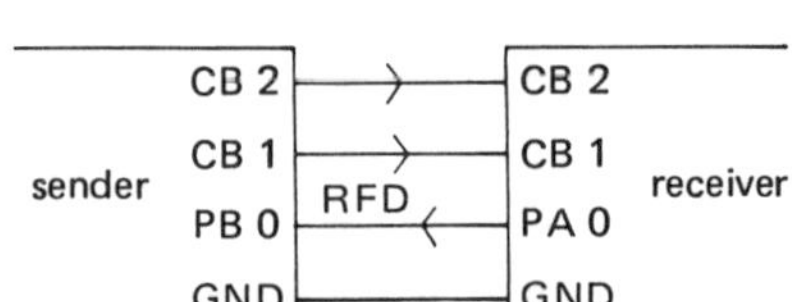

Figure 4.21 Serial data transfer

line starting with the most significant bit. At the same time the bit is shifted back into bit 0 of the SR. Thus after eight shifts, the byte in SR has been rotated completely. A new shift-out occurs when timer 2 reaches time-out, which depends upon the value loaded into T2LO initially. Note that T2HI is not used, so the timer is only eight bits wide, giving a maximum interval between shifts of 255 microseconds. The process is initiated by writing the byte to be sent into the serial register. After eight shifts the corresponding flag (bit 2) in the flag register is set. This can be used to give an interrupt, or alternatively as in this application, can simply be inspected until it goes HIGH. This can be the signal for the microcomputer to get the next byte to be shifted out. The flag is reset at the same time as the next byte is loaded into SR to begin the next byte transfer.

Time-outs on T2 cause the contents of the T2 latch to be reloaded into the timer itself ready for the next bit shift. At the same time a pulse is output through the CB1 control line for strobing the receiver. The CB1 line goes LOW when the next bit has stabilized at the CB2 output. Note that this is the only condition for which CB1 is an output.

3 Mode 110 – under the control of the system clock. This is similar to the method above, except that the shift-out rate is controlled by the system clock.
4 Mode 111 – under the control of external clock pulses. This time it is the external receiver that generates the clock pulses and sends these to the VIA through the CB1 control line.

There are similar ways for shifting the data into the SR in the receiving microcomputer (modes 001 to 011). In this application it is mode 011 that is used, which shifts the bits in from the CB2 line under the control of external clock pulses along the CB1 line. These are the clock pulses generated by mode 101 above. Thus the CB1 lines of the two machines are connected together to communicate the shift pulses, as are the CB2 lines, which are used to carry the data itself (Figure 4.21).

There has also to be some signal from the receiver to the sender to initiate the process each time. The line used is bit 0 of the user port in both cases. The receiver holds this line HIGH until it is ready to receive data and then it sends it LOW. The sender waits for its line to go LOW before loading its SR and thus starting to send the byte. In use, this allows characters to be typed in on one keyboard to appear on the screen of the other. It terminates when the character @ is typed in. It is necessary to generate a line feed whenever a carriage return is pressed and this is done by the subroutine at line 500.

```
 1 REM SERIAL TRANSFER-SENDER ROUTINE
10 BPRT = &FE60
20 DDRB = &FE62
30 T2LO = &FE68
40 SR = &FE6A
50 ACR = &FE6B
60 PCR = &FE6C
50 FLAG = &FE6D
60 IER = &FE6E
```

```
70
100 REM INITIALIZE VIA
110 ?DDRB=0:REM BIT 0 IS INPUT
120 ?IER=0:REM DISABLE SHIFT INTERRUPT
130 ?ACR=20:REM ACR IN SHIFT-OUT MODE
140 ?PCR=236:REM CB2 HIGH INITIALLY
150 ?T2LO=100:REM SHIFT OUT AT ONE BIT PER
    100 MICROSECONDS
160
200 REM SEND BYTE
210 A$=GET$
220 IF A$ = CHR$(13) THEN GOSUB 500
230 IF (?BPRT AND 1) THEN 230:REM WAIT FOR
    SIGNAL FROM RECEIVER
240 ?SR=ASC(A$):REM SEND BYTE
250 IF (?FLAG AND 4) = 0 THEN 250:REM WAIT FOR
    SHIFT-DONE FLAG
260 GOTO 200:REM GET NEXT BYTE READY
270
500 REM LINE FEED SUBROUTINE
510 IF (?BPRT AND 1) THEN 510:REM WAIT FOR
    SIGNAL FROM RECEIVER
520 ?SR=10:REM SEND LINE FEED
530 IF (?FLAG AND 4) = 0 THEN 530:REM WAIT FOR
    SHIFT-DONE FLAG
540 RETURN
```

```
1 REM SERIAL TRANSFER-RECEIVER ROUTINE
10 BPRT = &FE60
20 DDRB = &FE62
30 SR = &FE6A
40 ACR = &FE6B
50 FLAG = &FE6D
60 IER = &FE6E
70
100 REM INITIALIZE VIA
110 ?IER = 0:REM DISABLE INTERRUPTS
120 ?DDRB = 1: REM BIT 0 IS OUTPUT
130 ?ACR = 12:REM SHIFT IN MODE
140 ?BPRT = 1:REM NOT READY FOR DATA
156 X = ?SR:REM INITIALIZE FLAGS, ETC
160
200 REM GET BYTE
210 ?BPRT=0: REM READY FOR DATA
```

```
220  IF (?FLAG AND 4) = 0 THEN 220:REM WAIT FOR
     SHIFT-DONE FLAG
230  ?BPRT = 1:REM NOT READY FOR DATA
240  X = ?SR:REM COLLECT BYTE
250  IF X = 64 THEN STOP:REM @ CHARACTER IS END-OF-DATA
260  PRINT CHR$(X);
270  GOTO 200:REM GET READY FOR NEXT BYTE
```

Continuous pulse output

This is mode 100 mentioned above. It is very like mode 101 and utilizes T2LO in exactly the same way. The only difference is that once all eight bits have been output from SR along the CB2 line, the process is immediately restarted, so that the contents of SR are repeatedly output. The data in the serial register can thus be made to produce pulses of a particular shape continuously output via CB2 (Figure 4.22). To select this free running output requires ACR bits 4, 3 and 2 to be set to 1, 0 and 0 respectively and T2LLO should be loaded with the required time interval between the shift-outs of the individual bits. Suppose we require a frequency of 1 kHz for the selected pulse shape. With eight bits to be output, we require one bit every 125 microseconds, so we load the low byte of timer 2 with 124 (one less than 125) to get the correct time interval. The routine is as follows:

```
100  ?SR=15:REM SET UP SR WITH PULSE SHAPE
110  ?T2LLO=128:REM LOAD TIMER 2 LOW
120  ?ACR=16:REM SET UP ACR FOR FREE-RUNNING OUTPUT
```

To switch off these pulses, the simplest way is to load SR with zero, thus retaining the mode without outputting any pulses.

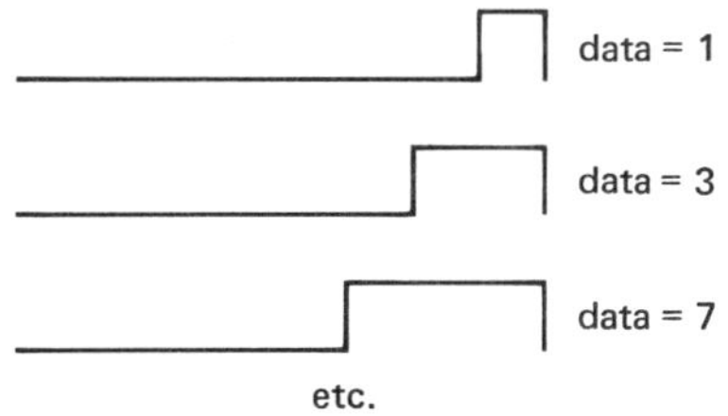

Figure 4.22 Pulse waveforms

Because this method only uses the low byte of timer 2, the lowest frequency available is when timer 2 is loaded with 255 and SR with 15, giving about 200 Hz. The maximum frequency is when timer 2 is loaded with 0, giving 31 kHz (since the routine takes 1 cycle per bit). This can be raised to 125 kHz if SR is loaded with four pulses at once, that is with 85 or 170. This is not as good as that available by using timer 1 and outputting through PB7, and so is not actually much use. Its main application is in providing asymmetric pulses.

The 1 MHz bus

As an alternative to connecting inputs and outputs to the user port, the BBC microcomputer provides the 1 MHz bus. In order to make use of this some knowledge of the way the microprocessor works is helpful. As we shall see in the next chapter, the microprocessor reads and writes to memory or to the user port through two sets of lines, called the **data bus** and the **address bus.** When the microprocessor wants to collect the contents of a particular location, it places the address of that location on the address bus. This consists of sixteen separate lines, each of which is made HIGH or LOW. For example, to read the user port, the microprocessor sets the lines of the address bus like this:

Address line	Status	Address
A15	HIGH	
A14	HIGH	F
A13	HIGH	
A12	HIGH	
A11	HIGH	
A10	HIGH	E
A9	HIGH	
A8	LOW	
A7	LOW	
A6	HIGH	6
A5	HIGH	
A4	LOW	
A3	LOW	
A2	LOW	0
A1	LOW	
A0	LOW	

These address lines go through a series of logic gates (in the ULA of the BBC microcomputer) and only the B-port of the 6522 VIA is enabled to respond. All other locations are ignored. This is called **decoding the address.** Since there are sixteen address lines, there are 65 536 possible locations that can be separately addressed.

When the addressed location sees its own address on the address bus, its response is of two kinds. Either the data in the location is read or new data is written into it. To tell the location which is to occur, the microprocessor signals along a separate R/NW line (read/not write). When this line is HIGH, the data will be read, when this line goes LOW, new data is written into the addressed location. Either way, it is the data bus which carries the data. This consists of eight separate lines, one for each bit of the data.

There also has to be careful control of when the data is available. In a data write instruction, the address is placed on the address bus, the data is placed on the data bus and the R/NW line is made LOW, but still nothing happens until the microprocessor sends the action signal. This is very much like an orchestra, where the conductor keeps everyone together by regular beats of the baton. The microprocessor does the same with clock pulses. These are carried to all parts of the microcomputer along the **clock pulse line (CLK).**

All of these lines appear at the connector of the 1 MHz bus. To add more memory or another device of our own to the microcomputer is ideally a matter of connecting the power supply, address, data, R/NW and CLK lines to the correct pins of the device. Unfortunately there are a few problems.

The first of these is that the selected address for the device must be different from any others that have already been chosen for the operating system of the microcomputer. This whittles the choice down from 65 536 to 63! Actually the BBC microcomputer sets aside 512 spare addresses, which run in the memory from &FC00 to &FDFF. Unfortunately some of these are scheduled to be used by add-on units, such as the teletext adaptor and the sideways ROM. Since you can never be sure which of these devices will be added to your machine in the future, it is safest to stick to the 63 that have not been booked (so far!). These are from &FCC0 to &FCFE. (&FCFF has a special use.)

All these addresses start with &FC, and so the BBC microcomputer automatically decodes the top eight address lines for us. When any location beginning with &FC is addressed, a special line in the 1 MHz bus connector (called FRED) goes LOW to signify the fact. FRED is therefore used instead of the top eight address lines. The lower eight address lines may be decoded as required.

To illustrate the principles, Figure 4.23 shows how sixteen separate select signals can be obtained from the SN74154 decoder. This has five inputs (address lines A4, A5, A6 and A7, and FRED) and produces sixteen device select lines — &FC0x to &FCFx ('x' can be any number from 0 to F). Of these only &FCCx, &FCDx, &FCEx and &FCFx can be used alongside the other add-on devices mentioned above. As the following truth table

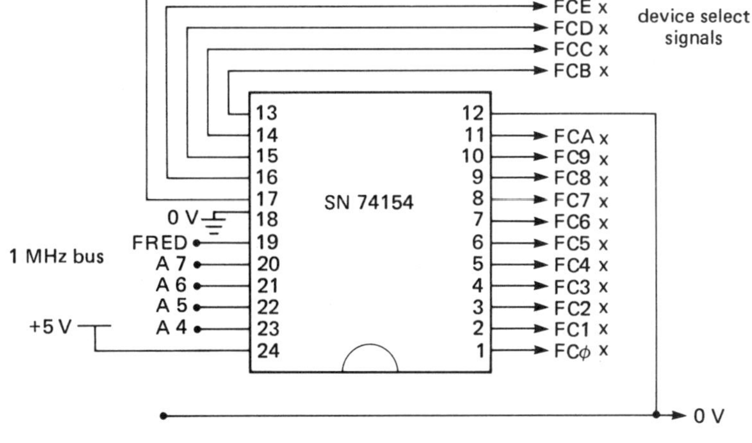

Figure 4.23 Decoding the 1 MHz bus

indicates, only one of these select lines goes LOW at any one time, when the binary address of the required line is sent to the address inputs (A4, A5, A6 and A7).

Inputs				Outputs															
A7	**A6**	**A5**	**A4**	**0**	**1**	**2**	**3**	**4**	**5**	**6**	**7**	**8**	**9**	**A**	**B**	**C**	**D**	**E**	**F**
0	0	0	0	L	H	H	H	H	H	H	H	H	H	H	H	H	H	H	H
0	0	0	1	H	L	H	H	H	H	H	H	H	H	H	H	H	H	H	H
0	0	1	0	H	H	L	H	H	H	H	H	H	H	H	H	H	H	H	H
0	0	1	1	H	H	H	L	H	H	H	H	H	H	H	H	H	H	H	H
0	1	0	0	H	H	H	H	L	H	H	H	H	H	H	H	H	H	H	H
0	1	0	1	H	H	H	H	H	L	H	H	H	H	H	H	H	H	H	H
0	1	1	0	H	H	H	H	H	H	L	H	H	H	H	H	H	H	H	H
0	1	1	1	H	H	H	H	H	H	H	L	H	H	H	H	H	H	H	H
1	0	0	0	H	H	H	H	H	H	H	H	L	H	H	H	H	H	H	H
1	0	0	1	H	H	H	H	H	H	H	H	H	L	H	H	H	H	H	H
1	0	1	0	H	H	H	H	H	H	H	H	H	H	L	H	H	H	H	H
1	0	1	1	H	H	H	H	H	H	H	H	H	H	H	L	H	H	H	H
1	1	0	0	H	H	H	H	H	H	H	H	H	H	H	H	L	H	H	H
1	1	0	1	H	H	H	H	H	H	H	H	H	H	H	H	H	L	H	H
1	1	1	0	H	H	H	H	H	H	H	H	H	H	H	H	H	H	L	H
1	1	1	1	H	H	H	H	H	H	H	H	H	H	H	H	H	H	H	L

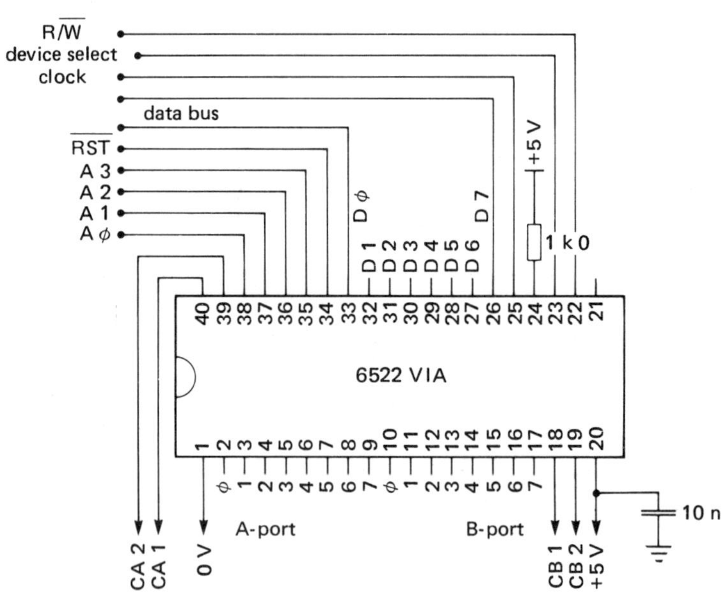

Figure 4.24 Connecting another VIA

If the other add-on units are not being used, each of these output lines can be used to select a different VIA, giving a possible 256 extra input/output lines for control. Figure 4.24 shows how one of these (address &FCC0) is connected to the device select input of just one of these VIAs. The lower four address lines are connected to the four address inputs of the VIA and the R/NW and CLK lines are connected too. Pin 21 of the VIA is left unconnected, it is an interrupt request line and the use of this has not been considered in this book. I have yet to find how the BBC interrupts work and, in any case, very few of my applications require interrupts. The technique of occasionally checking an input is nearly always satisfactory. Pin 34 of the VIA is connected to the RESET line. When the BREAK key of the BBC microcomputer is pressed, the RESET line goes temporarily LOW and clears all the registers of the VIA.

This VIA may now be used in exactly the same way as has just been described, except that it responds to different addresses, as follows:

Name	Function	Decimal	Hexadecimal
BPRT	B-port	64704	&FCC0
APRT	A-port (+ handshake)	64705	&FCC1
DDRB	Data direction reg B	64706	&FCC2
DDRA	Data direction reg A	64707	&FCC3
T1LLO	Low-byte Timer1-latch	64708	&FCC4
T1LHI	High-byte Timer1-latch	64709	&FCC5
T1CLO	Low-byte Timer1-count	64710	&FCC6
T1CHI	High-byte Timer1-count	64711	&FCC7
T2LO	Low-byte Timer2-latch	64712	&FCC8
T2HI	High-byte Timer2-latch	64713	&FCC9
SR	Serial register	64714	&FCCA
ACR	Auxiliary control reg	64715	&FCCB
PCR	Peripheral control reg	64716	&FCCC
FLAG	Interrupt flag reg	64717	&FCCD
IER	Interrupt enable reg	64718	&FCCE
APRT	A-port (no-handshake)	64719	&FCCF

There are other input/output devices that may be connected to the 1 MHz bus, but I am a firm advocate of the 6522 VIA. It is not much more expensive than simpler devices that just latch data in or out, yet it is far more powerful. In the next chapter we shall return to the 1 MHz bus to connect other devices also.

This chapter has tried to show the principles of environmental monitoring and control. Using the input and output buffers described in this chapter, almost any system can be either simulated or realized in a practical way. It is, however, most unlikely that a microcomputer would be used in a real situation. Chapter 9 discusses more realistic ways of producing control equipment.

Practical details

The practical wiring details for the two input board and the logic board are shown in Figures 4.25 and 4.26 respectively. The logic board requires two DS8833 quad line

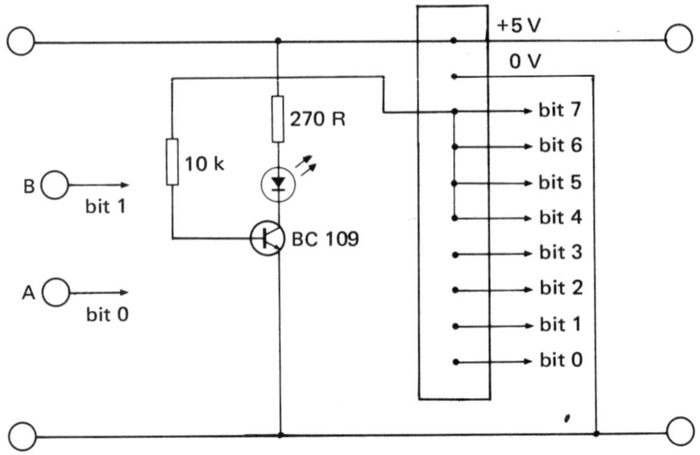

Figure 4.25 Two input board

transceivers (not available from RS Components but from Farnell Ltd). Each output driver is used to drive an LED indicator. The inputs of the four transceivers used for the output terminals are not used, so they are disabled. Connection to the BBC microcomputer user port is via a 20-way cable, each end which requires a 20-way cable mounting socket (RS 467-289). One end plugs into the user port and the other end plugs into a PCB mounting plug (RS 467-346), which may be soldered directly onto each logic board. The eight data lines and the +5 V and 0 V lines should then be connected as shown in Figure 4.26. The pin connections to the user port are shown in Figure 4.27. This configuration assumes that you have lifted up the front of the BBC microcomputer and are looking underneath at the socket directly from the front.

Specific applications of timing

Now that we have looked at the general principles of timing, let us examine a few specific timing applications in physics. The BBC microcomputer can be made to measure the time interval between logic level changes at either input. These changes can be caused by switches or, more importantly, with photocells, one connected to bit 0 and the other to bit 1 of the user port through a suitable op.amp. or transistor driver (Figures 4.9 and 4.10). For some programs only one of these is needed.

Events or logic level changes at the inputs are used to measure time intervals in exactly the same way as in CONTROL EXAMPLE 8. The inputs are read and stored in a memory location called **status.** The current state of the inputs are then monitored continuously and compared with status. Normally they will be the same, but when they are different, this is because one or other of the photocells has been activated. At this point the contents of a clock are noted. When the timing is finished, the time intervals involved can be calculated and displayed.

There are three ways of achieving the clock. The first is to make use of the BBC

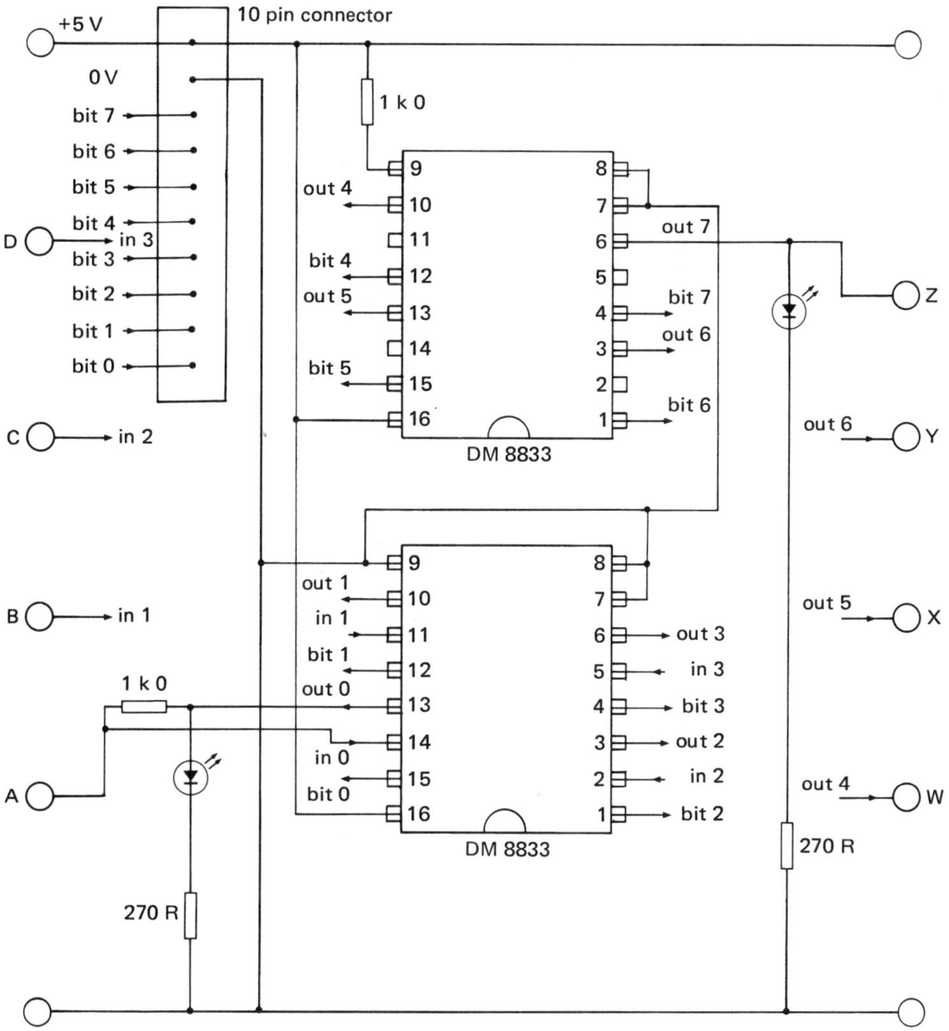

Figure 4.26 Logic board

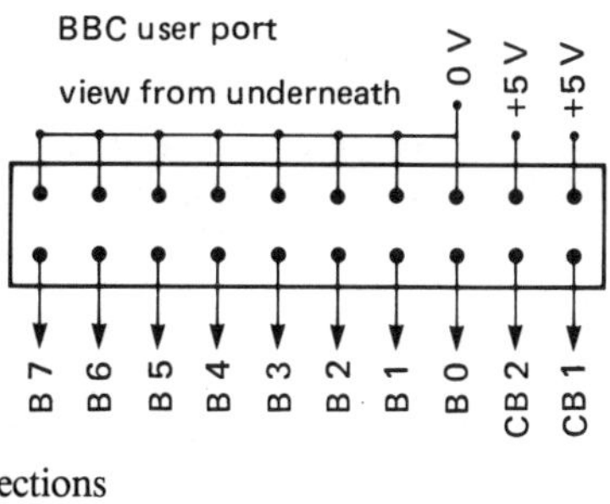

Figure 4.27 User port connections

microcomputer's own clock, which runs at 100 Hz, thus enabling time intervals of 10 ms to be counted. The technique is illustrated by this primitive reaction timer, which assumes a push button switch connected to one of the inputs.

```
  1 REM CONTROL EXAMPLE 10 – REACTION TIMER
 10 ?65122=60:REM CONFIGURE USER PORT
100 PRINT "WHEN THE SCREEN GOES BLANK,"
110 PRINT "PRESS THE SWITCH."
120 max = 5000 + RND(10000)
130 FOR T = 1 to max : NEXT T
140 CLS
150 now=TIME
160 status = ?65120 AND 3
170 IF status = ?65120 AND 3 THEN 170
180 PRINT "REACTION TIME = ";(TIME-now)/60
```

The more sophisticated REACTION TIMER (6) uses the same timing technique, but it displays the results in large digits for all to see (Plate 26). It also replaces the switch input with a keyboard input, so an interface is not needed for this program (Plate 25).

STOPCLOCK (5) accesses the same centisecond clock from machine code and continually updates the display to show the elapsed time. This has to be done with a machine code routine, because the display of the large digits would be too slow in BASIC. All the machine code routine in this section are described in Chapter 8, only their uses in teaching are discussed here. You do not have to be a machine code expert to make use of machine code programs, as long as you know how to call them and how to pass values from them back to BASIC. As already mentioned, programs like STOPCLOCK have many applications, for example they can replace centisecond timers in most instances. A simple photocell connected to bit 0 will operate STOPCLOCK for experiments on kinematics, etc.

Unfortunately, for intervals shorter than a second, the BBC centisecond clock is not sufficiently accurate. In this case the timers of the VIA can be used in the manner already discussed. A third way of timing relies on the fact that the BBC microcomputer is itself under the control of a crystal oscillator, which produces clock pulses at a rate of roughly 2 MHz. Each machine code operation of the microprocessor inside the BBC microcomputer requires a given number of such clock pulses. These can be counted, thus giving a measured time interval. This counting can be done with the VIA timers as discussed above, or by machine code loops as discussed in Chapter 8.

FAST TIMER (7) uses the latter technique to measure intervals up to 600 milliseconds in ten-microsecond units. It is of universal application and can easily be used in other programs without knowing how it works; for example:

i) Speed of a rifle pellet

Bits 0 and 1 should be grounded through the thin pieces of foil as in Figure 4.28. When the pellet breaks the first foil, the clock starts and when it breaks the second foil, the clock stops. The program will then stop the clock and display the elapsed time in large digits on the screen.

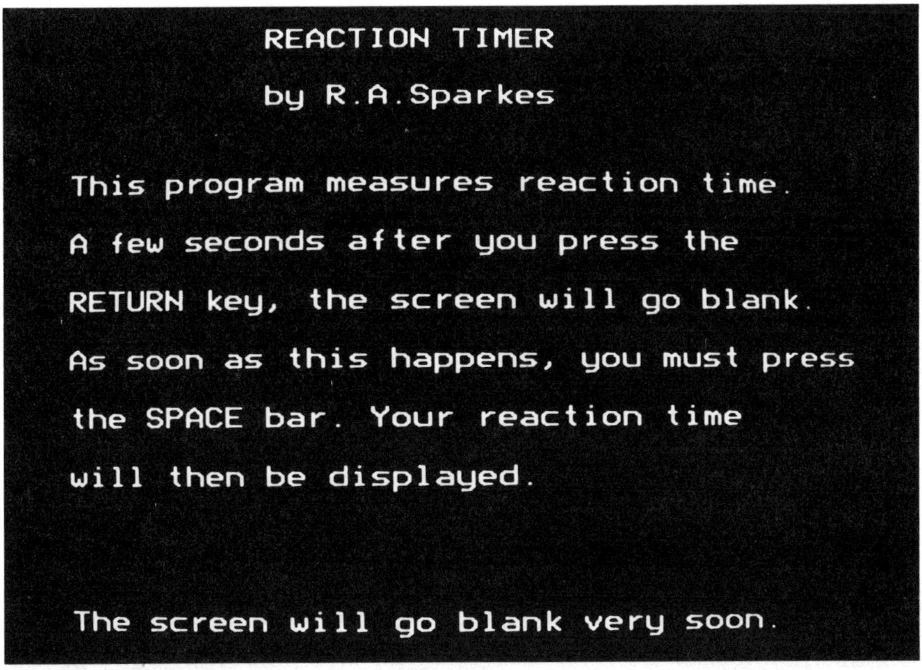

Plate 25 REACTION TIMER instructions

Plate 26 REACTION TIMER result

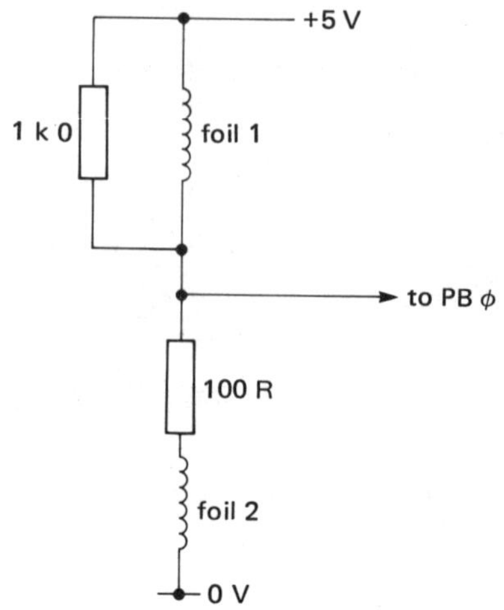

Figure 4.28 Foils

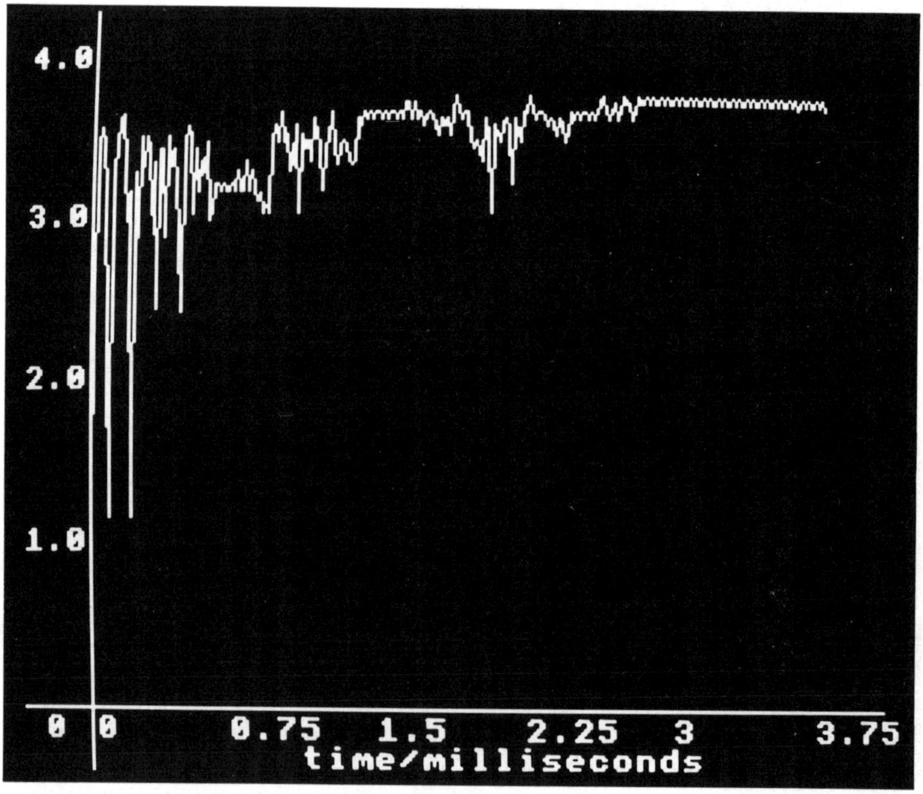

Plate 27 Contact bounce when a switch is closed

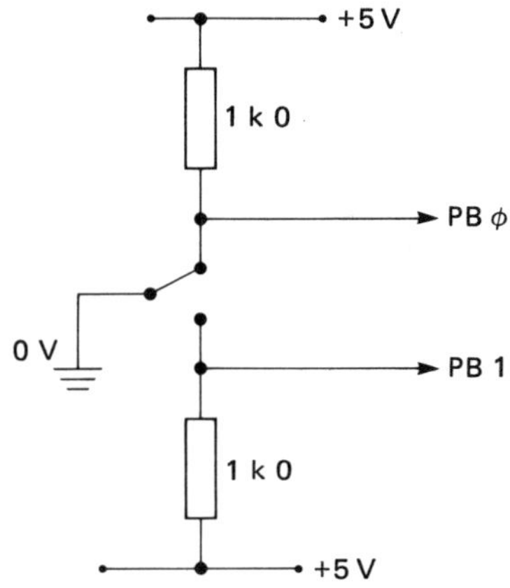

Figure 4.29 Switchover time of a switch

ii) Contact bounce

Some idea of the speed of the timing routine can be gained by using a single push button switch connected to one of the inputs. FAST TIMER is run and when the display says it is ready, the switch is pressed once. In most instances the program will display a result, indicating that at least two input changes have been detected. There were probably many more changes than this, caused by the contact bounce in the switch, when it is closed. FAST TIMER is more than fast enough to measure this contact bounce time. The same arrangement with a fast voltage measurement program (Chapter 5) produces Plate 27.

iii) Switchover time

Using this program with a two-way switch as indicated in Figure 4.29, enables the changeover time of this switch to be measured. An interesting experiment is to see if the switchover time is dependent upon the speed at which the toggle is operated.

iv) Camera shutter speed

Instead of switches to produce changes in the input status, this can also be done by the interruption of a beam of light focused on a photocell, with the photocell connected to one of the inputs. It then becomes possible to measure the effective shutter speed of a camera. The photocell should be mounted inside the camera at the image of an external light source. When the camera is operated, the time measured by this program is a good indication of the exposure time that the film receives.

v) Trolley speed measurement

If a card attached to a trolley crosses a light beam focused on the photocell, the time taken for it to do so may be measured by this program and displayed for all to see. In this instance both changes take place at the same input. If the length of the card is entered into the program beforehand, the microcomputer will automatically compute the speed of the trolley. Unfortunately this program cannot be used with two photocells, i.e. one connected to each input. This would be very useful, since the speed of the card could then be measured over a much greater distance. However, as the card crossed the first photocell, it would start and then stop the clock at this point. A more sophisticated timing routine is needed to measure the time between two different photocells.

Advanced timing

The advanced timing routine used in the following programs needs some explanation so that it can be used even without a knowledge of machine code. A full assembly listing is given in Chapter 8. To enable multiple measurements of speed for studying the law of conservation of momentum, there must be two photocells. Furthermore, in this experiment, it is possible for a second trolley to begin a transit of its photocell before the first has finished crossing the other photocell. Thus it must be possible to detect the two inputs independently and to keep their results separate. We still only need the one clock, but at the start or finish of an event, the time on the clock is copied into a store. In fact up to sixteen stores are available for each input. Thus, in the conservation of momentum experiment, it is possible to have two trolleys approach from different directions, to collide in the middle and both go off in one particular direction at different speeds. This involves two events at one input and six events at the other, but the routine can easily cope with this. (An event is any change in logic level at either of the inputs.)

This advanced timing routine can be called from a BASIC program in a variety of ways, to measure time and speed as above and also to measure period, frequency and acceleration. All measurements are displayed in large digits on the screen using the large digits machine code routine described in Chapter 7.

Program 8 (TIME, SPEED AND ACCELERATION METER) makes use of this routine for a number of purposes. Firstly, it measures time intervals of up to twelve minutes in units of fifty microseconds. Speed measurements are based upon the photocell technique using a card length of 40 mm. By changing lines 5070 and 6070 of the program this may be changed to any other length. However, there is considerable inaccuracy introduced by the photocells, because the point at which they switch on is not necessarily the same point at which they switch off. So a 40 mm card may not necessarily look like a 40 mm card to the photocell. The error is only a few mm, and this is only important if very short cards are being used. If great accuracy is desired, then 100 mm cards or longer should be used. The advantage of short cards is that some meaning can then be given to the difficult concept of 'instantaneous' velocity.

A double card such as that shown in Figure 4.30 enables acceleration to be determined and displayed directly. This quantity is computed from the standard equation

$$\text{acceleration} = (\text{final speed} - \text{initial speed})/\text{time taken}$$

An interesting experiment is simply to drop this double card vertically in front of a photocell using the acceleration option of program 8. The display gives the acceleration due to gravity directly (Plate 28). (But see the educational note later.) If different lengths are used for this double card, then line 5070 of the program should be changed. It is only the 40 mm lengths that are important, not the distance between them. The double card provides the two measurements of speed required in the calculation.

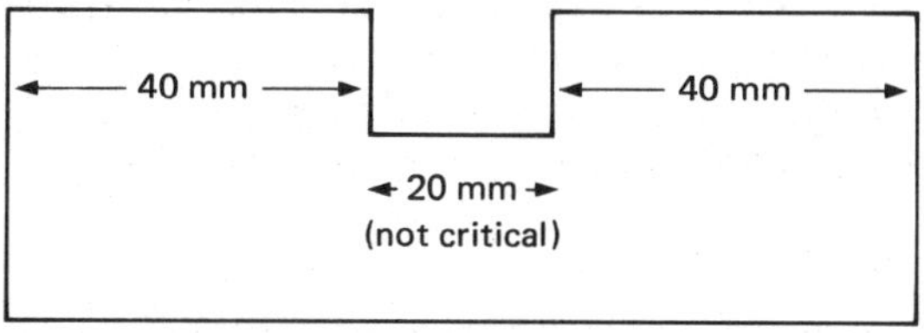

Figure 4.30 Double card

Plate 28 Measurement of acceleration due to gravity

By connecting two photocells in series, they can be placed any distance apart, and then a single card can pass in front of both photocells to provide the initial and final speeds for this calculation. This would be a good way to introduce the function of the double card.

The advanced timing routine of program 8 was designed to be used for measuring the speeds resulting from trolley collisions. It is used for this purpose in program 9 (CONSERVATION OF MOMENTUM). The same restrictions on card lengths apply as above. The speeds are displayed for each photocell separately, with the readings in chronological order for each separate channel (Plate 29).

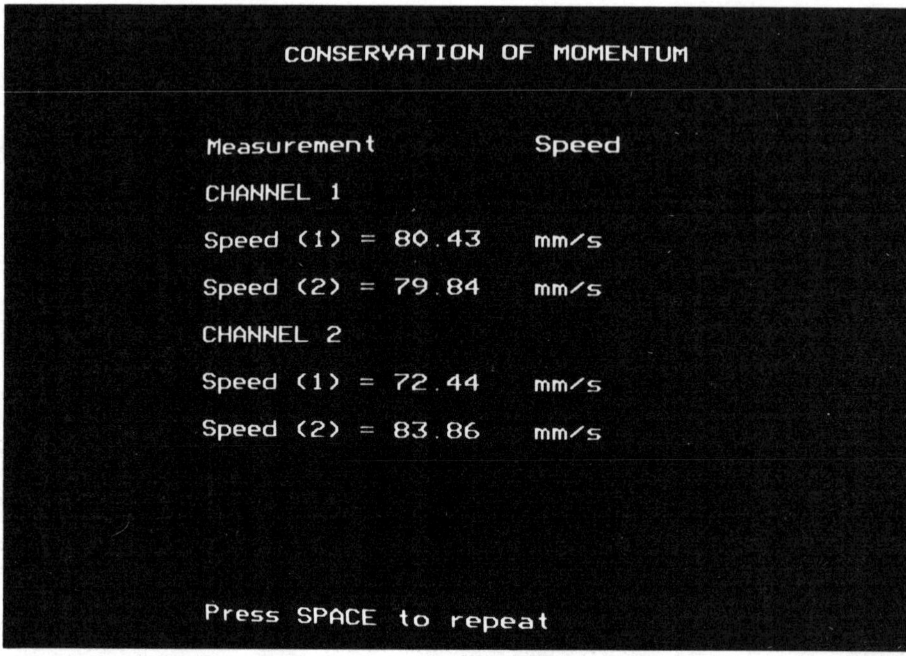

Plate 29 Speeds measured in the conservation of momentum experiment

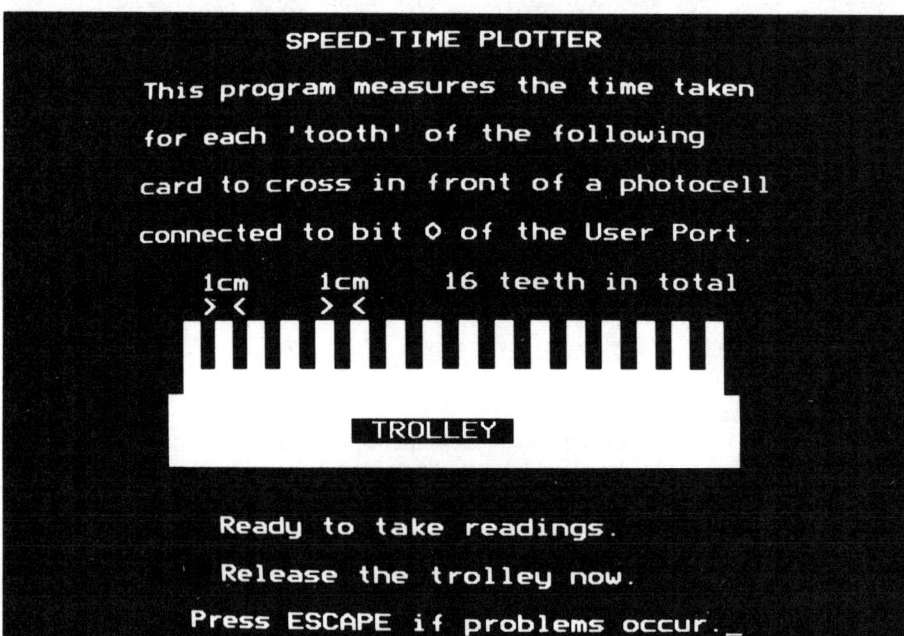

Plate 30 Speed-time plot of a moving trolley

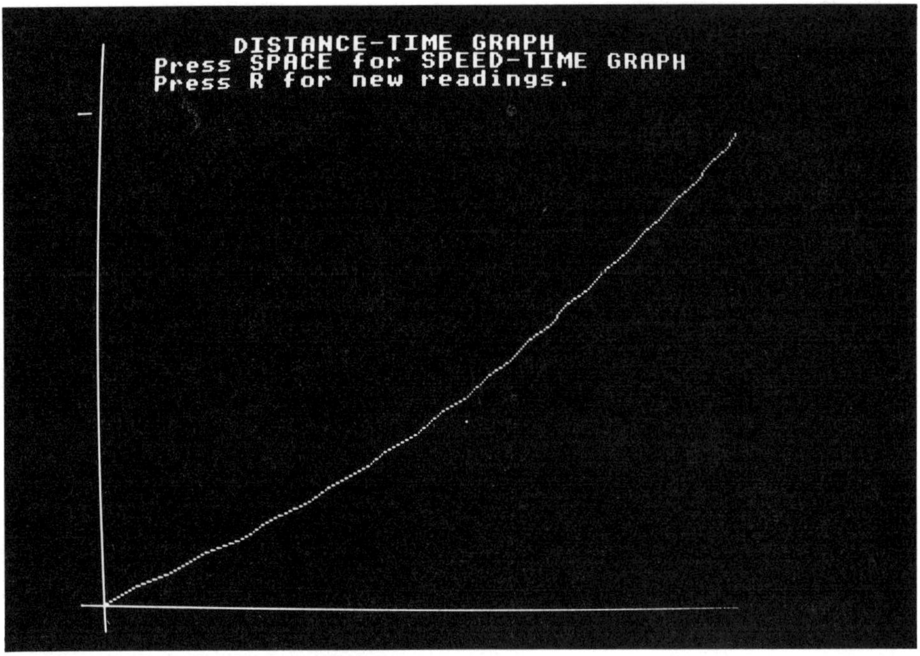

Plate 31 Result from SPEED-TIME PLOTTER

Using a 16-slot card (Plate 30) the speed of a trolley in front of a photocell can be measured several times and the distance-time and speed-time graphs can be plotted and displayed automatically (Plate 31). Program 10 (SPEED-TIME PLOTTER) uses this technique with the advanced timing routine to demonstrate the graphical relationships between distance, speed and acceleration.

Educational note

At this point a cautionary note must be made to discourage the over-zealous use of the microcomputer in the laboratory. The acceleration due to gravity experiment mentioned above can be carried out much more easily and accurately by the following program.

```
100 PRINT "Acceleration due to gravity = 9.81 metres per second squared"
```

This is not, of course, a measurement, but to a pupil who does not know how a microcomputer works, it is no less valid than the method described for program 8! It is essential that pupils understand what the microcomputer is doing, when it is taking measurements.

This does not require that pupils understand in the sense that they should know about programming and interfacing – that is clearly impracticable. What is needed is a demonstration that the microcomputer is giving the same results that could have been obtained by other, more longwinded, methods. The teaching sequence might be as follows:

i) Show the microcomputer as a measurer of time by getting pupils to press a switch for an estimated ten seconds, say.
ii) Show the microcomputer as a measurer of short time intervals using REACTION TIMER.
iii) Measure the time of transit of a card in front of a photocell using program 8. Use calculators to determine the speed of this card and then show that the microcomputer can carry out the same calculations automatically.
iv) Having shown how the microcomputer can calculate speed, allow it to measure the speed of a trolley at several different places as it runs down an inclined plane. The times of transit of the cards would be measured by the program and displayed as speeds, while the time intervals between these transits could be measured by a separate stopwatch. Pupils can again use their calculators to determine the acceleration of the trolley.
v) The principle of the double card should now be apparent; the microcomputer is measuring three time intervals and using them to compute the acceleration of the card. The acceleration due to gravity experiment can now be understood.
vi) Program 8 could now be used to demonstrate Newton's second law. Because acceleration is so easily measured, it is probable that pupils will get a better understanding of this law than they usually do with ticker timer measurements of acceleration.
vii) Conservation of momentum experiments are much more easily carried out using program 9, because it is no longer necessary to use stroboscopic techniques to measure the speeds of the colliding trolleys. Nor is it necessary to restrict the experiments to perfectly elastic or perfectly inelastic collisions.

At all times the teacher must be wary of using the microcomputer 'because it is there'. It must offer a clear advantage over the conventional ways of teaching before its use can be justified. The teaching of motion is an example of its advantage; the measurement of time in hours and minutes just to display it on the video screen is just a gimmick. A microcomputer should not be used for such purposes.

5 Analogue interfacing

'One side will make you grow taller, and the other side will make you grow shorter.'
(Lewis Carroll, *Alice's Adventures in Wonderland*)

Interfacing is the general name given to all connections between the microcomputer and other equipment. In Chapter 4 we looked at ways of connecting the user port of the BBC microcomputer to monitor and control the outside world using the logic board (digital interfacing). This chapter extends these ideas to analogue input and output too, showing how their use turns a microcomputer into a general purpose laboratory instrument.

Digital to analogue conversion

Measurements with laboratory instruments normally cover a whole range of values; examples are a spring balance, a meter rule and a thermometer. The word **analogue** is used to describe such measurements. A set of digital lines can produce analogue voltages using a digital to analogue converter (DAC). The DAC unit in this chapter has eight inputs, which give a set of 256 different voltages, each directly proportional to the input binary number. These voltages are in steps of 10 mV up to a maximum of 2.55 V. The DAC unit can be connected directly to the user port or, alternatively, a ZN428 device may be connected to the 1 MHz bus.

Digital to analogue converters

The easiest way to add a DAC is via the user port (Figure 5.1). The ZN425 device (RS Components 306-904 data sheet R/2911 March 1977) is still the best to use in this situation. It contains its own 2.5 V reference voltage and internal clock.

If you want to keep the user port free for other purposes, the DAC will need to be connected elsewhere. One obvious place is the printer port, which is already buffered. This is the A-port of the same VIA that runs the user port and is addressed at &FE61. Its associated data direction register is at address &FE63. In use it is just like the user port, except that it can only be used for output. The user guide shows the pin connections to this port.

If you need the printer port for other purposes, you will have to use the 1 MHz bus instead. The ZN425 DAC can be connected to a data latch (SN74LS373) or another 6522 VIA as described in Chapter 4. If you intend to hang a vast amount of hardware onto the 1 MHz bus, you will need to decode address lines 4 to 7 as shown in Figure 5.4.

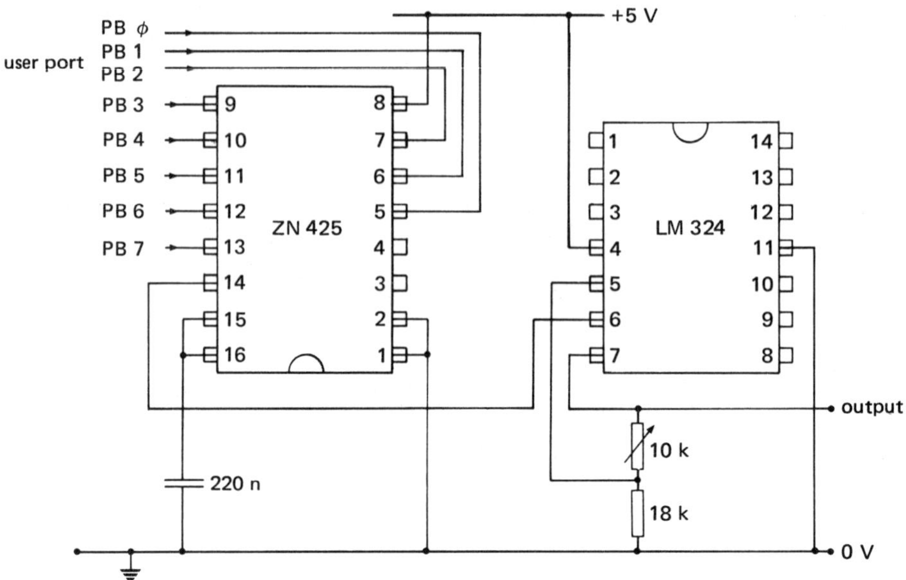

Figure 5.1 ZN425 DAC

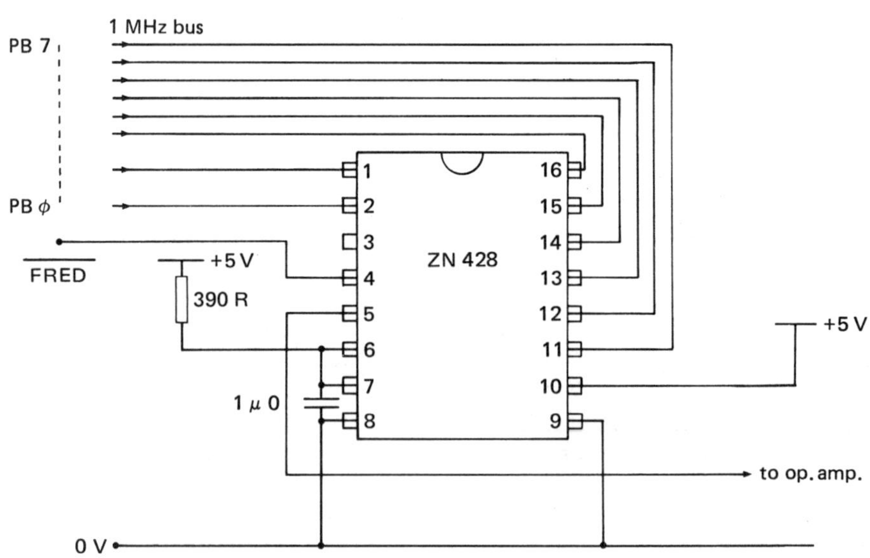

Figure 5.2 ZN428 DAC connected to the 1 MHz bus

A simpler method is to use a ZN428 device instead, which contains its own data latch. In Figure 5.2 the ZN428 DAC responds to any address from &FC00 to &FCFF, but again, further address decoding could be provided if necessary.

Applications of the DAC

The binary number to be converted is written into the user port address and the analogue voltage is produced at the output of the DAC a few microseconds later. The statement to do this is ?PRT = n where n is the decimal number between 0 and 255, which determines the final output voltage. To investigate this connect a 0 to 5 V voltmeter between the output terminal of the DAC unit and the 0 V line. Then connect the user port to the DAC through the ten-pin connector and configure the user port for output with ?DDR = 255. Now enter direct commands of the form ?PRT = n and observe the output voltage on the voltmeter. (Of course DDR and PRT will have to be declared previously using the appropriate addresses.)

As well as direct voltages, the DAC can also be used to produce alternating voltages of almost any waveform. This gives different waveforms, which are slow enough to be observed on the 0 to 5 V voltmeter. It is most convenient if one cycle of the waveform is produced by a single FOR...NEXT loop. This requires a conversion factor 'confac' to be chosen accordingly. For machine code programs the best number of loops per cycle is 256 (the limit of the X-INDEX). This gives confac a value of PI/128.

```
WAVEFORM OUTPUT
 10  DDR = 65122:REM DATA DIRECTION REGISTER
 20  PRT = 65120 :REM USER PORT
 30  confac = PI/128 :REM CONVERSION FACTOR FOR
     ONE CYCLE PER LOOP
100  ?DDR=255:REM ALL LINES AS OUTPUTS
110  FOR X = 0 TO 255
120  A = 128 + 127*SIN(X*confac)
130  ?PRT=A
140  NEXT X
150  GOTO 110
```

Different waveforms can be produced by altering the equation in line 120. For example,

```
120  A = 255 * ABS(X > 127) will give a square wave,
120  A = X will produce a ramp voltage and
120  A = ABS(128 - X) will give a triangular waveform.
```

The period of this oscillation is about 12 seconds. If a longer period is required then a delay can be included. For example,

```
125  FOR T = 1 TO 50: NEXT T
```

This principle may also be used to produce an output slow enough to be drawn using a chart recorder. The production of higher frequency oscillations is more difficult owing to the slow speed of BASIC. One way is to reduce the **resolution** of the waveform, by having fewer output points per cycle. This statement raises the frequency by a factor of 5:

```
110   FOR X = 0 TO 255 STEP 5
```

A better solution is to do all the calculations in BASIC beforehand and store the results in the memory as individual bytes. These can then be collected one by one from the memory and sent directly to the DAC using a machine code routine (PROGRAMMABLE OSCILLATOR, 13). This routine is described in Chapter 8.

Analogue to digital conversion

In Chapter 4 of *Microelectronics* I described how an analogue to digital converter converts a voltage in the range 0 to 2.5 V into a binary number from 0000 to 1111, with an accuracy of one in sixteen. By using all eight inputs of the user port the resolution can be increased to one in 256, thus giving greater accuracy. The built-in ADC of the BBC microcomputer gives twelve-bit resolution, an accuracy of one in 4096.

There are four channels for this A-to-D converter (Ch0 to Ch3), which continuously convert input analogue voltages into numbers from 0 to 65 520 (in steps of sixteen). These values are accessed with the statements

```
LET voltage1 = ADVAL(1):REM Channel 0
LET voltage2 = ADVAL(2):REM Channel 1
LET voltage3 = ADVAL(3):REM Channel 2
LET voltage4 = ADVAL(4):REM Channel 3
```

For the majority of applications the BBC microcomputer's own analogue to digital converter is satisfactory. It is very much easier to use and more accurate than the one I am about to describe. Its main fault is that it is slow (by microelectronic standards), since it takes several milliseconds to complete a conversion. The ZN427 device is a thousand times faster. Figure 5.3 shows how it may be connected to the 1 MHz bus and Figure 5.4 shows how further address decoding is achieved to allow this ADC to share the bus with other devices too.

Even better is the ZN448 device, which is similar to the ZN427, but may be triggered asynchronously (that is, out of step with the BBC microcomputer's own clock). The ZN448 also contains its own clock and reference voltage and may be connected directly to the 1 MHz bus as shown in Figure 5.5

There is little point in using either of these devices in BASIC, since the built-in ADC is more accurate and BASIC is too slow to take full advantage of the speed of these other ADCs. A description of how they might be used is therefore left until Chapter 8. The ZN448 device is single channel only. To allow different channels to be utilized, it should be preceded with an analogue multiplexer. This is rather like the rotary switch shown in Figure 5.6, except that the switching is done electronically. A useful analogue switch is the AD7590 (RS Components 303-595), which can switch one of four separate input voltages

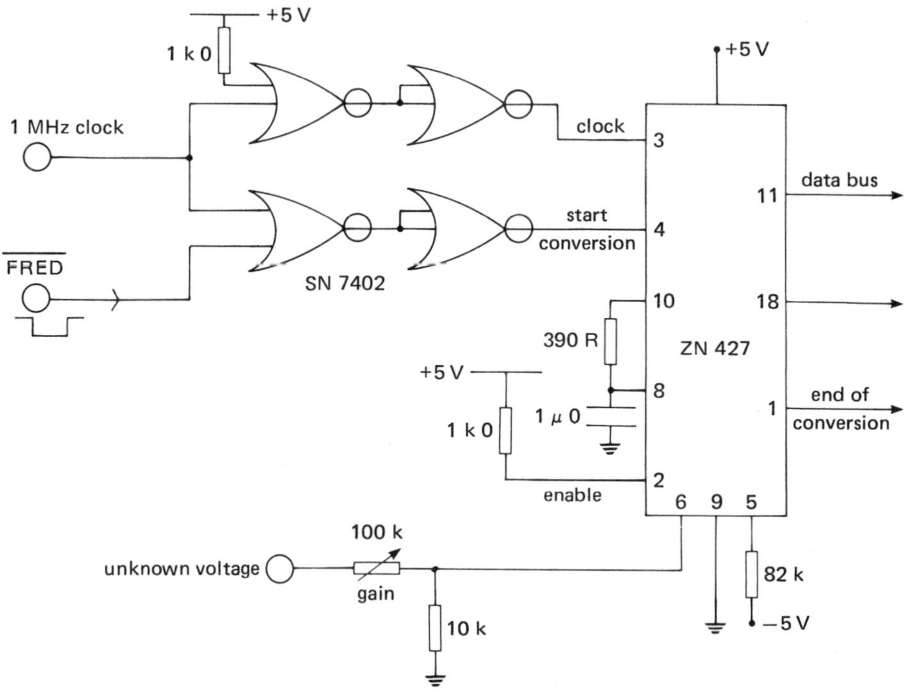

Figure 5.3 ZN427 ADC connected to the 1 MHz bus

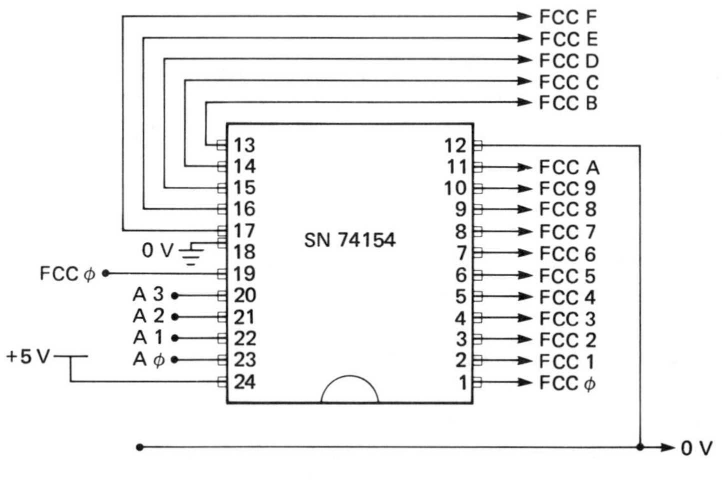

Figure 5.4 1 MHz bus address decoder

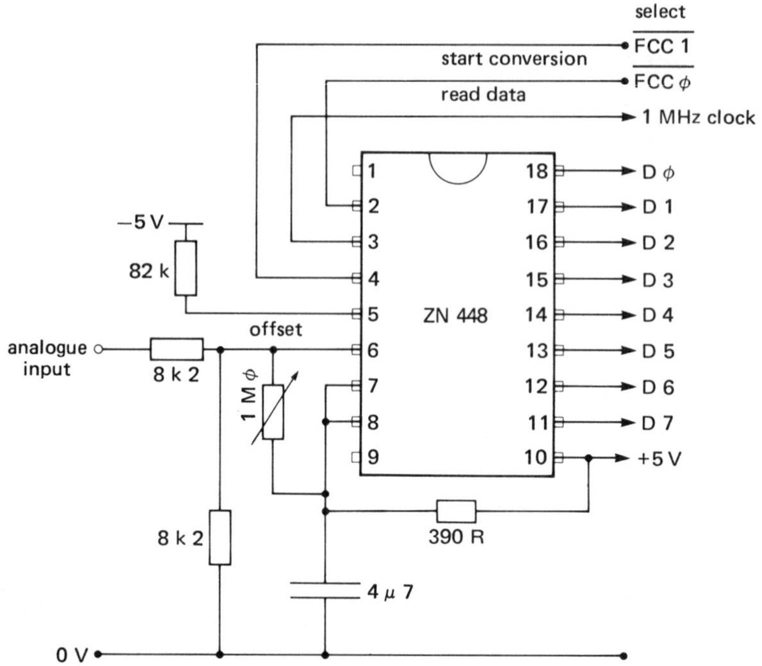

Figure 5.5 ZN448 ADC connected to the 1 MHZ bus

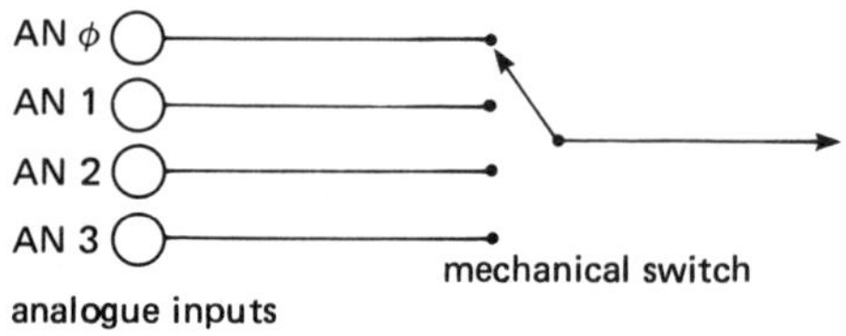

Figure 5.6 Mechanical switch

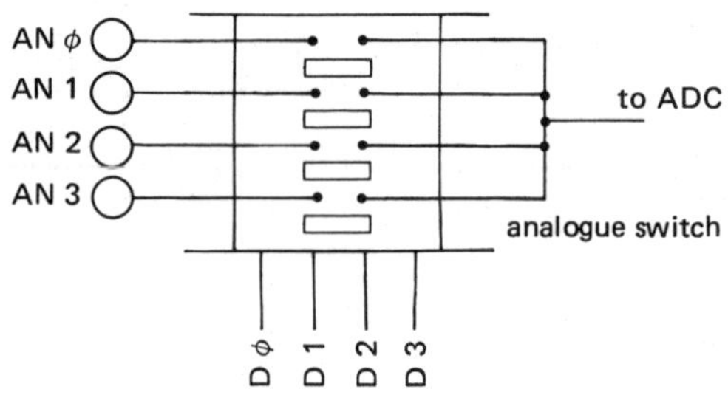

Figure 5.7 Analogue switch

to the ADC for conversion. Connected as in Figure 5.7, each channel is selected by the following statements:

Channel	
1	?&FCC2 = 254 (D0 goes LOW)
2	?&FCC2 = 253 (D1 goes LOW)
3	?&FCC2 = 251 (D2 goes LOW)
4	?&FCC2 = 247 (D3 goes LOW)

The converted voltage may then be read from the address &FCC2 ten microseconds later.

Alternatively the ZN448 can be connected to the user port (Figure 5.8) and the data latched in using the CB1 control line as described in Chapter 4. The device needs a start conversion pulse which can be provided by the CB2 line. Although this arrangement can be handled from BASIC, there is little point in doing this. A machine code program for using the ZN448 is listed as FAST ADC (15) in the Appendix and is also described in Chapter 8. A measure of the speed that can be obtained is shown in Plate 32, where the

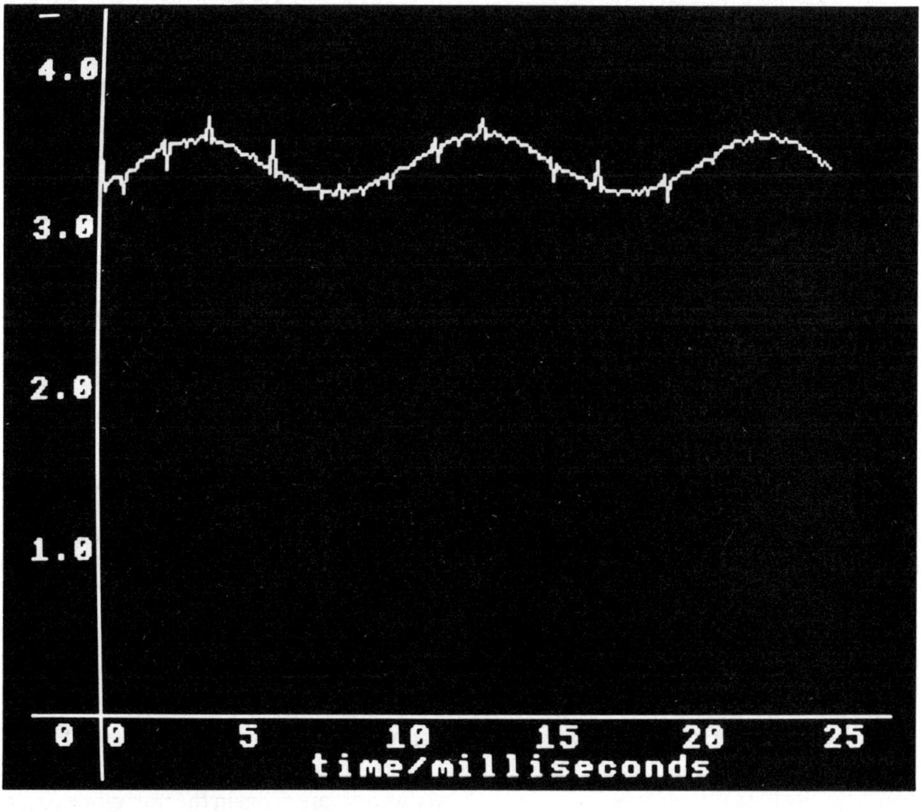

Plate 32 Light output from a mains driven lamp

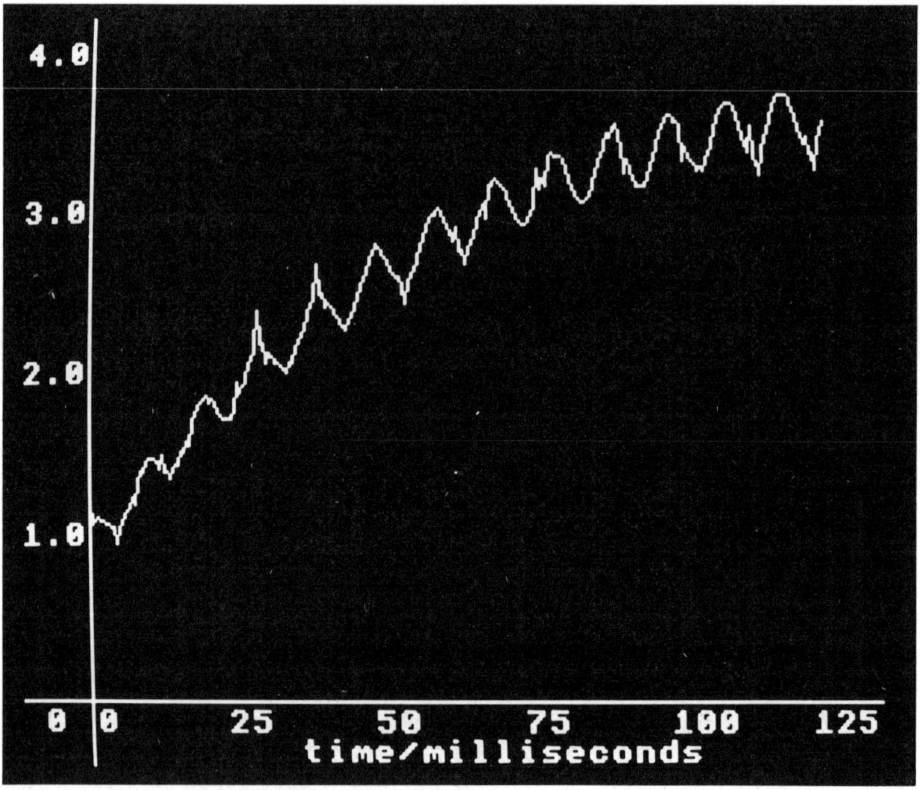

Plate 33 Light output from a lamp at switch on

light output from a mains-driven lamp is measured continuously and plotted. The 100 Hz fluctuation in the light intensity is readily observed. To obtain this plot the light output was sampled every 200 microseconds. At this sampling rate the variation in light output when the lamp is first switched on can easily be determined (Plate 33). FAST ADC is capable of sampling at fifteen microsecond intervals, if you can think of anything that goes that fast!

Voltage measurement

Measuring voltage with an ADC is obvious, but there are some pitfalls. A check should be made to see that the input voltage is within the acceptable range. If not, then the ADC will simply return the saturation values of 65 520 or 0. If the measured voltage is too large, it can be passed to a suitable voltage divider network to reduce it to the acceptable range. Likewise, if it is too small, a fixed gain op.amp. multiplier can be used to boost it. Figure 5.9 shows a universal input amplifier that can be connected to the BBC microcomputer analogue port for this purpose. Connections to this port are given in the user guide (page 499).

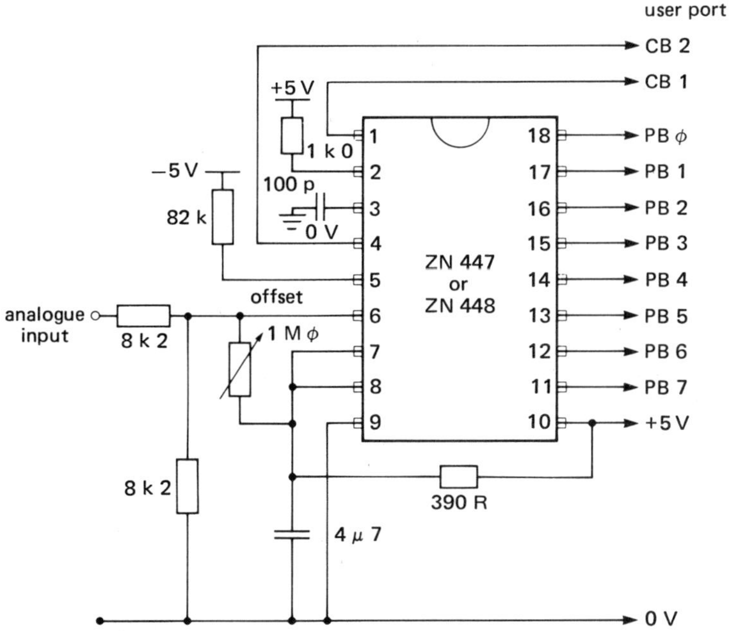

Figure 5.8 The ZN448 connected to the user port

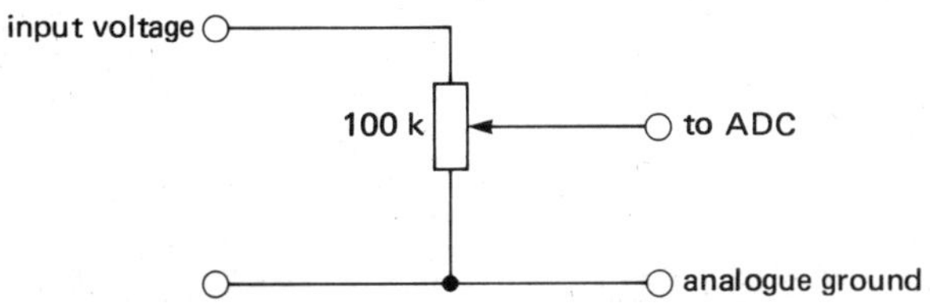

Figure 5.9 Voltage measurement

The following routine should initially be used to calibrate an ADC, allowing for different power supplies, etc. Connect the analogue input terminal to ground to produce an input voltage of 0 V and check that the voltage displayed on the screen reads zero. Next connect a voltage of 1.5 V to the input terminal (measured with a good voltmeter) and check that the value displayed on the screen is within a few millivolts of this. If not, adjust the conversion factor (confac in line 110 of the program) until it is.

```
100 REM ADC CALIBRATION
110 V = ADVAL(1) * confac
120 PRINT V
130 GOTO 110
```

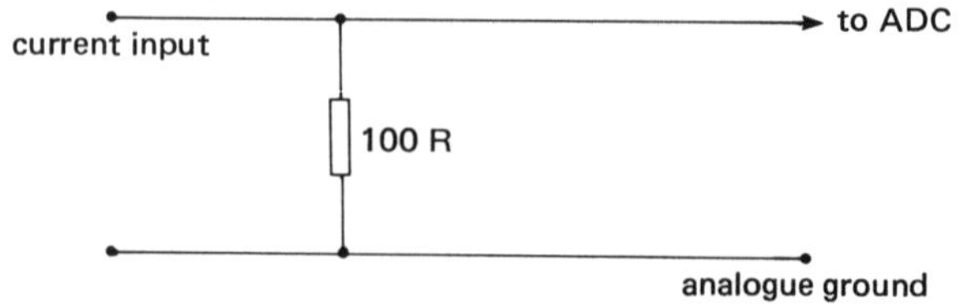

Figure 5.10 Current measurement

Current measurement

To measure current with an ADC, it should be allowed to flow through a known shunt resistor (Figure 5.10) and the voltage across that resistor measured by the ADC.

Resistance measurement

If both the voltage across a component and the current flowing through it are measured at the same time, their product gives the power developed in the component. Similarly, the resistance of the component can be calculated and displayed. This gives very effective demonstrations of the change of resistance of a lamp as it gets brighter. DIGITAL

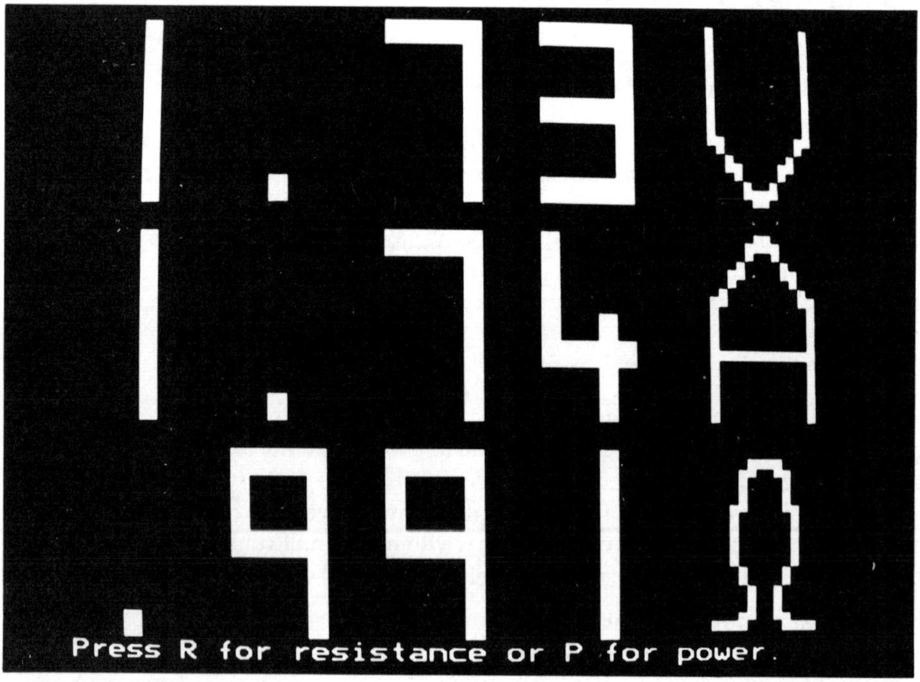

Plate 34 Digital multimeter

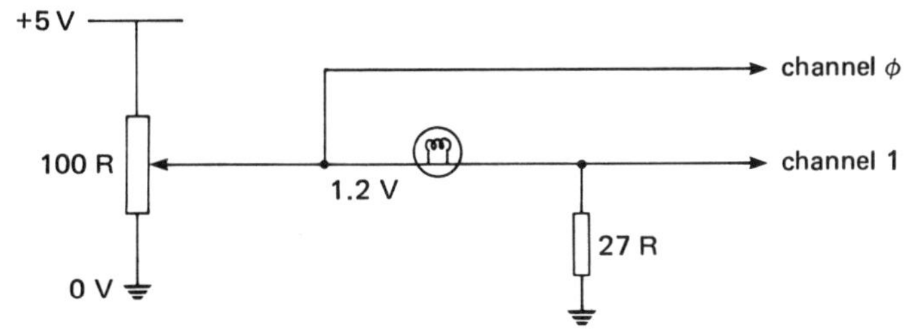

Figure 5.11 Resistance/power measurement

MULTIMETER (16) does this, displaying voltage, current, resistance or power in large digits (Plate 34). It requires a circuit like the one shown in Figure 5.11.

Other measurements
Any other physical quantity that can be turned into a voltage can be measured by the ADC too, provided it is turned into a voltage within the correct range. Devices that turn other physical quantities into voltages are called **transducers** and there are a large number of these available. Here are some examples from the current RS Components catalogue:

RS Stock No.	Measurement	Output Range
308-809	temperature	0 to 1 V
303-337	pressure	0 to 75 mV
304-267	magnetic field	0 to 400 mV
305-462	light intensity	0 to 1 V

In addition there exist transducers to measure force, displacement, wind speed, humidity, oxygen content, acidity and sound intensity. The last of these is called a microphone! This illustrates the point that alternating voltages are easily turned into direct voltages using a.c. to d.c. converters. The latter can be a diode rectifier or the more expensive r.m.s. to d.c. converter (RS Components AD536A). With this range of transducers, an ADC and a microcomputer, most laboratories will need no other instrument.

Many useful devices convert some physical quantity into a change of resistance. Examples of this are the thermistor (which changes its resistance with temperature) and the light-dependent resistor. These devices can be turned into transducers by putting them into a voltage divider network.

Another device in this category is the strain gauge, which converts the strain in a bar of metal into a voltage. Since strain is proportional to stress this allows force and hence weight to be measured too. Also by connecting a spring to the force transducer and an object to the other end of the spring, the displacement of this object may be measured too (replacing the metre rule?). There are commercially available movement sensors, which provide an output voltage proportional to the distance moved. With one of these connected to the bottom of an oscillating spring, it is possible to carry out measurements on simple and damped harmonic motion.

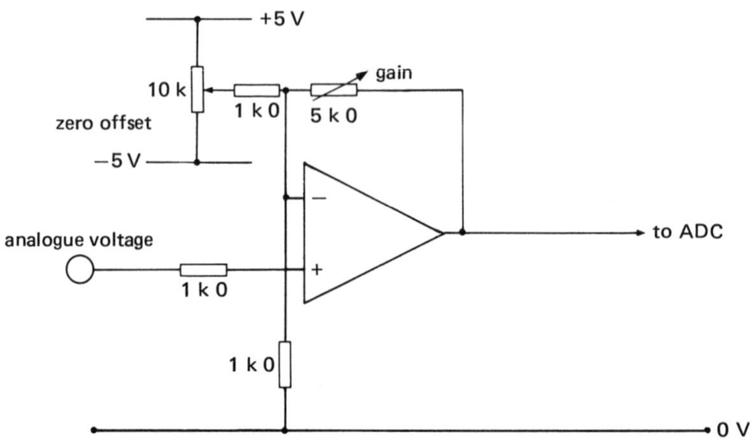

Figure 5.12 Transducer measurements

Potentiometer

This simple device is a transducer too. It is particularly easy to connect a potentiometer to the BBC microcomputer analogue input (Figure 5.13). Four such potentiometers may be mounted on a board side by side to simulate a control panel (Figure 5.15). The 'firing buttons' of the analogue port may also be connected to this control panel, enabling a range of industrial processes to be simulated. The control buttons are connected as shown in Figure 5.14 and monitored with ADVAL(0) as described in the user guide. The simulation of Millikan's experiment is much more satisfactory if voltages are entered via a control knob than by typing them in at the keyboard. This idea was suggested by M.Ryan and J.Stewart at the Dundee College National Course in 1982.

If two potentiometers are mounted perpendicularly the result is a joystick (RS Components 162-732). This allows the coordinates of a physical position (the knob of the joystick) to be plotted directly on the screen (which is what many video games are all about). The joystick is actually a displacement transducer but with two dimensional capabilities. A two dimensional plotter based on this idea is as follows:

```
10  REM ETCHASKETCHA
30  confac = 0.015:REM CONVERSION FACTOR
110 X = ADVAL(1) * confac
120 Y = ADVAL(2) * confac
125 PLOT5,X,Y
130 GOTO 110
```

Some devices do not produce values that are directly proportional to the quantity being measured. For example, a simple thermistor or LDR in a voltage divider circuit gives an ADC reading that is related to the physical quantity but not in a linear way. If twenty degrees produces an ADC value of 100, then forty degrees will not produce an ADC value

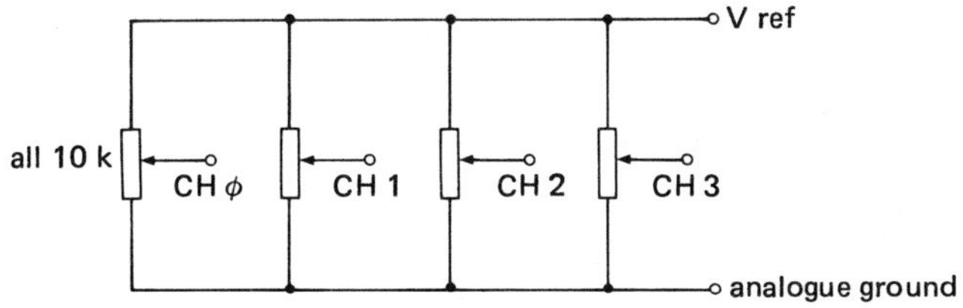

Figure 5.13 Potentiometer input

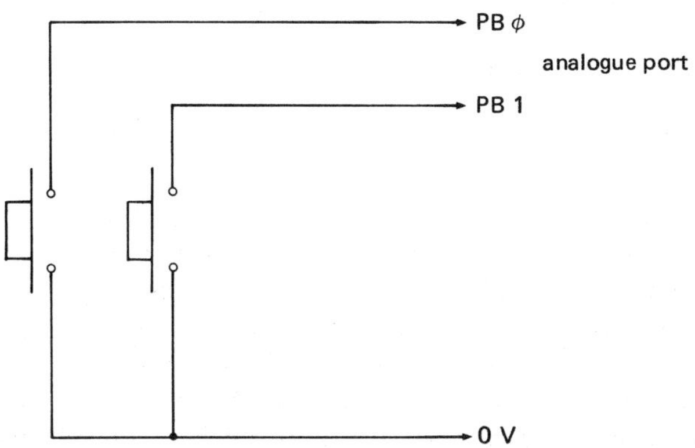

Figure 5.14 Connecting push buttons

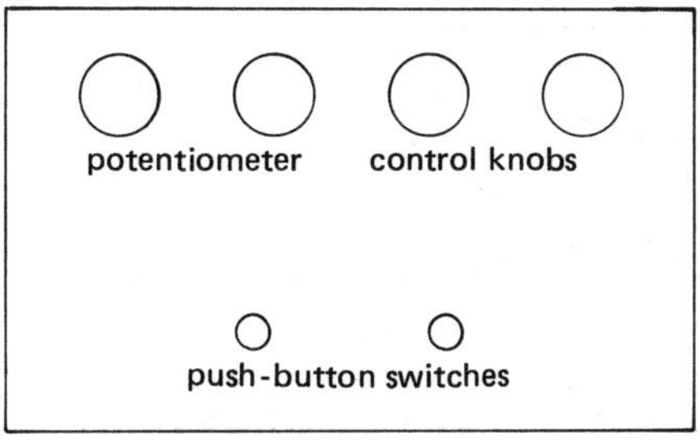

Figure 5.15 A simulated control panel

of 200. To obtain the true value (for temperature, etc.) a look-up data table needs to be created. The next example shows the general idea.

```
100  REM SET UP THE DATA TABLE
110  FOR I% = 0 TO 15
120  READ X$(I%)
130  NEXT I%
140  DATA "OUT OF RANGE"
150  DATA "IMPOSSIBLE TO MEASURE"
160  DATA "IMPOSSIBLE TO MEASURE"
170  DATA "22 degrees C"
180  DATA "24 degrees C"
190  DATA "27 degrees C"
200  DATA "30 degrees C"
210  DATA "34 degrees C"
220  DATA "37 degrees C"
230  DATA "41 degrees C"
240  DATA "46 degrees C"
250  DATA "50 degrees C"
270  etc.
3000 REM CONVERT READING AND DISPLAY IT
3010 X% = ADVAL(1)/4096
3020 PRINT "THE TEMPERATURE IS ";X$(X%)
3030 etc.
```

This program should obviously be expanded to 256 or more values to become sensible, otherwise a mercury thermometer is more accurate and easier to use. Care should always be taken not to use the microcomputer where an ordinary instrument does the job easier and more cheaply. The microcomputer is much more suited to areas where a simple instrument will not work. For example the speed of the microcomputer can be used to measure voltages several thousand times per second or to measure several different voltages repeatedly in rapid succession. The microcomputer memory can be used to store these voltage readings for later output to a cathode ray oscilloscope or to a chart recorder. The readings may be listed on the microcomputer screen or presented graphically as a bar chart or a graph. From there they can be printed out for everyone to see if screen copy facilities are available. This example shows how voltage changes can be measured and plotted immediately on a graph:

```
10  REM ADC GRAPHPLOT
20  LET X = 0
30  confac = 0.015:REM CONVERSION FACTOR
100 REPEAT
110 V = ADVAL(1) * confac
120 PLOT5,X,V
130 X = X + 1
140 UNTIL X>1279
```

The machine code routines for doing these things are discussed in Chapter 8.

This simple data acquisition routine can be speeded up by taking several hundred successive readings, storing them in an array and later outputting them to a chart recorder or a cathode ray oscilloscope using adaptations of the DAC programs described previously. If, instead, the data is displayed graphically on the VDU, this program is really carrying out the function of a storage oscilloscope. The microcomputer is being used as a **data memory**, later displaying the readings it has remembered.

This arrangement can replace the cathode ray oscilloscope in many instances. For some purposes it is even better, since it only needs to take a single set of readings, which can then be displayed indefinitely to allow measurements to be taken (for example, the gradient of the graph). There is also the possibility of overlaying two or more successive sets of results (Plate 35). Another example is the voltage-current characteristics of a transistor, which could be plotted for different values of the bias current. Plate 36 shows how the input/output voltage transfer curve may be plotted directly. Using transducers it

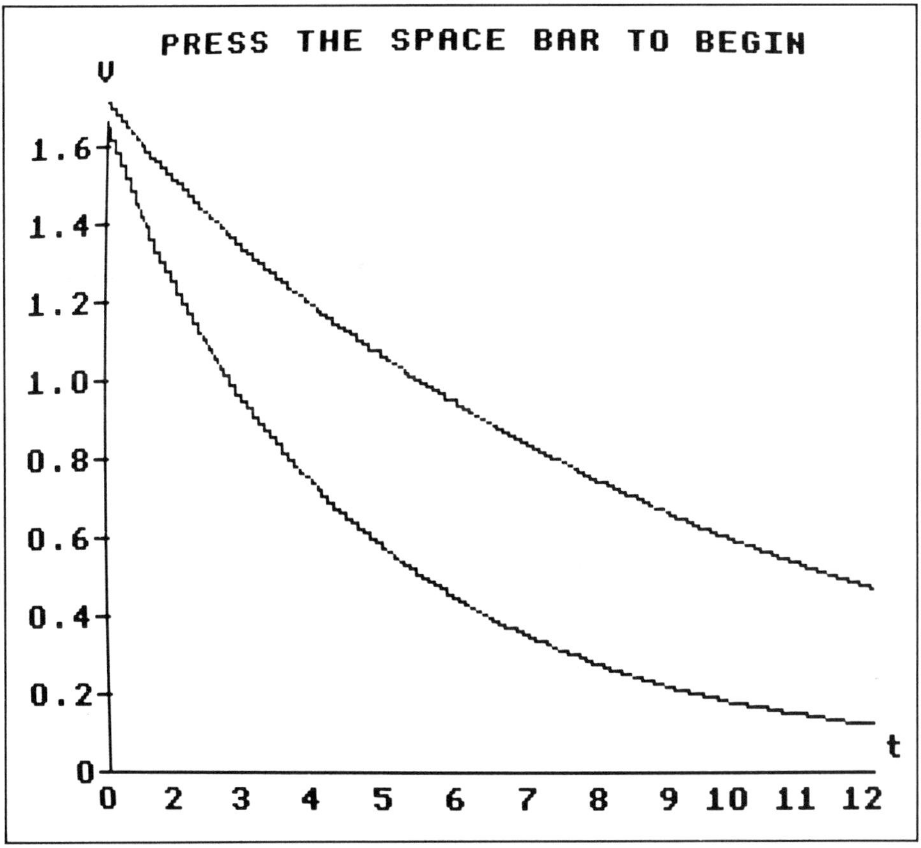

Plate 35 Capacitor discharge by practical measurement

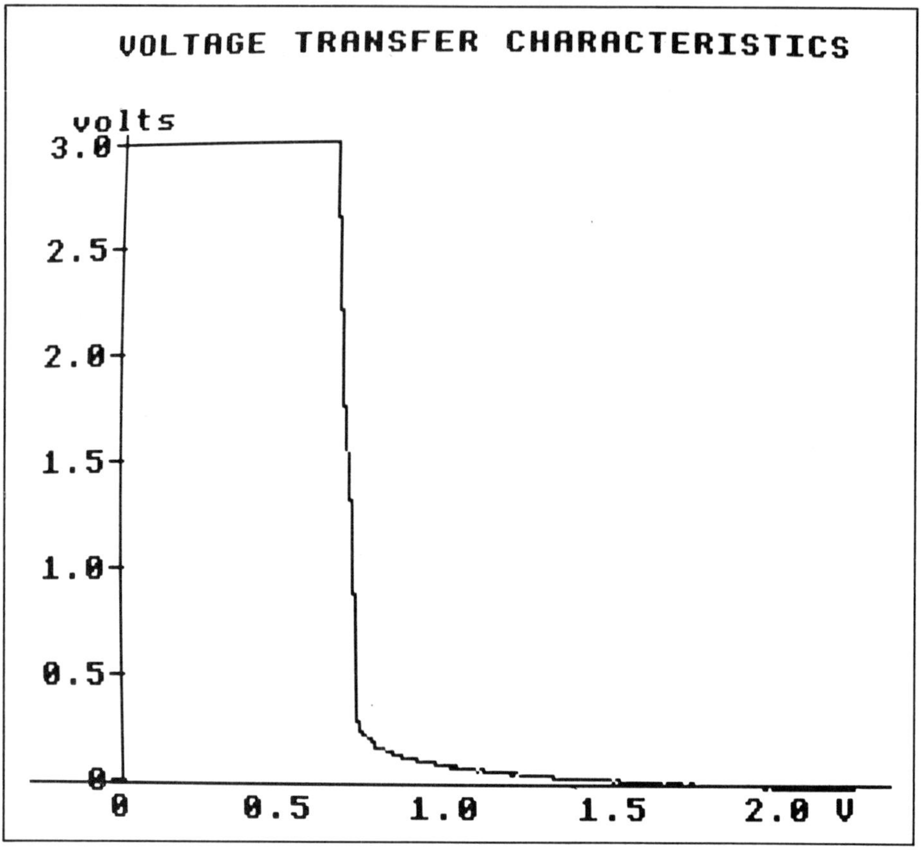

Plate 36 Using the DAC and ADC for automatic measurement

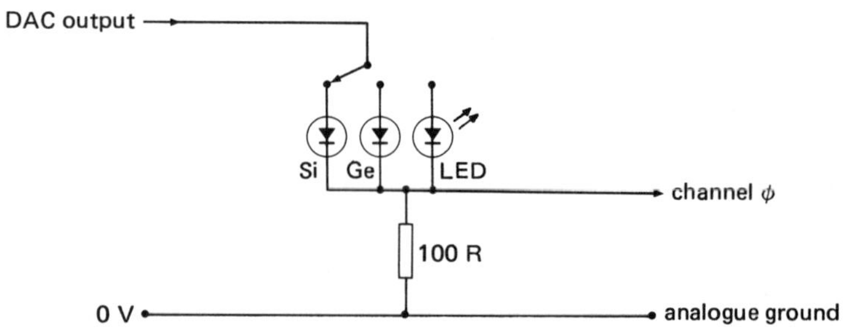

Figure 5.16 Diode characteristics

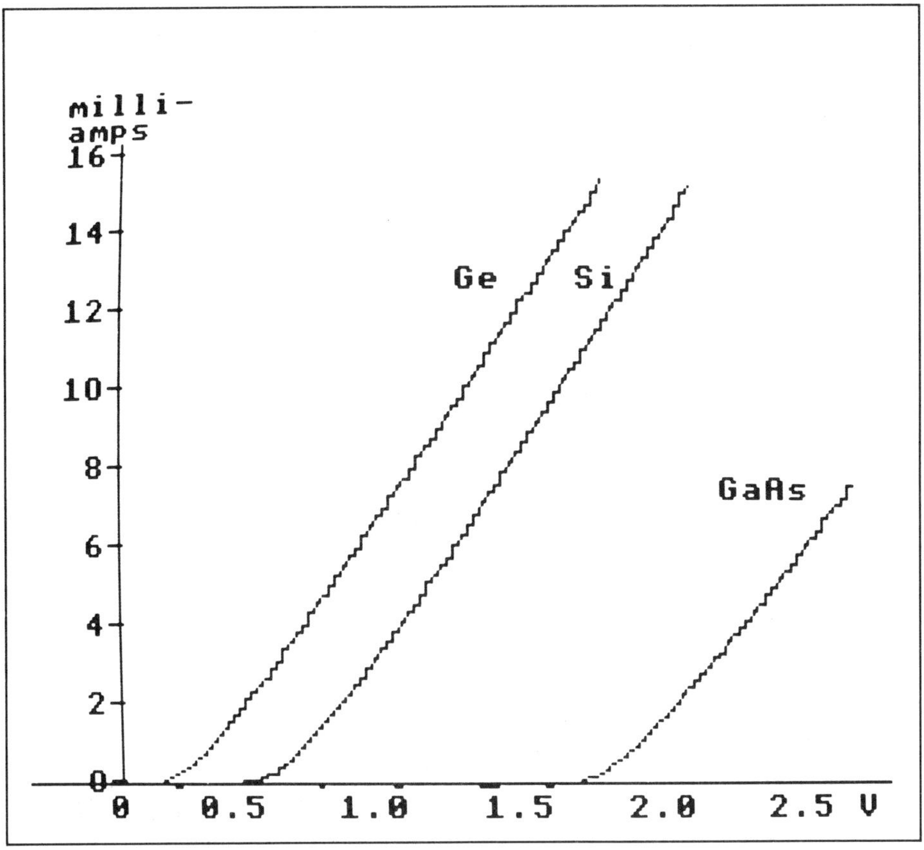

Plate 37 Diode characteristics by automatic measurement

would even be possible to plot pressure-volume curves of a gas at different temperatures (a three-dimensional CRO!).

The arrangement shown in Figure 5.16 allows the characteristics of three types of diode to be plotted automatically on the same graph. I-V PLOT (17) will carry out this task. The LED is particularly suitable for this, since it has a high turn-on voltage and it also lights up when it starts to conduct (Plate 37). Note how the output from the DAC is used to produce the steadily increasing voltage.

Programs like this allow a large number of measurements to be made in the science laboratory. Because the graphical results are quickly available, it is easier to see the science before it gets lost in the mathematics. Such a system is especially valuable for studying transient phenomena such as the discharge of a capacitor through a resistor (Plate 35). When the switch is pressed, the capacitor starts to discharge through the resistor (Figure 5.17). The effects of different starting voltages or different resistors are easy to investigate.

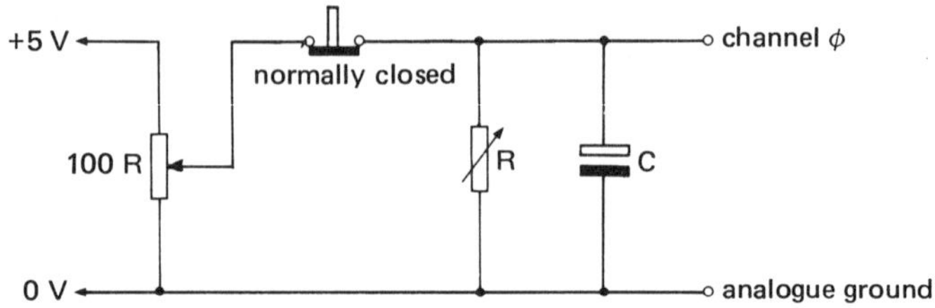

Figure 5.17 Capacitor discharge

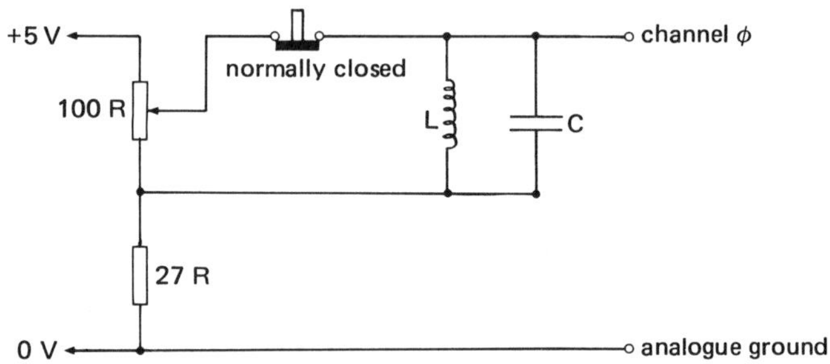

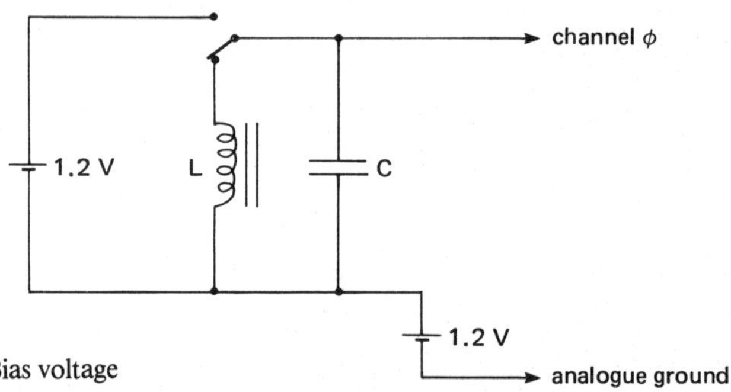

Figure 5.18 Bias voltage

If the resistor is replaced with an inductor, the voltage can go negative and a bias voltage must be added to prevent this using either of the methods shown in Figure 5.18.

For some purposes it is the peak value of an alternating voltage that is required. This can be achieved with a simple diode rectifier and smoothing circuit as in Figure 5.19. The values of R and C need to be chosen so that the time constant (RxC) is at least five times the period of the alternating voltage being measured (i.e. RxC > 5/freq.). For accurate measurement it may be worth the extra cost to obtain an r.m.s.-to-d.c. converter (RS Components 308-786) instead.

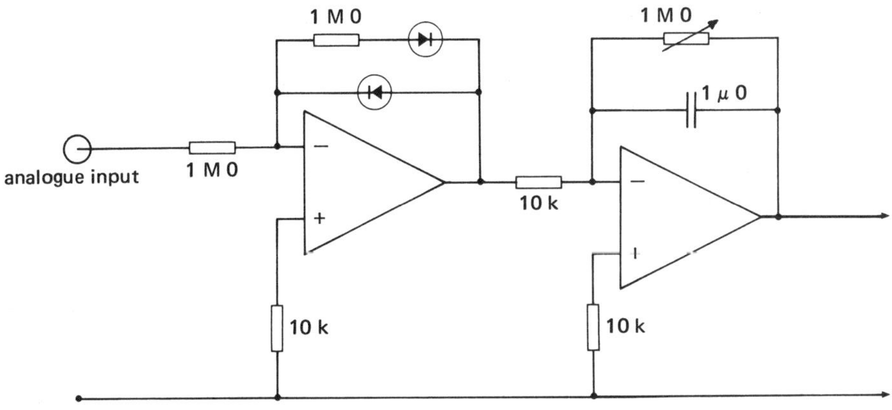

Figure 5.19 Peak voltage measurement

It is quite easy to make the display scroll slowly sideways at the same time that the four ADC channels are monitored and plotted. This produces a FOUR-CHANNEL CHART RECORDER (18) (Plate 38).

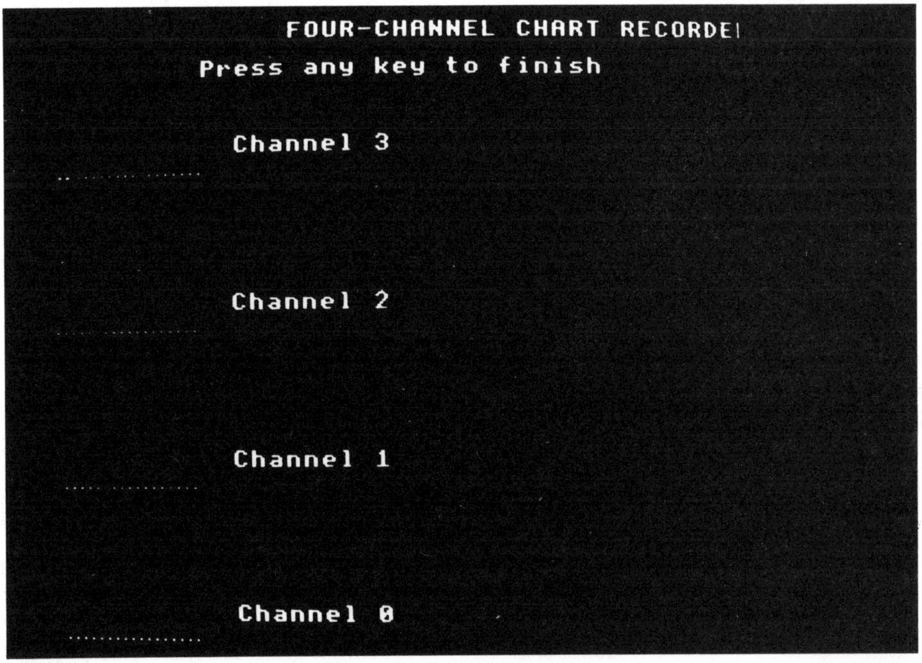

Plate 38 Scrolling the screen sideways

Two most interesting applications of DAC and ADC techniques were described by Paul Beverley at the 1982 MUSE Annual Conference. The first of these consists in applying the voltage from a DAC to the input terminals of a chart recorder. When the DAC output voltage is ramped (with the DAC treated like a binary counter) the pen of the chart recorder moves steadily along. The pen is replaced by a photocell and made to scan along the diffraction pattern produced by a laser. The photocell is connected to an ADC channel and a plot of intensity against position is made automatically on the VDU. The effect is magnificent!

The second application uses a DAC to produce a direct voltage, which is then fed to a waveform generator (RS Components 305-844)(Figure 5.20). The latter produces sine waves for feeding into a circuit and square pulses that can be accurately counted by the microcomputer. The frequency of these sine waves is proportional to the direct voltage fed to its input terminal. By ramping the DAC voltage a whole frequency spectrum is produced by the waveform generator. A range of 500 Hz to 20 kHz was produced with this arrangement.

The main problem of connecting the waveform generator to the DAC is that the direct voltage has to be applied to the former between its input and the + 15 V line, not its 0 V line. This is solved by tying its positive rail to 0 V and using an initial op.amp. circuit to convert the voltage output from the DAC to the right levels. The second op.amp. is to buffer the output from the waveform generator before it is fed to a 30 W power amplifier (HY 60). The sine wave voltage is input to a filter circuit, the output from which is connected to an ADC channel via an r.m.s.-to-d.c. converter, thus measuring the output

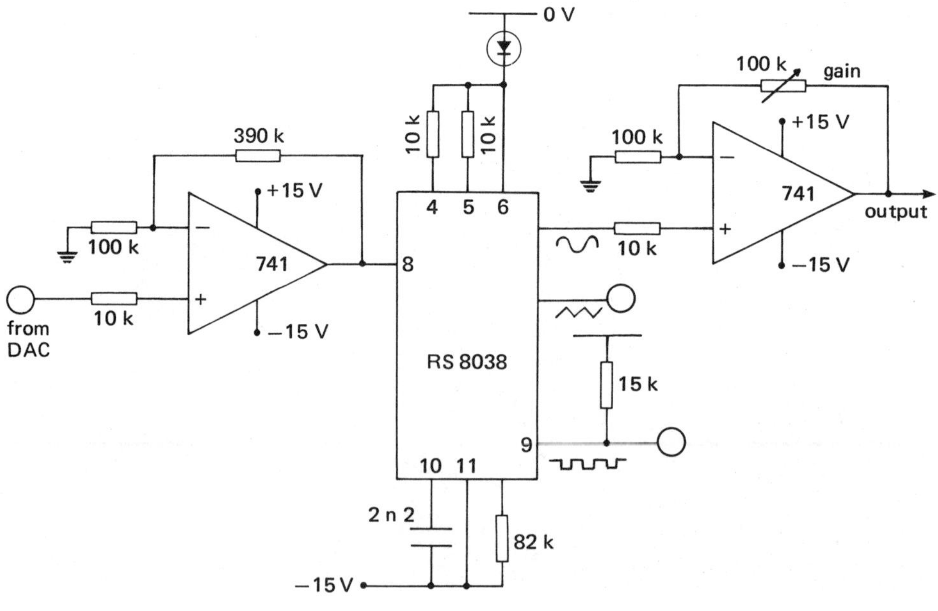

Figure 5.20 Waveform generator

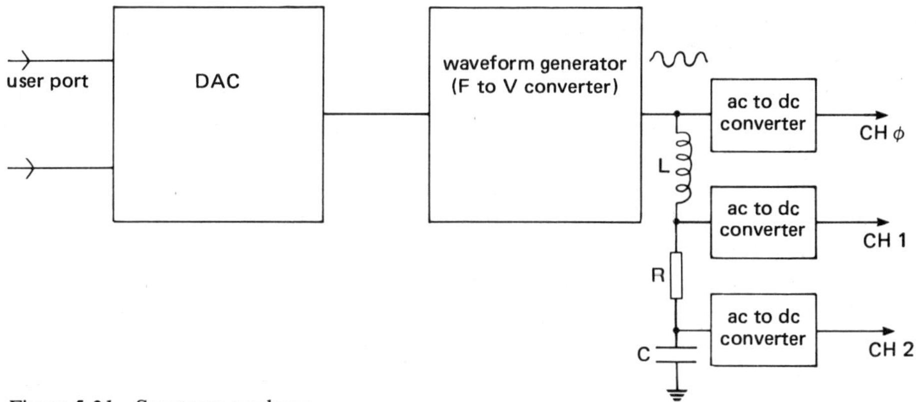

Figure 5.21 Spectrum analyser

voltage from the filter (Figure 5.21). A plot of the output voltage against frequency gives the frequency characteristics of the filter circuit. The idea is such a beautiful application of hardware and software techniques that it forms a fitting note on which to end this chapter.

6 The 6502 microprocessor

> 'When I make a word to do a lot of work like that,'
> said Humpty Dumpty, 'I always pay it extra.'
> (Lewis Carroll, *Through the Looking Glass*)

Under the lid of the microcomputer

The microprocessor is the manager of all the operations that the microcomputer undertakes. As in any organization the best results are obtained by talking directly to the manager! Unfortunately, this one does not speak English – communication with it is in the binary code. This chapter is an introduction to microprocessors and includes a detailed examination of one particular device, the Rockwell 6502. This is the microprocessor in the Apple, PET, VIC, Atom, UK101 and BBC microcomputers.

Programmed logic

In Chapter 3 of *Microelectronics* I showed how a set of bytes stored in RAM could be used to switch traffic lights on in their correct sequence. Each byte was an instruction to switch particular LEDs on or off, and each such instruction was executed when its address was sent to the memory (RAM). This is a primitive form of programmed logic. Now imagine a RAM driven by a binary counter with its output lines connected to the

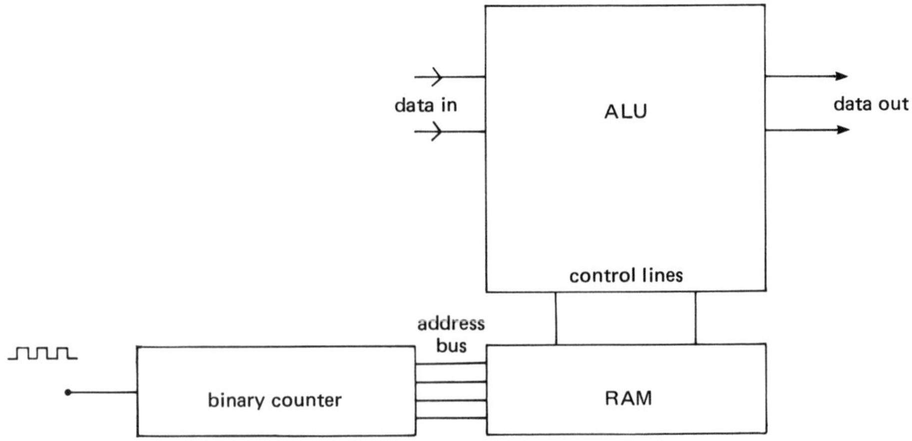

Figure 6.1 Programmed logic

the control lines of an **ALU (arithmetic and logic unit)** as in Figure 6.1. Each byte in the RAM can be regarded as an instruction to the ALU to perform some logical or arithmetic operation. Any instruction received by the ALU would be in **code** and the ALU would need to **decode** it to find out which instruction it was.

With only four bits the number of different instruction codes that can be given is limited to sixteen. This is enough for the traffic lights (which only need four different codes), but it is not enough for more complex control systems. If the RAM consisted of eight-bit bytes instead, then there could be 256 different instructions codes.

The microprocessor

Extend the above ideas still further, so that the RAM contains the data as well as the instructions and you have a system rather like a microcomputer. The instruction codes contained in the RAM are called a **program** and the binary counter, which points to each successive address in the RAM, is called a **PROGRAM COUNTER (PC).** Some of the instructions to the ALU tell it to collect its data from the RAM and some other instructions tell it what to do with that data. Of course there has to be some clever way for the ALU to distinguish between a binary number that is an instruction code and a binary number that is data. We shall see later how this is done.

This system is limited by the total number of instructions and data bytes that can be stored, which will affect the size of its program. A RAM with four address lines only has sixteen different addresses and can therefore only hold sixteen instruction codes (or data). If the number of address lines were increased to eight, this would allow a program of 256 steps, but even this would not be enough. The Rockwell 6502 microprocessor (Figure 6.2) has sixteen address lines, enabling it to address 65 536 different bytes each consisting of eight bits.

How the microprocessor works

In addition to an ALU a microprocessor contains several memories of its own called **registers.** Some of these are eight bits long and some sixteen. The address of the next instruction to be executed is contained in a sixteen-bit register called the PROGRAM COUNTER (PC). When the microprocessor is ready, it fetches the next instruction from

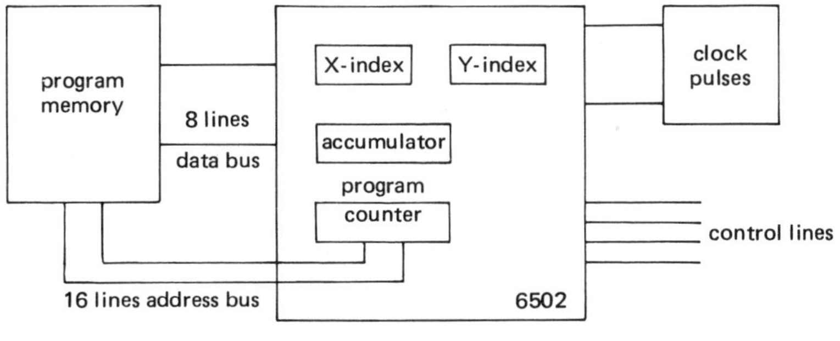

Figure 6.2 The 6502 microprocessor

the address indicated by the PC. To do this it switches on some of the lines of the address bus to point to the correct place (or **location**) in RAM; this is called putting the address on the address bus. It then sends a signal to the addressed location, which says 'Tell me what binary number you are storing'. This signal is called a **read signal** and the R/NW line of the microprocessor goes HIGH, indicating that a memory read is taking place. The addressed location responds by copying its contents onto the **data bus,** and the microprocessor collects them from there. It has now fetched the binary code for its next instruction.

The microprocessor now decodes this binary code to see which instruction is represented by it. Some instructions only affect the internal registers of the microprocessor, they are called **single byte instructions.** The microprocessor simply executes these instructions straightaway. Some other instructions require two bytes before they can be executed. When the microprocessor has fetched the first byte and has decoded it, it knows if it has to fetch the rest of the instruction. The program counter is increased by one (incremented) to point to the next address and the next byte is fetched from there. The first byte in any instruction is the **operation** to be carried out (like ADD or AND) and the second byte tells the microprocessor which data to use. This byte is called the **operand.** There are also cases where the information about the data cannot be contained in one byte and so two bytes are used for the operand and this gives a three-byte instruction.

In a microcomputer, a BASIC program is stored in RAM in a particular way. The microprocessor cannot just execute a BASIC program immediately, it must **interpret** it first. The microprocessor fetches each byte of the BASIC program and then asks its BASIC interpreter what to do with it. This interpreter is another program, but written in terms of the instruction codes that the microprocessor understands, that is, in **machine code.** This is why BASIC is so slow, relative to the great speed of the microprocessor itself. Every BASIC instruction is first translated into machine code before it can be executed and this wastes time. If you write the program directly in machine code, the microprocessor can get on with the job of executing it, without having to interpret it first.

Memory

The BASIC program can be changed by the user, so it is stored in RAM. The operating system of the microcomputer and the BASIC interpreter do not need to be changed, so they are frozen in **ROM** (which stands for **read only memory**). As the name implies, ROM can only be read, it cannot be changed. RAM is like a box that can be opened and the contents taken out and changed. ROM is like a sealed box with a glass lid; you can see what is in the box but you cannot change it. The advantage of ROM is that it is always there, even when the microcomputer has been switched off, whereas the contents of RAM disappear.

Because the user's program is in RAM, the amount of RAM in a microcomputer is a measure of its power. This is counted in **kilobytes(K),** hence there are 16K and 32K microcomputers available. In the context of computers a kilobyte of memory is actually 1024 bytes, not 1000. The reason for this is the binary system again, 1024 is an exact multiple of 256. It is useful to imagine the microcomputer's memory as being like the stamp locations in an album, with each location representing one byte. A particular binary number (i.e. a stamp) can be put into any location or taken out of it at any time. It is, of course, necessary to know where any particular stamp is stored, so that it can be found again. Hence every location in the microcomputer's memory is given a different address. For our purposes there are 256 pages in the album and 256 places (byte positions) on each page. To refer to any particular location we must specify its page number and its byte number within that page. Thus the fifty-first byte on page thirty-one would be referred to as byte 51, page 31. To find its position with respect to the first byte in the whole album, we need to calculate 256*page number + byte number. This is called its **decimal address.**

We noted above that the 6502 microprocessor has sixteen address lines, giving a possible 65 536 different addresses. It is convenient to regard each address as being made up from two eight-bit bytes, the high byte giving the page address and the low byte giving the address within that page. This is why some instructions take up three bytes – two bytes are needed to specify the sixteen-bit address of the data to be used.

In 16K microcomputers the RAM goes from page 0, byte 0 (or decimal address 0) to page 63, byte 255 (or decimal address 16383). However, each microcomputer uses some of the RAM for its own purposes, so not all addresses are available to the user. In the BBC microcomputer the bottom fourteen pages of RAM addresses (from 0 to 3583) are not used to store a normal BASIC program. Other machines are organized differently, but the same principles apply. When you write a BASIC program, the operating system of the microcomputer automatically stores it in a particular part of the memory and when you type RUN, the operating system goes to the start of this program and begins to collect and interpret it.

It is more difficult to write a machine code program. You may have to decide where to put the program in the memory and tell the microprocessor where your program has been placed. Thus there are two tasks to be performed:

1 Enter the instruction codes into their correct locations.
2 Tell the microprocessor where to go to execute these instructions.

Before you can do either of these tasks, you need to know what sort of instructions can be given to the microprocessor. The rest of this chapter is devoted to a description of the 6502 instruction set. In Chapter 7 we shall return to these two tasks so that you will be able to run real machine code programs.

Why use machine code ?

We ought first to ask why anyone wants to write programs in machine code at all: isn't BASIC good enough? The answer is that BASIC is good enough for some purposes but not for all; there is no alternative if you want to have complete control over the microprocessor. With this control you gain speed; machine code programs run up to 400 times faster than their BASIC equivalents. You also gain compactness; a machine code program occupies only a fraction of the memory space needed to run an equivalent BASIC program. Thirdly, you gain freedom; you become independent of the operating system of your microcomputer and become able to add extra facilities, which are not implemented by your machine. Finally, it even becomes possible to build your own microcomputer for a particular task, one that is self-contained with its own operating system, memory, program and microprocessor. Such a system is said to be **dedicated** and can be produced comparatively cheaply (see Chapter 9).

Many people start to learn how to write machine code programs. Unfortunately, there are so many things to be learned to begin with, that some get discouraged. After studying hexadecimal coding, addressing modes and indexation, the usual conclusion is, that machine code programming is too difficult. This introduction tries to overcome these initial problems, by reducing the number of ideas that have to be learned at the beginning. Each of the instructions of a microprocessor is described in a visual way, so that its effects can be more easily observed, thus making this introduction as easy as possible. *But,* machine code programming is not simple!

Some people use the words 'microprocessor' and 'microcomputer' interchangeably, but they should be distinguished. The microprocessor is the silicon chip which acts as the brain of a computer. A microcomputer contains a microprocessor, but it contains other chips too, especially memory and I/O chips. (I/O stands for INPUT-OUTPUT, and refers to devices used for getting information into and out of the microprocessor.) Usually a microcomputer will have a keyboard and a TV screen controller too, but this is not always true. Confusion between the two words arises because a dedicated system may contain a microprocessor, I/O and memory all inside a single package called a **single chip microcomputer.** Yet from the outside this single chip microcomputer looks just like a microprocessor. Nevertheless I shall reserve the word 'microcomputer' for complete machines like the PET, the BBC microcomputer and the Apple and 'microprocessor' for the processing unit inside each microcomputer that makes it work.

In this book we consider one particular microprocessor, the Rockwell 6502, which is found inside many different microcomputers (Apple, PET, VIC, Atom, UK101 and BBC). There are several other microprocessors, another popular one being the Zilog Z80, which is used in the RML 380Z and the Sinclair ZX 81 and ZX Spectrum microcomputers. The instruction set and the codes used for the 6502 are not the same as for other microprocessors, so, unfortunately, you will not be able to use this book to guide you in programming them.

To study machine code programming some sort of microprocessor development system can be used, but I am assuming that most readers will not have access to one of these. Instead you may use a microcomputer for this purpose, but that is not until the next chapter. In this chapter we shall only be using a simulation of how the 6502 microprocessor behaves. One of the problems of real microprocessors is that they have to be programmed exactly in the right way, or they can cause the microcomputer to crash. The advantage of a simulation run from BASIC is that mistakes can be trapped to prevent such disasters.

This program, called 6502 SIMULATION, uses the graphics capability of the microcomputer to show what happens inside the 6502 microprocessor. With its aid you can write machine code instructions immediately and thus learn more quickly, what each instruction does. The listing of this program is given in the Appendix (MICSIM, 4). The simulation does not attempt to deal with all of the instructions that the 6502 can handle, only the more important ones. Also 6502 SIMULATION only deals with one-byte and two-byte instructions; most three-byte instructions left until Chapter 7.

What is a machine code program?
In all cases a microprocessor is told what to do by a program. This is a list of instructions, 'do this' or 'do that', in many ways similar to BASIC statements. The microprocessor carries out these instructions one by one, fetching each instruction from the program memory when it is required. It is because this program can be changed by the user, that the microprocessor can be made to do so many different things.

Both the 6502 and the Z80 are eight-bit microprocessors. This refers to the size of the binary numbers that they can handle. These binary numbers (data) are the information that is being processed by the microprocessor. An eight-bit binary number can be any value from 0000 0000 to 1111 1111 (0 to 255 in decimal). All of the different things that are done by a microprocessor are done with binary numbers like this. (Even letters of the alphabet are turned into binary numbers so that the microprocessor can handle them. Each letter is represented by a special binary number, called its **ASCII code.**) The microprocessor has special places inside itself for the temporary storage of such data called **registers.** We shall now look at the different registers in the 6502 microprocessor and see what each one does (Plate 39). The three most important registers are the ACCUMULATOR, the X-INDEX and the Y-INDEX.

The ACCUMULATOR is the most used register. The results of logic or arithmetic operations are stored in the ACCUMULATOR after they have been executed. The ACCUMULATOR is an 8-bit register, so it can store any binary number from 0000 0000 to 1111 1111. From the ACCUMULATOR this binary number (data) can be sent to other parts of the microcomputer, such as the user port, the TV screen or RAM.

The X-INDEX and the Y-INDEX are both similar to the ACCUMULATOR; they too are eight-bit registers. They are often used as counters, but their most important purpose is to point to different memory locations.

There are three other registers that are used by the microprocessor, although the programmer is not usually aware of them, these are the PROGRAM COUNTER, the DATA REGISTER and the ADDRESS REGISTER. These are used by the microprocessor like a diary, to keep notes of what it has to do next. The most important of these is the PROGRAM COUNTER, which is a 16-bit register and can store numbers from 0000 0000 0000 0000 to 1111 1111 1111 1111 (0 to 65 535 in decimal).

The purpose of the PROGRAM COUNTER (PC) is to point to the instruction that is being executed. (More accurately the PC contains the address of the location in memory where the code for the next instruction is stored.) These may be instructions written by the user or instructions from the BBC microcomputer operating system. In any microcomputer there are instructions to tell the microprocessor how to read the keyboard, how to display letters on the TV screen, how to interpret BASIC statements, etc. These fixed instructions are stored in ROM and cannot be changed by the microcomputer user. On the other hand you will want to write any machine code program you wish, so your instructions have to be stored in memory locations that can be changed, i.e. RAM.

The microprocessor does not care whether its instructions come from RAM or from ROM, it treats them both in the same way. But it has to know which instruction to do next and this is the purpose of the PROGRAM COUNTER. This holds the 16-bit binary number or address of the memory location where the next instruction can be found. After this instruction has been completed, the PROGRAM COUNTER is incremented (increased by one) to point to the address of the following instruction. In this way the microprocessor executes a series of instructions continuously.

Each location holds an eight-bit binary number (or byte) which is the code for an instruction. After an instruction code has been fetched from the memory, it is decoded by the microprocessor to find out what it is required to do. Some simple instructions only need one byte to tell the microprocessor all it needs to know. For example, the code 1010 1010 tells the microprocessor to copy the data in the ACCUMULATOR into the X-INDEX; no other information is required. Some instructions require two bytes. The code to tell the microprocessor to put the number 0001 1001 (25 in decimal) into the ACCUMULATOR is 1010 1001 0001 1001. The first byte (the operation) tells the microprocessor *what* to do, while the second byte (the operand) tells it what data to use.

Some instructions expect the data to be collected from a location in the memory. When the microprocessor wants to collect data from a particular location, it puts the address of that location into its ADDRESS REGISTER. This register is connected to the outside memory via the address bus. Each external location looks at the address bus, but only one location responds, the one that sees its own address on the address bus. This is like calling the class register in school; all the pupils hear the name being called out, but only the pupil with that name responds.

The addressed location can respond in two ways. If it is being read, then it places a copy of the data it contains onto the data bus. This data bus is connected to the DATA REGISTER in the microprocessor, so the data in the addressed location is copied into this DATA REGISTER. If the instruction to the microprocessor is to load the ACCUMULATOR with this data, then the DATA REGISTER transfers this data into the ACCUMULATOR. The whole instruction is called loading the ACCUMULATOR from memory. Note that the data is not removed from the addressed memory location, it is only copied into the DATA REGISTER. From there it is moved into the ACCUMULATOR and any data already in the ACCUMULATOR will be destroyed.

If the instruction is 'store the contents of the ACCUMULATOR in memory', the data moves the opposite way. A copy of the data in the ACCUMULATOR is first placed in the DATA REGISTER and it travels along the data bus to the addressed location in the memory. Only this addressed location will capture the data being sent. This is called a **write** instruction. Note that the data in the ACCUMULATOR is not destroyed by this instruction, it is only copied into the addressed memory location. Clearly though, any data that was in the addressed location before the write instruction will be lost, replaced by the new data.

Since the microprocessor only handles eight-bit data, the DATA REGISTER is only an eight-bit register. The data bus thus consists of only eight lines, one for each bit of the data. The PROGRAM COUNTER and the ADDRESS REGISTER are sixteen-bit registers, because they are concerned with addresses rather than data. They allow the microprocessor to collect data from any of 65 536 available addresses and the address bus consists of sixteen lines going to different parts of the microcomputer. To simplify matters 6502 SIMULATION does not use these full sixteen-bit addresses, but only the lower eight bits of this address. The proper method of addressing is discussed later.

Mnemonic instruction codes

The instructions to the microprocessor are themselves binary numbers. The microprocessor interprets them according to a special code. For example, the code to instruct the microprocessor to load the decimal number 25 into the ACCUMULATOR is

1010100100011001

It is clear that codes like this are difficult to remember and it would be easy to make a mistake when programming a microprocessor with them. To make life easier a special language has been developed, called **mnemonic language.** The mnemonic for 1010100100011001 is LDA #25, which means load the ACCUMULATOR with the number 25. As you can see, the mnemonic is easier to interpret than the binary code.

The instruction LDA #25 consists of two parts, the operation, which tells the microprocessor what to do and the operand, which tells it what data to use. In this instruction the operand itself contains the data to be used, so it can be immediately transferred to the ACCUMULATOR. It is therefore called a **load immediate instruction.** The # symbol is used to show that it is an immediate instruction.

Another instruction is load from memory. This has the mnemonic LDA 2. The operation has the same mnemonic (LDA) but the operand is different, it does not contain the # symbol. This tells the microprocessor that the operand is not itself data but is an address, where the desired data can be found. LDA 2 means load the ACCUMULATOR with the data which is in memory at the address number 2 (i.e. at memory location 2). The data is collected from location 2 by putting the number 2 on the address bus and collecting the data via the data bus, exactly as described above.

To write data into a memory location the **store** instruction is used. STA 2 means 'copy the data from the ACCUMULATOR into memory location 2'. There is no instruction like STA #25, because #25 is not an address, it is data. You can only store the contents of the ACCUMULATOR in an addressed location.

This means that if you want to change the contents of memory location 2 to the value 25, you must do it in two stages. First you must load the value into the ACCUMULATOR with the instruction LDA #25 and then you must store it in location 2 with the instruction STA 2.

If you want the data in location 2 to be copied into location 1, you must also do it in two stages. First you copy the data from location 2 into the ACCUMULATOR with LDA 2. Next you copy it from the ACCUMULATOR into location 1 with the instruction STA 1.

Load and run the simulation program called 6502 MICROPROCESSOR SIMULATION, which is listed in the Appendix. If you do not have a disk system, execute PAGE = lC00 before entering this program. Plate 39 shows how this program displays the following registers:

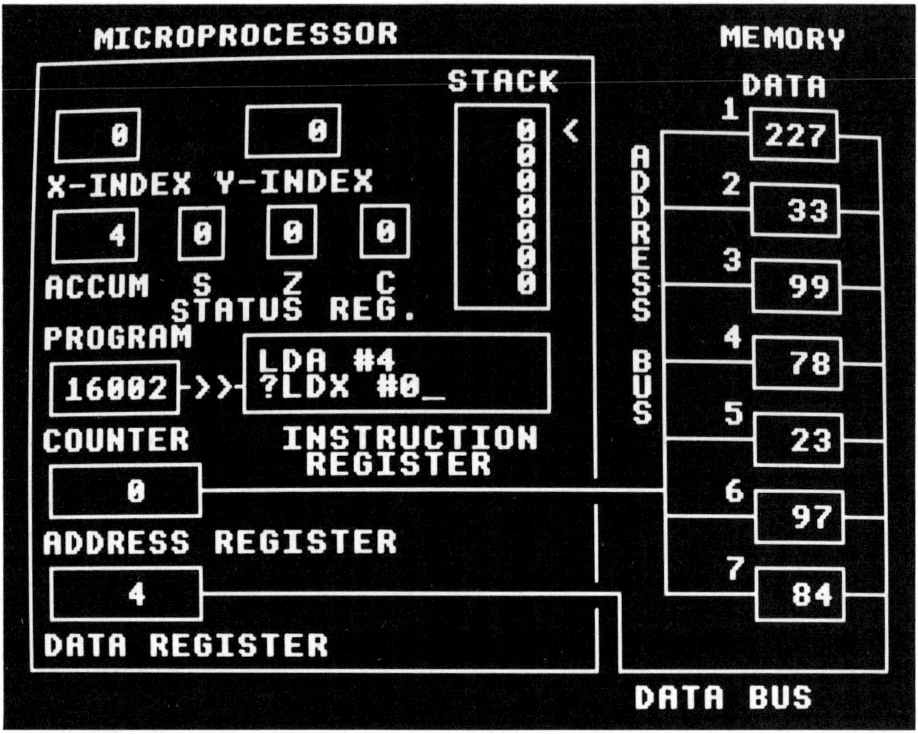

Plate 39 Microprocessor simulation

X-INDEX
Y-INDEX
ACCUMULATOR
PROGRAM COUNTER
ADDRESS REGISTER
DATA REGISTER

It also shows the STATUS REGISTER and the STACK, but we shall not deal with these just yet. The microprocessor is connected to the external memory via the data bus and the address bus. Only seven memory locations are shown but all memory locations from 0 to 255 can be addressed. In a real microcomputer any of 65 536 locations can be addressed. In this respect, our simulation is invalid. The change to full sixteen-bit addressing will be made later.

In the middle of the screen is the INSTRUCTION REGISTER containing the current instruction. Normally this instruction has been fetched from the program memory at the address pointed to by the PROGRAM COUNTER. We shall, however, enter instructions one at a time, so the PROGRAM COUNTER will not actually be used in this way. Each instruction is shown in mnemonic language, so that it can be more easily understood, but remember that each instruction would really be stored as a binary number. After each instruction has been executed, the INSTRUCTION REGISTER will display the old instruction on the line above, thus creating a space for the next instruction.

Type in the following instruction:

```
LDA #25
```

If you make a mistake while typing, you can rub it out by using the DELETE (DEL) key. Repeated pressing of this key will erase the whole line and a new one can be re-typed. The cursor movement keys cannot, however, be used. Some obvious typing errors are trapped by this program, so if the display does not change when you press certain keys, this is because the 6502 SIMULATION refuses to accept what you are typing.

When you have typed LDA #25 correctly, press the RETURN key to tell the microprocessor that you have finished. The simulation program will then attempt to execute your instruction. If you have typed it wrongly (for example, if you have typed LAD #25), the simulation program will tell you that your instruction is not valid by displaying ERROR 1. A list of the different error codes is given at the end of the chapter. If you do get one of these, press RETURN to clear a space for the correct instruction. After entering an instruction press the RETURN key, you should observe the number 25 enter into the ACCUMULATOR. The ADDRESS REGISTER will not be affected, because it is not used for this instruction.

Now type STA 2 and press <RETURN>. You should see that the number 25 in the ACCUMULATOR is copied into location 2. The original data in location 2 is destroyed, but the 25 in the ACCUMULATOR is not lost. Because the data and the address buses are used to do this, their corresponding DATA and ADDRESS REGISTERS are affected. Finally copy the contents of location 2 to location 1. Type:

```
LDA 2 <RETURN>
STA 1 <RETURN>
```

Continue this investigation for yourself. Try changing the operand #25 to other values in the range #0 to #255 and the operands 1 and 2 to other addresses in the range 1 to 255 (values outside these ranges will produce an ERROR). Only locations 1 to 7 are visible, so you should use these only at first.

The index registers

The X-INDEX can be used in the same way as the ACCUMULATOR. LDX loads the X-INDEX and STX stores the contents of the X-INDEX in memory. The X-INDEX may be used instead of the ACCUMULATOR to put the value 30 into location 6. Type:

```
LDX #30
STX 6
```

The Y-INDEX behaves the same way as the X-INDEX. The mnemonics LDY and STY are used for the Y-INDEX. Type:

```
LDY #10
STY 5
```

Now try the following problems, the solutions to which are given at the end of the chapter:

1 Type in a series of instructions to make the contents of location 2 equal to 50.
2 Type in a series of instructions to make the contents of location 6 equal to the contents of location 7, but do *not* change the contents of location 7.
3 Type in a series of instructions to make the contents of location 1 equal to the number 1, the contents of location 2 equal to 2 and the contents of location 3 equal to 3.
4 What is the effect of a succession of STA instructions to different locations? Can you make all the locations contain the data 0 by this method? You only need to carry out the instruction LDA #0 once.
5 Load the Y-INDEX with 5, store this in memory location 1. Then load the contents of this memory location into the X-INDEX.
6 What is the difference between the *contents* of location 5, the *address* of location 5 and data with the *value* of 5?
7 What is the difference between a 'write to memory' and a 'read from memory'? Which occurs when the instruction LDA 2 is executed?

LDA #10 is called an **immediate** instruction to distinguish it from LDA 10, which is an **addressed** instruction.

Microprocessor arithmetic

Addition

In the 6502, addition is performed by adding data to the current contents of the ACCUMULATOR. The instruction ADC #30 will add 30 to the existing contents of the ACCUMULATOR. The instruction ADC 4 will fetch the contents of location 4 and add them to the existing contents of the ACCUMULATOR. In both cases the result of the addition is left in the ACCUMULATOR and the original contents of the ACCUMULATOR are destoyed.

To add together the numbers 5 and 6, we first of all execute the instruction LDA #5, followed by the instruction ADC #6. You can try this for yourself using the simulation program. You will see that the result (11) is left in the ACCUMULATOR.

```
LDA #5 <RETURN>
ADC#6 <RETURN>
```

The numbers added may also be obtained from the external memory. For example,

```
LDA   1 <RETURN>
ADC   2 <RETURN>
```

will add the contents of location 1 to the contents of location 2, leaving the result in the ACCUMULATOR.

Enter each of these instructions in turn. After each one, note the effect on the contents of the ACCUMULATOR.

```
LDA #5 <RET>
STA   1 <RET>
LDA #6 <RET>
STA   3 <RET>
LDA   1 <RET>
ADC   3 <RET>
STA   5 <RET>
```

Repeat this with some of your own numbers.

Now try

```
LDA #255 <RETURN>
ADC #1   <RETURN>
```

The result 0 remains in the ACCUMULATOR. A moment's thought will explain this. The largest number that the ACCUMULATOR can store is 1111 1111 (or 255 in decimal). If we try to exceed this number, it starts again from zero. (For the mathematically minded, the microprocessor is counting in modulo 256.) This is like the milometer in a motor car, when the distance exceeds 99 999 miles, the milometer starts again from zero. Although it is possible to tell from the appearance of a car, whether it has travelled ten or 100 010 miles, the ACCUMULATOR does not age in the same way. To show that the ACCUMULATOR has exceeded 255 a special CARRY bit is used in the STATUS REGISTER. If the result of the addition is greater than 255 then this CARRY bit is set to logic 1. If the result of the calculation is not greater than 255, then this CARRY bit is cleared to 0. Check this by entering the following instructions:

```
CLC        <RET>
LDA #100 <RET>
ADC #100 <RET>
ADC #100 <RET>
ADC #100 <RET>
ADC #100 <RET>
```

The CARRY bit is particularly useful, since it enables the microprocessor to add large numbers, (it would be very inconvenient if it could not handle numbers greater than 255). First of all, how does the microprocessor store such numbers? This problem has to be solved in the decimal system too, since a set of decimal digits can only count up to nine. To count higher numbers we use more sets of digits, arranged in columns and called hundreds, tens and units. The decimal number 23, is really 2 x 10 + 3.

Similarly we can use two eight-bit bytes to store numbers larger than 256. This is not simple because the two columns are not tens and units, but 256s and units. The first column is called the **high byte** and the second is called the **low byte.** Converting a two byte binary number to decimal requires the following formula:

decimal = 256 * high byte + low byte.

A further complication is that the 6502 needs to collect the number in the order low byte followed by high byte. We shall stick to this practice, even though we shall not be dealing with the microprocessor directly for some time yet.

The decimal number 4100 becomes 4,16 when written in this order as a two byte binary number: (16 x 256 + 4 = 4100). Other examples are 3,12, which is 12 x 256 + 3 = 3075 and 250,255 which is 255 x 256 + 250 = 65 530. To convert a decimal number to a two byte number, divide the number by 256; the integer part remaining is the high byte. Multiply this by 256 and subtract it from the original number to get the low byte. BBC BASIC is ideal for carrying out these calculations; n DIV 256 gives the high byte and n MOD 256 gives the low byte.

Try these problems

8 Convert each of the following low byte/high byte numbers to decimal:

(i) 0,2
(ii) 10,12
(iii) 200,40
(iv) 0,80
(v) 96,234

9 Convert each of the following decimal numbers to low byte/high byte numbers:

(i) 256
(ii) 1024
(iii) 4097
(iv) 8000
(v) 65 535

Numbers larger than 255 are added in the following way. Each number is held in two successive locations, low byte and high byte. First the low bytes of the two numbers are added together and the result is stored. Then the high bytes are added together and the result is stored also. If the CARRY bit was set after the low byte addition, it will be added in with the high bytes. The instruction **ADC** means just that, **add with CARRY.**

There is one problem with this ADC instruction; when the low bytes are added, the CARRY bit is also added in automatically. This may already have been set to 1 by a previous unrelated instruction. We therefore clear it to 0 before the low byte addition to prevent any mistake from being made. This is done with the single byte instruction **CLC (clear the CARRY bit).**

Since we cannot store both the high byte and the low byte together in the ACCUMULATOR, we make use of the memory. This is illustrated in Figure 6.3. We put the number 4100 in the two locations 1 and 2, with the low byte (4) in location 1 and the high byte (16) in location 2. Then we put the number 510 into the next two locations (254 into location 3 and 1 in location 4).

Next we clear the CARRY bit and then add together the low bytes of the two numbers (like adding up the units in a decimal addition). Because the result is greater than 255, the CARRY bit will be set (like the decimal addition 5 + 8 = 3, carry 1). We store the result of this low byte addition in location 5.

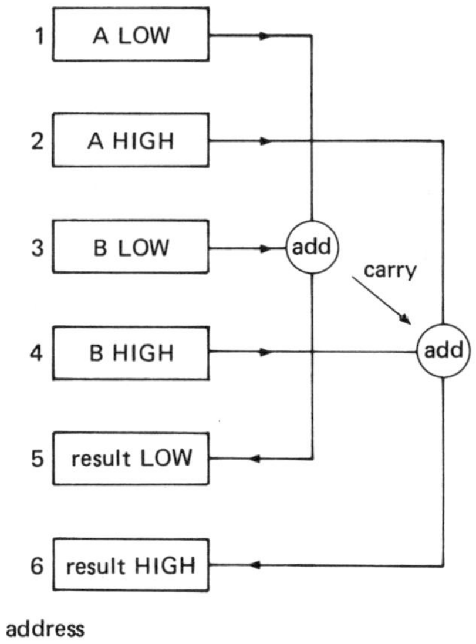

Figure 6.3 Double byte addition

Then we add together the high bytes. As we do this the CARRY bit from the low byte addition is added in as well (as in decimal addition, when we get to the tens column we add in the carry from the units) (Figure 6.3). The final result is then stored in location 6. The whole set of instructions for this double byte addition is given below. Enter each of these instructions in turn. As each instruction is entered and executed, note what happens to the CARRY bit in the STATUS REGISTER and to the contents of the ACCUMULATOR. The first eight instructions are simply setting up the memory locations with the correct numbers.

```
LDA #4    <RET>
STA  1    <RET>
LDA #16   <RET>
STA  2    <RET>
LDA #254  <RET>
STA  3    <RET>
LDA #1    <RET>
STA  4    <RET>
CLC       <RET>
LDA  1    <RET>
ADC  3    <RET>
STA  5    <RET>
LDA  2    <RET>
ADC  4    <RET>
STA  6    <RET>
```

The result is stored in locations 5 and 6, is it the result you expected?

Continue this investigation with large and small numbers. You will get the correct answer as long as the result is not greater than 65 535. What happens if the result is larger than this? (Clue, look at the CARRY bit when all the instructions have been executed.)

Try these problems:

10 Add together the numbers 45 and 54 (single byte addition) without using any external memory locations (Clue: use the immediate mode.)

11 Add together the contents of locations 4 and 5 (single byte addition) and put the result in location 3.

12 Add together the numbers 450 and 540 using double byte addition. Put one double byte number into locations 1 and 2 and the other into locations 3 and 4. Then add the numbers and put the result in locations 5 and 6.

13 Put the single byte number 225 into location 1 and 100 into location 2. Then add up the numbers and put the result into locations 3 and 4. The result is greater than 255, so be very careful about what happens to the CARRY bit.

14 Put the double byte number 1000 into locations 5 and 6. Now add 1 in immediate mode to the contents of locations 5 and 6, storing the result in the same locations. Consider how you will cope with the situation where the low byte addition results in the CARRY bit being set.

15 What two decimal numbers can be added together, using double byte addition, to give the result 0? (Clue: there are 32 768 different answers!)

Subtraction

Subtraction can also be performed using the immediate mode or the addressed mode. The instruction SBC #1 will subtract 1 from the contents of the ACCUMULATOR, leaving the result in the ACCUMULATOR. The instruction SBC 1 will subtract the contents of location 1 from the contents of the ACCUMULATOR, again leaving the result in the ACCUMULATOR.

The effect on the CARRY bit is however different from the addition case. If the second number is larger than the first, then 1 is borrowed from the next column. In the units column this 1 becomes 256, and the result in the ACCUMULATOR is larger than before. For example,

```
LDA #10
SBC #11
```

will result in the number 255 being left in the ACCUMULATOR and a 1 being borrowed from the next column. This 'borrow' is shown by the CARRY bit being cleared to 0. If there is no borrow as in the following case:

```
LDA #11
SBC #10
```

then the CARRY bit is set to 1 after the subtraction.

It is interesting to ask why the CARRY bit in subtraction works the opposite way from addition. Rather than have a special set of gates in the ALU of the microprocessor to carry out subtraction, this operation is accomplished by the method known as **twos complement addition.** First we need to explain what is meant by the **complement** of a binary number. Complement is, in fact, another word for inversion, where all the ones become zeros and all the zeros become ones. Thus the complement of 0000 1011 is 1111 0100 and the complement of 1111 1111 is 0000 0000.

The complement of a number may be found by EXCLUSIVE-ORing it with 1111 1111. This is done bit by bit, so wherever the original number contains 1, this becomes a 0, and wherever it contains 0, this becomes 1. The twos complement is obtained by adding one to the complement of the number. Thus the twos complement of 0000 1011 is 1 + 1111 0100 (which is 1111 0101). The twos complement of 1111 1111 is 1 + 0000 0000 (or 0000 0001). Another way of looking at this is that the complement of a number is the same as subtracting it from 1111 1111 (or 255 in decimal) and the twos complement is the same as subtracting it from 256.

Subtracting a binary number B from a binary number A is accomplished by adding A to the twos complement of B. For example, consider the subtraction of 0000 1011 from 0000 1111 (which is 15–11 in decimal). First the twos complement of B is found, which is 1111 0101. This is then added to A, giving 0000 1111 + 1111 0101, or 1 0000 0100. The '1' at the beginning of the answer is in the ninth column, which in our eight-bit subtraction will be left as the CARRY bit. Since this cannot be stored in an eight-bit ACCUMULATOR, the result is 0000 0100 (or 4 in decimal). Thus, although we did not need to borrow any digits from the next column, the CARRY bit is still set to 1 at the end of the subtraction.

Now see what happens if the subtraction is done the other way round, that is 11–15. The twos complement of 15 is 1111 0001, so the subtraction becomes 0000 1011 + 1111 0001, which is 0 1111 1100 (or 252 in decimal). It is significant that the CARRY bit in the ninth column is 0 this time. Now why do we get this answer? If we had tried to do this in decimal subtraction, we should have started with the units and said '1–5, you can't, so borrow 1 from the tens column'. In the decimal system this '1' is actually worth ten.

In binary subtraction we do exactly the same, except that the '1' we are borrowing is taken from the CARRY bit (the ninth column, which is worth 256). Thus our result is really the answer to the decimal problem 11 + 256 – 15, which is, of course, 252. This is the answer that our twos complement addition actually produced. The fact that we have borrowed from the sixteens column is shown by the CARRY bit. Thus if the CARRY bit is set to 1 after a subtraction then no borrow has occurred. If it is cleared to 0, then a borrow has been made.

The operation SBC automatically 'pays back' the CARRY bit (in the same way that ADC automatically adds in the CARRY bit). To avoid errors, therefore, the first SBC instruction must be preceded by SEC (set the CARRY bit), which signifies that there is no borrow to be repaid. Check the above ideas by entering each of the following instructions, and note the status of the CARRY bit each time.

```
SEC        <RET>
LDA   #11  <RET>
SBC   #10  <RET>
```

```
SEC          <RET>
LDA   #10 <RET>
SBC   #11 <RET>
```

Note how the following instructions

```
SEC         <RET>
LDA   #0  <RET>
SBC   #1  <RET>
```

leave 255 in the ACCUMULATOR, thus indicating that 255 is equivalent to −1 in this arithmetic.

If the process involves double byte subtraction, the 'borrow' is repaid during the high byte subtraction. If the CARRY bit is set to 1, there is no 'borrow' to be repaid. But if the CARRY bit is cleared to 0, then the result of the high byte subtraction is reduced by 1 to pay back the 1 that was borrowed during the low byte subtraction. Enter each of the following instructions in 6502 SIMULATION and observe their effect on the various registers:

Place the number 3,2 (decimal 515) into locations 1 and 2. Then subtract 5,1 (decimal 261) from the first number in immediate mode and place the result in locations 3 and 4.

```
LDA   #3  <RET>
STA    1  <RET>
LDA   #2  <RET>
STA    2  <RET>
SEC       <RET>
LDA    1  <RET>
SBC   #5  <RET>
STA    3  <RET>
LDA    2  <RET>
SBC   #1  <RET>
STA    4  <RET>
```

Now try these problems:

16 Load a number into the ACCUMULATOR. Then subtract this number from itself, leaving the result in the ACCUMULATOR. Do you get the result 0? If the CARRY BIT is initially cleared then you will not get the expected result. Perform SEC before your subtraction to get the correct result.

17 Place a single byte number into location 1 and another number into location 2. Subtract the contents of location 2 from the contents of location 1, placing the result in location 3.

18 Place a double byte number in locations 1 and 2. Add this number to itself and put the result in locations 3 and 4. Then subtract the number in locations 1 and 2 from the number in locations 3 and 4, leaving the result in locations 3 and 4. What do you notice about this result?

19 Place 0 into the locations 1 and 2. Treat this as a double byte number and subtract 1 from it in immediate mode, leaving the result in locations 1 and 2. What do you notice about the result?

Counting

Counting can be done by adding one repeatedly to the location being used as a counter, but it can also be done with the single instruction **increment.** The instruction, **INC 3,** fetches the content of location 3 from memory, adds one to it, and places it back in the original memory location. The ACCUMULATOR is not involved in this, so it is not changed.

The **decrement** instruction, **DEC 3,** does the same, except that the content of location 3 is reduced by one instead. In both cases no account is taken of the CARRY bit, so this does not have to be cleared or set before the INC or DEC instruction. The CARRY bit is not affected if the register is incremented above 255. The register becomes zero but the CARRY bit is not altered. Likewise, if the register is at zero and it is decremented, it becomes 255 but the CARRY bit is unchanged. Because INC and DEC involve storing the data after it has been incremented or decremented, then these instructions cannot be used in the immediate mode.

Both instructions are used a great deal in counting. It is often necessary in a program to repeat an instruction or a set of instructions several times (like the FOR...NEXT loop in BASIC). Suppose we want to repeat it eight times. The location being used as a counter is initially made equal to eight. After each cycle of the required instructions, this counter is decremented. When it reaches zero, the cycle has been repeated eight times.

The register most often used for counting is the X-INDEX. The single byte instructions to increment and decrement the X-INDEX are **INX** and **DEX** respectively. **INY** and **DEY** do the same for the Y-INDEX. None of these affect the CARRY bit in any way. It is not possible to increment or decrement the ACCUMULATOR directly, but this can be done by adding or subtracting 1 in the immediate mode. However, in this case the normal rules regarding the CARRY bit will apply.

Investigate this set of instructions:

```
LDX  #0 <RET>
LDA  #3 <RET>
STA   5 <RET>
INX     <RET>
DEC   5 <RET>
INX     <RET>
DEC   5 <RET>
INX     <RET>
DEC   5 <RET>
INX     <RET>
DEC   5 <RET>
```

Now try this problem:

20 Place 0 in the X-INDEX and 5 in the ACCUMULATOR. Now increment the

X-INDEX and decrement the ACCUMULATOR (by subtracting one) until the latter reaches zero. What value is left in the X-INDEX?

Logic instructions

As well as its arithmetic instructions, the microprocessor can also perform logic operations on data. Since each byte of data consists of eight bits, the microprocessor has to perform eight logic operations at a time. Consider the series of instructions:

```
LDA #5
AND #6
```

The second data in this case is the binary number 0000 0110. This is ANDed with the data already in the ACCUMULATOR, which is the binary number 0000 0101. These two bytes are ANDed one bit at a time and the result is put into the ACCUMULATOR.

```
6 is    0 0 0 0 0 1 1 0
5 is    0 0 0 0 0 1 0 1
Result  0 0 0 0 0 1 0 0
```

The result has a logic 1 only where there is a logic 1 in both of the corresponding bit positions of the two bytes being ANDed. This is the bit 2 position, so the result of ANDing 5 and 6 is 4.

ANDing is a good way of clearing particular bits to 0 without affecting the other bits at the same time. If the ACCUMULATOR contained the value 3 (binary 0000 0011) and we wanted to turn bit 0 off, we could perform the instruction AND #254 (binary 1111 1110), which would only affect bit 0.

```
LDA #3   <RET>
AND #254 <RET>
```

If location 5 contained the value 7 (binary 0000 0111) and we wanted to switch off bit 1 only, we could first load the contents of location 5 into the ACCUMULATOR, then AND it immediately with 253 and finally store the result back in location 5. There is, however, another way. We could load the ACCUMULATOR with the number 253 and AND it with the contents of location 5, using the instruction AND 5. As before the result (0000 0101) can then be stored in location 5.

```
LDA #7   <RET>
STA  5   <RET>
LDA  5   <RET>
AND #253 <RET>
STA  5   <RET>
```

or

```
LDA #7   <RET>
STA  5   <RET>
LDA #253 <RET>
AND  5   <RET>
STA  5   <RET>
```

The other use of the AND instruction is to **mask** an input (say from the user port) to inspect one particular bit (say bit 0). If we load the contents of location 5 into the ACCUMULATOR and perform the instruction AND #1, the result will be 1 if bit 0 of location 5 was set and 0 if bit 0 was cleared. This is the equivalent of the BASIC statement Q = ?5 AND 1 on the BBC microcomputer. In a similar way

```
LDA  #127 <RET>
STA    5  <RET>
LDA    5  <RET>
AND  #128 <RET>
```

leaves 0 in the ACCUMULATOR.

```
LDA  #255 <RET>
STA    5  <RET>
LDA    5  <RET>
AND  #128 <RET>
```

leaves 128 in the ACCUMULATOR.

Logical OR is carried out with the ORA operation, which can take an immediate (#) or an addressed mode operand.

```
LDA  #6   <RET>
ORA  #5   <RET>
```

The ACCUMULATOR contains 6 and this is ORed with 5, so the result is 7, as follows:

```
6 is    0  0  0  0  0  1  1  0
5 is    0  0  0  0  0  1  0  1
Result  0  0  0  0  0  1  1  1
```

There is a logic 1 in the result if there is a logic 1 in either of the corresponding bit positions of the two starting numbers.

The main use of ORA is to switch a particular bit on, without affecting the other bits. To turn on bit 7 of location 5, we load the contents of location 5 into the ACCUMULATOR, OR it with 1000 0000 (decimal 128) and store the result back in the user port (the exact equivalent of ?5 = (?5 OR 128) in BASIC).

```
LDA  #127 <RET>
STA    5  <RET>
LDA    5  <RET>
ORA  #128 <RET>
```

leaves 255 in the ACCUMULATOR.

In Chapter 4 we looked at the EXCLUSIVE-OR function and noted that there is a logic 1 output if the two inputs to the gate are different. The EXCLUSIVE-OR output goes to logic 0 if its two inputs are the same. The BBC BASIC EOR works in the same way. The microprocessor operation which does this is also EOR. This too can be used in the immediate mode and in the addressed mode:

```
LDA  #6   <RET>
EOR  #255 <RET>

6 is     0  0  0  0  0  1  1  0
255 is   1  1  1  1  1  1  1  1
Result   1  1  1  1  1  0  0  1
```

EOR has one special property that makes it particularly useful. If the contents of location 5 are loaded into the ACCUMULATOR and then EXCLUSIVE-ORed with 1111 1111, each bit that was previously on will be turned off, and each bit that was previously off will be turned on. This can be seen from a comparison of the two numbers above. If the data collected from location 5 is 6, the result shows a logic 0 in each bit position where it was previously a logic 1, and vice versa. The instruction EOR #255 is thus the equivalent of the BASIC statement Q = NOT Z.

Try each of the following sets of instructions:

```
LDA  #255 <RET>     ;This instruction will switch all
STA   5   <RET>     ;bits of location 5 on.

LDA   5   <RET>
AND  #16  <RET>     ;This will switch off all
STA   5   <RET>     ;bits except bit 4.

ORA  #128 <RET>
STA   5   <RET>     ;This will turn on bit 7 also.

EOR  #240 <RET>     ;This will turn bits 4 and 7 off and
STA   5   <RET>     ;bits 5 and 6 on.
```

Enter each of the following instructions in turn. Before each one, try to predict what the result in the ACCUMULATOR will be. Then see if you were correct.

```
LDA  #170 <RET>
STA   1   <RET>
LDA  #15  <RET>
AND  #10  <RET>
ORA  #15  <RET>
EOR  #10  <RET>
AND   1   <RET>
STA   2   <RET>
LDA  #0   <RET>
ORA   1   <RET>
AND   2   <RET>
EOR  #255 <RET>
```

Now try these problems:

21 What is the result of ANDing 85 with 45?
22 What is the result of ORing 85 with 45?
23 What is the result of EXCLUSIVE-ORing 85 with 45?
24 How do you switch off bits 1 and 2 of location 5 without changing the state of the other bits?
25 How do you switch bits 0, 1, 2, 3, 4, 5 and 6 of location 5 on, yet not affect bit 7?

Indexed addressing

We mentioned above that the X-INDEX is often used as a pointer to memory locations. We use this when we want to point to a table of values. For example location 1 could contain the square of the number 1, location 2 could contain the square of the number 2 and so on. Then, to find the square of a number in a machine code program, we only have to look it up in this table. We do this with **indexed addressing.**

The instruction LDA 1,X loads the ACCUMULATOR with the contents of a memory location. The chosen location is obtained by adding the X-INDEX to the address specified in the operand. Thus if the X-INDEX is equal to 5, the chosen location would have the address 1 + 5, which is, of course, location 6. The contents of this location would thus be loaded into the ACCUMULATOR.

```
LDX #5   <RET>
LDA   1,X <RET>
```

Since the X-INDEX cannot be greater than 255, the desired location must be within 255 of the operand address. The instruction LDA 0,X can fetch data from any of the locations 0 to 255. However 6502 SIMULATION only displays the locations 1 to 7, so it is not possible to give indexed addressing a full test. All arithmetic and logic instructions so far described can be used with indexed addressing as well as immediate or ordinary addressed modes.

The advantage of indexing will not yet be apparent, because we have not discussed how to repeat a series of instructions. Let us first learn how to use the indexed address mode. The address that occurs in the operand is taken as the starting address for working out where the chosen location should be. The operand indicates the indexed addressed mode by the ',X' that occurs after this starting address.

The following program will put the value 1 into location 1, the value 2 into location 2 and so on. Enter this series of instructions and see what happens each time. Note especially what happens to the ADDRESS REGISTER.

```
LDX #1   <RET>
LDA #1   <RET>
STA   0,X <RET>
INX       <RET>
LDA #2   <RET>
STA   0,X <RET>
INX       <RET>
```

```
LDA #3   <RET>
STA  0,X <RET>
INX      <RET>
LDA #4   <RET>
etc.
```

This program can be greatly simplified with a new set of single byte instructions, that are used to copy data from one register to another:

```
TXA  copy data from the X-INDEX to the ACCUMULATOR
TAX  copy data from the ACCUMULATOR to the X-INDEX
TYA  copy data from the Y-INDEX to the ACCUMULATOR
TAY  copy data from the ACCUMULATOR to the Y-INDEX
```

Here is the same program but using TXA. Note now how the *same* set of instructions is repeated over and over again. Clearly the machine code equivalent of a FOR...NEXT loop will make this a very simple program, when we come to it.

```
LDX #1   <RET>
TXA      <RET>
STA  0,X <RET>
INX      <RET>
TXA      <RET>
STA  0,X <RET>
INX      <RET>
TXA      <RET>
STA  0,X <RET>
INX      <RET>
TXA      <RET>
etc.
```

Repeat this procedure, but change the store instructions to 1,X instead of 0,X. What difference does it make?

Rewrite the above program to read the contents of each memory location into the ACCUMULATOR, to add 1 and to store the result back in the same location. The program should use indexed addressing to point to each location in turn.

The PROGRAM COUNTER

Although 6502 SIMULATION is useful for demonstrating the different instructions available in the 6502 microprocessor, it is only possible to make it run a few types of program. So far we have not asked it to carry out a set of instructions automatically. It is as if in BASIC we could only enter statements one at a time into a microcomputer. We need a way of storing a whole series of instructions that the microprocessor can execute one by one. This is the only way that we shall be able to repeat a cycle of instructions for a given number of times.

Up till now we have not bothered particularly about the PROGRAM COUNTER, henceforth called the PC. This is a sixteen-bit counter that points to the address of the next instruction. Try each of these instructions and note how each single byte instruction increments the PC by one and each double byte instruction increases it by two.

```
CLC       <RET>
SEC       <RET>
LDX #5    <RET>
LDA #0    <RET>
TXA       <RET>
TAY       <RET>
```

The address in the PC starts at 16000, which is roughly where most of my BBC machine code programs begin. If you enter a large number of instructions you could get this to increase to 65535. Further increases cause it to reset to zero. 65535 is the maximum number that a sixteen-bit register can hold. In the memory a segment of a program would be stored sequentially like this.

```
16100   LDX #5
16102   TXA
16103   CLC
16104   LDA 5
```

Notice how the PC seems to be giving each instruction a number as in BASIC. But it is not at all like BASIC: these numbers are the address of the first byte of the instruction, some of which are two byte and some of which are one byte instructions. Here is the same program written out one byte at a time:

```
16100   LDX
16101   #5
16102   TXA
16103   CLC
16104   LDA
16105   5
```

The line numbers must be consecutive and none may be omitted. This is annoying when writing machine code programs, because if you later want to insert another instruction, you have to move all the others down by one or two bytes (which is one of the reasons why BASIC is a better language than machine code). In BASIC the next statement fetched is the one with the next highest number, and it does not matter if some numbers are omitted. The line numbers in machine code programming represent the addresses in memory where the codes for the instructions are stored. They are the values taken by the PROGRAM COUNTER to get each new instruction. Each time the PC executes an instruction it is simply incremented to fetch the next instruction. If we put our next instruction in the wrong place, the microprocessor will not notice, it will still fetch its next instruction from the next location in memory. It is quite possible that this wrong instruction collected by the microprocessor will cause the whole system to crash.

Using the address of the program counter, it is common to write out machine code programs like this:

```
16100        LDX  #5    ;set the counter to 5
16102        LDA  #0    ;set ACCUMULATOR to 0
16104 .rpt   STA   0,X  ;clear the location
16106        DEX        ;next value of X
16107        BNE  -5    ;do next location
```

We have not yet dealt with how this program works, we are just looking at the method of writing it.

The first column is the value of the PC as before, which is the address of the operation part of each instruction.

The second column of the program listing is the name or **label** of the cycle of instructions to be repeated (.rpt). This way of labelling the program is to show us where the cycle (or loop) begins. The microprocessor takes no notice of labels, because it uses the PC to determine where this loop is. 6502 SIMULATION likewise uses numbers to determine the next instruction. The label is only included for our information (and it cannot be entered as any part of an instruction in 6502 SIMULATION).

The third column has the mnemonic of the instruction as before. The remainder of the line, after the semi-colon, is the **comment** column. This is used to explain what is going on, rather like the REM statement in BASIC. 6502 SIMULATION will not recognize such comments, even if there is room to put them in, so these too should not be entered. In the BBC assembler comments are indicated by the backslash (\ ) character.

Program jumps

BASIC has two methods of jumping to a different part of the program, **GOTO** and **GOSUB.** There are exact equivalents in machine code too, **JMP (jump)** and **JSR (jump to subroutine).** The instruction JMP 12000 loads the address 12000 into the PROGRAM COUNTER and the next instruction is fetched from that address. Execution then continues line by line from this new position. JMP therefore transfers control completely to this new part of the program. The microprocessor loses all knowledge of where it has come from and it has no way of getting back to it (unless, that is, the new part of the program sends it back with another JMP instruction). JMP and JSR are three byte instructions so you might expect to see the PC increase by three when they are used. However these instruction change the address in the PC, so you cannot really see this happen. The operand is a two byte address (written in the low byte, high byte order). We can treat it as a decimal number, however, and let 6502 SIMULATION take care of the two bytes. Enter these instructions and watch especially how the PC changes its address:

```
       JMP  12000  <RET>
12000  JMP  10000  <RET>
```

JSR 12000 behaves almost the same, but there is one important difference. After jumping to line 12000 execution continues until the single byte instruction **RTS (return from subroutine)** is met. Control then returns to the line immediately after the original JSR instruction. The microprocessor keeps a note of the address of the JSR instruction (called the return address) in a special register called the **STACK.** When the RTS instruction is encountered, this return address is pulled off the STACK and put back into the PC. The latter is then incremented and execution continues from the new address.

When the following instructions are tried out, watch the STACK as well as the PC. Note that both the low byte and the high byte of the return address are stored on the STACK and note how the **STACK POINTER (the arrow)** moves up and down, pointing to the last entry in the STACK. Note the relationship between the number pushed onto or pulled off the STACK and the PC address, when the JSR and the RTS instructions are executed.

```
      JSR  12000  <RET>
12000 LDA  #1     <RET>
12002 RTS         <RET>
```

Do you see the difference between the JMP and JSR instructions?

Try these problems:

26 What address would be left in the PC after the following instructions had been executed?

```
      JMP  12000  <RET>
12000 JMP  10000  <RET>
```

27 What would a microprocessor do if it met this instruction?

```
12000 JMP  12000  <RET>
```

Conditional jumps

In BASIC the IF...THEN statement allows the program to choose between alternatives:

```
1000 IF Y=0 THEN GOTO 5000
1010 X=2
```

If Y is zero at statement 1000, this causes a jump to line 5000. If Y is not zero, the program continues with statement 1010. In machine code the BRANCH instructions have the same purpose. After nearly every instruction a special bit in the STATUS REGISTER, called the **ZERO bit,** is changed. It is set to 1 if the result of the instruction is zero, it is cleared to 0 if the result is not zero. Watch the effect on the ZERO bit (Z) in the 6502 SIMULATION, when each of the following is executed:

```
LDA #0  <RET>
LDY #0  <RET>
TAX     <RET>
INY     <RET>
LDA #1  <RET>
```

The **BNE** instruction **(branch if not equal to zero)** tests this ZERO bit and if it is cleared to 0 (i.e. the result of the previous instruction was not zero), the branch is obeyed. If the ZERO bit is set to 1, then the result of the previous instruction was zero, so the branch is not obeyed and execution continues with the next line.

The **BEQ** instruction **(branch if equal to zero)** is the opposite of this: the branch is obeyed when the ZERO bit is set and is not obeyed when the ZERO bit is cleared.

The operand of the branch instruction is the number of lines to be skipped over. Unlike the JMP instruction, it is not the actual address to which the PC is changed. The operand is called a **displacement** and it is the number of bytes to be added to the PROGRAM COUNTER. This displacement can be positive (a forward jump) or negative (a backward jump). For 6502 SIMULATION we signify this with the + or – symbols, which must be included. A real microprocessor has a special way of distinguishing positive and negative numbers – we shall deal with this later.

Let us now see how this conditional branching is used. It is assumed that the following program begins at 16100. You can get to this address by entering JMP 16100 <RET>. Remember not to type in the label or the comment columns.

```
16100       LDY #20  Set counter    <RET>
16102       LDX #1   Set pointer    <RET>
16104 .rpt  TXA      Get value      <RET>
16105       STA 0,X  Save value     <RET>
16107       INX      Next location  <RET>
16108       DEY      Dec counter    <RET>
16109       BNE -7   Repeat cycle   <RET>
16111          remainder of program
```

In this program the BNE –7 instruction tells the microprocessor to go back seven bytes to the address 16104, labelled (.rpt). BNE stands for 'branch if the result of the previous instruction is not zero'. In this case the previous instruction was DEY (decrement the Y-INDEX). Since the Y-INDEX starts at twenty, every time it is decremented it becomes smaller, but not equal to zero. So the branch condition is obeyed and the program branches back to line 16104 each time. It does this by adding –7 to the PC, thus making it point to the previous address. After the twentieth decrement, the Y-INDEX finally becomes zero, so the ZERO bit is set and the branch condition is not obeyed. Now the PC is incremented to 16111 and the next instruction is fetched from address 16111.

The reason for jumping back seven bytes and not six is as follows. Look at what happens if the ZERO bit is set so that the branch condition is not obeyed. The BNE –7 instruction is a two byte instruction, starting at address 16109. After it has fetched the operand (–7), the PC is equal to 16110. The branch condition fails, so this instruction has now been completed and the PC is incremented to point to the next instruction, which is at address 16111.

Now suppose that the Y-INDEX was not zero so that the ZERO bit is cleared. In this case the branch condition will be obeyed and –7 will be added to the PC, which will thus become 16103, since 16110 + (–7) = 16103. This is the end of the current instruction, so the PC is incremented (to 16104) and the next instruction is fetched from line 16104. This is exactly where we want to be. The rule, therefore, is as follows: all BRANCH instructions must branch to the address immediately before the desired address.

Let us see how this applies to the following program, which achieves the same as the one above:

```
16100        LDY  #20   ;Set counter     <RET>
16102        LDX  #0    ;Set pointer     <RET>
16104 .next  TXA                         <RET>
16105        STA  0,X                    <RET>
16107        INX        ;Inc pointer     <RET>
16108        DEY        ;Dec counter     <RET>
16109        BEQ  +2    ;Branch to end   <RET>
16111        JMP  104   ;Go to next      <RET>
16113        end of program
```

This time line 16109 is a forward jump BEQ +2. This is after the instruction DEY and will thus be obeyed whenever the Y-INDEX is zero. This does not occur for the first nineteen loops, so the PC is incremented to point to address 16111, which is a JMP to address 16104. On the twentieth loop the Y-INDEX becomes zero so the branch is obeyed and the PC becomes 16112 (i.e. 16110 + 2). This is the end of the current instruction, so the PC is incremented to point to the next instruction at address 16113. Note once again that the displacement added to the PC makes it point to the address immediately in front of the desired address. This is to allow for the fact that the PC is incremented before the next instruction is fetched. Of all ideas in machine code programming, this is probably the most difficult to get right.

Comparison

So far we have only looked at counting down to zero; this is too restrictive. To enable us to count up as well, the ability to compare two sets of data is essential. The **CMP (compare)** instruction performs this function. The instruction CMP #5 carries out the following steps:

i) The CARRY bit is set to 1 initially, as for a subtraction.
ii) The data in the operand is subtracted from the data in the ACCUMULATOR and the result is held in the DATA REGISTER. The data in the ACCUMULATOR is not changed.
iii) If the operand data is equal to the ACCUMULATOR data then the result will be zero and the ZERO bit will be set, otherwise it will be cleared. Thus if CMP #5 is followed by BEQ, the branch will be obeyed if the ACCUMULATOR also contains 5.
iv) If the operand data is greater than the ACCUMULATOR data, then the CARRY bit will be cleared, indicating that a borrow has occurred. If the operand data is not greater than the ACCUMULATOR data then the CARRY bit will be set. These conditions can be detected by the branch instructions BCC (branch if the CARRY bit is cleared) and BCS (branch if the CARRY bit is set).

To summarize:
CMP #5 followed by BCS will branch if the ACCUMULATOR data is greater than or equal to 5.
CMP #5 followed by BCC will branch if the ACCUMULATOR data is less than 5.

CMP #5 followed by BEQ will branch if the ACCUMULATOR data is equal to 5. CMP #5 followed by BNE will branch if the ACCUMULATOR data is not equal to 5. The CMP operation can have an operand in the immediate, the addressed or the indexed modes. In all cases the data (immediate or from an external memory location) will be compared with the ACCUMULATOR data.

The X-INDEX is tested by the **CPX** operation. This usually has operands that are in immediate or addressed mode (indexing an INDEX is possible, but is a special case).

The Y-INDEX has a similar instruction, **CPY**, which also can have an operand in the immediate mode or the addressed mode.

Try each of the following sets of instructions. Make sure that you understand why the branch operands have the values they do. Try to predict what each program should do, then see if you were correct. You will have to re-enter the instructions in the loop (16208 to 16216) three times over, because 6502 SIMULATION will not remember them. Later we shall see how to enter these instructions into a program.

Program to place the square of the number 3 into location 5

```
16000        LDA  #0  ;Set result to      <RET>
16002        STA   5  ;zero               <RET>
16004        LDY  #3  ;Set counter        <RET>
16006        STY   7  ;Keep value         <RET>
16008 .loop  CLC                          <RET>
16009        LDA   7  ;Get value          <RET>
16011        ADC   5  ;Add result         <RET>
16013        STA   5  ;Keep new result    <RET>
16015        DEY      ;Dec counter        <RET>
16016        BNE -10  ;Repeat loop        <RET>
```

The loop adds together the contents of location 7, called value and location 5, called result. This loop is performed a total of three times, initially set by the counter. The final result at the end will thus be 3 + 3 + 3 or three squared.

Try these problems:

28 What would happen if the BNE −10 instruction in line 16016 were replaced by BNE −9, or by BCC −10?

29 Write a series of instructions to put 100 into location 1, 99 into location 2, 98 into location 3 and so on, to 91 in location 10. You will need to increment the location pointer, but decrement the value being placed in each successive location.

Negative numbers

So far we have written −5, say, to indicate a backward jump. The microprocessor knows nothing about the negative sign and needs some other way of indicating whether a number is positive or negative. It does this by the coding technique known as twos complement discussed earlier. This relies on the phenomenon that 256 is actually equivalent to 0 if the CARRY is ignored. Hence 255, which is one less than zero, is equivalent to −1, which is also one less than zero. A table of some of these equivalents shows this more clearly.

Pos. decml.	Positive binary	2s compl. binary	Equiv. decml.	Neg. decml.
128	1000 0000	1000 0000	128	−128
127	0111 1111	1000 0001	129	−127
126	0111 1110	1000 0010	130	−126
125	0111 1101	1000 0011	131	−125
41	0010 1001	1101 0111	215	−41
40	0010 1010	1101 1000	216	−40
39	0010 1011	1101 1001	217	−39
38	0010 1100	1101 1010	218	−38
30	0001 1110	1110 0010	226	−30
20	0001 0100	1110 1100	236	−20
10	0000 1010	1111 0110	246	−10
2	0000 0010	1111 1110	254	−2
1	0000 0001	1111 1111	255	−1
0	0000 0000	0000 0000	0	0

An inspection of the table shows that we can now represent both positive and negative numbers with binary numbers, depending upon which form of binary coding is being used. Twos complement coding represents numbers in the range −128 to + 127 only, and it is possible to distinguish the negative numbers, because their most significant bit (bit 7, at the left end) is always 1. For all positive numbers this bit is 0. Thus we need only test the most significant bit position to see if it is a 1 or a 0. The 6502 microprocessor is aware of this need and sets the SIGN bit in the STATUS register to tell us if a number is positive or negative. We do not have to bother about this unless we want to make use of twos complement coding. The numbers behave quite 'normally' and it is up to us to decide what we want those numbers to represent. The operand of a BRANCH instruction is the number of bytes of the machine code program to be skipped over. This is not difficult to calculate, provided you remember that the program counter is incremented immediately before the next byte of an instruction is fetched from memory. So a BRANCH must go to the byte immediately preceding the desired instruction.

In the case of forward branching, one counts up in the normal way until one reaches this preceding byte. The number obtained is the required operand. For example,

```
16100   LDX #0     <RET>
16102   BEQ +2     <RET>
16104   yyy  zz
16106   ppp  qq
```

After BEQ + 2, the PC is at memory location 16103. To this is added + 2, giving 16105 and the PC is then incremented to 16106. The next instruction is fetched from 16106. Instruction ppp qq will be executed next after the branch instruction.

For backward branching the operand should really be a twos complement number, but 6502 SIMULATION has been programmed to accept negative numbers instead. Later we shall have to do this properly, but for the moment we can ignore this.

An idea of twos complement numbers enables us to do a simple check on bit 7 of any location. If bit 7 is set to 1, then the number in the location is regarded as negative, if bit 7 is 0 then the number is regarded as positive. So the operation **BMI (branch if minus)** will succeed if bit 7 is a 1 and the operation **BPL (branch if plus)** will succeed if bit 7 is cleared to 0. For example,

```
16100   LDX  #255   <RET>
16102   BMI  +2     <RET>
16104   yyy  zz     <RET>
16106   ppp  qq     <RET>
```

will cause instruction ppp qq to be executed next after the branch instruction, whereas

```
16100   LDX  #255   <RET>
16102   BPL  +2     <RET>
16104   yyy  zz     <RET>
16106   ppp  qq     <RET>
```

will cause instruction yyy zz to be executed next after the branch instruction.

Shift instructions

This set of instructions is often used in binary multiplication and division. Multiplying by ten with decimal numbers holds no terrors, we simply add a 0. Similarly in binary, multiplication by two is accomplished by adding a 0. The instruction to do just that is **ASL (arithmetic shift left).** This causes each bit in the specified location (or the ACCUMULATOR) to move into the next position left, with 0 loaded into the lowest bit. If the number was originally greater than 127 (or negative in twos complement coding) then the 1 originally in bit 7 is shifted into the CARRY bit.

```
LDA #81  <RET>
ASL A    <RET>
```

(The ACCUMULATOR now contains 162.)

```
ASL A    <RET>
```

(The ACCUMULATOR contains 68 and the CARRY bit contains 1, which is really 256 and 256 + 68 = 324.)

Two byte shifting can also be performed, by allowing the CARRY bit to be shifted into bit 0 of the high byte (Figure 6.4). This is done with **ROL (rotate left).** This causes the CARRY bit (if any) from the low byte to be shifted into bit 0 of the high byte.

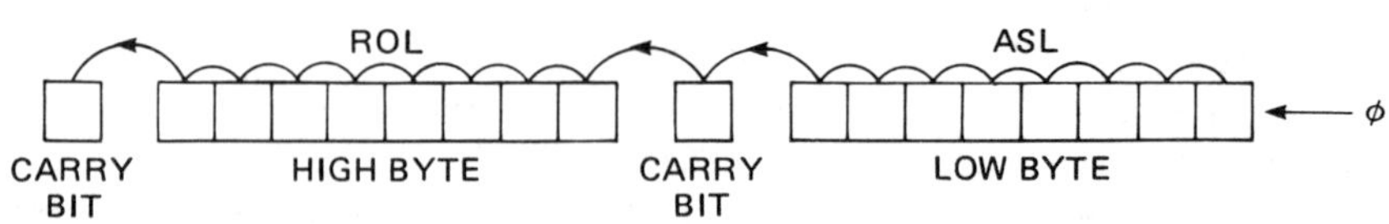

Figure 6.4 Left shifting on two bytes

```
LDA #181   <RET>
STA 1      <RET>
LDA #0     <RET>
STA 2      <RET>
ASL 1      <RET>
ROL 2      <RET>
ASL 1      <RET>
ROL 2      <RET>
ASL 1      <RET>
ROL 2      <RET>
```

will cause the original two byte number (181,0) to be multiplied by 8.

A similar set of instructions can be used to divide by two. This time the routine starts with the high byte and performs an **LSR (logical shift right)** on it. Bit 7 becomes 0, bit 6 becomes equal to the previous value of bit 7, etc. and the contents of bit 0 are shifted into the CARRY bit. This instruction can be followed by an **ROR (rotate right)** and the CARRY bit is pushed into bit 7 of the low byte (Figure 6.5). Bit 0 of the low byte is pushed into the CARRY bit itself. (This is very useful for determining if the original number was odd or even, since only an odd number leaves the CARRY bit set to 1.)

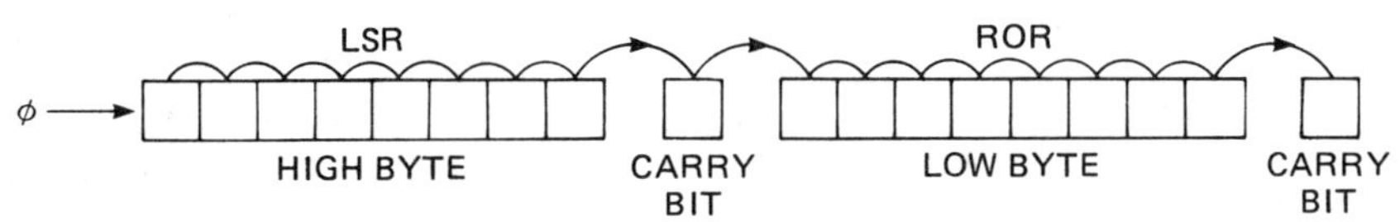

Figure 6.5 Right shifting on two bytes

The STACK

Another set of instructions is concerned with the STACK. The single byte instruction **PHA** makes the stack pointer move down to point to the next STACK position and then pushes the contents of the ACCUMULATOR onto the STACK for temporary storage. The reverse instruction **PLA** will pull the contents of the current position off the STACK into the ACCUMULATOR and make the stack pointer move up one. Try these examples:

```
LDA #5     <RET>
PHA        <RET>
LDA #0     <RET>
PHA        <RET>
LDA #255   <RET>
PLA        <RET>
PLA        <RET>
PLA        <RET>
```

and watch the movement of the stack pointer in each case.

No operation

The most mystifying instruction must surely be **NOP (no operation).** It simply causes the microprocessor to waste time. None of the registers is affected in any way, except for the PROGRAM COUNTER, which is incremented by 1, to point to the next instruction. The main use of NOP is to adjust delay loops to get the correct delay time. Try it for yourself and see its lack of effect.

Break

This instruction **(BRK)** performs a special task. When encountering it the microprocessor treats it rather like a JSR instruction. It saves the current address of the PC on the STACK and looks at locations 65532 and 65533 to collect an address. These often contain the start address for the microprocessor (the one it jumps to when first switched on). When building a dedicated system, one often needs to use this instruction while debugging. It is also useful to BBC microcomputer users, since it allows us to access the error messages of BASIC to add our own. Its use is desciribed in the user guide (page 464). In 6502 SIMULATION the start address is assumed to be 16000. When using this instruction, note how the PC address is pushed onto the STACK for future reference.

Running a program

So far instructions have been entered one at a time just like BASIC in command mode. To run a BASIC program you have to store the commands (called **statements**) in a series of lines. 6502 SIMULATION behaves in the same way, except that the line numbers must follow consecutively, allowing one number for each byte of the instruction. In our case this is not too difficult. Single byte instructions use a single mnemonic with no operand. The only three byte instructions I have implemented are JMP and JSR (and these can only be three bytes). In 6502 SIMULATION (though not in the real microprocessor) all other instructions require two bytes. All programs should start from the address 16000, which will be where the simulation will expect to begin. To illustrate the techniques, carry out the following instructions carefully. In this respect 6502 SIMULATION is somewhat fragile and gives unpredictable results if it meets situations it was not programmed to handle.

First type NEW and press RETURN. The simulation display will disappear and be replaced by some instructions on how to use the programming mode. Press SPACE to begin. Then type:

```
16000  LDA  #5  <RETURN>
16002  LDX  #5  <RETURN>
16004  CLC      <RETURN>
16005  ADC  #5  <RETURN>
16007  DEX      <RETURN>
16008  BNE  -5  <RETURN>
```

If you make a mistake, just retype the offending line again. To delete a line just type its number and press RETURN exactly as with BASIC. To run this program type CALL

<RETURN> and watch what happens to the X-INDEX and the ACCUMULATOR. You can type CALL from within the simulation to re-run the same program.

Notice how some lines of this program occupy two bytes while others only take up one byte (CLC and DEX). Note too how the last line (BNE –5) branches back to line 16005 (ADC #5). If you try your own programs, you will need to work out such offsets very carefully, or the simulation will crash. You should always be able to recover by pressing the ESCAPE key, but your program will then be lost. In this respect the simulation is quite accurate, the microprocessor also gets lost if you tell it to fetch its next instruction from the wrong place. The ESCAPE key can also be used if you get yourself into an infinite loop. For example:

```
16000  JMP  16000
```

will keep going for ever.

If you wish to write a new program, type NEW from within the simulation. It will send you to the programming mode and wipe out any existing program at the same time. To edit an existing program, do not type NEW, but type PROG instead. This returns you to the programming mode and displays your current program, which may then be edited. To return to the direct command mode at any time, type COMMAND.

You may wish to try out any of the programs that you have already entered one instruction at a time. Then try out your own ideas using 6502 SIMULATION. Apart from the restriction on memory locations (single bytes only) the simulation supports most 6502 instructions (and also a few that are not implemented on the 6502, but this is a mistake on my part). In particular 6502 SIMULATION will allow indirect-indexed and indexed-indirect addressing of a sort (subject to the single byte limitation). A list of the most useful 6502 instruction codes is given at the end of this chapter, so try them out for yourself. There is no doubt that the ability to handle the mnemonics properly does speed up the writing of assembly language programs later.

I do not guarantee that your programs will work, since the programming mode of 6502 SIMULATION was an afterthought. It is in fact a perfect example of poor programming style – structured programs are planned from the start as described in Chapter 2. However, 6502 SIMULATION does work to some extent. If you want a crash-proof version, you will have to wait until it has been rewritten.

Sixteen-bit addressing

This brief tour of the 6502 microprocessor has shown some of the available instructions and their effects on the internal registers of the microprocessor. You should now be able to move on to the more exciting challenge of putting these instructions into a real machine code program and seeing their overall effect. There are, though, a few more general ideas that need to be understood, before the next chapter can be tackled.

So far we have assumed that the external memory has only consisted of addresses 0 to 255. In fact this is not so. The PC has to address memory locations from 0 to 65535 (that is &0000 to &FFFF). The address bus thus consists of sixteen lines and the PC and ADDRESS REGISTER are sixteen-bit registers. To store data in an address, the ADDRESS REGISTER sends the chosen address as two bytes: the low byte and the high byte. A convenient way to think of the memory, is to imagine it divided into a series of **pages** each containing 256 bytes. The high byte of the address is the page number and the low byte is the address within the chosen page. The STA instruction will thus need two bytes to specify the address and not just the one as we have so far assumed. For example,

Hex code	**Mnemonic**
8D 00 80	STA 32768 (&8000)

(&8000 is the hexadecimal equivalent of the decimal address 32768).

One of the quirks of the 6502 microprocessor is that it requires this double byte address to be stored in the program with the low byte first followed by the high byte. The screen address 32768 is byte 0, page 128, which is therefore sent as 0,128 (&00,&80 in hex). The hex code for 'store the contents of the ACCUMULATOR in a two-byte address' is &8D, so the instruction becomes 8D 00 80 in hex.

Review of addressing modes

i) Immediate mode
The operand is the actual number to be loaded into the accumulator.

Decimal code	**Hex. code**	**Mnemonic**
169,42	A9 2A	LDA #42

The # sign used in the mnemonic indicates this mode of addressing. This is followed by a single byte, which is the data to be loaded. There can only be one because the ACCUMULATOR can only store a single byte at a time.

ii) Absolute mode
If we want to load the ACCUMULATOR with the contents of a particular memory location, we use the absolute addressing mode, in which the operand is an address. The microprocessor goes to that address to find the number to be loaded into the ACCUMULATOR. Since there are so many different addresses, the operand consists of two bytes, the low byte of the address followed by the high byte. As an example, we could fetch the contents of address 32768 (&8000).

173,0,128	AD 00 80	LDA 32768

The absence of a # sign indicates the ABSOLUTE addressing mode. Note that the numeric code is different from the code for the immediate addressing mode.

iii) Zero page mode
If the required data is on page 0 of the memory (locations 0 to 255), it could be fetched with the absolute mode thus:

173,2,0	AD 02 00	LDA 2

which means, 'load the ACCUMULATOR with the contents of memory location 2'. The zero page mode enables the same instruction to be executed faster and it also takes up less space to write because it is a two byte instruction only. The microprocessor understands from the operation code that the location is on page zero.

165,2	A5 02	LDA 2

The mnemonic codes for both modes are identical, it is only the numeric codes that show the difference.

iv) Indexed addressing
This has also been described above. The final address is calculated by adding the X-INDEX to the operand address. The microprocessor then goes to this final address to get the desired data.

```
189,0,128        BD 00 80        LDA 32768,X
```

The ',X' in the mnemonic indicates this mode. Alternatively this same mode may be used with the Y-INDEX instead of the X-INDEX.

```
185,0,128        B9 00 80        LDA 32768,Y
```

v) Other addressing modes
This by no means exhausts the addressing modes available to the 6502 microprocessor; another very important one (indirect indexed) will be introduced in the next chapter. Most of the others are zero page modes and there are very few zero page locations available in our chosen microcomputers, so these modes can rarely be used. For a fuller discussion refer to the texts described in the Bibliography.

Disassembly
Program 37 (DISASSEMBLER) allows you to look at other machine code programs. This program is in BASIC and is very slow, but it does work. Disassembling the operating

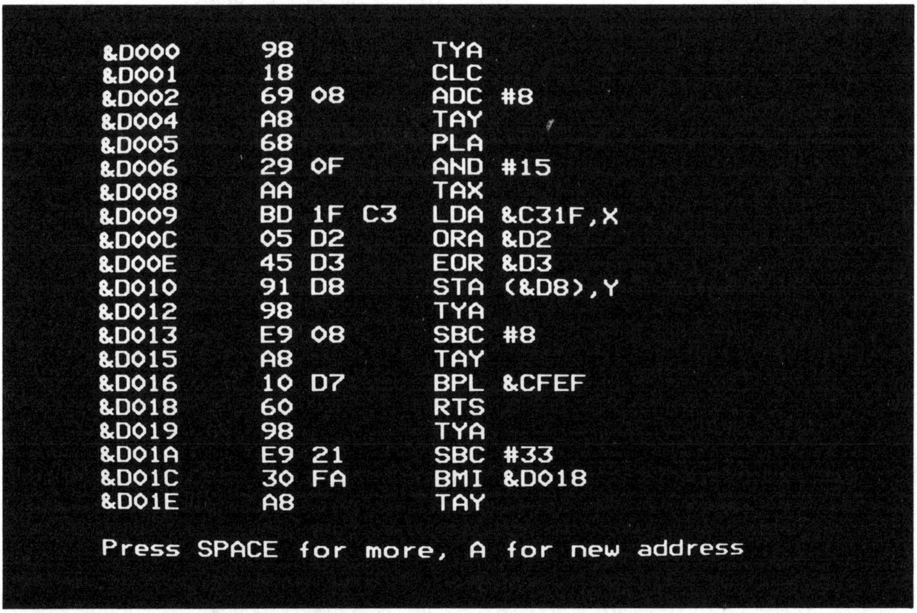

Plate 40 The DISASSEMBLER in use

system of the BBC microcomputer is a life's work, so do not be too ambitious (Plate 40). It is useful to do this for some parts of the ROM, particularly to see if there are ways of using any routines there. The user guide gives a great deal of information about using operating system (OS) calls, and there is little to be gained by trying to be too clever. I have found it useful for one or two discoveries, which will be revealed in Chapter 8. You may likewise like to play with it.

Some 6502 instructions

The first code is hexadecimal, the second is decimal.

Part 1 Arithmetic and logic instructions

ADC – Add with carry

Adds operand data to ACCUMULATOR and adds in the CARRY bit too, the result is left in the ACCUMULATOR.

Affects SIGN, CARRY and ZERO bits.

Codes:

Immediate	69	105	2 bytes	2 cycles
Absolute	6D	109	3 bytes	4 cycles
Absolute indexed with X	7D	125	3 bytes	4 cycles
Absolute indexed with Y	79	121	3 bytes	4 cycles
Zero page	65	101	2 bytes	2 cycles
Zero page indexed with X	75	117	2 bytes	4 cycles
Indirect indexed with Y	71	113	2 bytes	5 cycles
Indexed indirect with X	61	97	2 bytes	6 cycles

AND – Logical AND

Performs the AND function on the operand data and the ACCUMULATOR. The result is left in the ACCUMULATOR.

Affects SIGN and ZERO bits.

Codes:

Immediate	29	41	2 bytes	2 cycles
Absolute	2D	45	3 bytes	4 cycles
Absolute indexed with X	3D	61	3 bytes	4 cycles
Absolute indexed with Y	39	57	3 bytes	4 cycles
Zero page	25	37	2 bytes	3 cycles
Zero page indexed with X	35	53	2 bytes	4 cycles
Indirect indexed with Y	31	49	2 bytes	5 cycles
Indexed indirect with X	21	33	2 bytes	6 cycles

ASL – Arithmetic shift left
Shifts each bit one place to the left. 0 enters bit 0 and the previous bit 7 enters the CARRY bit.
Affects SIGN, CARRY and ZERO bits.
Codes:

ACCUMULATOR	0A	10	1 byte	2 cycles
Absolute	0E	14	3 bytes	6 cycles
Absolute indexed with X	1E	30	3 bytes	7 cycles
Zero page	06	06	2 bytes	5 cycles
Zero page indexed with X	16	22	2 bytes	6 cycles

CMP – Compare with the ACCUMULATOR
The operand data is subtracted from the ACCUMULATOR, but the ACCUMULATOR is not altered. The CARRY bit is cleared if the ACCUMULATOR is less than the operand data, otherwise it is set. The ZERO bit is set if the ACCUMULATOR is equal to the operand data, otherwise it is cleared. The SIGN bit is set if the final result is negative.
Affects SIGN, CARRY and ZERO bits.
Codes:

Immediate	C9	201	2 bytes	2 cycles
Absolute	CD	205	3 bytes	4 cycles
Absolute indexed with X	DD	221	3 bytes	4 cycles
Absolute indexed with Y	D9	217	3 bytes	4 cycles
Zero page	C5	197	2 bytes	3 cycles
Zero page indexed with X	D5	213	2 bytes	4 cycles
Indirect indexed with Y	D1	209	2 bytes	5 cycles
Indexed indirect with X	C1	193	2 bytes	6 cycles

CPX – Compare with the X-INDEX
The operand data is compared with the X-INDEX. The SIGN, CARRY and ZERO bits are affected in the same way as for CMP.
Codes:

Immediate	E0	224	2 bytes	2 cycles
Absolute	EC	236	3 bytes	4 cycles
Zero page	E4	228	2 bytes	3 cycles

CPY – Compare with the Y-INDEX
The operand data is compared with the Y-INDEX. The SIGN, CARRY and ZERO bits are affected in the same way as for CMP.
Codes:

Immediate	C0	192	2 bytes	2 cycles
Absolute	CC	204	3 bytes	4 cycles
Zero page	C4	196	2 bytes	3 cycles

DEC – Decrement

The contents of the specified register or memory location are decremented by one and put back in the same place.
Affects SIGN and ZERO bits, but not the CARRY bit.
Codes:

Absolute	CE	206	3 bytes	6 cycles
Absolute indexed with X	DE	222	3 bytes	7 cycles
Zero page	C6	198	2 bytes	5 cycles
Zero page indexed with X	D6	214	2 bytes	6 cycles
DEX (Decrement X-INDEX)	CA	202	1 byte	2 cycles
DEY (Decrement Y-INDEX)	88	136	1 byte	2 cycles

EOR – EXCLUSIVE-OR

Performs the EXCLUSIVE-OR function with the operand data and the ACCUMULATOR. The SIGN and ZERO bits are affected but not the CARRY bit.
Codes:

Immediate	49	73	2 bytes	2 cycles
Absolute	4D	77	3 bytes	4 cycles
Absolute indexed with X	5D	93	3 bytes	4 cycles
Absolute indexed with Y	59	89	3 bytes	4 cycles
Zero page	45	69	2 bytes	3 cycles
Zero page indexed with X	55	85	2 bytes	4 cycles
Indirect indexed with Y	51	81	2 bytes	5 cycles
Indexed indirect with X	41	65	2 bytes	6 cycles

INC – Increment

The contents of the specified register or memory location are incremented by one and put back in the same place.
Affects SIGN and ZERO bits, but not the CARRY bit.
Codes:

Absolute	EE	238	3 bytes	6 cycles
Absolute indexed with X	FE	254	3 bytes	7 cycles
Zero page	E6	230	2 bytes	5 cycles
Zero page indexed with X	F6	246	2 bytes	6 cycles
INX (Increment X-INDEX)	E8	232	1 byte	2 cycles
INY (Increment Y-INDEX)	C8	200	1 byte	2 cycles

LDA – Load the ACCUMULATOR

The operand data is loaded into the ACCUMULATOR.
Affects SIGN and ZERO bits but not the CARRY bit.
Codes:

Immediate	A9	169	2 bytes	2 cycles
Absolute	AD	173	3 bytes	4 cycles

Absolute indexed with X	BD	189	3 bytes	4 cycles
Absolute indexed with Y	B9	185	3 bytes	4 cycles
Zero page	A5	165	2 bytes	3 cycles
Zero page indexed with X	B5	181	2 bytes	4 cycles
Indirect indexed with Y	B1	177	2 bytes	5 cycles
Indexed indirect with X	A1	161	2 bytes	6 cycles

LDX – Load the X-INDEX
The operand data is loaded into the X-INDEX.
Affects SIGN and ZERO bits, but NOT the CARRY bit.
Codes:

Immediate	A2	162	2 bytes	2 cycles
Absolute	AE	174	3 bytes	4 cycles
Absolute indexed with Y	BE	190	3 bytes	4 cycles
Zero page	A6	166	2 bytes	3 cycles
Zero page indexed with Y	B6	182	2 bytes	4 cycles

LDY – Load the Y-INDEX
The operand data is loaded into the Y-INDEX.
Affects SIGN and ZERO bits, but NOT the CARRY bit.
Codes:

Immediate	A0	160	2 bytes	2 cycles
Absolute	AC	172	3 bytes	4 cycles
Absolute indexed with X	BC	188	3 bytes	4 cycles
Zero page	A4	164	2 bytes	3 cycles
Zero page indexed with X	B4	180	2 bytes	4 cycles

LSR – Logical shift right
The contents of the specified memory location or the ACCUMULATOR are shifted one bit to the right. Bit 7 becomes 0 and the previous bit 0 is shifted into the CARRY bit.
Affects SIGN, CARRY and ZERO bits.
Codes:

ACCUMULATOR	4A	74	1 bytes	2 cycles
Absolute	4E	78	3 bytes	6 cycles
Absolute indexed with X	5E	94	3 bytes	7 cycles
Zero page	46	70	2 bytes	5 cycles
Zero page indexed with X	56	86	2 bytes	6 cycles

NOP – No operation
A 'filler' or 'time-waster'; it affects nothing but just uses up one byte and takes two cycles.
Does not affect SIGN, CARRY or ZERO bits.
Code:

NOP (No operation)	EA	234	1 byte	2 cycles

ORA – Logical-OR
Performs the OR function with the operand data and the ACCUMULATOR.
Affects SIGN and ZERO bits, but NOT the CARRY bit.
Codes:

Immediate	09	9	2 bytes	2 cycles
Absolute	0D	13	3 bytes	4 cycles
Absolute indexed with X	1D	29	3 bytes	4 cycles
Absolute indexed with Y	19	25	3 bytes	4 cycles
Zero page	05	5	2 bytes	3 cycles
Zero page indexed with X	15	21	2 bytes	4 cycles
Indirect indexed with Y	11	17	2 bytes	5 cycles
Indexed indirect with X	01	1	2 bytes	6 cycles

ROL – Rotate left
The contents of the specified location or the ACCUMULATOR are shifted left by one bit. The CARRY bit is shifted into bit 0 and the previous bit 7 is shifted into the CARRY bit.
Affects SIGN, CARRY and ZERO bits.
Codes:

ACCUMULATOR	2A	42	1 bytes	2 cycles
Absolute	2E	46	3 bytes	6 cycles
Absolute indexed with X	3E	62	3 bytes	7 cycles
Zero page	26	38	2 bytes	5 cycles
Zero page indexed with X	36	54	2 bytes	6 cycles

ROR – Rotate right
The contents of the specified location or the ACCUMULATOR are shifted right by one bit. The CARRY bit is shifted into bit 7 and the previous bit 0 is shifted into the CARRY bit.
Affects SIGN, CARRY and ZERO bits.
Codes:

ACCUMULATOR	6A	106	1 byte	2 cycles
Absolute	6E	110	3 bytes	6 cycles
Absolute indexed with X	7E	126	3 bytes	7 cycles
Zero page	66	102	2 bytes	5 cycles
Zero page indexed with X	76	118	2 bytes	6 cycles

SBC – Subtract with carry
The operand data is subtracted from the ACCUMULATOR. If the CARRY bit is initially cleared, then a further '1' is subtracted from the result. The final result is stored in the ACCUMULATOR. If a borrow occurs durung the subtraction, the CARRY bit is cleared to 0, otherwise it is set to 1.
Affects SIGN, CARRY and ZERO bits.
Codes:

Immediate	E9	233	2 bytes	2 cycles
Absolute	ED	237	3 bytes	4 cycles
Absolute indexed with X	FD	253	3 bytes	4 cycles
Absolute indexed with Y	F9	249	3 bytes	4 cycles
Zero page	E5	229	2 bytes	3 cycles
Zero page indexed with X	F5	245	2 bytes	4 cycles
Indirect indexed with Y	F1	241	2 bytes	5 cycles
Indexed indirect with X	E1	225	2 bytes	6 cycles

STA – Store the ACCUMULATOR contents
The contents of the ACCUMULATOR are stored in the specified memory location. The SIGN, CARRY and ZERO bits are not affected.
Codes:

Absolute	BD	189	3 bytes	4 cycles
Absolute indexed with X	9D	157	3 bytes	5 cycles
Absolute indexed with Y	99	153	3 bytes	5 cycles
Zero page	85	133	2 bytes	3 cycles
Zero page indexed with X	95	149	2 bytes	4 cycles
Indirect indexed with Y	91	145	2 bytes	6 cycles
Indexed indirect with X	81	129	2 bytes	6 cycles

STX – Store the X-INDEX contents
The contents of the X-INDEX are stored in the specified memory location. The SIGN, CARRY and ZERO bits are not affected.
Codes:

Absolute	8E	142	3 bytes	4 cycles
Zero page	B6	182	2 bytes	3 cycles
Zero page indexed with Y	96	150	2 bytes	4 cycles

STY – Store the Y-INDEX contents
The contents of the Y-INDEX are copied into the specified memory location. The SIGN, CARRY and ZERO bits are not affected.
Codes:

Absolute	8C	140	3 bytes	4 cycles
Zero page	84	132	2 bytes	3 cycles
Zero page indexed with X	94	148	2 bytes	4 cycles

Part 2 Jump and branch instructions
None of the branch or jump instructions has any affect on the SIGN, CARRY or ZERO bits. Each branch instruction takes 2 cycles if it is not obeyed. If it is obeyed, it takes 3 cycles, plus one further cycle if a page boundary is crossed.

BCC (if the CARRY bit is 0)	90	144	2 bytes
BCS (if the CARRY bit is 1)	B0	176	2 bytes
BEQ (if the ZERO bit is 1)	F0	240	2 bytes

BNE (if the ZERO bit is 0)	D0	208	2 bytes	
BMI (if the SIGN BIT is 1)	30	48	2 bytes	
BPL (if the SIGN BIT is 0)	10	16	2 bytes	
JMP – Jump to operand address	4C	76	3 bytes	3 cycles
JSR – Jump to subroutine	20	32	3 bytes	6 cycles
RTS – Return from subroutine	60	96	1 byte	6 cycles
BRK – Break	00	0	1 byte	7 cycles

Execution of the program stops and the PROGRAM COUNTER is loaded with the contents of memory locations 65534 and 65535. A jump to this address then occurs. In the BBC microcomputer control passes to a special routine (see page 464 of the guide).

Part 3 Internal microprocessor register instructions

CLC – Clear the CARRY bit	18	24	1 byte	2 cycles
SEC – Set the CARRY bit	38	56	1 byte	2 cycles
CLI – Clear the INTERRUPT bit	58	88	1 byte	2 cycles
SEI – Set the INTERRUPT bit	78	120	1 byte	2 cycles

The following transfer instructions copy the contents of the first register into the second. The SIGN and ZERO bits are affected, but not the CARRY bit.

TAX – ACCUMULATOR to X-INDEX	AA	170	1 byte	2 cycles
TAY – ACCUMULATOR to Y-INDEX	A8	168	1 byte	2 cycles
TXA – X-INDEX to ACCUMULATOR	8A	138	1 byte	2 cycles
TYA – Y-INDEX to ACCUMULATOR	98	152	1 byte	2 cycles

The following instructions increment or decrement the internal registers. The SIGN and ZERO bits only are affected.

DEX – Decrement the X-INDEX	CA	202	1 byte	2 cycles
DEY – Decrement the Y-INDEX	88	136	1 byte	2 cycles
INX – Increment the X-INDEX	E8	232	1 byte	2 cycles
INY – Increment the Y-INDEX	C8	200	1 byte	2 cycles

This list is not complete. Several instructions involving interrupts exist, but the BBC microcomputer uses the interrupt system for its own purposes. It is difficult for another user to construct his own interrupts because of conflicts. These instructions are thus not described.

There are also instructions involving decimal addition and subtraction. There is no point in the user writing machine code programs involving these instructions, it is nearly always easier to use BASIC and to pass the results to a machine code routine later.

Number notation

Binary	Decimal	Hexadecimal
0000 0000	0	00
0000 0001	1	01
0000 0010	2	02
0000 0011	3	03
0000 0100	4	04
0000 0101	5	05
0000 0110	6	06
0000 0111	7	07
0000 1000	8	08
0000 1001	9	09
0000 1010	10	0A
0000 1011	11	0B
0000 1100	12	0C
0000 1101	13	0D
0000 1110	14	0E
0000 1111	15	0F
0001 0000	16	10
0001 0001	17	11
0001 0010	18	12
0001 0011	19	13
0001 0100	20	14
0001 0101	21	15
0001 0110	22	16
0001 0111	23	17
0001 1000	24	18
0001 1001	25	19
0001 1010	26	1A
0001 1011	27	1B
0001 1100	28	1C
0001 1101	29	1D
0001 1110	30	1E
0001 1111	31	1F
0010 0000	32	20
0011 0000	48	30
0100 0000	64	40
0101 0000	80	50
0110 0000	96	60
0111 0000	112	70
1000 0000	128	80
1001 0000	144	90
1010 0000	160	A0

1011 0000	176	B0
1100 0000	192	C0
1101 0000	224	D0
1110 0000	232	E0
1111 0000	240	F0
1111 1111	255	FF

Solutions to problems

The following are not necessarily the only solutions. The test of any solution is whether it actually works. 6502 SIMULATION lets you try out your own ideas in 99 per cent of all cases.

```
1 LDA #50
  STA  2
2 LDA  7
  STA  6
3 LDA #1
  STA  1
  LDA #2
  STA  2
  LDA #3
  STA  3
4 LDA #0
  STA  1
  STA  2
  STA  3
  etc.
5 LDY #5
  STY  1
  LDX  1
```

6 The contents of location 5 are the data contained in the memory at the address number 5. This data can have any value from 0 to 255. The address of location 5 is in fact 5 (the fifth address).

7 Data write: the data is copied from the ACCUMULATOR, or the X- or Y-INDEX into the addressed location in memory.

Data read: the data in a memory location is copied into the ACCUMULATOR, or the X- or Y-INDEX. LDA 2 is a data read instruction.

8 (i) 512
(ii) 3082
(iii) 10440
(iv) 20480
(v) 60000

9 (i) 0,1
(ii) 0,4
(iii) 1,16
(iv) 64,31
(v) 255,255

10
```
CLC
LDA #45
ADC #54
```
11
```
CLC
LDA  4
ADC  5
STA  3
```
12
```
LDA #194
STA  1
LDA #1
STA  2

LDA #28
STA  3
LDA #2
STA  4

CLC
LDA  1
ADC  3
STA  5
LDA  2
ADC  4
STA  6
```
13
```
LDA #225
STA  1
LDA #100
STA  2

CLC
LDA  1
ADC  2
STA  3
LDA #0
ADC #0
STA  4
```
14
```
LDA #232
STA  5
LDA #3
STA  6
```

```
    CLC
    LDA   5
    ADC #1
    STA   5
    LDA   6
    ADC #0
    STA   6
15  32768 + 32768
    32769 + 32767
    32770 + 32766
    32771 + 32765
    etc.
16  SEC
    LDA #25
    SBC  #25
17  LDA #15
    STA   1
    LDA #45
    STA   2

    SEC
    LDA   1
    SBC   2
    STA   3
18  LDA #15
    STA   1        Place the number
    LDA #3         in the stores
    STA   2
    CLC
    LDA   1
    ADC   1
    STA   3        Add the number
    LDA   2        to itself
    ADC   2
    STA   4

    SEC
    LDA   3
    SBC   1
    STA   3        Subtract the first
    LDA   4        number, hopefully
    SBC   2        leaving the same
    STA   4        number in both stores.
```

19 LDA #0
STA 1
STA 2
SEC
LDA 1
SBC #1
STA 1 — The result is 255,255
LDA 2 — the two-byte
SBC #0 — equivalent of −1.
STA 2

20 5
85 is 0 1 0 1 0 1 0 1
45 is 0 0 1 0 1 1 0 1

21 85 AND 45 is 5

22 85 OR 45 is 125

23 85 EOR 45 is 120

24 LDA 5
AND #249
STA 5

25 LDA 5
ORA #127
STA 5

26 10000...the last JMP instruction

27 A crash; the program continually jumps back to repeat itself (just like 100 GOTO 100 in BASIC).

28 BNE −9 causes a branch back to line 16209, thus omitting the CLC instruction. This would cause an error if the CARRY bit had been set, but there is no danger of that here, so the result will be the same as with BNE −10.

BCC −10 will cause about eighty-five repeats of the loop, since the CARRY bit will not become set until the addition exceeds 255. The DEY instruction has no effect on the CARRY bit.

7 Assembly language programming

'If you want to get somewhere else, you must run at least twice as fast as that!'
(Lewis Carroll, *Through the Looking Glass*)

Microcomputers are not designed for running machine code programs in the same way that they are for BASIC. There are generally more problems in entering, saving, loading and running such programs. In particular machine code programs contain no error checking procedures like BASIC. If you ask the microcomputer (in BASIC) to GOTO a non-existent line, it will stop and tell you that this is not possible. If you tell a microprocessor to JMP to the wrong address, it will still jump and may cause a crash. This may mean that you lose all control of the machine and have to reset to regain control.

Crashes are quite common in machine code programming. Fortunately, the BBC microcomputer can recover from such events without loss of program in most cases. The BREAK key will usually regain control over the microprocessor. Then, if OLD is typed, the original program will usually be restored too. The exceptions are when the crash has written rubbish into the part of memory used by BASIC. The message 'Bad program' might then appear, so that it has to be reloaded. This is not a disaster provided you saved the program on cassette tape or disk before it was run.

Machine code graphics

Machine code graphics give a particularly good introduction to machine code programming in general, as well as being important in their own right. The screen gives a visible record of the contents of the memory locations, so direct observations on the course of the program can be made. In Chapter 2 we looked at BASIC methods of making the *-character move around the screen. We shall now study how to do this in machine code.

A program to place 40 *-characters along the top line of the screen (in MODE 7) is relatively simple. To begin with we write it in the way we used in Chapter 6.

```
      LDX #0         ;first screen position
      LDA #42        ;get value for *-character
.next STA &7C00,X    ;place * in screen position
      INX
      CPX #40        ;All positions done?
      BNE -8         ;No, do next position
      RTS            ;Yes, so finish
```

This now has to be converted into the binary codes that the microprocessor understands. With most other microcomputers there are three ways of doing this, two of which involve hand compilation. Each mnemonic is looked up in a table and converted into the correct decimal or hexadecimal code. Branch displacements or offsets must be carefully worked out and actual addresses calculated and split into their high byte, low byte components. Finally, the codes must be entered into the memory from BASIC. The BBC microcomputer user is most fortunate in having an assembler to do this instead and therefore can ignore hand compilation altogether.

Assembler

The BBC assembler allows a mnemonic program to be entered as part of a BASIC program. Only those who have had to use microcomputers without an assembler can appreciate the value of this. Its inclusion puts the BBC microcomputer designers into the genius class.

The method of using this assembler is shown below. Each instruction is preceded by a line number, as in BASIC, but these numbers have no significance for the machine code program itself; they are simply there as a programming aid, to allow the insertion of extra lines, deletions or for listings, etc. You cannot GOTO any of these line numbers from BASIC, nor JMP to them in machine code. In Chapter 6 our line numbers represented the memory locations where the instructions (or rather their binary codes) were stored. This is not true for the BBC assembler.

This is how the 40-* program looks when listed in any MODE other than MODE 7. (In MODE 7 the [and] brackets are printed as left and right arrows, also the backslash character becomes the symbol for one half.)

```
   1  MODE 7
   2  HIMEM = &4000:REM RESERVE SPACE FOR MACHINE CODE
      PROGRAM
   3
1000  FOR pass = 0 TO 3 STEP 3
1010  P% = &4000:REM START ADDRESS OF MACHINE CODE
      PROGRAM
1020  [OPT pass
1030                              \STARS
1040                              \THIS PROGRAM PLACES 40
                                   *-CHARACTERS
1050                              \ON THE TOP LINE OF THE SCREEN
1060
1070  .stars    LDX #0             POINT TO FIRST POSITION
1080            LDA #42            GET *-CHARACTER
1090  .nxtpos   STA &7C00,X        SEND IT TO SCREEN
1100            INX
1110            CPX #40            ALL POSITIONS DONE?
1120            BNE nxtpos         NO DO NEXT POSITION
1130            RTS                YES SO FINISH
```

```
1140  ]
1150  NEXT pass
1160  FOR T=1 TO 2000:NEXT T:REM Delay to emphasize the rapidity of
      the machine code routine
1190  CLS
1200  CALL stars
```

There are several points to be noted about this listing. Firstly, line 1010 sets the program counter (P%) to the desired starting address of the machine code routine. This is where the machine code is placed when the program is run. This facility enables us to put different parts of the program into different locations, particularly to keep tables apart from the program. To prevent BASIC from competing with our machine code program, we tell BASIC not to use any locations at or above HIMEM. Thus line 2 of the program sets HIMEM to the desired limit for BASIC. This instruction must be placed very early in the program, preferably immediately after setting the MODE. Care must also be taken not to be too greedy, or BASIC will die of starvation! HIMEM = &4000 leaves BASIC with at least eight kilobytes, which is enough for most purposes. It gives us fifteen kilobytes for our machine code programs in MODE 7, at least six kilobytes in MODE 4, 5 and 6 and practically nothing at all for the other modes (so if you want to use them with machine code programs, you will need to set HIMEM lower still).

BBC BASIC does not allow a variable (or **label** as it is called in this case) like nxtpos to be used before it has been declared. In this particular program nxtpos is declared first and afterwards line 1120 of the machine code routine makes reference to it, so there is no problem. In the case of a forward branch, however, the label would be referred to before being declared and the program would signal an error. This is prevented by making two **passes** through the assembly listing, the first time with OPT 0 selected and the second time with OPT 3 selected. OPT 0 allows the listing to be assembled but suppresses the error messages caused by any such forward referencing. The first pass through the listing does, however, assign addresses to the labels, so that during the second pass all labels can be referenced without error. If P% is declared before entering the FOR...NEXT loop, BASIC compiles the assembly language routine into two different places and this may cause complications later. The format given above should therefore be adhered to every time.

Note too that the BASIC statement to run this machine code routine **(CALL stars)** is reached after the machine code has been assembled. It is more usual to have such CALLs at the start, in which case the assembly language routine could be placed as a subroutine at the end of the program and compiled from a GOSUB at the beginning. Most of the programs to be described later are like this.

Because of the peculiar nature of the BBC microcomputer screen memory, machine code graphics routines should be called after clearing the screen with CLS. If this is not done, then the address &7C00 may not be at the top of the screen, and the result will be rather different from that expected.

It can be seen that it is not necessary to calculate the branch displacement (offset) in line 1120. The place in the program to where we intend to branch is already labelled '.nxtpos'.

We simply state BNE nxtpos and leave the assembler to work out the offset for us. If the branch exceeds the limits of −128 to + 127, the assembler will tell us of this error during pass 3.

Note, finally, the ability to put comments into the source program. These must be placed after the backslash (\ ) and they behave just like BASIC REM statements. The microprocessor ignores them, but they are invaluable for explaining how the program works. This is essential, not only for others, who may wish to read the program to see how it works but also for the programmer; it is incredible how incomprehensible an undocumented program becomes after even a few weeks. Note that the backslash is only essential if the comment is the only thing on a particular line. After an instruction it is not always needed – if there is a space between the operand and the comment and if the comment begins with an alphabetic character then all is well.

When this program is run, it first compiles the assembly language part (between the [ ] brackets) into machine code and stores these codes in the memory starting at location &4000 (as we instructed in line 1010). During OPT 3 the assembled routine is printed on the screen like this:

```
>RUN
4000                OPT pass
4000               \ STARS
4000               \ THIS PROGRAM PLACES 40 *-CHARACTERS
4000               \ ON THE TOP LINE OF THE SCREEN
4000
4000   A2 00        .stars LDX #0 POINT TO FIRST POSITION
4002   A9 2A        LDA #42 GET *-CHARACTER
4004   9D 00 7C     .nxtpos STA &7C00,X SEND IT TO SCREEN
4007   E8           INX
4008   E0 28        CPX #40 ALL POSITIONS DONE?
400A   D0 F8        BNE nxtpos NO DO NEXT POSITION
400C   60           RTS YES SO FINISH
```

The mnemonic instructions and comments are unchanged, but now they are preceded by new sets of numbers. The first numbers (4000 etc.) are the memory locations where the machine codes for the instructions are now placed. This is exactly the same as in 6502 SIMULATION. Because some instructions take two bytes and others take three bytes, these memory locations are apparently not consecutive, but they are. Note that these numbers are in hexadecimal.

The second set of numbers are the codes themselves, also in hexadecimal. Since the BBC assembler does all the work for us, you need not bother with these, but spare a thought for those who still have to compile programs by hand. They have to look up each instruction code and work out each branch offset with pencil and paper. What lucky people we are!

We are still, however, making very little use of the power of the assembler. Here is a better version of STARS:

```
   1  MODE 7
   2  HIMEM = &4000:REM RESERVE SPACE FOR MACHINE CODE
      PROGRAM
   3
 900  char = 42
 910  screen = &7C00
 920  max = 40
 930
1000  FOR pass = 0 TO 3 STEP 3
1010  P% = &4000:REM START ADDRESS OF MACHINE CODE
      PROGRAM
1020  [OPT pass
1030                                \BETTER STARS
1040                                \THIS PROGRAM PLACES 40
                                     *-CHARACTERS
1050                                \ON THE TOP LINE OF THE SCREEN
1060
1070  .charput  LDX #0               POINT TO FIRST POSITION
1080            LDA #char            GET *-CHARACTER
1090  .nxtpos   STA screen,X         SEND IT TO SCREEN
1100            NX
1110            CPX #max             ALL POSITIONS DONE?
1120            BNE nxtpos           NO DO NEXT POSITION
1130            RTS                  YES SO FINISH
1140  ]
1150  NEXT pass
1160  FOR T=1 TO 2000:NEXT T
1190  CLS
1200  CALL charput
```

This ability to use **symbols,** as they are called, to refer to different quantities is of no advantage in a short program. But in a long program we might want to refer to 'char' many times. Later, we might wish to replace this by a different character. It would be time consuming to go through the whole program, changing every 42 to 81 say, but a single change to line 900 (char = 81) achieves the same end. The same is true about the screen position for these characters **(screen)** and the number to be placed there **(max).**

Direct coding

There are other ways of entering binary codes into memory for the BBC microcomputer. One of these is via BASIC and is particularly useful for loading tables into the memory. Suppose, for example, you wanted to use the sine functions of numbers from 0 to 255 in a machine code program. It is easy to do this from BASIC with the following routine:

```
10  FOR i = 0 TO 255
20  ?(&4200 + i)=128 + 127 * SIN(i*PI/128)
30  NEXT i
```

This constructs a sine table of one cycle stored in 256 successive bytes of memory. The numbers can then be accessed from this table in machine code. The number of degrees being looked up in the table is first loaded into the X-INDEX and the sine value retrieved with

```
LDA &4200,X
```

We shall see several examples of this technique in later programs. In particular it is used in the wave motion programs and the large digits routine described later in this chapter.

This method can also be used for entering machine code routines directly into the memory. The program above could be written as follows:

```
 10  FOR location = &4000 TO &400C
 20  READ code
 30  ?location = code
 40  NEXT location
 50  DATA 162,0,169,42,157,0,124,232,224,40,208,248,96
100  CLS
200  CALL &4000
```

Apart from using up less memory (of doubtful value) the only advantage of this is that it hides your program from others. However, a determined poacher could easily load it and disassemble it to see how it works. This technique is thus only of historical interest now. REACTION TIMER (6) uses this technique because that program was written before I learned how to do forward referencing by making two passes through the assembler.

A DISASSEMBLER (37) is listed in the Appendix for those who wish to use it for the purposes mentioned above. Its main application is for investigating the operating system of the BBC microcomputer itself. This may reveal several possible ways of making use of the operating system in user-written programs, particularly its keyboard handling and display routines. However, since the user guide is so helpful in providing these details, I am not sure that it will yield much new information.

Description of the 40-* program

The initial line numbers are used to refer to particular lines. Lines 900, 910 and 920 declare the values of the variables to be used in the assembly language program. Some of these are decimal and some are hexadecimal, but BASIC will take care of this. Line 1070 is the start of the assembly language program, so it is given its name with the label '.charput'. LDX #0 sets up the X-INDEX as a pointer, initializing it to the first screen position (0). In line 1080 the ACCUMULATOR is loaded with the screen value of the character to be displayed — in this case the *-character. The # symbol in front of the symbol 'char' shows that it is the value of char that is loaded (that is, char is not an address). The instruction **LDA char** means **'load the ACCUMULATOR from the address called char'.** This difference between immediate and memory addressing is exactly as described in Chapter 6, except that there we used numbers instead of symbols.

In line 1090 the value of char is sent to its screen position using the indexed address mode; the value of the X-INDEX is added to the value of the operand, which is called

screen. This value is an address (which was chosen in line 910). Line 1090 is labelled 'nxtpos' so that a BRANCH can be made to it later.

Next, in line 1100, the X-INDEX is incremented to point to the next adjacent screen position. Line 1110 compares the new value of the X-INDEX with the maximum allowable value ('max', which was initially set to 40, because there are forty columns on the screen). If the two values are equal, then the routine finishes, returning control to BASIC with RTS. But this only happens after forty *s have been printed. Initially the X-INDEX will be smaller than max, in which case the branch condition will succeed and the program counter will go back eight bytes to the label 'nxtpos'. The value of char will next be stored in screen + 1, then, during the next loop in screen + 2 and so on. This will happen a total of forty times, giving a whole row of *-characters.

Branching

In Chapter 6 we had a brief look at branching, but this is such a vital concept that we must now study it more deeply. A branch is not a direction to jump to a particular place, it is more like a jump over a particular number of bytes. The numerical operand of a branch instruction is the number of bytes to be missed out. This branching, or **skipping** as it is also called, can occur in the forward direction or in the reverse direction. The purpose of a BRANCH is to perform the equivalent of IF...THEN...ELSE in BASIC. In the above program we required:

IF the X-INDEX is not equal to max, THEN go back to nxtpos, ELSE return to BASIC.

With this sort of BRANCH the ZERO bit in the STATUS register is inspected and whether the branch is obeyed (succeeds) or whether the branch is ignored (fails) depends upon whether the ZERO bit is set or cleared. We have already mentioned the STATUS register bits that are used in this way, they are as follows:

	Set to 1 by	**Cleared to 0 by**
The CARRY bit	addition, or subtraction, or shifting	addition, or subtraction, or shifting
The SIGN bit	Negative result	Positive result
The ZERO bit	Zero result	Non-zero result

By 'result' in this context is meant the result of any operation, whether loading, storing, adding or subtracting to the ACCUMULATOR, the X-INDEX or the Y-INDEX. The only exceptions are INCREMENT and DECREMENT, which do not affect the CARRY bit, although these operations do affect the other two bits.

Here are the more useful 6502 BRANCHING operations:

```
BEQ   BRANCH IF EQUAL TO ZERO          (if the ZERO bit is set to 1)
BNE   BRANCH IF NOT EQUAL TO ZERO      (if the ZERO bit is cleared)
BCC   BRANCH IF CARRY BIT IS CLEARED
BCS   BRANCH IF CARRY BIT IS SET
BPL   BRANCH IF PLUS                   (if the SIGN bit is cleared)
BMI   BRANCH IF MINUS                  (if the SIGN bit is set)
```

The OPERAND of a branch instruction is the number of bytes of the machine code program to be skipped over. This is not difficult to calculate, but it is far more convenient to use labels. There will not then have to be a recalculation every time that extra instructions are inserted. The only problem is that forward branches cannot occur over more than 127 bytes. Backward branches cannot go more than 128 bytes. This means that the position to be branched to must not be too far ahead nor too far behind the position of the branch instruction. If this happens error 1 (out of range) will occur during the second pass through the assembler.

This restriction is overcome by using a JMP instruction. For example, the 40-* program might contain a large number of extra instructions, making it impossible to branch back to nxtpos. The relevant part might look like this:

```
1070  .charput   LDX #0
1080             LDA #char
1090  .nxtpos    STA screen,X
1100  (many more instructions here)
1200  ............................
1300  ............................
1400  ............................
1500  ............................
1600  ............................
1700  ............................
1710             INX
1720             CPX #max     ALL POSITIONS DONE?
1730             BEQ done     YES SO FINISH
1740             JMP nxtpos   NO DO NEXT POSITION
1750  .done      RTS
```

Because the JMP can be to anywhere in the memory, this structure will always work. Program 26 (MOLECULAR MOTION) shows several examples where this has become necesssary.

One advantage of a BRANCH over a JMP is that the latter must refer to a particular place in the memory. Once the assembly language routine has been compiled, the position of this particular place cannot be changed. A JMP operand refers to one particular memory location, so, if the compiled machine code routine is **relocated** (put) somewhere else, say beginning at location &5000, then the JMP operand will have to be recalculated and changed. Since the assembler does this automatically you rarely need to bother about it in normal progams. You would tend to use JMP instructions for unconditional jumps and BRANCH instructions otherwise.

But, if you ever intend to burn your program into EPROM (see Chapter 9) all JMP operands will need to be changed to fit the new addresses. In such instances unconditional jumps are better made by setting the correct STATUS bit to a known value and branching accordingly. For example, the 40-* program could be written as follows:

```
1070  .charput LDX #0           POINT TO FIRST POSITION
1080           LDA #char        GET * CHARACTER
1090  .nxtpos  STA screen,X     SEND IT TO SCREEN
1100           INX
1110           CPX #max         ALL POSITIONS DONE ?
1120           BEQ done         YES SO FINISH
1130           CLC
1140           BCC nxtpos       DO NEXT POSITION
                                (UNCONDITIONAL BRANCH)
1150  .done    RTS
```

Line 1130 now contains the CLC instruction (clear the CARRY bit) and this is followed by BCC (branch if the CARRY bit is cleared). Well of course the CARRY bit is cleared, so this condition will always succeed! This technique implements the unconditional branch found on some other microprocessors (e.g. the Z80). In the previous version of this program we achieved the same result by a simple JMP instruction. The only advantage of this second method is that the BRANCH occurs over the required number of bytes, irrespective of where the whole routine is located. It can thus be placed anywhere in the memory, in particular, it can be burned into an EPROM without any changes. Note, however, that this only works if the number of bytes skipped over is less than 128.

Screenfill

The X-INDEX can only point to screen positions that are no more than 255 away from the address called 'screen'. How then can we fill the whole screen with *-characters? The solution lies in being able to change the value of screen while the program is being run. This is done in the following **self-modifying** program:

```
   1  MODE7
   2  HIMEM=&4000:REM RESERVE SPACE FOR MACHINE CODE
      PROGRAM
   3
 900  star     = 42
 910
1000  FOR pass = 0 TO 3 STEP 3
1010  P% = &4000:REM START ADDRESS OF MACHINE CODE
      PROGRAM
1020  [OPT pass
1030                             \STARS
1040                             \THIS PROGRAM FILLS THE SCREEN
1050                             \WITH STARS
1100  .begin   LDA #&00           SET OPERAND TO LOW BYTE
```

```
1110            STA &400F       ADDRESS
1120            LDA #&7C        SET OPERAND TO HIGH BYTE
1130            STA &4010       ADDRESS
1140            LDX #4          FOUR PAGES TO BE SENT
1150            LDA #star       GET *-CHARACTER
1160  .nxtpos   STA &FFFF       SEND TO SCREEN
1170            INC &400F       DO NEXT POSITION
1180            BNE nxtpos      ALL DONE ON THIS PAGE?
1190            INC &4010       YES TURN TO NEXT PAGE
1200            DEX             ALL PAGES DONE?
1210            BNE nxtpos      NO DO NEXT PAGE
1220            RTS             FINISH
1230]
1300  NEXT pass
1350  CLS
1360  FOR T=1 TO 2000:NEXT T
1400  CALL begin
```

The effect of this program is quite electrifying, a thousand stars hit the screen simultaneously! A picture, or screenful of text could be flashed on and off the screen just as quickly (as in FAST SCREEN TRANSFER, 36). We now have to see how it works. To aid this discussion the compiled routine is reproduced in the form that the assembler displays it, but with the comments omitted.

```
4000  A9 00      .begin       LDA #&00
4002  8D 0F 40   STA &400F
4005  A9 7C      LDA #&7C
4007  8D 10 40   STA &4010
400A  A2 04      LDX #4
400C  A9 2A      LDA #star
400E  8D FF FF   .nxtpos      STA &FFFF
4011  EE 0F 40   INC &400F
4014  D0 F8      BNE nxtpos
4016  EE 10 40   INC &4010
4019  CA         DEX
401A  D0 F2      BNE nxtpos
401C  60         RTS
```

The first task is to discover where the machine code program has stored the value of the screen address operand. A look at the assembly listing indicates that the binary code for this operand is placed in locations &400F and &4010. The numbers in the left column are where the machine code instructions are stored in the memory. These are consecutive, because the microprocessor will fetch each one in turn and execute it. The numbers in the next columns are the hexadecimal machine codes that are placed into the successive memory locations by the assembler. In a single column they look like this:

```
4000  A9
4001  00
4002  8D
4003  0F
4004  40
4005  A9
4006  7C
4007  8D
4008  10
4009  40
400A  A2
400B  04
400C  A9
400D  2A
400E  8D
400F  FF   (low byte of screen address)
4010  FF   (high byte of screen address)
4011  EE
4012  0F
4013  40
4014  D0
4015  F8
4016  EE
4017  10
4018  40
4019  CA
401A  D0
401B  F2
401C  60
```

Location &400F contains the low byte of the operand address for screen and location &4010 contains the high byte address. To begin with these locations contain &FF and &FF which is clearly the wrong address altogether. When the routine is executed **(CALL begin)** the routine first places &00 in location &400F and then puts &7C in location &4010. Thus when the program reaches the '.nxtpos STA screen' instruction, the operand address has been correctly set to &7C00.

Later the low byte of this address is incremented to &01 to point to the next screen location at &7C01 and the routine returns to nxtpos once again. This is repeated a total of 256 times until location &400F contains &00 again. At this point the first 'BNE nxtpos' instruction fails and the high byte of the screen position is incremented to &7D to point to the next page of 256 bytes. This continues for a total of four pages, counted by the X-INDEX. Throughout the execution of this routine the program thus changes itself, so that it contains a different screen address every time.

Having now explained how to do it, we shall now abandon this technique in favour of a better one! There are two reasons for this. Firstly this routine would be tied forever to RAM, it would never be possible to burn it into EPROM, because locations &400F and &4010 (or whatever they became) could not then be altered whenever the routine is executed. Secondly, and of very great importance, programs that change themselves are very difficult to interpret later. Explaining what a program does is as important as doing it in the first place, because no program is ever absolutely error-free, and you may wish to return to it weeks or even years later to change it. A properly laid out and documented program will save many hours of frustration later.

There are instances where self-modifying programs give the best results, particularly if speed is at a premium. The SCROLL routine described later in this chapter is a good example of this, so it is worth noting the technique. Be very sparing in its use, however, or you will make your programs almost unintelligible.

Indirect-indexed addressing

If we do not allow ourselves to use the self-modifying technique, how can we address all 1000 screen positions? The solution lies in a new and very powerful addressing mode that we have not yet mentioned – indirect-indexed addressing. This mode uses only page zero addresses and only works with the Y-INDEX. For example,

```
LDA (&80),Y
```

The operand consists of a single byte, which is an address on page zero of the memory. This address does not contain data, but the low byte of another address, called the **interim address.** The adjacent location on page zero (which is location &81) contains the high byte of this interim address. The microprocessor gets the two parts of this interim address and uses them to calculate the final address it is looking for.

An analogy may help to explain what is going on. If a postman delivers a letter to a particular house in a street, that is absolute addressing. If, however, he does not know the final address, he might take it to the corner shop and ask, 'Where should I deliver this?'. At the corner shop (the page zero address in the mnemonic) the postman is told an interim address which he could use to find the correct final address. This is the meaning of 'indirect', the corner shop contains information about the final address, it is not itself the final address. In the corner shop the postman might be told, 'The house you want is five houses further down than Mr Smith's'. In this analogy, Mr Smith's is the interim address. Note that the interim address is in two parts, the low byte being in the zero page location specified by the operand, while the high byte is in the next higher zero page location.

It now remains to use this idea in conjunction with indexed addressing. The interim address that has been collected from the the zero page address is not the final address. To obtain this, the value of the Y-INDEX is added to produce the required final address. A concrete example should help to remove any remaining mystery:

```
 900  screen = &80:REM zero page address
 910  !screen = &7C00:REM fix interim address
 920
1000  [
```

```
1100  .............
1140  LDY #&19          Set the Y-INDEX to 25
1150  LDA #42           Get screen value of *-character
1160  STA (screen),Y    Place character on screen
1170  RTS               Finish
```

Line 900 sets up two adjacent memory locations (&80 and &81) as the low byte and high byte respectively of the zero page location we are calling 'screen'. The instruction in line 910 puts the correct interim address into the successive zero page locations &80 and &81, (low byte, high byte order). The ! operator actually puts four bytes into the four successive locations &80 to &83. &00 goes into location &80 (the low byte of the screen address), &7C goes into location &81 (the high byte of the screen address) and &00 goes into &82 and &83. The assembly routine contains an instruction to set the value of the Y-INDEX to 25 (hex &19). The next instruction puts the screen value of the *-character into the ACCUMULATOR and the next in line 1160 places this value where we want it on the screen. Where is that?

The microprocessor goes to locations &80 and &81 on zero page and gets the interim address from there. Location &80 contains &00 and location &81 contains &7C, so the interim address is &7C00. The Y-INDEX contains &19 which is added to the interim address to give the final address &7C19. This is the screen address where the *-character should appear.

We can now use this instruction to fill the whole screen with stars. The machine code routine to do this follows. The screen consists of nearly four pages of memory (not quite 1024 bytes). This number is kept in a location called 'pages'. Indirect-indexed addressing is used to place the * in the first position, then the Y-INDEX is incremented to point to the next position and so on until the Y-INDEX reaches 256. This is, of course, the same as 0, so BNE nxtpos (line 1150) finally fails. The page counter (X-INDEX) is then reduced by one and the process repeats until all four pages have been done. The significant difference between this program and the previous self-modifying version is that the screen address, which is changed every 256 times, is now kept separate from the program itself. Even if the above program were stored permanently in ROM, it would still work. When this program is run, see how long it takes between the screen's going blank (CLS in line 1350) and the 1000 stars being printed. Again, it is virtually instantaneous.

Screenfill

```
   1  MODE7
   2  HIMEM = &4000:REM RESERVE SPACE FOR MACHINE CODE
      PROGRAM
   3
 900  star = 42
 910  pages = 4:       REM Number of pages to be sent
 920  screen = &80:  REM Low/high bytes of interim address of screen
 930  !screen = &7C00
 940
1000  FOR pass = 0 TO 3 STEP 3
```

```
1010  P% = &4000:REM START ADDRESS OF MACHINE CODE
      PROGRAM
1020  [OPTpass
1030                               \STARS
1040                               \THIS PROGRAM FILLS THE SCREEN
1050                               \WITH STARS
1100  .begin   LDX #pages           SET COUNTER TO 4 PAGES
1110  .nxtpage LDY #0               POINT TO FIRST POSITION
1120  .nxtpos  LDA #star
1130           STA (screen),Y       SEND IT TO SCREEN
1140           INY                  MOVE TO NEXT POSITION – END OF
                                    PAGE?
1150           BNE nxtpos           NO DO NEXT POSITION
1160           INC screen+1         DO ANOTHER SCREEN PAGE
1180           DEX                  ALL PAGES DONE?
1190           BNE nxtpage          NO DO NEXT PAGE
1200           RTS                  FINISH
1210]
1300  NEXT pass
1310  FOR T=1 TO 2000:NEXT T
1350  CLS
1400  CALL begin
```

OS calls

We noted before, the dire warnings made to those who address memory directly, rather than use the 'proper' methods. But as I pointed out then, there is no alternative, if you want fast graphics. This point of view will now be justified. First, here is a BASIC program to carry out the screenfill described above.

```
100   MODE7
110   FOR row = 0 TO 24
120   PRINT TAB(0,row);"****************************************";
130   NEXT row
```

Next here is a BASIC version that uses the forbidden direct memory access (to illustrate the principles).

```
100   MODE 7
110   FOR I=&7C00 TO &7FE7
120   ?I=42
130   NEXT I
```

As you will see the second program is slower than the first and also it will not work when a second processor is added to the BBC microcomputer. The addresses &7C00 to &7EF7 will not be the screen memory from the point of view of the second processor. Programs thus ought to be written using the operating system calls. Here is a machine code version that obeys the BBC microcomputer user guide rules. Instead of accessing memory directly, the stars are sent via 'oswrch', which is a routine located at &FFEE in ROM. The program is fundamentally that on page 315 of the guide. The X and Y-INDEXES are acting only as counters, they do not 'point' to the screen in any way.

```
  1  MODE7
 10  oswrch = &FFEE
 20  DIM P% 100
 30  [OPT0
 40  .start   LDA #42
 50           LDX #4       FOUR PAGES
 60           LDY #0       256 BYTES PER PAGE
 70  .loop    JSR oswrch
 80           DEY          DO NEXT POSITION
 90           BNE loop
100           DEX          DO NEXT PAGE
110           BNE loop
120           RTS
130]
200  CLS
210  CALL start
```

Load and run all three versions of this screenfill program. In the BASIC programs the screen starts to fill straightaway. The machine code program has to be compiled first, which takes half a second, and then the screen clears and the screenfill routine is called. It can be seen that there is little to choose between any of these programs (the direct write to memory in the second program is the slowest). Compared with the other two machine code routines already discussed, these latter programs are positively snail-like. So if you want fast graphics, you can forget about the OS calls.

Instant pictures

The screenfill routine can be used to paint instant pictures. The picture to be placed on the screen is first drawn with the methods described in Chapter 2. It is then transferred to a different part of the memory (say &7000 to &73E7) with the BASIC routine:

```
  1  HIMEM = &7000
  2
100  FOR i = 0 TO 999
110  ?(i + &7000) = ?(i + &7C00)
120  NEXT i
```

This program should be loaded beforehand and run to copy the contents of the screen memory to the new locations. The following machine code routine will transfer the picture back to the screen when it is called:

Flash

```
   1  MODE7
   2  HIMEM = &4000:REM RESERVE SPACE FOR MACHINE CODE
      PROGRAM
   3
 910  pages = 4: REM Number of pages to be sent
 920  screen = &80:REM Low/high bytes of interim address of screen
 930  !screen = &7C00
 940  source = &84:REM Low/high bytes of interim address of source
 950  !source = &7000
 960
1000  FOR pass = 0 TO 3 STEP 3
1010  P% = &4000:REM START ADDRESS OF MACHINE CODE
      PROGRAM
1020  [OPTpass
1030                                \PAINT
1040                                \THIS PROGRAM TRANSFERS A
                                     PICTURE
1050                                \FROM &7000 UPWARDS TO THE
                                     SCREEN
1100  .paint    LDX #pages           SET COUNTER TO 4 PAGES
1110  .nxpage   LDY #0               POINT TO FIRST POSITION
1120  .nxtpos   LDA (source),Y       GET BYTE
1130            STA (screen),Y       SEND IT TO SCREEN
1140            INY                  MOVE TO NEXT POSITION – END OF
                                     PAGE?
1150            BNE nxtpos           NO DO NEXT POSITION
1160            INC screen+1         DO ANOTHER SCREEN PAGE
1170            INC source+1
1180            DEX                  ALL PAGES DONE?
1190            BNE nxpage           NO DO NEXT PAGE
1200            RTS                  FINISH
1210]
1300  NEXT pass
1350  CLS
1400  CALL paint
```

The technique used here also works with the high resolution modes, except that it takes much longer. An example is given in program 36, where the 'flashed' pictures are just big words. The same routine will also work with pictures, except that you rapidly run out of memory for storing the pictures.

Animation

By adjusting the starting position and the number of bytes transferred, the 'flash' routine in MODE 4 can produce excellent animation for small pictures. If several different versions of, say, an animal, are saved in successive blocks of memory, each one can be called in succession, placed on the screen for a few centiseconds and then replaced with the next picture. This is the traditional way of making cartoons and animated diagrams become relatively easy with this technique. More usually, it is parts of pictures that are to be moved to the screen in this way (for example the piston in the cylinder of a motor car, or a happy face for reinforcement of a correct answer in a quiz program).

Low resolution part-pictures can be transferred in the same way as described in Chapter 2, with two tables, one to hold the character (what) and the other to hold the relative place for that character (where).

Engine

```
  1 MODE7
  2 HIMEM=&4000:REM RESERVE SPACE FOR MACHINE CODE
    PROGRAM
 10 GOSUB 900
 20
100 REM LOAD DATA INTO TABLES
110 max = 35
120 FOR i=1 TO max
130 READ position
140 ?(where+i) = position
150 READ character
160 ?(what+i) = character
170 NEXT i
180 DATA 0,32,1,252,2,252,3,32,4,32,5,32,6,32
190 DATA 40,32,41,234,42,255,43,240,44,240,45,240,46,244
191 DATA 80,32,81,234,82,255,83,255,84,255,85,255,86,255
192 DATA 120,32,121,250,122,255,123,255,124,255,125,255,126,255
193 DATA 160,32,161,32,162,79,163,32,164,32,165,79,166,32
194
200 REM SET UP SCREEN FOR GRAPHICS
210 CLS
220 FOR i=31744 TO 32703 STEP 40
230 ?i=151
240 NEXT i
250 REM MOVE PICTURE
260 FOR place = 1 TO 30
270 !screen = !screen + 1
280 CALL partpic
285 FOR T = 1 TO 30:NEXT T:REM DELAY
290 NEXT place
300 END
310
```

```
900  REM assembly language subroutine
910  max = 35 :REM number of characters
920  screen = &80:REM Low/high bytes of interim address of screen
930  !screen = &7CC9
940  what     = &7000
950  where    = &7100
960
1000 FOR pass = 0 TO 3 STEP 3
1010 P% = &4000:REM START ADDRESS OF MACHINE CODE
     PROGRAM
1020 [OPTpass
1030                             \PAINT
1040                             \THIS ROUTINE TRANSFERS
                                  CHARACTERS
1050                             \FROM &7000 UPWARDS TO THE
                                  SCREEN
1060                             \AT ADDRESSES DETERMINED BY
1070                             \THE CONTENTS OF &7100 UPWARDS
1100 .partpic  LDX #max           SET POINTER TO NUMBER OF
                                  CHARACTERS
1110 .nxchar   LDY where,X        GET POSITION
1120           LDA what,X         GET CHARACTER
1130           STA (screen),Y     SEND IT TO SCREEN
1140           DEX                ALL CHARACTERS DONE?
1150           BNE nxchar         NO DO NEXT CHARACTER
1200 RTS       FINISH
1210]
1300 NEXT pass
1400 RETURN
```

It would be a simple matter to increment the contents of location &80 (screen) in machine code to transfer the engine to its adjacent position. The inclusion of the blank character (32) at the start of each line ensures that bits of the engine do not remain behind as it is moved along. However, in machine code the movement would be much too rapid. Later we shall discuss ways of slowing down a machine code routine, but for now it is easiest to do this from BASIC; line 285 controls the speed of the engine.

Particle motion

One of the earliest applications of microcomputers in science was the use of fast machine code animations to simulate wave motion and the movement of molecules etc. We have already seen how the top line of the screen can be filled with the *-character. Let us now look at how the motion of this character may be achieved in machine code graphics. The obvious way of achieving horizontal motion is to paint the character successively one screen position further to the right each time as we did in the BASIC program in Chapter 2.

The following program will place the *-character into the 40 contiguous positions at the top of the screen. It is similar to the program discussed before, except that this time the Y-INDEX is used as a pointer instead.

Stars

```
   1  MODE7
   2  HIMEM = &4000:REM RESERVE SPACE FOR MACHINE CODE
      PROGRAM
   3
 900  star = 42
 910  max = 40
 920  screen = &7C00:REM absolute address of screen
 930
1000  FOR pass = 0 TO 3 STEP 3
1010  P% = &4000:REM START ADDRESS OF MACHINE CODE
      PROGRAM
1020  [OPTpass
1030                                 \ STARS
1040                                 \ THIS PROGRAM PLACES 40 *'s
1050                                 \ ACROSS THE TOP OF THE SCREEN
1110  .stars    LDY #0                 POINT TO FIRST POSITION
1120  .nxtpos   LDA #star
1130            STA screen,Y           SEND IT TO SCREEN
1140            INY                    MOVE TO NEXT POSITION
1150            CPY #max               END OF LINE ?
1160            BNE nxtpos             NO DO NEXT POSITION
1200            RTS                    YES FINISH
1210]
1300  NEXT pass
1350  CLS
1400  CALL stars
```

When you run this program, you will not get motion but merely a set of stars. The reason is not too hard to find, but it requires a little more knowledge about the microprocessor.

Because so many things are happening in the microcomputer, everything is under the control of the system clock, which beats away regularly at 500 nanosecond intervals (half a microsecond). Single byte instructions require two machine cycles, so they take one microsecond to be executed. If the operation requires an operand, then the execution time is increased. Some instructions need one byte for the operand while others need two. An example of a three byte instruction is STA &7C00 (store to an absolute address). An example of a two byte instruction is LDA #42 (load the number 42 immediately). Two byte instructions are generally executed in three cycles, while three byte instructions take one cycle longer (for the extra byte to be fetched and decoded). Thus it is easy to predict how long a particular program will take. The whole routine to place 40 *-characters on the screen takes 40 times 6 = 240 microseconds. From a human point of view this is instantaneous, hence the absence of motion. The solution is obvious, we must find a means of making the microprocessor waste time.

There is a single byte instruction in the 6502 set, which performs just this function; NOP (no operation). It takes two cycles to execute and causes absolutely nothing else to happen. Unfortunately, we are looking for a much longer delay than this and must look elsewhere. The most efficient time wasting technique is to ask the microprocessor to count up to 256 every time before proceding with the rest of its instructions. This is known as a **delay loop.** Its use in BASIC is quite common:

```
100   FOR T = 1 TO 1000:NEXT T
```

In machine code the simplest delay loop uses one of the indexes and since we are using the Y-INDEX as a pointer, we shall have to use the X-INDEX instead. Here is a delay loop routine:

```
        LDX #0      Initialize X-INDEX
LOOP    INX         2 cycles
        BNE LOOP    3 cycles if successful
                    2 cycles otherwise
etc.
```

The X-INDEX is initialized to 0. Then it is incremented and a test is made to see if it is equal to zero. If it is not equal to zero, then the PROGRAM COUNTER jumps back to the second instruction, labelled 'loop'. When the X-INDEX is incremented on the 256th time, it becomes 0000 0000 and the looping is then terminated. The execution times for each instruction are shown in the comment column, and it can be seen that this loop takes five cycles per loop or 1279 cycles in total. Note: not 1280, which is 256*5, because on the last loop, the branch condition is not successful, so the execution time is reduced by one cycle.

An alternative way is to decrement the X-INDEX instead with DEX, which makes absolutely no difference to this program, because it still requires 256 loops. However, if we were counting 100 loops, then the decrement method would be advantageous as we shall see later.

With either of these delay loops in the program, the time to place all forty *s on the screen would be increased to around fifty milliseconds, which is still practically instantaneous to us. Our delay loop will thus have to be extended, but we are already at the limit for the X-INDEX. The solution is to make the microprocessor go round the inner delay loop again, several times if necessary. This requires an outer loop and a loop counter to go with it. Since we have now run out of internal registers in the microprocessor, the obvious choice is an external memory location called **temp.** We could either increment this counter or decrement it. The increment method would be:

```
limit=100
LDA #0       Initialize temp
STA temp
```

```
.o loop  LDX #0        Initialize X-INDEX
.i loop  DEX
         BNE i loop    Do inner loop 256 times
         INC temp
         LDA temp
         CMP # limit   All loops done?
         BNE o loop    No do next outer loop
etc.
```

The decrement method requires less code, since it removes the need to load temp and compare it with the required limit each time. This time we load temp with a variable number each time before starting the countdown. We use another location called **count** for this, since its purpose is to count the number of inner delay loops to be executed each time. Initially count can be chosen in BASIC before execution of the machine code program. The delay routine thus becomes:

```
         temp = &8C
         count= &8D
.delay   LDA count     Get outer loop count
         STA temp      and keep in temporary store
.oloop   LDX #0        Set inner loop counter
.iloop   DEX           All done ?
         BNE i loop    No do the next inner loop
         DEC temp      Yes. All outer loops done?
         BNE o loop    No do the next outer loop
         RTS           Yes, so finish
```

The number written into count before the routine is called can be varied from 1 to 255, thus resulting in a delay each time of between about 0.5 ms and 150 ms. The total time needed to place the forty *s on the screen can thus be varied from about 20 ms to a few seconds. Longer delays than this are unnecessary, since the program would then be slow enough for BASIC, but they could be achieved with an additional outer counting loop.

How do we insert this delay routine into our machine code program? It could be fitted in after the * has been sent to its screen position and before the pointer is incremented to the next position, but there is a strong reason for not doing that. It is possible that the routine for producing a delay will need to be used several times more and every time we use it, it will have to be written out again. So a better technique is to place the delay loop in a separate subroutine very much like GOSUB 5000 in BASIC. The mnemonic for this is **JSR (jump to subroutine)** and the numeric code contains the address at which the subroutine starts. The memory locations in the delay program have been chosen to run from the end of the previous routine upwards and it too ends with **RTS (return from subroutine).**

The *-fixing program that we started with must now be altered to take account of this delay subroutine. In addition each star must be erased from the screen after it has been placed there, to produce the illusion of motion. We do this by placing a blank character (value 32) into each screen location soon after the * character. I say 'soon after' and not 'immediately after' because we want to leave the * long enough to be able to see it. The best place is therefore after the delay subroutine as follows. The value for count is written directly into its proper location from BASIC and this sets the speed at which the star moves across the screen.

Moving star

```
   1  MODE7
   2  HIMEM=&4000:REM RESERVE SPACE FOR MACHINE CODE
      PROGRAM
   3
 900  star = 42
 910  blank = 32
 920  max = 40
 930  screen = &7C00:REM absolute address of screen
 940  temp = &8C
 950  count = &8D
 960
1000  FOR pass = 0 TO 3 STEP 3
1010  P% = &4000:REM START ADDRESS OF MACHINE CODE
      PROGRAM
1020  [OPTpass
1030                                \STARS
1040                                \THIS PROGRAM MOVES A STAR
1050                                \ACROSS THE TOP OF THE SCREEN
1110  .starmv   LDY #0               POINT TO FIRST POSITION
1120  .nxtpos   LDA #star
1130            STA screen,Y         SEND IT TO SCREEN
1140            JSR delay            WAIT A BIT
1150            LDA #blank
1160            STA screen,Y         SEND IT TO SCREEN
1170            JSR delay            WAIT A BIT
1180            INY                  MOVE TO NEXT POSITION
1190            CPY #max             END OF LINE?
1200            BNE nxtpos           NO DO NEXT POSITION
1210            RTS                  YES FINISH
1215
1220  .delay    LDA count            GET OUTER LOOP COUNT
1230            STA temp             AND KEEP IN TEMPORARY STORE
1240  .oloop    LDX #0               SET INNER LOOP COUNTER
1250  .iloop    DEX                  ALL DONE?
1260            BNE iloop            NO DO THE NEXT INNER LOOP
1270            DEC temp             ALL OUTER LOOPS DONE?
1280            BNE oloop            NO DO THE OUTER LOOP
```

```
1290            RTS                 YES SO GO BACK
1300]
1310  NEXT pass
1350  CLS
1360  INPUT TAB(0,5) "ENTER SPEED (range 10 to 100) ";S
1370  ?count = 101 - S
1400  CALL starmv
```

So far we have only considered what happens when the pointer to the next screen position (the Y-INDEX) is increased. You can probably guess that if we were to decrease the pointer instead, then the star would move backwards across the screen from right to left. The instruction to decrement the Y-INDEX is just DEY, and when executed, the Y-INDEX is reduced by 1 and points to the previous screen position, rather than the next one.

What we shall do is wait until the star reaches the fortieth screen position and then, instead of finishing with the RTS as at present, we shall decrement the Y-INDEX successively until it reaches the beginning again. We can easily detect when it gets there, because the pointer will become zero. The BNE condition will succeed until the Y-INDEX reaches zero, and then it will fail, and we can stop the program at that point. The extra instructions to do this are listed below, starting from the location where they are different from the previous listing.

```
1201           DEY            MOVE TO END OF LINE AGAIN
1202  .nxtrev  LDA #star
1203           STA screen,Y   SEND IT TO SCREEN
1204           JSR delay      WAIT A BIT
1205           LDA #blank
1206           STA screen,Y   SEND IT TO SCREEN
1207           JSR delay      WAIT A BIT
1208           DEY            MOVE TO NEXT POSITION
1209           BNE nxtrev     DO NEXT POSITION UNLESS AT END
```

Instead of a return to BASIC in line 1210, a BRANCH to the start of the program will keep the star in continuous motion. But how then would we ever leave this program? It would continue for ever until the BREAK key is pressed and this is not an elegant way to finish. A better way is to look at the keyboard to see if any key is being pressed and, if so, to return to BASIC with RTS. If this keyboard routine is placed at the end of the main program it will only be effective when the star reaches the left side of the screen. A better way would be to place the keyboard routine inside the delay routine so that the keyboard will be checked more often. Unfortunately, this means that we cannot then immediately return to BASIC with RTS, because we are still in a subroutine. We must first pull two bytes off the STACK to get at the BASIC return address. The keyboard causes the CA2 line of the keyboard VIA to trigger a flag, which is sensed at the location &FE4D. The following additional sequence will check if a key is being pressed and, if so, will cause a return to BASIC:

```
1281            LDA &FE4D     GET FLAG REGISTER
1282            AND #1        MASK TO GET CA2 FLAG
1283            BNE finish    FINISH IF IT IS SET
1284            RTS           CARRY ON IF NO FLAG
1285  .finish   PLA           PULL STACK TO FIND THE
1286            PLA           RETURN ADDRESS TO BASIC
1287            RTS
```

With this keyboard sensing routine the star can now bounce back and forth until you stop it by pressing the SPACE key. At some speeds the motion of the particle is rather jerky because the screen refresh rate is out of synchronization with the display of the particle. There ought to be a way of preventing this by maintaining control over when the screen is refreshed, but I have yet to discover how. In the interim period just use those speeds that produce the smoothest motion (70 is very good).

Molecular motion

Now we can start to move the *-character all over the screen as we did in Chapter 2, but this time with machine code. First, let us consider a single molecule:

```
   1  MODE 7
   2  HIMEM = &4000
  10  GOSUB 10000:REM ASSEMBLY LANGUAGE ROUTINE
 100  REM MOTION OF A MOLECULE
 130  CLS
 140  PROCwalls
 150  INPUT " Temperature (range 1 to 10) " S%
 160  IF S%>10 OR S%<1 THEN 130
 165  LET S%=15-S%
 170  ?count=S%:?tptr=S%
 190  ?oposlo=32500 MOD 256
 191  ?oposhi=32500 DIV 256
 192  ?drtn = 215
 195  PRINT TAB(3,0);"Press SPACE to alter temperature"
 200  CALL onemol
 205  IF INKEY$(0)=" " THEN 130
 210  GOTO 200
 220
5000  DEF PROCwalls
5010  REM DRAW WALLS
5020  REM LEFT SIDE IS GRAPHICS WHITE CHARACTER (151)
5030  REM LEFT WALL IS CHARACTER 234
5040  REM RIGHT WALL IS CHARACTER 181
5050  FOR 32064 TO 32083 STEP 40
5060  ?I=151:?(I+1)=234:?(I+39)=181
5070  NEXT I
5080
```

```
5090  REM TOP SIDE IS CHARACTER 240
5100  REM BOTTOM SIDE IS CHARACTER 163
5110  FOR I = 32065 TO 32103
5120  ?I=240
5130  ?(I+640)=163
5140  NEXT I
5150  ENDPROC
5160
10000 REM MOLECULE ASSEMBLY LANGUAGE ROUTINE
10010
10020 oposlo=&70
10030 oposhi=&71
10040 nposlo=&72
10050 nposlo=&73
10060 tptr =&74
10070 drtn =&75
10080 count =&76
10220
11000 FOR pass = 0 TO 2 STEP 2
11010 P%=&4000
11020 [OPT pass
11030                 \SINGLE MOLECULE ROUTINE
11040
11050 .onemol  DEC count        IS COUNT AT ZERO?
11060          BEQ domol        YES CARRY ON
11065          RTS              NO RETURN TO BASIC
11070 .domol   LDA tptr         BEGIN
11080          STA count        RESET COUNT
11090          LDY #0           INITIALIZE POSITION POINTER
11100          CLC
11110          LDA oposlo       GET OLD POSITION
11120          ADC drtn         ADD DISPLACEMENT
11130          STA nposlo       KEEP RESULT
11140          LDA drtn         IS DISPLACEMENT NEGATIVE?
11150          BMI negdr        YES DO SUBTRACTION
11160          LDA oposhi
11170          ADC #0
11180          STA nposhi       KEEP RESULT
11190          BNE cont         UNCONDITIONAL BRANCH
11200 .negdr   LDA oposhi
11210          SBC #0
11220          STA nposhi
11230 .cont    LDA (nposlo),Y   LOOK AT NEW POSITION
11240          CMP #32          IS IT EMPTY?
```

```
11250          BNE wall      NO IT MUST BE THE WALL
11260          JMP empty     YES IT IS EMPTY
11270
11280 .wall    CMP #240      TOP WALL?
11290          BEQ top       YES
11300          CMP #234      LEFT?
11310          BEQ left      YES
11320          CMP #181      RIGHT?
11330          BEQ right     YES
11340                       \IT MUST BE THE BOTTOM WALL
11470          LDA drtn
11480          CMP #39       SOUTH-WEST?
11490          BEQ sw        YES
11500          CMP #40       SOUTH?
11510          BEQ s         YES
11520                       \IT MUST BE SOUTH-EAST
11530          LDA #217      GO NORTH-EAST
11540          STA drtn
11550          BNE exit
11560 .sw      LDA #215      GO NORTH-WEST
11570          STA drtn
11580          BNE exit
11590 .s       LDA #216      GO NORTH
11600          STA drtn
11610          BNE exit
11620 .top                  \DO NORMAL REFLECTION FROM
                             TOP
11630          LDA drtn
11640          CMP #215      NORTH-WEST?
11650          BEQ nw        YES
11660          CMP #216      ORTH?
 1160          BEQ n         YES
11680                       \IT MUST BE NORTH-EAST
11690          LDA #41       GO SOUTH-EAST
11700          STA drtn
11710          BNE exit
11720 .nw      LDA #39       GO SOUTH-WEST
11730          STA drtn
11740          BNE exit
11750 .n       LDA #40       GO SOUTH
11760          STA drtn
11770          BNE exit
11780 .left                 \DO NORMAL REFLECTION FROM
                             LEFT
```

```
11790          LDA drtn
11800          CMP #215     NORTH-WEST?
11810          BEQ lnw      YES
11820          CMP #255     WEST?
11830          BEQ lw       YES
11840                      \IT MUST BE SOUTH-WEST
11850          LDA #41      GO SOUTH-EAST
11860          STA drtn
11870          BNE exit
11880  .lnw    LDA #217     GO NORTH-EAST
11890          STA drtn
11900          BNE exit
11910  .lw     LDA #1       GO EAST
11920          STA drtn
11930          BNE exit
11940  .right                \DO NORMAL REFLECTION FROM RIGHT
11950          LDA drtn
11960          CMP #217     NORTH-EAST?
11970          BEQ rne      YES
11980          CMP #1       EAST?
11990          BEQ re       YES
12000                      \IT MUST BE SOUTH-EAST
12010          LDA #39      GO SOUTH-WEST
12020          STA drtn
12030          BNE exit
12040  .rne    LDA #215     GO NORTH-WEST
12050          STA drtn
12060          BNE exit
12070  .re     LDA #255     GO WEST
12080          STA drtn
12090          BNE exit
12100
12170  .empty  LDA #32      ERASE OLD MOLECULE
12180          STA (oposlo),Y
12190          LDA #79      GET MOLECULE CHARACTER
12200          STA (nposlo),Y
12210          LDA nposlo
12220          STA oposlo
12230          LDA nposhi
12240          STA oposhi   SAVE NEW POSITIONS
12250  .exit   RTS
15000]
16000  NEXT pass
17000  RETURN
```

Although this routine is alarmingly long, it is relatively straightforward. First, the walls of the container are drawn, each using a different graphics character. The old screen position of the molecule is kept in two locations – **oposlo** which holds the low byte of the screen position and **oposhi** which holds the high byte. The displacement of the molecule is kept in **drtn.** This value can have one of eight possible directions as follows:

Value	Direction
1	East
41	South-east
40	South
39	South-west
255	West
215	North-west
216	North
217	North-east

Values greater than 127 represent negative directions, the contents of the screen address are reduced when added to it. To ensure that this happens there has to be a check that the high byte of the screen address (oposhi) is also reduced when the CARRY bit is set following the low byte addition. The instructions from 11140 to 11230 do this. Another way of doing this would be to use two bytes to store the displacement, containing the following values:

Value	Direction
1	East
41	South-east
40	South
39	South-west
65535	West
65495	North-west
65496	North
65494	North-east

The displacement would then be contained in drtnlo and drtnhi and would be added to oposlo and oposhi each time. This would automatically ensure that the screen position was reduced for movement in a negative direction. This technique is used in WAVE REFLECTION (25).

Once the new position for the molecule has been computed, a check is made to see if it is empty. If not, then this can only be because the molecule has reached the wall. We therefore look to see which wall it is and we bounce off according to the normal laws of relection. The new direction is stored in drtn and the routine is quitted without changing anything else. Next time, the original oposlo and oposhi will have the new value of drtn added to them and another check made as to the suitability of the new position. Eventually, the new position will be empty, so the molecule is erased from its old position and replaced in its new position. Only then are the values of oposlo and oposhi changed to record the new position. The routine then returns to BASIC, where a keyboard check is made, before returning to the routine for the next move.

While not particularly exciting this routine is the foundation of many simulations of molecular movement. It is not difficult to manage the movement of up to 256 different molecules at the same time. One addition must first be made to the single molecule routine to cover a new eventuality. We need to handle the situation where two molecules collide. This can be done by checking that the new position for any molecule does not already contain the character 79 for a different molecule. If so, we simply ignore it! The conservation laws tell us that the two molecules would swap directions anyway and the principle of indistinguishability means that we need not bother about which molecule is which either. This neat solution unfortunately is not applicable to other cases. If we want the gas molecules to condense to a liquid, we have to be more careful about allowing them apparently to pass through each other. The program KINETIC MODEL (not listed here but available separately) looks after this problem by giving the molecules different properties below a certain temperature (obviously our critical temperature!).

For moving many molecules 'onemol' is treated as a subroutine, which is applied to each molecule in turn. The delay routine at the start of onemol is not needed for each separate molecule, so this is deleted from there and placed in the main program. The latter collects the values of position and displacement for each molecule in turn from three tables poslo, poshi and dr. These are passed to the onemol subroutine through the locations oposlo, oposhi and drtn. On returning from this routine these values may well be different, so they are stored in the table of values in place of the old ones. The main program loops once for each new molecule and then exits to BASIC to check on the keyboard.

A flag is set when any molecule strikes the left wall. On return to BASIC if this flag is set, then a noise is made to simulate this collision. The program therefore allows students to observe the greater number of collisions when the temperature is increased or the number of molecules is increased. The complete program for MOLECULAR MOTION is listed in the Appendix (program 26, called MOLMOT).

The program KINETIC MODEL uses the same techniques to demonstrate what happens to gas molecules under conditions of expansion and contraction and at different temperatures. Sufficiently low temperatures cause the molecules to condense into liquids and solids. The added bonus here is the regular crystalline shape produced when the molecules reach the solid phase. The inclusion of a partition to divide the container into two parts allows a discussion of entropy. Students can be challenged to alter the direction of entropy change by collecting all the molecules onto one side of the partition (playing the part of Maxwell's demon by opening and closing the hole in the partition). Similar routines are used in BROWNIAN MOTION (not the same as program 27) to simulate the movement of a smoke particle under the bombardment of gas molecules. Neither of these programs is listed in this book, but both are available separately. The reason for this is because they have been carefully checked to make them crash-proof and have had extensive evaluation.

The display of large screen characters

One useful application of machine code graphics is the display of large digits and letters on the screen. This enables the whole class to see the results of a voltage measurement or some other reading. It is used extensively in measurement and timing programs. The principle is based upon the normal method used by the microcomputer to display characters on the screen. Each character is made up from a matrix of 8 x 8 pixels. If the same matrix is used to display a matrix of 8 x 8 screen positions instead, then each character is eight times larger.

Because there are 40 squares across the screen (5 times 8) and there are 25 down the screen (3 times 8, nearly) then the choice of an 8 by 8 matrix allows fifteen different large digit positions on the screen, or three rows each of five digits. Even with a negative sign and a decimal point, this is enough. Each digit actually only occupies five columns and seven rows of the matrix, thus allowing a border to separate each large character from its neighbour. The appearance of the characters as they occur in TSA METER (8) is shown in Figure 7.1.

We need eight bytes to store the rows of any one large digit, using one bit for each column position in each row. If the bit at, say, position 7 is a 1, then the screen square corresponding to that position in the matrix is turned on (white square). If the bit in position 7 is a 0 then the corresponding screen position is turned off (blank square). Thus a row of eight blank and white squares can be stored in a single byte. The byte values for each of the digits in the diagram is shown alongside each line. The sets of eight bytes for each digit are stored sequentially in a table called bittbl. The first part of the program gets the digit code (which is passed via BASIC in a location called dgtval), multiplies it by eight and enters bittbl to collect the eight bytes of the selected digit. These are kept in a set of eight temporary stores temp.

The starting position for each large digit is specified and there are two ways in which this can be done. Either the digit can be placed almost anywhere on the screen, in which case the full screen address must be passed to the machine code subroutine, or alternatively the full screen can be considered as having 3 by 5 possible destinations only. Then it is only necessary to pass to the machine code subroutine a single value from 0 to 14 corresponding to the ultimate destination of the large digit. We shall adopt the latter practice.

In this case the screen destination of a particular digit is passed via a location called **dest** as one of the numbers 0 to 14, each corresponding to a screen position. This is converted into the correct screen values which are kept in two successive locations called **screen** and **screen + 1.**

Having obtained the bytes of the digit to be displayed and its screen position, it remains to look at each bit of each byte in turn and to send a blank or a white character to the appropriate position on the screen. This is done using the **ASL** instruction **(arithmetic shift left)** and looking at the CARRY bit to see if it is a 0 or a 1. The routine needs three counters, one to keep the screen position (Y-INDEX), one to count the eight bytes of each digit (X-INDEX) and a third to keep track of the bits within each byte (a location called **bitcnt**).

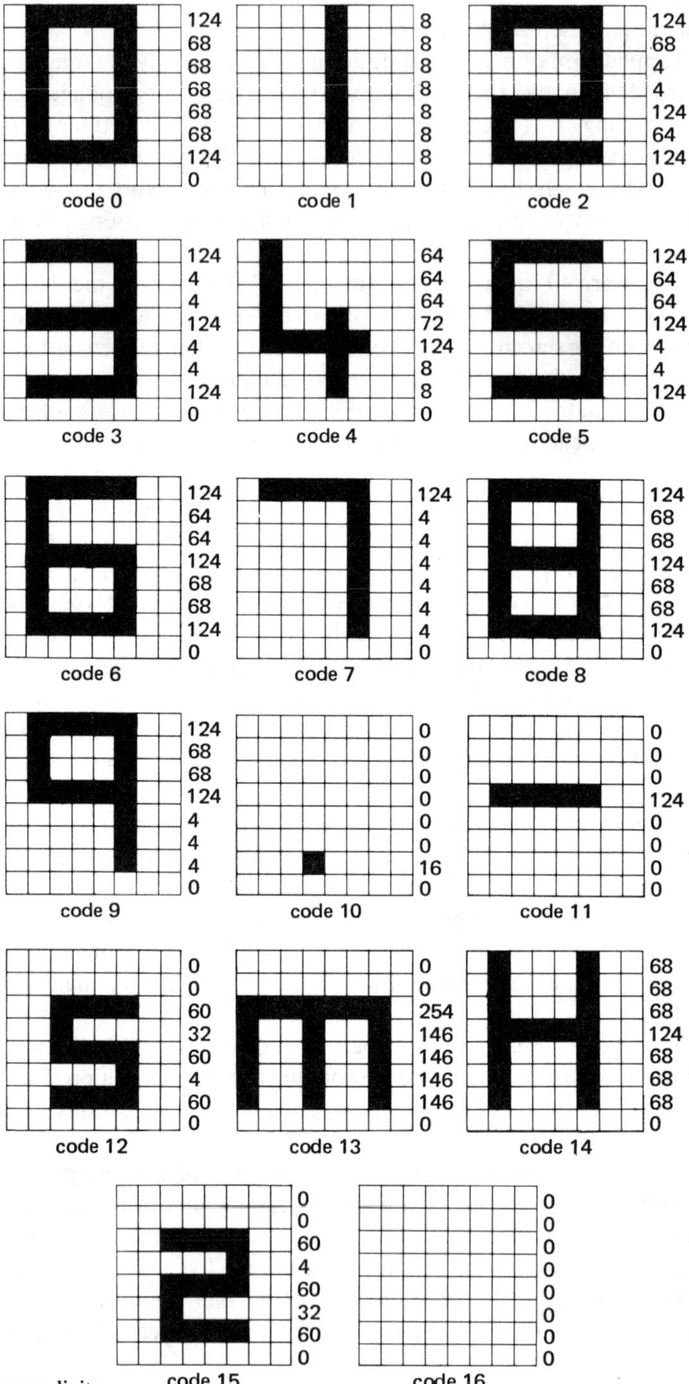

Figure 7.1 Large digits

```
10000  REM Large digit display
10010  REM BASIC loader for
10200  REM digits table
10210  FOR I = &7100 TO &716F
10220  READ X
10230  ?I = X
10240  NEXT I
10250  DATA 124,68,68,68,68,68,124,0:REM DIGIT 0
10260  DATA 8,8,8,8,8,8,8,0:REM DIGIT 1
10270  DATA 124,68,4,4,124,64,124,0:REM DIGIT 2
10280  DATA 124,4,4,124,4,4,124,0:REM DIGIT 3
10290  DATA 64,64,64,72,124,8,8,0:REM DIGIT 4
10300  DATA 124,64,64,124,4,4,124,0:REM DIGIT 5
10310  DATA 124,64,64,124,68,68,124,0:REM DIGIT 6
10320  DATA 124,4,4,4,4,4,4,0:REM DIGIT 7
10330  DATA 124,68,68,124,68,68,124,0:REM DIGIT 8
10340  DATA 124,68,68,124,4,4,4,0:REM DIGIT 9
10350  DATA 0,0,0,0,0,0,16,0:REM DECIMAL POINT
10360  DATA 0,0,0,124,0,0,0,0:REM NEGATIVE SIGN
10370  DATA 0,0,60,32,60,4,60,0:REM LETTER S
10380  DATA 0,0,127,73,73,73,73,0:REM LETTER M
11000  REM Large digit display
12000  REM assembly language routine
12001  dest=114
12002  dgtval=115
12003  screen=112:REM AND ALSO 113
12004  bitcnt=116
12005  temp=&7080:REM AND NEXT 7 BYTES
12006  bittbl=&7100:REM AS LISTED ABOVE
12007
12008  FOR pass = 0 TO 2 STEP 2
12010  P% = %7000
12020  [OPT pass
12030  .display  LDA dest       GET DESTINATION
12040            CMP #10        BOTTOM ROW ?
12050            BPL bottom     YES
12060            CMP #5         MIDDLE ROW?
12070            BLP middle     YES
12080            ASL A          MUST BE TOP ROW
12090            ASL A
12100            ASL A          MULTIPLY BY 8
12110            STA screen     KEEP NOTE OF POSITION
12120            LDA #&7C       SCREEN ADDRESS
12130            STA screen+1
```

```
12140           BNE begin        UNCONDITIONAL BRANCH
12150
12160 .bottom   SEC
12170           SBC #10
12180           ASL A
12190           ASL A
12200           ASL A
12210           ADC #128         MOVE TO PROPER PLACE
12220           STA screen       AND SAVE IT
12230           LDA #&7E
12240           STA screen+1
12250           BNE begin        UNCONDITIONAL BRANCH
12260 .middle   SEC
12270           SBC #5
12280           ASL A
12290           ASL A
12300           ASL A
12310           ADC #64          MOVE TO PROPER PLACE
12320           STA screen       AND SAVE IT
12330           LDA #&7D
12340           STA screen+1
12250
12360                           \GET BITS FOR DIGIT
12370 .begin    LDX #0           INITIALIZE BYTE POINTER
12380           LDA dgtval       GET DIGIT CODE
12390           ASL A
12400           ASL A
12410           ASL A            MULTIPLY BY 8
12420           TAY              POINT TO TABLE OF BITS
12430 .bytget   LDA bittbl,Y     GET BYTE
12440           STA temp,X       KEEP IN TEMP STORE
12450           INY              ADVANCE TABLE POINTER
12460           INX              ADVANCE BYTE POINTER
12470           CPX #8           8 BYTES COLLECTED?
12480           BNE bytget       NO – GET THEM
12490           LDY #223         SET SCREEN POINTER TO −32
12500           LDX #255         SET ROW POINTER TO −1
12510 .nxtrow   INX              READY FOR NEXT ROW
12520           CPX #7           ALL ROWS DONE?
12530           BEQ finish
12540           LDA #8           INITIALIZE BIT POINTER
12550           STA bitcnt
12560           CLC
12570           TYA              GET SCREEN POINTER
```

```
12575               ADC #32          ADVANCE TO NEXT ROW
12580               TAY              RESTORE SCREEN POINTER
12590   .nxtbit     INY              NEXT SCREEN POSITION
12600               ASL temp,X       SHIFT BIT INTO CARRY STORE
12610               BCC empty        BIT IS ZERO
12620               LDA #255         BIT IS ONE – SEND WHITE BLOCK
12630               BNE send         UNCONDITIONAL BRANCH
12640   .empty      LDA #151         SEND BLANK BLOCK
12650   .send       STA (screen),Y   SEND TO SCREEN
12660               DEC bitcnt       ALL BITS SENT?
12670               BEQ nxtrow       YES DO NEXT ROW
12680               BNE nxtbit       NO DO NEXT BIT
12690
12700   .finish RTS:]
12800   NEXT pass
12900   RETURN
```

The way that this routine is called can best be seen by studying one of the programs that uses it, particularly TSA METER (8). I find it of universal value in displaying digits to a whole class, where a BASIC equivalent takes too long to paint each digit in turn. STOPCLOCK (5) updates the digits every ten milliseconds and this is not possible in BASIC.

High resolution plotting

It is occasionally necessary to plot points on the screen in machine code. An example is in STANDING WAVES (23)(Plate 41), where the screen picture has to be changed quite often to give the appearance of motion. Let us first look at the algorithm used to do this.

The high resolution screen of MODE 4 runs from &5800 (top left corner) to &7FFF. Adjacent screen positions are not contiguous in the memory. Running the following program shows that each character position (8 by 8 bits) is made from eight consecutive bytes. The next set of eight bytes is next door to this and so on. After 320 bytes (40 columns) the next row is started and so on to the bottom of the screen.

```
  1  MODE 4
100  FOR I = &5800 TO &7FFF
110  ?I = 255
120  NEXT I
```

The algorithm to plot the point (X,Y) directly is thus:

```
byte number = &5800 + 320*(Y DIV 8) + 8*(X DIV 8) + (Y MOD 8)
```

The position within this byte is just (X MOD 8). This is not quite right because the top left of the screen is now the origin (0,0). This is a situation that Apple users have long been used too. For most programs it is not a serious problem, the point (X,256-Y) has to be plotted instead. For wave motion programs this complication is ignored completely.

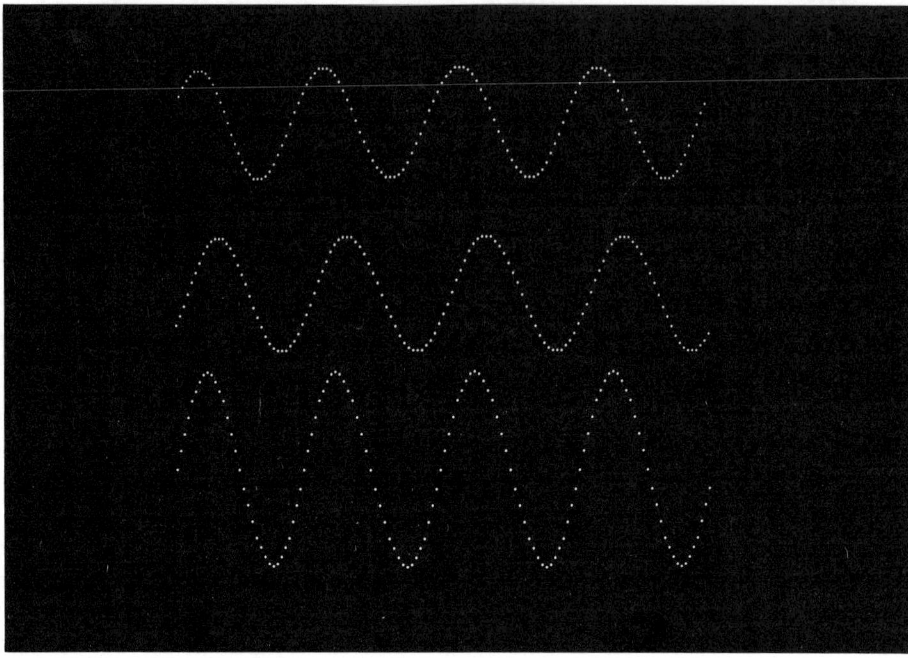

Plate 41 Interference between two waves of different phase angle

The machine code routine that achieves the above algorithm is as follows:

```
10000 REM MACHINE CODE PLOTTING ROUTINE
10010 y=&70:REM Y-COORDINATE
10020 x=&71:REM X-COORDINATE
10030 Xval=&72:REM TEMPORARY STORE FOR X-INDEX
10040 scrlo=&73
10050 scrhi=&74
10060 temp=&75
10070 FOR pass = 0 TO 3 STEP 3
10075 P%=&4000
10080 [OPT pass
10090 .find  STX Xval    KEEP CURRENT X-INDEX
10095        LDA y       CONVERT Y-COORDINATE
10150        LSR A
10160        LSR A
10170        LSR A       y DIV 8
10190        STA scrlo   TEMPORARY STORE
10210        CLC
10220        ADC #&58    ADD TOP-OF-SCREEN ADDRESS
10230        STA scrhi   y DIV 8 EFFECTIVELY MULTIPLIED BY 256
```

```
10232          LDA #0
10240          LDX #6       SIX SHIFTS OF y DIV 8 IS
10250  .next   ASL scrlo    EQUIVALENT TO MULTIPLYING BY 64
10252          ROL A
10254          DEX
10256          BNE next
10270          ADC scrhi    GIVING EQUIVALENT OF MULTIPLYING BY
                            320
10280          STA scrhi
10300
10320          LDA y
10330          AND #7       EQUIVALENT TO y MOD 8
10333          STA temp
10380
10400          LDA x
10410          AND #&F8     EQUAL TO (x DIV 8) * 8
10420          ADC temp     ADD IN PREVIOUS CALCULATIONS
10425          ADC scrlo
10430          STA scrlo    KEEP LOW BYTE OF SCREEN ADDRESS
10440          LDA scrhi
10450          ADC #0       ADD CARRY BIT TO HIGH BYTE
10460          STA scrhi
10470          LDY #0       DETERMINE BIT POSITION WITHIN BYTE
10480          LDA x
10490          AND #7
10500          TAX
10505          SEC          SHIFT CARRY BIT DOWN ACCUMULATOR
10512          LDA #0       UNTIL CORRECT BIT POSITION IS
                            REACHED
10515  .shift  ROR A
10516          DEX
10520          BPL shift
10530          STA temp
10535          LDX Xval     RESTORE X-INDEX
10536
10540          RTS
```

On returning from this routine the locations scrlo and scrhi contain the screen address of the byte in which the dot was found and the ACCUMULATOR contains the bit position itself. To plot a point without erasing any other points in the same byte requires that byte to be ORed with the new bit, thus:

```
12760          JSR find       GET BIT AND BYTE
12770          ORA (scrlo),Y
12780          STA (scrlo),Y
```

To erase the dot requires the inverse of the ACCUMULATOR contents to be ANDed with the current screen byte in this way:

```
12430     JSR find      GET BIT AND BYTE
12440     EOR #255      INVERT BIT
12450     AND (scrlo),Y
12460     STA (scrlo),Y
```

This routine is used extensively in the programs listed in the Appendix. A slightly different version is used for CHART RECORDER (18), because that only needs to determine the y-coordinate. This is plotted on the extreme left of the screen, which is then scrolled across.

STANDING WAVES is a machine code version of what is essentially a simple process. To create a wave on the screen we need to plot a sine wave, erase it and replot it one pixel to the left or right. In BASIC this takes far too long and wave motion is not apparent. Unfortunately, a machine code routine to work out sines is beyond my capabilities. The solution is to use BASIC to work out the sines beforehand. These values are then stored in a table (sintbl), which is accessed in machine code using the X-INDEX as a pointer. If the X-INDEX contains the value 25, then LDA sintbl,X will retrieve the sine of 25 from the table. The table is loaded with the correct values by a program like this:

```
20000 REM SET UP SINE TABLE
20010 REM CONTAINS 256 DATA ITEMS
20020 FOR I=0 TO 255
20024 LET angle=I*PI/128
20025 LET val=SIN(angle)
20035 ?(&4A00+I)=INT(20*val)
20090 NEXT I
```

This produces sines with an amplitude of 20. When I started to write my wave motion programs, I wanted the option of choosing different amplitudes. To produce waves of different amplitudes requires each sine value in the table to be multiplied by some factor. The following multiplication routine was developed for the purpose.

```
13000
13010                          \MULTIPLICATION ROUTINE
13020                          \RESULT IN ACCUMULATOR
13030 .mult     LDA #0          PRODUCT
13050           LDY #8          8 SHIFTS
13060 .nxmult   ASL A           MULTIPLY RESULT BY TWO
13070           ASL mult1       FIRST NUMBER
13080           BCC cont        IF CARRY BIT IS CLEAR IGNORE REST
13085           CLC
13090           ADC mult2       ADD SECOND NUMBER
13100 .cont     DEY             ALL SHIFTS DONE?
13110           BNE nxmult      NO, DO NEXT BIT
13120           RTS             YES ALL DONE
```

This subroutine takes two numbers stored in mult1 and mult2, multiplies them together by a shift and add method and returns with their product in the ACCUMULATOR. Clearly this product must be less than 255 or the ACCUMULATOR will overflow. In the cases where this subroutine is being used, this is always true. It is an interesting point to note one reason why compiled BASIC is still too slow to cope with fast graphics: it is too universal and cannot adapt itself to particular cases in the way that I have done here.

Unfortunately, all this effort proved to be in vain. The time taken to use this routine for each dot on the wave turned out to be too great. I had to choose the alternative technique of using several sine tables, each for a different amplitude. Fortunately, the total number of amplitudes needed was sufficiently low that this could be done. A look at the listing for STANDING WAVES will show exactly how.

The algorithm used to draw the waves is rather like that used to plot the molecules. For each x-coordinate the present y-value of the wave is kept in a table (opos) and accessed via the X-INDEX. This value is retrieved and passed to the erasing routine above. The current x-position is then multiplied by a constant (called wvln) and another constant (time) is subtracted to give the position so far reached in the table. The current amplitude for the wave is used to point to the correct sine table and the sine value is retrieved from it. To this is added an offset to get the wave to the correct height and the new point is plotted. It is also put back into the table of positions ready to be erased the next time round.

Fundamentally we are computing the wave displacement from the equation

```
displacement = amplitude*SIN(wvln*x-time)
```

Physicists will appreciate that the constant called ‘wvln’ is actually the reciprocal of the wavelength. This can be altered before the routine is called to change the number of waves that appear on the screen (and hence their wavelength). By adjusting the constant called time at the completion of each cycle, the wave can be made to move through the table faster or slower. This is a means of adjusting the speed of the waves. The third variable (frequency) depends upon both speed and wavelength and cannot be independently altered.

The great advantage of this technique is the ease with which the wave can be made to travel backwards. The constant (time) is added instead of subtracted to produce the result. The two displacements for the two waves are then added together to produce the standing waves. Close inspection of the listing in the STANDING WAVES program will reveal exactly how this is done. If you want both waves to travel in the same direction, producing interference when the waves have the same wavelength and beats when they are different, change this program to the following:

```
12520  CLC
12530  ADC time
```

You now have the capability to produce your own wave motion programs for a variety of purposes.

Ripple tank simulations

The plot routine can be used to make the plane (or circular) wavefronts of water waves travel across the ripple tank and be reflected from a plane (or circular) barrier. For practical purposes the time to set up the starting conditions is too long to make this idea a viable simulation program (although I am working on this problem). Again the basic method is similar to that of moving molecules around the screen. Because the screen locations are not contiguous, it is not possible to add a constant to move a particular dot up or down. Instead the x- and y-coordinates are handled separately. As before though, the current positions are stored in two sets of tables (X-POSITION HIGH, X-POSITION LOW etc.). The displacement added each time to the current positions are also held as double-byte numbers (INITIAL Y-SPEED HIGH, INITIAL Y-SPEED LOW, etc.). This allows each dot on a wavefront to move independently of all the others. If all the dots are initially lined up and given the same displacement, they will progress across the screen as a plane wave.

Upon reaching the barrier each dot is given a different displacement, so that it then moves off in a different direction. Simulations of spherical wavefronts colliding with spherical barriers are thus quite possible. The only price to be paid is the setting up of some twelve tables initially, each consisting of 256 elements. Once this has been done the result is reasonably satisfactory. WAVE REFLECTION (25) gives the full listing.

Brownian motion

More satisfactory from my point of view is the ease of simulating the Brownian motion of smoke particles. I am indebted to W. Jeffries (Jordanhill College of Education) for bringing this idea to my attention. Each smoke particle is a dot on the screen, which is then given a random displacement in one of the usual eight directions. A random number which can be +1, 0 or —1 is added to the x-coordinate and another is added to the y-coordinate, thus giving the eight directions (plus the possibility of not moving at all).

These random numbers cannot be generated in machine code quickly enough, so we resort to trickery, by setting timer1 in the VIA ticking away in microseconds and accessing its lower two bits. These are ORed with 1 to produce numbers 1, 2 or 3 and 254 is added to them to give the required displacements. By my reckoning this ought to produce a bias in the results towards −1, but it doesn't seem to have that effect. The clock for the VIA is asynchronous with that running the microprocessor and this seems to produce the necessary randomness. The whole program is listed as BROWNIAN MOTION (27).

Screen scroll

The layout of the screen makes it possible to shift each pixel into the neighbouring position, using the ROR instruction. This has several applications as we shall see later. I was first alerted to this possibility by S. Rushbrook-Williams of the Microelectronics Educational Development Centre in Paisley. What will upset some purists is my use of a modified address for the current screen byte being shifted. This program is not, therefore, relocateable.

```
    1 MODE 4
    2 HIMEM=&4000
10020 rowcnt=&71
```

```
11000  FOR pass = 0 TO 3 STEP 3
11005  P% = &4000
11010  [OPT pass
11012  .scroll  LDA # &58
11014           STA &4018
11016           LDA # &00
11018           STA &4017    RESTORE STARTING ADDRESS OF
                             SCREEN
11020           LDA #32      COUNT 32 ROWS
11030           STA rowcnt
11040  .nxrow   LDY #40      COUNT 40 COLUMNS
11050           CLC          SHIFT BLANK INTO LEFTMOST BIT
11060           LDA #0       ACCUMULATOR KEEPS ALL RIGHTMOST
                             BITS
11070  .nxcol   ROR A
11080           LDX #8       8 LINES PER COLUMN
11090  .nxlin   ROR &FFFF    MODIFIED SCREEN ADDRESS
11100           ROR A
11110           INC &4017    INCREMENT MODIFIED SCREEN
                             ADDRESS
11120           BNE cont
11130           INC &4018
11140  .cont    DEX
11150           BNE nxlin    DO NEXT LINE IN SET OF EIGHT
11160           DEY
11170           BNE nxcol    DO NEXT SET OF EIGHT
11180           DEC rowcnt
11190           BNE nxrow    DO NEXT ROW
11200           RTS
11500  ]
12400  NEXT pass
20000  CALL scroll
20010  GOTO 20000
```

Each row of the MODE 4 screen contains 320 bytes arranged as forty rows of eight lines. Each of the eight lines is rotated in turn into the ACCUMULATOR and any bit 0 positions that contain a 1 will place that bit in bit 7 of the ACCUMULATOR. This is repeated eight times for each set of lines in a column. At the end of eight shifts the ACCUMULATOR has collected all these bits and shifted them down to the other end. At the same time, any bits which dropped off the end of previous bytes are shifted out of the ACCUMULATOR into the bit 7 position of each screen byte. This happens for all forty column positions, except for the first, which has a 0 shifted into its bit 7 position. The whole routine can be repeated for as many lines as required by setting the initial starting address to the beginning of any row and by adjusting the value stored in rowcnt.

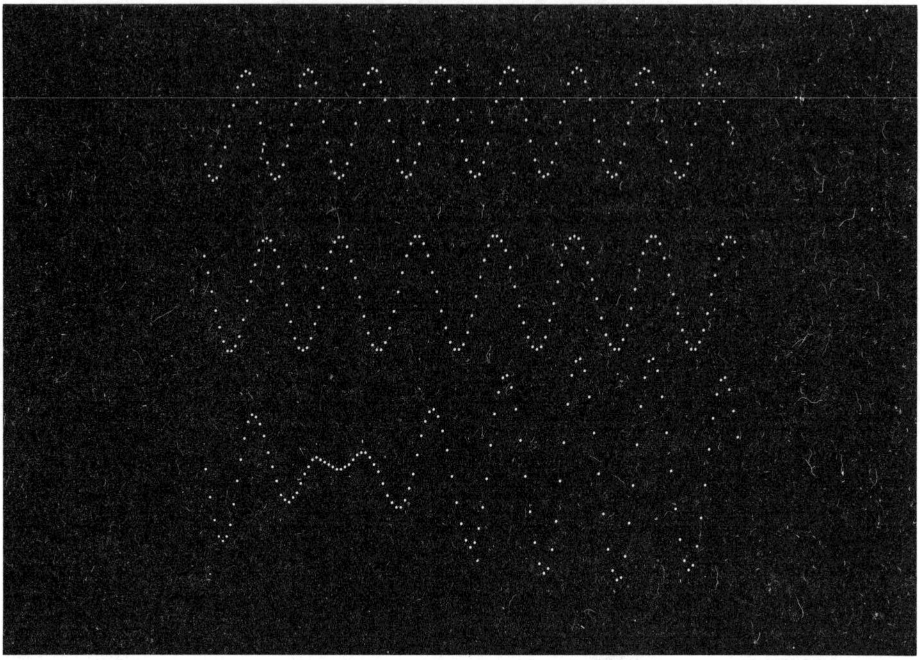

Plate 42 Beats between two waves of differing frequency

When the whole screen is shifted, as above, the result is rather slow, although it is quite adequate for FOUR-CHANNEL CHART RECORDER (18).

If the extreme left positions are plotted with the displacements of a sine table, then waves will be produced as the screen scrolls across. This is used in WAVE SUPERPOSITION (24) to provide a different technique for demonstrating beats and wave interference (Plate 42). Although slower, it is more powerful than STANDING WAVES, since its calculations are in BASIC and give finer tuning of the beat frequency, wavelengths and phase relationship between the waves. A faster machine code version of this program is currently being prepared.

This chapter has come a long way and some readers may well feel that it is not for them. I did warn that machine code programming was not easy, but no matter. Study the program listings to see the way that each routine is used and you should then be able to make use of them yourself, even if you cannot see how they work.

8 Interfacing in machine code

'Now! Now!' cried the Queen. 'Faster! Faster!'
(Lewis Carroll, *Through the Looking Glass*)

This chapter brings together previous ideas to produce very useful routines for making fast measurements. First, let us look at the VIA from the point of view of machine code. It is assumed that we are using the B-port, since this is the normal user port of the BBC microcomputer. The address of this VIA is &FE60, referred to as the **BASE address.**

Using the B-port for output

```
LDA   #&FF      All B-port lines as outputs
STA   BASE + 2  Data direction register
LDA   #&80      B-port line 7 HIGH, all others LOW
STA   BASE + 0  B-port
```

Using the B-port for input

```
LDA   #&00      All B-port lines as inputs
STA   BASE + 2
LDA   BASE + 0  Read B-port
```

Using the B-port for inputs and outputs and looking at bit 0 only

```
LDA   #&F0      Lines 0 to 3 as inputs, others as outputs
STA   BASE + 2
LDA   BASE + 0  Read inputs
AND   #1        Mask to get bit 0 only
```

The VIA timers may be accessed in just the same way to produce machine code versions of the programs described in Chapter 4.

Using machine code versions of these progams gives faster results and turns the microcomputer into a very powerful laboratory aid. One example of this is STOPCLOCK, listed as program 5 in the Appendix. It prints the current value of a centisecond clock on the screen in large digits, which is updated one hundred times a second. This 'clock' is actually the internal clock of the BBC microcomputer, which is accessed in machine code through location 594 (OS 0.1) or location 662 (OS 1.0). The BBC microcomputer's own operating system interrupts the program every hundredth of a second to update this clock. It is important, therefore, not to disable the operating system, or this clock will not work. The position of this clock seems to depend upon which operating system you have. OS 0.1 uses location 594 as stated above, but OS 1.0

appears to have moved it to location 662. If STOPCLOCK does not work with your system, change line 1010 to:

```
1010  CSLO = 662
```

An alternative timing technique is to use timer 1 of the VIA to provide accurate time-outs at predetermined intervals. This could then generate its own interrupts at whatever time interval might be required. However, centiseconds are ideal for the present purposes, so the use of timer 1 is an unnecessary complication.

Rather than use the interrupt system of the microcomputer, it is also quite easy just to inspect bit 6 of the flag register to see if it is set. If so a time-out has occurred and T1LHI can be reloaded to start a new countdown. When the countdown reaches zero, it sets a flag in the flag register, reloads itself from the latch and carries on counting down. If the latch contains the number 10 000 (actually 9998 to allow for the reloading time), because the VIA clock runs at 1 MHz, timer 1 gives out a steady stream of one centisecond signals.

A final alternative would be to use a timing loop lasting exactly ten milliseconds. In this application, though, we need to update the display at the same time and it is quite awkward to do both tasks simultaneously. The chosen technique is therefore the best in this instance.

The clock is started by an **event** (a change in logic level) at either bit 0 or bit 1 of the user port. The current time is displayed in minutes, seconds and centiseconds in large digits on the screen, using the machine code subroutine developed in Chapter 7. Another event stops the clock, which then displays the elapsed time. Pressing a key halts the display, while allowing the clock to continue counting. The whole program illustrates the freedom given by using the VIA instead of delay loops to do the timing. The microprocessor can then get on with other tasks, like sorting out where the digits have to go and displaying them.

The full program is listed in the Appendix. The following brief description may help to explain it, since comments in that listing are rather sparse.

2025 to 2049: the special codes for the large letters m, s and the decimal point are sent to the large digit subroutine. Each of these characters is placed in turn into dgtval and its position is placed in dest and the routine is called by JSR display.

2050 to 2125: the minutes, seconds and centiseconds are initialized to zero and then displayed on the screen by JSR showtimes.

2130 to 2195: bits 0 and 1 of the user port are collected and stored in status. The program then sits at this point until one or other of these bits changes.

2200 to 2610: the centisecond store is cleared and the timing begins. Every centisecond the BBC operating system adds one to location 594 (called CSLO). If this location contains a number less than ten, the routine jumps to see if any key on the keyboard is being pressed. If not the current time measured by the clock is displayed. If a key is being pressed, the showtimes routine is bypassed and the clock display freezes at its previous value. After the current time has (or has not) been displayed, the routine checks the user port to see if any input has changed. If so, a return to BASIC is made. If not, the routine goes back to check the current value of CSLO.

When CSLO exceeds ten, it is reset to zero and CSHI is incremented, thus effectively

counting ten centiseconds. When it reaches ten, it too is reset and one second is added to the time. This process continues up to 100 minutes or until the input status changes. The clock stores continue to be incremented every hundredth of a second even if the display is temporarily frozen. It would be more difficult to do this if a timing loop was being used to generate the centisecond intervals.
2620 to 3170: the showtimes subroutine collects the contents of each of CSLO, CSHI, etc. and displays each in its correct position with the display subroutine.

Timing loop routines

We saw in Chapter 4 how user port outputs may be switched on for controlled intervals of time using simple delay loops in BASIC. The maximum rate at which an output (other than PB7 and CB2) can be switched on and off in this way is limited to about 100 Hz and this is inadequate for most purposes. A better way is to use the timers of the VIA to control outputs on PB7, but there is an alternative, which is to use machine code delay loops, as we did when moving characters across the screen in Chapter 7. However, we were not then interested in accuracy.

Since timing loops are used extensively for accurate measurement of short intervals, they will now be described. We shall use them to switch user port outputs rapidly on and off to produce sound in a suitable loudspeaker. (This particular application, chosen only to illustrate the principles, is not a sensible one because better ways of producing sound already exist in the BBC microcomputer.) The algorithm is as follows:

i) Switch the output on
ii) Delay for half-period
iii) Switch the output off
iv) Delay for other half-period
v) Go back to step i

The delay routine is half a millisecond, based upon counting the number of machine cycles needed to execute each instruction.

```
        LDX count    ;2 cycles
DLY2    LDY #198     ;2 cycles
DLY1    DEY          ;2 cycles
        BNE DLY1     ;2 or 3 cycles
        NOP          ;2 cycles
        NOP          ;2 cycles
        DEX          ;2 cycles
        BNE DLY2     ;2 or 3 cycles
```

The loop DLY1 takes five cycles to complete if the conditional branch BNE DLY1 succeeds. After the last decrement the branch fails, so it then takes two cycles and makes the last loop four cycles in total. Since DLY1 is executed 198 times it takes 198*5 – 1 or 989 cycles. The other instructions in the loop DLY2 take 11 cycles (except for the last loop which is one less than this), so every time that the X-INDEX is decremented a total delay of 1000 cycles is introduced (which is half a millisecond).

When this delay routine is used in the algorithm above to cause the delay between switching the user port lines alternately HIGH and LOW, a frequency of about 1 kHz will obviously be produced if the location called count contains a value of one. Changing count allows different (lower) frequencies to be produced.

Time measurement by counting machine cycles

The principle of measuring time intervals is as follows. The user port is read and stored in a memory location called **status.** The current state of the user port is then monitored continuously and compared with status. Normally it will be the same, but when it is different, this is because an input has been activated. A clock is then started and the new status of the user port is saved in status. When the user port again changes state, the current contents of the clock are noted and copied into a store. The time interval involved can then be calculated and displayed. We saw how this routine was used with the internal clock to produce a centisecond timer in BASIC.

Accurate timing of short intervals is only possible using machine code routines, since BASIC is too slow to respond to input changes. Although it is possible to use the VIA timers in machine code, the use of timing loops is still a good way to measure time intervals and this will now be described. It works because it takes exactly the same length of time to add one unit to a chosen (zero page) location (called **clock**). During each loop the user port is checked to see if it has changed its status and, if so, the program jumps out of the timing loop.

Initialization

```
.begin  SEI
        LDA #0
        STA clock
        STA errflag
        LDA PRT
        STA status
```

Wait for input status to change

```
.wait   LDA PRT
        CMP status
        BEQ wait
        STA status   Keep new status
```

Timing loop

```
.loop   INC clock    5 cycles
        BEQ error    2 cycles usually
        LDA PRT      4 cycles
        CMP status   3 cycles
```

```
        BEQ loop      3 cycles usually
        CLI
        RTS
.error  LDA #1
        STA errflag
        CLI
        RTS
```

The timing loop interval is seventeen cycles. The instruction BEQ error is normally unsuccessful, so it takes two cycles. BEQ loop is successful until the input status changes, so it takes three cycles. Each cycle takes 500 nanoseconds to be executed, giving a loop of 8.5 microseconds. There is not usually any need to make this a round number (like ten) since it may have to be processed by BASIC later anyway.

Note the following further points. The interrupt system is disabled (with SEI) to prevent the BBC microcomputer's operating system from interrupting the timing routine and causing timing errors. At the end of the routine the interrupt system is restored with CLI. The maximum interval that can be measured is 256 loops x 8.5 microseconds (2.176 ms). If the interval exceeds this an error will be flagged through the location called **errflag.** On return to BASIC this will be zero if the timing was satisfactory and one if the maximum interval was exceeded. This can be checked by a BASIC routine and the operator informed of a timing error if necessary.

The timing of longer intervals may be achieved with a two byte clock. Using the increment method is now more difficult because the high byte of this clock is only incremented whenever the low byte of the clock reaches zero (i.e. 256). This takes an additional five cycles so a 5-cycle delay has to be incorporated to compensate for the 255 occasions when the high byte is not incremented. To achieve the greatest speed the X-INDEX (low byte) and the Y-INDEX (high byte) are used for the clock.

Initialization

```
.begin  SEI
        LDA #0
        STA errflag
        TAX
        TAY
        LDA PRT
        STA status
.wait   LDA PRT       Wait for input status to change
        CMP status
        BEQ wait
        STA status    Keep new status
.loop   INX           Timing loop 2 cycles
        BNE delay     3 cycles usually
        INY           2 cycles
        BNE cont      3 cycles usually
        LDA #1        Error condition
```

```
        STA errflag
        CLI
        RTS
.delay  NOP          2 cycles
        NOP          2 cycles
.cont   LDA PRT      4 cycles
        CMP status   3 cycles
        BEQ loop     3 cycles usually
        CLI
        RTS
```

The delay of two NOP instructions compensates for not incrementing the high byte of the clock. Branching to this delay also involves one extra cycle, thus giving a total of five cycles, which is equivalent to the time taken to increment the high byte of the clock and to see if it has exceeded its limit. The total 19-cycle timing loop thus takes 9.5 microseconds and can measure intervals up to 600 milliseconds. Intervals exceeding this cause the overflow error which is detected in BASIC later. This routine is the basis of FAST TIMER (7). The accuracy of this program depends upon the accuracy of the 1 MHz clock rate. If it is not exact, then the 0.0095 factor in line 405 of this program can be altered accordingly.

For still longer time intervals a three-byte clock may be used. The incrementing method now needs so many compensatory delays that it is better to use the technique of adding one unit to the clock during each loop instead. The CARRY bit from the low byte addition may be added in to the next byte by adding in zero each time. The three bytes for the clock are kept on zero page and called CLOCKLO, CLOCKMID and CLOCKHI. This 24-bit clock can count up to 16 777 216 and for a 50-cycle loop can measure times up to several minutes.

Count subroutine

```
COUNT  CLC             2 cycles
       LDA CLOCKLO     3 cycles
       ADC #1          2 cycles
       STA CLOCKLO     3 cycles
       LDA CLOCKMID    3 cycles
       ADC #0          2 cycles
       STA CLOCKMID    3 cycles
       LDA CLOCKHI     3 cycles
       ADC #0          2 cycles
       STA CLOCKHI     3 cycles
       LDA KEYBRD      4 cycles
       CMP KEY         2 cycles
       BNE CHK         3 cycles unless timing has finished
       BEQ DONE
CHK    LDA APRT        4 cycles
```

```
AND #3          2 cycles
TAY             2 cycles
CMP STATUS      4 cycles
BEQ COUNT       3 cycles unless timing has finished.
```

Using the tables given at the end of Chapter 7 to convince yourself that it takes fifty cycles to complete this loop and that the clock will have increased by one unit in the process.

Once entered, this loop continously counts time in units of fifty cycles. There are two ways of leaving the loop. If the keyboard is pressed during the timing then the keyboard flag in the VIA will be set and will terminate the loop. Alternatively, if there has been some change at the user port so that it no longer compares with STATUS, then the microprocessor goes off to find out what caused the change. Because the maximum time interval is so great, the overflow checking routine can now be abandoned. This routine could be used virtually as it is to measure short time intervals. In programs 8 to 12 it has, however, been replaced by the alternative technique of waiting for time-outs on timer 1.

The original version of this program was developed on the PET and no timers are available there. The BBC microcomputer has both timer 1 and timer 2, so that they are free for a user program. Timer 1 is set to provide continuous 50 microsecond timeouts (approximately), which is quite long enough for the routine to update its clock and check its flags, etc. After this the routine waits for the timeout, resets the flag and continues. The timing continues even when the routine goes off to store the clock data after an event, although this is too short to make a lot of difference. Hence there is little to choose between this technique and loop counting, except that it is easier to adjust the timing interval when using timer 1. In both cases the time interval measured is not quite 50 microseconds and an adjustment is made in BASIC later, when the readings are processed. The amount of this adjustment was determined by accurate measurement over several minutes with a stopwatch (digital, I hasten to add!).

These advanced timing routines can be used in a variety of programs. For example a photocell connected to bit 0 of the user port could be mounted inside a camera to measure how long its shutter remains open. The timing routine actually used in programs 8 to 12 has been made even more powerful by including extra facilities. Firstly, it allows up to sixteen different time intervals to be measured consecutively. This means that it can be used for a variety of purposes, particularly the measurement of an a.c. frequency (which requires several cycles to be counted), the measurement of the speeds of a trolley as it runs down an inclined plane and the measurement of acceleration. TSA METER (8) uses this advanced timing routine and the large digits subroutine to display the results.

To allow the measurements of speed when studying the laws of collision between two trolleys, there must be two photocells. It is possible for the second trolley to begin a transit of its photocell before the first has finished crossing the other. Thus it must be possible to detect two inputs independently and to keep their results separate. We still only need the one clock, but at the start or finish of a transit, the time on the clock is copied into a store. In fact, up to sixteen stores are available for each input and the pointers (ptr) keep track of which status change is currently being timed. Thus in the collision experiment it would be possible to have two trolleys approach from different directions, to collide in the middle and both go off in one particular direction at different speeds. This involves two events at one input and six events at the other, but the routine can easily cope with this. (In this context an event is any change at either of the inputs.)

The whole routine has a method for deciding how long it has to continue taking readings, since the number of events is kept in a location (evntctr) beforehand. It also has an escape route, for the occasion when you run the program and find that the photocell is not working. This is achieved by the keyboard detect routine.

The final part of the routine (.done) is a means of converting the recorded clock times into time intervals. This is carried out for all of the stores even if most of them are empty.

```
15000 REM ADVANCED TIMER
15005 REM MACHINE CODE ROUTINE
15010 ptr = &6880:REM CHANNEL 1 POINTER IS &6880
15020                 REM CHANNEL 2 POINTER IS &68C0
15030 store = &6800:REM UP TO &687F
15040 status = &6881:REM INPUT STATUS
15050 evntctr = &6882:REM NUMBER OF EVENTS
15060 clocklo = &70
15070 clockmid = &71
15080 clockhi = &72
15090 PRT = &FE60:REM USER PORT
15100 DDRB = &FE62:REM DATA DIRECTION REGISTER
15110 flag = &FE6D:REM FLAG REGISTER
15120 T1LLO = &FE64:REM TIMER 1 LATCH LOW
15130 T1LHI = &FE65:REM TIMER 1 LATCH HIGH
15140 ACR = &FE6B:REM AUXILIARY CONTROL REGISTER
15150 ?ACR = 64:REM GENERATE CONTINUOUS TIMEOUTS
      (TIMER 1)
15160 ?&FE6E = 127:REM DISABLE ALL INTERRUPTS FROM VIA
15170 ?T1LLO = 48:?T1LHI = 0:REM TIMEOUTS AT 50
      MICROSECOND INTERVALS
15200 keyboardflag = &FE4D:REM TO DETECT KEY CLOSURE
16000 REM ASSEMBLY LANGUAGE ROUTINE
16010 FOR pass = 0 TO 3 STEP 3
16020 P% = &6000
16030 [OPT pass
16040 .timer   SEI
16050          CLD
16055                        \CLEAR ALL STORES
16060          LDX #127       POINTER TO STORES
16070          LDA #0
16080          STA clocklo
16090          STA clockmid
16100          STA clockhi
```

```
16110  .nxtclr  STA store,X
16120           DEX           ALL DONE ?
16130           BPL nxtclr    NO DO NEXT
16140           STA DDRB      USER PORT IS FOR INPUT
16150           LDA #252      SET POINTERS TO -4
16160           STA ptr       SAVE CHANNEL 1 POINTER
16170           STA ptr+64    SAVE CHANNEL 2 POINTER
16180           LDA PRT       GET CURRENT INPUT STATUS
16190           AND #3        MASK FOR BITS 0 AND 1
16200           STA status    KEEP CURRENT STATUS
16210  .wait    LDA PRT       GET CURRENT INPUT STATUS
16220           AND #3        MASK FOR BITS 0 AND 1
16230           TAY           KEEP STATUS TEMPORARILY
16240           CPY status    SAME STATUS ?
16250           BEQ wait      WAIT UNTIL IT CHANGES
16255                         STATUS HAS CHANGED
16256                         DETERMINE WHICH CHANNEL
16260  .query   TYA           RETRIEVE STATUS
16270           EOR status    WHICH CHANNEL?
16280           STY status    KEEP NEW STATUS
16290           CMP #1        CHANNEL 1?
16300           BEQ chan1     YES
16310           CMP #2        CHANNEL 2?
16320           BEQ chan2     YES
16330           TYA           BOTH CHANNELS
16340           EOR #2        IGNORE CHANNEL 2 THIS TIME
16350           STA status
16360  .chan1   LDX #0        POINT TO CHANNEL 1 EVENT
                              COUNTER
16370           BEQ cont      UNCONDITIONAL BRANCH
16380  .chan2   LDX #64       POINT TO CHANNEL 2 EVENT
                              COUNTER
16390  .cont    LDA ptr,X     GET CORRECT EVENT POINTER
16400           CLC
16410           ADC #4        MOVE DOWN 4 BYTES
16420           STA ptr,X     AND PUT IT BACK
16430           CLC
16440           TXA           GET CHANNEL POINTER
16450           ADC ptr,X     ADD EVENT POINTER
16460           TAX           POINT TO NEXT EMPTY STORE
16470           LDA clocklo   STORE CURRENT CLOCK READING
16480           STA store,X
16490           LDA clockmid
16500           STA store+1,X
```

```
16510            LDA clockhi
16520            STA store+2,X
16530            DEC evntctr      ALL EVENTS DONE?
16540            BEQ done         QUIT IF FINISHED
16550            DA keyboardflag CLEAR FLAG FOR KEYBOARD
16551            STA keyboardflag
16559                            \TIMING ROUTINE
16560  .count    CLC
16570            LDA clocklo      INCREMENT CLOCK
16580            ADC #1
16590            STA clocklo
16600            LDA clockmid
16610            ADC #0
16620            STA clockmid
16630            LDA clockhi
16640            ADC #0
16650            STA clockhi
16660            LDA keyboardflag
16665            AND #1           KEY PRESSED?
16668            BNE done         YES SO FINISH
16670  .timewait LDA flag         TIMEOUT?
16672            AND #64
16674            BEQ timewait
16675            STA flag         RESET TIMER FLAG
16700            LDA PRT          HAS INPUT STATUS CHANGED?
16710            AND #3
16720            TAY              KEEP TEMPORARILY
16730            CMP status
16740            BEQ count        NO CHANGE CONTINUE TIMING
16750            BNE query        YES FIND OUT WHICH CHANNEL
16760  .done     LDX #120         CONVERT STORES TO TIME
                                  INTERVALS
16770  .nxtstore SEC
16780            LDA store+4,X
16790            SBC store+0,X
16800            STA store+4,X
16810            LDA store+5,X
16820            SBC store+1,X
16830            STA store+5,X
16840            LDA store+6,X
16850            SBC store+2,X
16860            STA store+6,X
16870            DEX
16880            DEX
```

```
16890              DEX
16900              DEX
16910              BPL nxtstore
16920              CLI
16930              RTS:]
16940    NEXT pass
16950    RETURN
```

Fast digital to analogue conversion

In Chapter 5 we noted that the frequency of the alternating voltage produced by a DAC via BASIC was limited to a few hertz. I stated then that for higher frequencies it is necessary to do all the calculations in BASIC beforehand and store the results in the memory as individual bytes. These are then collected one by one from the memory and sent directly to the DAC using a machine code routine. The waveform is created by BASIC before the machine code routine is called. This gives a table of numbers between 0 and 255 held in a set of locations called **store.** The machine code routine outputs these numbers to the DAC one by one. A delay routine similar to that used before will alter the rate at which the numbers are sent to the DAC and thus change the frequency of the waveform. The length of this delay is loaded from BASIC into a location called **count** before the DAC output routine is called.

PROGRAMMABLE OSCILLATOR (13) is based upon this routine. As with the BASIC programs already discussed, different waveforms are produced by altering the defining equation. The waveform can be inspected by connecting the DAC output to a cathode ray oscilloscope or turned into sound with a suitable amplifier and loudspeaker.

```
.begin   LDX #0
.next    LDA store,X 4   cycles
         STA PRT         4 cycles
         LDY count       3 cycles
.delay   DEY             2 cycles
         BNE delay       2 or 3 cycles
         INX             2 cycles
         BNE next        2 or 3 cycles
         BEQ begin       3 cycles
```

The delay loop can range from 4 to 1279 cycles, depending upon the value in count; 1 to 256 (which is, in fact, 0). Including the remaining instructions, the rate of output to the DAC thus ranges from 20 to 1295 cycles and the period for the whole waveform is between about 2.5 ms and 160 ms (highest frequency 400 Hz).

Higher frequencies can still be obtained by putting more than one cycle of the waveform into store to begin with, although this will reduce the resolution obtained. Even so, a mere eight voltage levels per waveform cycle still gives acceptable sound, in which case the frequency can be as high as 12 kHz.

The above routine suffers from one fault; it is not possible to get out of it! PROGRAMMABLE OSCILLATOR contains a method of quitting the routine by having the keyboard flag checked regularly. When the flag goes up, the routine returns to BASIC.

Applications

This DAC is very useful for producing alternating voltages. From an electronic engineering viewpoint, its waveform can have almost any shape, so it can be used to analyse the behaviour of filter circuits. For this purpose the output from the DAC can be boosted as described in Chapter 5.

Fast analogue to digital conversion

In Chapter 5 we saw how readings from the ADC may be plotted on the screen. If the measured voltages are changing rapidly however, BASIC is too slow and a machine code routine is needed to collect the readings and to store them for future use. The built-in ADC is itself rather slow, but if it is restricted to channel 0 only (*FX16,1 in version 1.0 of BBC BASIC), then it may be accessed up to a hundred times per second. Rather than address the built-in ADC directly (which creates an interrupt) the locations used by the operating system to store the reading obtained should be used instead. This is 652 for the low byte and 656 for the high byte (adjacent locations store the results for the other channels). Alternatively the analogue port can be accessed with the OSBYTE call as described in the user guide (page 429).

Much faster results are obtained by using the ZN448 device described in Chapter 5. A single delay loop provides data acquisition rates between 1000 and 100 000 readings per second. Since the screen is not much more than 256 pixels wide (actually 320) a single page of stores can be accessed by indexed addressing to save the readings until a BASIC routine later plots them on the screen.

If this ADC is connected to the 1 MHz bus (Figure 5.5) or the user port (Figure 5.8), it has to be triggered to start a conversion. If the ADC is connected to the user port as in the program listed in the Appendix, the start conversion pulse is obtained from CB2. At the end of the conversion the data is latched into the user port with a strobe on CB1.

The way to achieve the maximum data acquisition rate is to start the next conversion before storing the results of the previous one. The data acquisition time can then be reduced to 15 microseconds. This is ideal for fast transient phenomena such as the light output from a flashgun.

Fast ADC

```
.go     SEI
        LDY #0
.wait   LDA BPRT      Clear latch
        STA BPRT      Start conversion
        NOP
```

```
        NOP
        NOP
        NOP
        NOP
        NOP
        LDA BPRT
        STA BPRT       Begin next conversion
        CMP thrshld    Ready to start ?
        BCC wait       No wait for change
.new    LDA BPRT       Start taking readings
        STA BPRT       Begin next conversion
        STA store,Y    Save present sample
        LDX delay      Get delat time
.dly    NOP            2 cycles
        LDA delay      3 cycles dummy load
        DEX            2 cycles
        BNE dly        3 cycles usually
        INY            Total delay 10 cycles
        BNE new
        CLI
        RTS
```

The minimum time between starting and completing a conversion is about ten microseconds, which is the best that can be achieved with this device. Because of the time needed to collect the results the minimum delay between readings is thirty cycles or fifteen microseconds. The maximum delay is 2590 cycles or 600 readings per second. To decrease this further is simply a matter of putting extra NOP instructions in the .dly loop. If fewer readings per second are needed then an inner loop of say 120 microseconds can be provided in place of the NOP instruction in the manner shown in Chapter 7.

```
.next   LDY delay      3 cycles
.dly    LDA #30
        STA temp
.i loop DEC temp       5 cycles
        BNE i loop     2 or 3 cycles
        DEY            2 cycles
        BNE dly        2 or 3 cycles
```

This provides a minimum delay of about 125 microseconds (8000 readings per second) and a maximum of about 30 ms (33 readings per second). Lower rates than this can conveniently be handled from BASIC.

At full speed the time required to collect all 256 readings is about 2.5 ms. There thus has to be some means of telling the routine when to begin taking readings. One software solution to this problem is based on the assumption that nobody is interested in the voltage until it starts to change. So the routine waits until it changes, before beginning to store its readings regularly. In practice, ordinary fluctuations due to electrical noise means that the required change should be substantial, a change in the lower three bits at least. This is a little complicated, since the change may be positive or negative, so the absolute value of the change must be retrieved before the comparison can be made. The following listing gives the general idea:

```
        LDA BPRT     Keep note of present reading
        STA status
.wait   LDA BPRT     Check reading for change
        SBC status
        BPL pos
        EOR #255     Negative – so complement
.pos    AND #240     Mask to ignore lower four bits
        BEQ wait     Wait till change is significant
.go     SEI
etc.
```

In FAST ADC the simpler technique of just comparing the measured ADC value with a previously declared threshold is used. This does mean that the voltage cannot be used with, say, capacitor discharge, where the voltage approaches the threshold from the other direction. In such cases the BCC of the FAST ADC routine must be replaced by BCS. The method above covers both eventualities, but takes too long for some purposes (e.g. the light output from a flashgun). Which technique is used depends on the application.

Connecting the ZN448 device to the user port does prevent the latter being used with a DAC at the same time (although I use the printer port for this instead), but it does make the programming simpler. Using the 1 MHz bus as described in Chapter 5, requires different addresses for the VIA, but the same program may be used otherwise. The full listing for FAST ADC is given in the Appendix (15). Once taken the readings are plotted on the screen by BASIC in the normal way. One peculiarity is worth a mention, the need to write to the user port to start the conversion. This is the only way to make the CB2 line go LOW for a single cycle. The CA2 line, on the other hand, will also go LOW as the data is read from the A-port. This would save one whole microsecond. If this is important to you, connect the ZN448 device to the A-port of your 1 MHz bus VIA and you will be able to get 100 000 readings per second. I can't think what you will use it for!

9 Dedicated systems

'I see you're admiring my little box,' the knight said in a friendly tone. 'It's my own invention.'
(Lewis Carroll, *Through the Looking Glass*)

Permanent programs

Most microprocessors spend their time doing one set of tasks only. It is only the few that find their way into personal or school microcomputers, that are given different tasks from day to day at the whim of the programmer. The microprocessor inside a calculator has been preprogrammed to carry out calculations only. It will not be asked to play tunes or measure time intervals or temperatures etc. The microprocessor in a supermarket checkout will not be asked to play space invaders as well. The microprocessors in these systems are said to be **dedicated** to their one function. The programs that run these dedicated systems are usually frozen in ROM, because there is no need to change them once they have been written and debugged.

ROM is produced by a silicon chip manufacturer exactly as requested by the purchaser. The program is placed in the ROM by a process called **mask programming.** An individual ROM may contain 32 000 or more bytes, which is 256 000 different bits. Each bit of every byte in the ROM is initially switched on. Then, by a photographic process, each individual bit is marked, either as one to be left on, or one to be switched off. The final process then permanently switches each bit off, or leaves it on, according to the information printed on it. Once the program has been produced in this way, it is not possible to alter it later. The program remains in the ROM even if the power supply to the equipment is later switched off. When this ROM is coupled to a microprocessor, the latter will only carry out the program in the ROM.

The making of the masks for a ROM is a very expensive business and it is not done unless several thousand such ROMs are required. In the development stage, therefore, before the bugs have been ironed out, a different form of ROM is used, called programmable ROM. One version of this is especially useful; it is called **EPROM** or **electrically programmable ROM.** This allows programs to be burned in, just as with ROM, but it is also possible to erase this program and burn in a different one, if the first is found to contain bugs. The equipment needed to burn a program into an EPROM is not too expensive (fifty pounds or so for an add-on unit to the BBC microcomputer), but it is probably not worth the average user getting such equipment. Local polytechnics and FE colleges usually possess it and are willing to let visitors make use of it under supervision.

EPROM enables the programmer to store machine code routines permanently in his or her microcomputer, which can then be called from BASIC in the usual way **(CALL**

nnnnn). The exact value for 'nnnnn' depends upon where in the memory space the EPROM is placed. The most convenient EPROM is the 2516 (also known as the single-rail 2716), which can hold 2048 eight-bit bytes. A larger EPROM is the 2532, which can hold 4096 bytes. The older 2708 EPROM is less useful since it needs a separate −5 V supply, not always available.

Because of the many facilities offered, the BBC microcomputer has very little space available for such EPROMs in its 65 536 addressable locations. Only &FC00 to &FDFE are free and some of these are earmarked for future expansion. One useful facility, therefore, allows the user to switch different sets of memory into the memory space using a separate latch. Thus three EPROMs could be plugged into the spare sockets and the routines contained in them could be accessed with an *FX call. This is how the graphics chip, word processor chip and the speech chip are added. I expect it will thus be possible for users to add their own chips with the same technique, although details of this are not available at the time of writing.

Unfortunately these sockets are themselves earmarked for other uses, particularly the word processor chip, Econet interface chip, LOGO chip and so on. The Acorn publication *BBC Microcomputer Applications,* Note 1 – The 1 MHz Bus, describes how another 64K of RAM, ROM or EPROM may be connected to the 1 MHz bus. Only 256 bytes of this can be accessed directly at any one time through the JIM addresses (&FD00 to &FDFF). What happens is this. The desired page of the extra memory is selected by writing the page number into an eight-bit data latch at the address &FCFF. Thus

```
?&FCFF = &80
```

will select page 128 of the extra memory. This number is retained by the latch and used to set up the top eight lines of the address bus. The bottom eight lines are selected by the microprocessor in the usual way in conjunction with the JIM address. Thus

```
LET x = ?&FD90
```

will read the contents of the extra memory at the actual address &8090. The &80 comes from the data latch and the &90 from the lower eight address lines. To switch to the next page of memory the data latch must be separately loaded with the next address with

```
?&FCFF = &81
```

and so on through the whole of the 65 536 addresses (256 pages) available.

For physics teachers an **obvious resident** program for an EPROM is the timing routine discussed in the last chapter. To get such a routine into the EPROM, the hexadecimal code is usually typed into an EPROM burner and checked. Then a freshly erased EPROM is placed in one socket and the burn commences. Each binary code in turn is sent to its correct address and stored there by sending a voltage pulse along the program line. It takes one or two minutes for this process, after which the EPROM can be installed in the microcomputer. An EPROM can be erased again (for example, if a mistake has been made or if a better version has been developed) by exposing it to the correct dose of ultra-violet radiation. Any establishment with an EPROM burner will probably possess such a UV eraser too. EPROM burners are also currently being developed for use with the BBC microcomputer.

If this sounds a little complicated, then there is **EAROM (electrically alterable ROM).** This too can be programmed and retains its program after the power has been switched off. Its program can be changed later, without having to erase the whole program first, since each memory location can be changed independently. EAROM is unfortunately much more expensive than EPROM, but does not need special equipment to program it. It is simply placed into the ROM socket and treated like ordinary RAM, only it retains its program after the machine is switched off.

RAM has such tiny power requirements that a suitable battery can maintain a program in it for years after it has been programmed. Some RAM units, therefore, have a built-in battery to retain a program after the main power has been switched off. Here too, it is not necessary to buy special burner and eraser equipment, since the device behaves like any other RAM from the point of view of the microcomputer.

A stand-alone system

The above system is still just a microcomputer with some special resident routines. It would be possible to buy a microcomputer, add an EPROM and use it purely as a dedicated system. Fundamentally this is what has happened to some older microcomputers; for example my PET is now used exclusively for word processing. However, the manufacturers of, say, video games, are not going to do it like this. For them most of the microcomputer, such as the BASIC interpreter and the keyboard are unnecessary. Their procedure is to design each system specially, using only those components necessary for the task required. This is also a technique which we can use too.

Requirements

A dedicated system will need some means of collecting data and giving information back to the user. In a microcomputer this is the typewriter keyboard and video display. In a control system this could be a sensor and a few switches for input and an elecromagnetic relay as an output (for example, in a system to open the garage doors automatically upon the arrival of a motor car). In both cases, however, some sort of input/output chip, like a VIA, will be needed and the techniques discussed in Chapter 4 are relevant in this context.

The system will also need a microprocessor and some RAM for storing variable data. The amount of RAM depends upon the system, a garage doors system may only need a few bytes, whereas a programmable electronic organ may need thousands. Finally, the dedicated system will need its program stored in ROM or EPROM. Small dedicated systems can be developed around multi-purpose chips, such as the RRIOT (which contains ROM, RAM, input and output lines and a timer). The user's program is burned into the ROM when it is manufactured. This is combined with a microprocessor to give a two-chip system. The ultimate is a single chip containing all the RAM, ROM and I/O and the microprocessor as well. Such a chip is called a **single-chip microcomputer.**

These reductions in chip count give an obvious saving in cost, since the interconnections between the different parts of the system have already been made. All that is needed is a small printed circuit board to take the remaining components and a socket for the single-chip microcomputer and the complete system is ready.

This brings us right up to the present in microelectronic technology, since it is the use of such dedicated systems that is so profoundly affecting our lives. They are found in washing machines, sewing machines, knitting machines, motor cars, supermarket checkout points, video games and electric train sets. They control robots in factories, word processing equipment in the office and automatic stock delivery and despatch in the warehouse. What else they will do in the future is speculation, but I think it is safe to bet that those who can understand and program microelectronic systems are more likely to be employed than those who cannot.

This book was originally intended to be a part of a complete introduction to microelectronics, beginning with transistors and ending with complete single-chip microcomputers. This proved to be too ambitious and the emphasis was thus changed to using an existing microcomputer (in this case the BBC microcomputer) to do most of the tasks that a microprocessor normally does. I do want to complete the picture, however, and to encourage some of you to build your own dedicated systems (even your own microcomputer).

The first problem with any dedicated system is the number of connections needed. By the time an EPROM, a VIA, RAM, address decoders and a microprocessor are connected together, the resulting forest of wires is quite alarming. A printed circuit board (PCB) is a much better proposition. It isn't difficult to make a PCB but it probably isn't worth the effort either, since commercial boards with connections for these chips already exist. I use the 'Cubit', which is available from Control Universal Ltd. Their board contains space for the 6502 microprocessor, a single rail 2716 EPROM, address decoding circuits, 2114 memory chips and a VIA. There are hundreds of simple systems that could be produced with this board, although some expertise in machine code programming and a good knowledge of the 6502 are needed before such a project is tackled. Some possible means of putting data into and getting it out of such a system are as follows:

Keyboard

The simple and cheap hexadecimal keyboard contains the numerals 0 to 9 and the keys A to F. There are two different versions of it, one of which has sixteen separate switches, each operated by one of the keys. The way to use this keyboard is to run it from the a four-to-sixteen demultiplexer (SN74LS154) described in Chapter 4. This device switches on one of sixteen possible lines when the binary address of the required line is sent to the address inputs (A0, A1, A2, A3). Only one of the outputs goes LOW at any time, depending on the binary number at the inputs. These inputs would be driven by four lines of the VIA to select any of the sixteen output lines. Each of these output lines is connected to one of the keys of the keyboard. If any of the keys is depressed, while its line is being held LOW (or strobed), then the output from the keyboard will itself be driven LOW. If this keyboard output is connected to a VIA input line, it can be sensed by the microprocessor.

The keyboard scan procedure is to put each of the numbers 0000 to 1111 in turn into the demultiplexer and to look at the keyboard output each time. When it is LOW, the

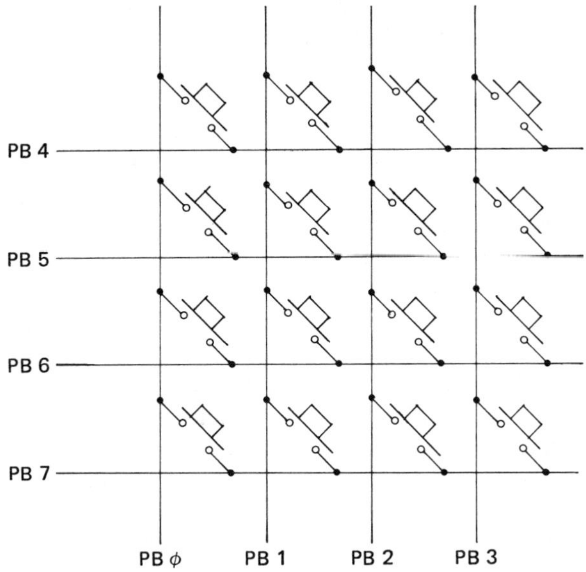

Figure 9.1 Matrix keyboard

number currently being output to the demultiplexer is the key that is being pressed. The obvious line for the keyboard output is bit 7, since that can be detected with the single operation BPL, which will only be obeyed if one of the keys is being pressed.

An alternative is the 4 x 4 matrix keyboard of Figure 9.1, which connects to the eight lines of the user port, configured to make PB0 to 3 into inputs and PB4 to 7 into outputs. Each line of PB 4 to PB7 is then made to go LOW and each of PB0 to PB3 is checked to see if it has gone LOW. If so, the key at the intersection of the two chosen lines must have been pressed.

Display

If the display only needs to show a few digits at a time and simple words, an ideal device is the eight-digit seven-segment LED display, just like that found in most calculators. Different characters are displayed by controlling each segment of each digit independently. Calculator-style displays also have the advantage of being inexpensive. Each line **(segment)** of the display is an LED and all eight segments have a common cathode (or anode). The seven segments of the digit are labelled a, b, c, d, e, f and g and there is also a decimal point dp. When any segment is taken HIGH and its cathode is taken LOW, that segment will light up. To display digits different codes need to be sent to the segments. By alternating between upper and lower case letters, it is even possible to display enough letters of the alphabet to present such words as 'rEAdy', 'yES' and 'no', as well as the responses A, b, C, d and E. The codes for these are calculated just like those for the digits.

At first sight it looks as if the requirements of the eight-digit, seven-segment display are impossible to meet. The number of segments is actually eight, because of the decimal point, and this might imply that 8 x 8 or 64 lines are needed to drive all eight digits. In practice, only one digit is displayed at any one time and only the segments needed for that particular digit are switched on. This technique is called **multiplexing** and is the standard procedure for this type of display. (If the number 8888888888 is entered into a pocket calculator, which is then waved about, it becomes obvious that this is happening.) With this method we can use the same eight lines to run the segments for all of the digits and we only need eight more lines, one for each digit.

The same demultiplexer that drives the sixteen-key keyboard, can be used to provide these digit drives. As each keyboard position is strobed, it applies a LOW to the cathode of one of the display digits. The required segments are then driven HIGH at the same time, so that the desired character is displayed in its correct position. Each position is strobed in turn so that, in fact, up to sixteen digits could be displayed by this method. All of them could appear to be showing a different digit or character.

This technique means that the segment drive and the selected digit have to be held for a few milliseconds, to give the user time to see the displayed character. Although this slows up the rate of scanning the keyboard, there is really no problem because an operator is unlikely to press a key for less than several centiseconds. There is plenty of time to strobe the keyboard as well as to display all eight digits. This method therefore only needs thirteen lines of the VIA to run the keyboard and display. The remaining lines may be used for switch inputs or other outputs.

Memory

To provide temporary storage for input data and to allow a working space for the operating system some RAM is necessary. On the Cubit board RAM comes in blocks of 1K up to a maximum of 4K. The obvious place to put this 1K is on pages zero to three of the memory map so that we can use zero page addressing modes and make savings in execution time. To make use of subroutines, we also need to create a STACK in RAM, which, for the 6502 microprocessor, must be on page one. This leaves the remainder for data storage. As we saw above, only one VIA is required to handle all the I/O. The VIA address on the Cubit is chosen to be &9000 to &900F.

The program needed to run the operating system will need routines for handling the keyboard input and display output, for sending and receiving the data and for processing the data entered from the keyboard. This might sound a great deal, but in fact machine code is very sparing in its use of memory, so the two kilobytes of a single 2716 EPROM are more than enough. Its 2048 bytes take up the memory space from &F800 to &FFFF. This is essential because the 6502 will need addresses &FFFC and &FFFD, which is where the microprocessor will look for its first jump address after being switched on. We shall put the starting address of our program into the locations &FFFC and &FFFD and the microprocessor will jump to the start of our program every time we switch on or reset the terminal.

Our memory map will therefore look like this:

Memory	**User address**
RAM	&0000-&03FF
VIA	&9000-&900F
EPROM	&F800-&FFFF

The Cubit board itself has switches to decide where the ROM and RAM are to go. A simple system like ours does not need these switches, wires are soldered instead to choose block zero for RAM and block F for ROM (or EPROM in our case).

VIA usage

The keyboard and display require only thirteen I/O lines. The 6522 VIA has 16 available I/O lines, so there is a little choice. We could use the C1 and C2 control lines too if this is found to be unnecessary. The whole of the B-Port is chosen to drive the segments and the lower four bits of the A-Port are connected to the four-to-sixteen demultiplexer to provide the digit select and keyboard scan. Bit 7 of the A-Port is chosen for the input from the keyboard. The remaining lines could be used for other purposes such as communication with other systems or for input sensors or relay outputs:

```
B-port: bits 0 to 7 : segment select (to segment drivers)
A-port: bits 0 to 3 : digit select (to inputs of SN74154)
                    : and key select on the keyboard
               bit 7: input from keyboard
```

Programming

I have made several stand-alone systems based upon the Cubit board, which I find exceptionally easy to use. I actually wrote the programs for these systems using an Apple II microcomputer. The address and data lines from an Apple connector socket were connected to a VIA and the outputs from this went to the keyboard, display and I/O lines of my system. The program was written in the Apple's memory accessing the VIA through the address &C0C0. When the program had been debugged, the hexadecimal codes were copied out by hand and the VIA address changed to &9000 to fit the Cubit system. The Cubit board was constructed and its VIA connected to the keyboard, display and I/O lines in exactly the same way as the other VIA had been. The program codes were then taken to Glasgow University and typed into their EPROM burner. The EPROM was then plugged into the final system. To my utter astonishment it worked first time! One of the systems I made using the Apple was a simple microprocessor tutor, now marketed by Griffin and George Ltd as the Mini-microprocessor. I have been hooked on dedicated systems ever since.

There is no reason why the same arrangement I developed for the Apple would not also work with a VIA connected to the 1 MHz bus of the BBC microcomputer. However a much better way to do the development is to use an **emulator.** This is a small board that fits the BBC microcomputer and terminates in a twenty-four pin plug. This plug is pin-compatible with the 2516 EPROM and it is fitted into the EPROM socket of the Cubit board. A suitable program in the BBC microcomputer turns that microcomputer and the emulation board into a simulated 2516 EPROM. The routines to run the Cubit board can then be written using the BBC assembler and the Cubit board system can be run to try them out. Debugging is quick and easy and when the program has been fully developed, it can be burned into an EPROM. This can then be plugged into the stand-alone Cubit board system.

At the time of writing a great deal of work is being done to produce emulators and EPROM burners for coupling to the BBC microcomputer (for example, Control Universal Ltd). They will make the development of dedicated systems quite easy and perfectly feasible projects for fifth and sixth year students. There is something very pleasing about inventing and producing your very own computer; it is real microelectronics. May I wish you the same success and joy in any of your ventures into dedicated systems.

Suppliers

At the time of writing several commercial interfaces are available for the BBC microcomputer. Soon there will be an overwhelming supply. What criteria should be used in selecting one for use in the science laboratory?

First and foremost is cost. Some interfaces for the Apple cost a few hundred pounds and offer less than is standard in the BBC microcomputer, so the cost of an interface is no guide to its facilities. There is no point in duplicating the facilities already offered on the BBC microcomputer, so a slow analogue converter is not needed. Similarly, unbuffered inputs and outputs are available at the user port, so these are no use either.

A useful laboratory interface would have a fast analogue converter, preferably with up to four channels. A data acquisition rate of at least 10 000 readings a second is needed for measuring transients. The inputs may be a.c. or d.c. and it should be possible to alter the sensitivity and the bias, so that, for example, the voltage across a capacitor could be measured as it discharged through an inductor. A useful facility would allow the alteration of the threshold level at which the measurements begin to be taken.

The interface ought also to provide a digital to analogue converter with sufficient power output to drive current through an LCR circuit or a lamp. Even better would be an a.c. output with controllable frequency as described in Chapter 5.

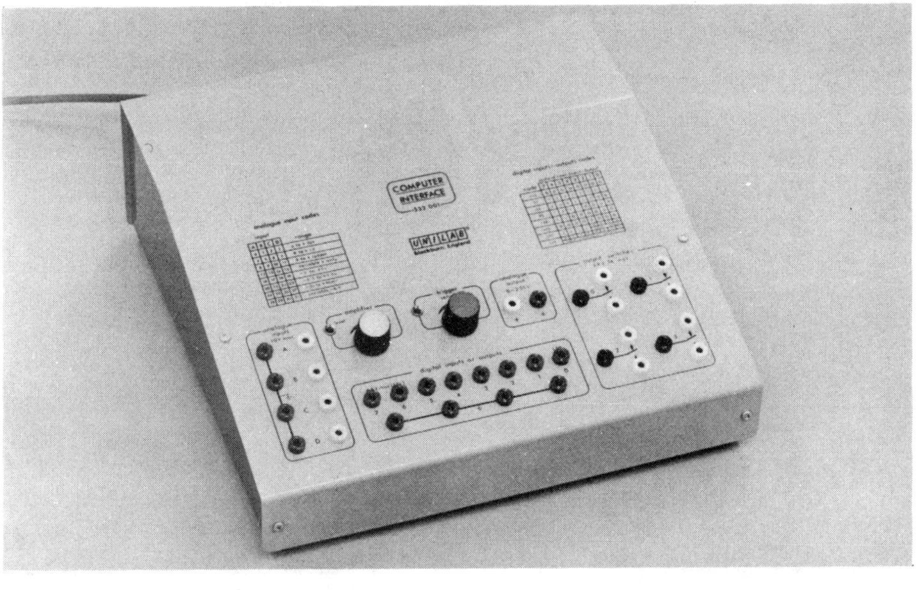

Plate 43 Unilab interface

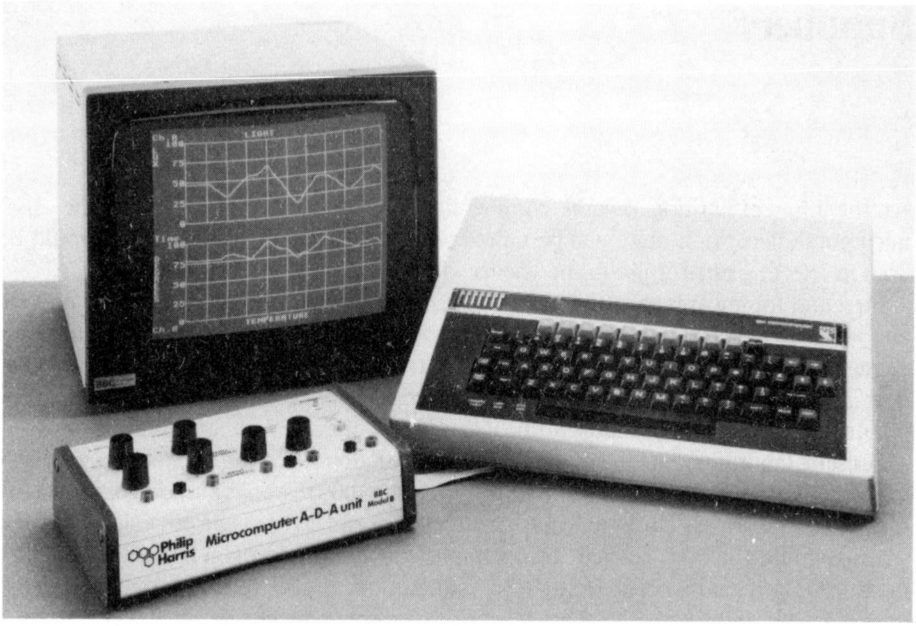

Plate 44 Philip Harris analogue interface

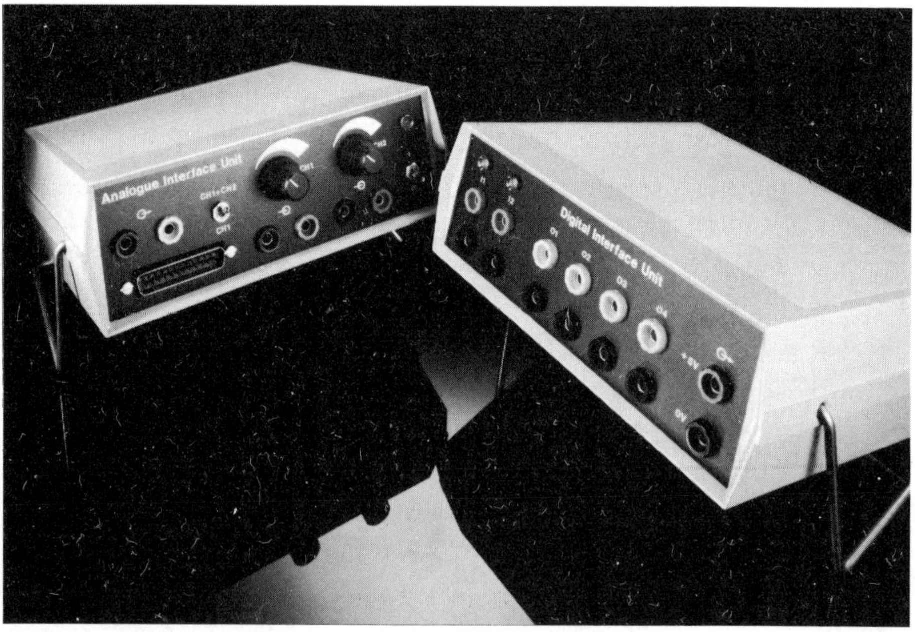

Plate 45 Griffin interface units

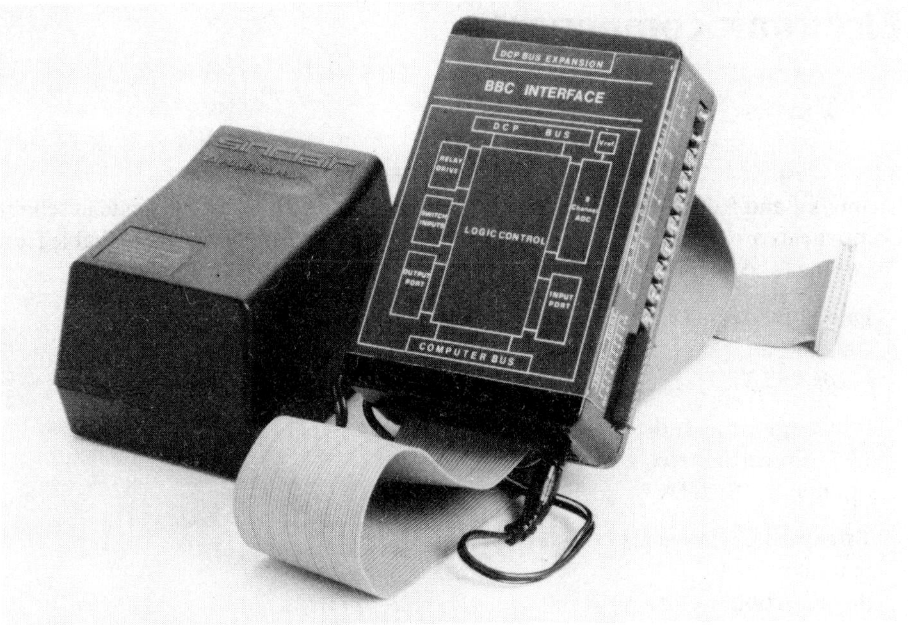

Plate 46 BBC Interface

The digital side should have relay outputs for driving motors and heaters and TTL outputs for driving other integrated circuits. Inputs that can be driven directly from a switch or a photocell are also desirable. A minimum number of outputs is four and at least two inputs would be needed. Eight of each is very nice if the expense can be justified.

There is no commercially available interface that yet fulfils all of these requirements. A good contender is that produced by Unilab Ltd (Plate 43). Those sold by Philip Harris are also very good, although a full set would be rather expensive (Plate 44). Griffin and George Ltd have their digital and analogue units (Plate 45) which are satisfactory, if costly. An exciting development is a new, very cheap interface available through Griffin and George Ltd, which is close to my specification above. It is called the BBC Interface (Plate 46)

For further details contact

Griffin and George Ltd
Ealing Road
Wembley HA0 1HJ

Unilab Ltd
Clarendon Road
Blackburn BB1 9TA

Philip Harris Ltd
Lynn Lane
Shenstone WS14 0EE

Electronic components

Chapters 4 and 5 describe several interfacing circuits that can easily be made in school. Components are the biggest problem, but those mentioned are normally available from one of the following suppliers:

Farnell Electronic Components Ltd
Canal Road
Leeds LS2 2TU

RS Components Ltd
13-17 Epworth Street
London EC2P 2HA

Verospeed Components
Stansted Road
Boyatt Wood
Eastleigh
Hants SO5 4ZY

Concept keyboard

The best known is obtainable from:

Star Microterminals Ltd
22 Hyde Street
Winchester
Hants SO23 7DR

Cubit PCB

The PCBs for dedicated microcomputers based upon the Cubit system are obtainable from:

Control Universal Ltd
Unit 2
Andersons Court
Newnham Road
Cambridge CB3 9EZ

Bibliography

Introductory

J. McGregor and A. Watt, *The BBC Micro Book,* Addison-Wesley

T. Hartnell, *Let your BBC Micro Teach you to Program,* Interface

N. and P. Cryer, *Basic Programming on the BBC Microcomputer,* Prentice Hall

P. Williams, *Programming the BBC Microcomputer,* Newnes Technical Books

Microcomputer graphics

J. Cownie, *Creative Graphics on the BBC Microcomputer,* Acornsoft

R. E. Myers, *Microcomputer Grphics with Apple II examples,* Addison-Wesley

Advanced

J. McGregor and A. Watt, *Advanced Programming Techniques for the BBC Micro,* Addison-Wesley

L. Poole and M. Borchers, *Some Common BASIC Programs,* Osborne/McGraw Hill

J. S. Coan, *Advanced BASIC,* Hayden Book Co. Inc.

J. S. Gilder, *BASIC Computer Programs in Science and Engineering,* Hayden Book Co. Inc.

Assembly language

I. Birnbaum, *Assembly Language Programming for the BBC Microcomputer,* Macmillan

J. Ferguson and A. Shaw, *Assembly Language Programming on the BBC Micro,* Addison-Wesley

L. A. Levethal, *6502 Assembly Language Programming,* Osborne/McGraw Hill

Electronics

Malmstadt, Enk and Crouch, *Electronics and Instrumentation,* Benjamin/Cummings Pub. Co. Inc. California

On education

C. Doerr, *Microcomputers and the 3Rs,* Hayden Book Co. Inc.

National BBC user clubs

Beebug
374 Wandsworth Road
London SW3 4TE

Laserbug
18 Dawley Ride
Colnbrook
Slough
Berks SL3 0QH

Program listings

LOGIC GATES - PROGRAM 1

```
LIST
    1 MODE 7
   10 REM LOGIC GATES
   20 PRT=&FE60:REM USER PORT
   25 DDR=&FE62:REM DATA DIRECTION REGISTER
   80 SR=&7C00:REM SCREEN VALUE
   90 ?DDR=240:REM BITS 0 TO 3 ARE INPUTS, BITS 4 TO 7 ARE OUTPUTS
  100 REM
  110 CLS
  120 PRINT TAB(12,0);"LOGIC GATES"
  121 PRINT TAB(0,2);"SELECT DESIRED GATE BY PRESSING ONE"
  122 PRINT TAB(0,4);"OF THE FOLLOWING NUMBERS."
  123 PRINT TAB(6,6);"1     AND"
  124 PRINT TAB(6,8);"2     OR"
  125 PRINT TAB(6,10);"3     NOT"
  126 PRINT TAB(6,12);"4     EXCLUSIVE-OR"
  127 PRINT TAB(6,14);"5     EQUIVALENCE"
  128 PRINT TAB(6,16);"6     NAND"
  129 PRINT TAB(6,18);"7     NOR"
  140 LET S$=GET$
  145 S%=VAL(S$)
  150 IF S%<1 OR S%>7 THEN 140
  151 PRINT TAB(0,20);"YOUR SELECTION IS"
  152 IF S%=1 THEN PRINT TAB(20,20);"AND"
  153 IF S%=2 THEN PRINT TAB(20,20);"OR"
  154 IF S%=3 THEN PRINT TAB(20,20);"NOT"
  155 IF S%=4 THEN PRINT TAB(20,20);"EXCLUSIVE-OR"
  156 IF S%=5 THEN PRINT TAB(20,20);"EQUIVALENCE"
  157 IF S%=6 THEN PRINT TAB(20,20);"NAND"
  158 IF S%=7 THEN PRINT TAB(20,20);"NOR"
  160 PRINT :PRINT"Press RETURN to confirm"
  165 PRINT :PRINT"or press SPACE to try again.";
  170 IF GET$<>CHR$(13) THEN 110
  250 IF S%<>3 THEN 490
  260 CLS:PRINT TAB(0,2);"THE 'NOT' FUNCTION HAS ONE INPUT."
  270 PRINT:PRINT"WHICH INPUT?  PRESS A OR B"
  420 I$=GET$
  430 IF I$<>"A" AND I$<>"B" THEN 420
  460 REM **********************
  470 REM DISPLAY FUNCTION AND TERMINALS
  480 REM **********************
  490 CLS
  500
  510 GOSUB 1000:REM DISPLAY FUNCTION
  530 ON S% GOSUB 1100,1200,1300,1400,1500,1600,1700
  540 PRINT TAB(13,8);P$
  550 PRINT TAB(30,8);"( ) OUTPUT"
  590 REM DISPLAY INPUTS
  600 IF S%=3 THEN GOSUB 5000 ELSE GOSUB 5100
```

```
 620 PRINT TAB(0,20);"Press F for different gate, or E to end."
 630 A$=INKEY$(0)
 640 IF A$="F" THEN 110
 650 IF A$="E" THEN END
 660 REM GET DATA
 670 LET A%=?PRT AND 1
 680 LET B%=(?PRT AND 2)DIV 2
 720
 730 REM CHANGE INPUT VALUES ON SCREEN
 740 FOR PN=5TO 15
 750 SC=SR+PN*40
 760 J=?SC-64
 770 IF J=1 THEN ?(SC+2)=A%+48
 780 IF J=2 THEN ?(SC+2)=B%+48
 790 NEXT PN
 800 REM CALCULATE OUTPUT DATA
 910  ON S% GOSUB 3100,3200,3300,3400,3500,3600,3700
 920 REM SEND OUTPUT TO USER PORT
 930  ?PRT= 128*VO%
 940 REM SEND LOGIC LEVEL TO SCREEN
 950 PRINT TAB(31,8);VO%
 990 GOTO 630
1000 REM BOX DISPLAY
1010 PRINT TAB(11,6);CHR$(151);CHR$(55);CHR$(96);CHR$(96);CHR$(96);CHR$(96);
CHR$(96);CHR$(96);CHR$(107);CHR$(135)
1020 PRINT TAB(11,7);CHR$(151);CHR$(53);"      ";CHR$(106);CHR$(135)
1030 PRINT TAB(11,8);CHR$(151);CHR$(53);"      ";CHR$(106);CHR$(44);CHR$(44);
CHR$(44);CHR$(44);CHR$(44);CHR$(44);CHR$(44);CHR$(44);CHR$(44);CHR$(135)
1040PRINT TAB(11,9);CHR$(151);CHR$(53);"      ";CHR$(106);CHR$(135)
1050PRINT TAB(11,10);CHR$(151);CHR$(117);CHR$(112);CHR$(112);CHR$(112);CHR$
(112);CHR$(112);CHR$(112);CHR$(122);CHR$(135)
1060 RETURN
1100 P$="  AND":RETURN
1200 P$="  OR":RETURN
1300 P$="  NOT":RETURN
1400 P$="EX OR":RETURN
1500 P$="EQUIV":RETURN
1600 P$=" NAND":RETURN
1700 P$=" NOR":RETURN
3000 REM DETERMINE OUTPUTS FOR EACH FUNCTION
3100 REM AND FUNCTION
3110 VO%=A% AND B%
3150 RETURN
3200 REM OR FUNCTION
3210 VO%=A% OR B%
3250 RETURN
3300 REM NOT FUNCTION
3310 IF S%=3 AND I$="A" THEN VO%=(NOT A%) AND 1
3320 IF S%=3 AND I$="B" THEN VO%=(NOT B%) AND 1
3330 RETURN
3400 REM EXCLUSIVE-OR FUNCTION
3410 VO%=((A% AND NOT B%) OR (NOT A% AND B%)) AND 1
3430 RETURN
3500 REM EQUIVALENCE FUNCTION
3510 VO%=((A% AND B%) OR (NOT A% AND NOT B%)) AND 1
3530 RETURN
3600 REM NAND FUNCTION
3610 VO%=NOT(A% AND B%) AND 1
3620 RETURN
3700 REM NOR FUNCTION
```

```
 3710 VO%=NOT(A% OR B%) AND 1
 3760 RETURN
 5000 REM APPEND THE INPUTS
 5010 REM ONE INPUT
 5020 PROCline(8,I$)
 5030 RETURN
 5100 REM TWO INPUTS
 5110 PROCline(7,"B")
 5120 PROCline(9,"A")
 5130 RETURN
 6000 DEFPROCline(K,G$)
 6010 PRINT TAB(0,K);G$;"( )";CHR$(151);CHR$(44);CHR$(44);CHR$(44);CHR$(44);
CHR$(44);CHR$(44);CHR$(44)
 6020 ENDPROC
```

LOGIC TEST - PROGRAM 1A

```
    1 MODE 7
   10 ON ERROR GOTO 110
   20 REM TURN CURSOR OFF
   30 VDU23;8202;0;0;0
  100 DIM unused(10)
  110 REM LOGIC TEST
  120 PRT=&FE60:REM USER PORT
  130 DDR=&FE62:REM DATA DIRECTION REGISTER
  140 LET score=0
  150 FOR I=0 TO 9:LET unused(I)=TRUE:NEXT I
  160 LET question=0
  170 ?DDR=240:REM BITS 0 TO 3 ARE INPUTS, BITS 4 TO 7 ARE OUTPUTS
  180 REPEAT
  190 LET status=1000:REM INITIALIZE INPUT STATUS
  200 CLS
  210 LET attempt=FALSE:LET correct=FALSE:LET question=question+1
  220 PROCselect
  230 PROCgate:GOSUB 5100:REM APPEND TWO INPUTS
  240 PRINT TAB(0,6)
  250PRINT:PRINT"Which of these functions is the board"
  260PRINT:PRINT"now producing? Choose by pressing        "
  270 PRINT"one of these numbers."
  280 PRINT:PRINT"0    A AND B           1    A OR B"
  290 PRINT:PRINT"2    NOT A             3    NOT B"
  300 PRINT:PRINT"4    (A AND NOT B) OR (NOT A AND B)"
  310 PRINT:PRINT"5    (NOT A AND NOT B) OR (A AND B)"
  320 PRINT:PRINT"6    NOT(A AND B)      7    NOT(A OR B)"
  330 PRINT:PRINT"8    NOT A AND B       9    NOT A OR B";
  340 PROCdogate
  350 LET S%=INKEY(0)-48
  360 IF S%=17 THEN LET line=15:CLS:GOTO 650
  370 IF S%<0 OR S%>9 THEN 340
  380 PRINT TAB(0,8);"                                        "
  390 PRINT TAB(0,10);"                                       "
  400 PRINT TAB(0,12);"                                       "
  410 PRINTTAB(0,8);"Your selection is ";
  420 IF S%=0 THEN PRINT TAB(18,8);"A AND B"
```

```
 430 IF S%=1 THEN PRINT TAB(18,8);"A OR B"
 440 IF S%=2 THEN PRINT TAB(18,8);"NOT A"
 450 IF S%=3 THEN PRINT TAB(18,8);"NOT B"
 460 IF S%=4 THEN PRINT TAB(2,10);"(NOT A AND B) OR (A AND NOT B)"
 470 IF S%=5 THEN PRINT TAB(2,10);"(NOT A AND NOT B) OR (A AND B)"
 480 IF S%=6 THEN PRINT TAB(18,8);"NOT(A AND B)"
 490 IF S%=7 THEN PRINT TAB(18,8);"NOT(A OR B)"
 500 IF S%=8 THEN PRINT TAB(18,8);"NOT A AND B"
 510 IF S%=9 THEN PRINT TAB(18,8);"NOT A OR B"
 520 PRINT:PRINT"RETURN to confirm   or  T to try again."
 530 PROCdogate
 540 LET K$=INKEY$(0)
 550 IF K$=CHR$13 THEN 580
 560 IF K$="T" THEN 240
 570 GOTO 530
 580 REM CHECK ANSWER
 590 IF S%<>N% THEN PROCwrong:GOTO 340
 600 LET correct=TRUE
 610 LET line=15:REM Initialize row
 620 CLS
 630 IF attempt=0 THEN PRINT TAB(6);"CORRECT FIRST TIME" ELSE PRINT TAB(6);
"CORRECT THIS TIME"
 640 IF attempt=0 THEN score=score+1
 650 PROCgate
 660 PROCnamegate
 670 PROCtable
 680 PRINT TAB(0,22);"Press N for next question."
 690 REPEAT
 700 PROCshow
 710 UNTIL INKEY$(0)="N"
 720 UNTIL question=10
 730 REM SHOW SCORE
 740 CLS
 750 PRINT TAB(8,1);"LOGIC GATES"
 760 PRINT:PRINT:PRINT"Your score is ";score
 770 PRINT:PRINT:PRINT"Press SPACE to begin again."
 780 REPEAT UNTIL GET$=" "
 790 GOTO 110
 800
1000 DEF PROCgate
1010 PRINT TAB(11,2);CHR$(151);CHR$(55);CHR$(96);CHR$(96);CHR$(96);CHR$(96);
CHR$(96);CHR$(96);CHR$(107);CHR$(135)
1020 PRINT TAB(11,3);CHR$(151);CHR$(53);"      ";CHR$(106);CHR$(135)
1030 PRINT TAB(11,4);CHR$(151);CHR$(53);"      ";CHR$(106);CHR$(44);CHR$(44);
CHR$(44);CHR$(44);CHR$(44);CHR$(44);CHR$(44);CHR$(44);CHR$(44);CHR$(135)
1040PRINT TAB(11,5);CHR$(151);CHR$(53);"      ";CHR$(106);CHR$(135)
1050PRINT TAB(11,6);CHR$(151);CHR$(117);CHR$(112);CHR$(112);CHR$(112);CHR$
(112);CHR$(112);CHR$(112);CHR$(122);CHR$(135)
1060 PRINT TAB(30,4);"( ) OUTPUT"
1070 ENDPROC
1200 P$="  AND":RETURN
1210 P$="   OR":RETURN
1220 P$=" NOT A":RETURN
1230 P$=" NOT B":RETURN
1240 P$="EX OR":RETURN
1250 P$="EQUIV":RETURN
1260 P$=" NAND":RETURN
1270 P$=" NOR":RETURN
1280 P$=CHR$11+" NOT A"+CHR$8+CHR$8+CHR$8+CHR$8+CHR$8+CHR$10+CHR$10+"AND B":
RETURN
```

```
 1290 P$=CHR$11+" NOT A"+CHR$8+CHR$8+CHR$8+CHR$8+CHR$8+CHR$10+CHR$10+" OR B":
RETURN
 1400 DEF PROCnamegate
 1410 ON (N%+1) GOSUB 1200,1210,1220,1230,1240,1250,1260,1270,1280,1290
 1420 PRINT TAB(13,4);P$
 1430 REM DISPLAY INPUTS
 1440 IF N%=2 OR N%=3 THEN GOSUB 5000 ELSE GOSUB 5100
 1450 ENDPROC
 2000 DEF PROCselect
 2010 REPEAT
 2020 LET N%=RND(10)-1
 2030 UNTIL unused(N%)
 2040 LET unused(N%)=FALSE
 2050 IF N%=2 THEN LET I$="A"
 2060 IF N%=3 THEN LET I$="B"
 2070 ENDPROC
 3000 REM DETERMINE OUTPUTS FOR EACH FUNCTION
 3001 REM AND FUNCTION
 3010 VO%=A% AND B%
 3020 RETURN
 3100 REM OR FUNCTION
 3110 VO%=A% OR B%
 3120 RETURN
 3200 REM NOT A FUNCTION
 3210 VO%=(NOT A%) AND 1
 3220 RETURN
 3300 REM NOT B FUNCTION
 3310 VO%=(NOT B%) AND 1
 3330 RETURN
 3400 REM EXCLUSIVE-OR FUNCTION
 3410 VO%=((A% AND NOT B%) OR (NOT A% AND B%)) AND 1
 3430 RETURN
 3500 REM EQUIVALENCE FUNCTION
 3510 VO%=((A% AND B%) OR (NOT A% AND NOT B%)) AND 1
 3530 RETURN
 3600 REM NAND FUNCTION
 3610 VO%=NOT(A% AND B%) AND 1
 3620 RETURN
 3700 REM NOR FUNCTION
 3710 VO%=NOT(A% OR B%) AND 1
 3760 RETURN
 3800 REM NOT A AND B FUNCTION
 3810 VO%=(NOTA% AND B%) AND 1
 3820 RETURN
 3900 REM NOT A OR B FUNCTION
 3910 VO%=(NOTA% OR B%) AND 1
 3920 RETURN
 4000 DEF PROCtable
 4010 PRINT TAB(8,8);CHR$(151);CHR$(183);CHR$(163);CHR$(163);CHR$(163);CHR$
(183);CHR$(163);CHR$(163);CHR$(163);CHR$(183);CHR$(163);CHR$(163);CHR$(163);
CHR$(163);CHR$(163);CHR$(163);CHR$(163);CHR$(163);CHR$(235)
 4020 PRINT TAB(8,9);CHR$(151);CHR$(53);CHR$(32);CHR$(193);CHR$(32);CHR$(53);
CHR$(32);CHR$(194);CHR$(32);CHR$(53);CHR$(32);CHR$(207);CHR$(213);CHR$(212);
CHR$(208);CHR$(213);CHR$(212);CHR$(32);CHR$(234)
 4030 PRINT TAB(8,10);CHR$(151);CHR$(117);CHR$(240);CHR$(240);CHR$(240);CHR$
(117);CHR$(240);CHR$(240);CHR$(240);CHR$(117);CHR$(240);CHR$(240);CHR$(240);
CHR$(240);CHR$(240);CHR$(240);CHR$(240);CHR$(240);CHR$(250)
 4040 PRINT TAB(8,11);CHR$(151);CHR$(53);CHR$(32);CHR$(32);CHR$(32);CHR$(53);
CHR$(32);CHR$(32);CHR$(32);CHR$(53);CHR$(32);CHR$(32);CHR$(32);CHR$(32);CHR$
(32);CHR$(32);CHR$(32);CHR$(32);CHR$(106)
```

```
 4050 PRINT TAB(8,12);CHR$(151);CHR$(53);CHR$(32);CHR$(207);CHR$(32);CHR$
(53);CHR$(32);CHR$(207);CHR$(32);CHR$(53);CHR$(32);CHR$(32);CHR$(32);CHR$(32);
CHR$(32);CHR$(32);CHR$(32);CHR$(32);CHR$(234)
 4060 PRINT TAB(8,13);CHR$(151);CHR$(53);CHR$(32);CHR$(32);CHR$(32);CHR$(53);
CHR$(32);CHR$(32);CHR$(32);CHR$(53);CHR$(32);CHR$(32);CHR$(32);CHR$(32);CHR$
(32);CHR$(32);CHR$(32);CHR$(32);CHR$(106)
 4070 PRINT TAB(8,14);CHR$(151);CHR$(53);CHR$(32);CHR$(207);CHR$(32);CHR$
(53);CHR$(32);CHR$(201);CHR$(32);CHR$(53);CHR$(32);CHR$(32);CHR$(32);CHR$(32);
CHR$(32);CHR$(32);CHR$(32);CHR$(32);CHR$(234)
 4080 PRINT TAB(8,15);CHR$(151);CHR$(53);CHR$(32);CHR$(32);CHR$(32);CHR$(53);
CHR$(32);CHR$(32);CHR$(32);CHR$(53);CHR$(32);CHR$(32);CHR$(32);CHR$(32);CHR$
(32);CHR$(32);CHR$(32);CHR$(32);CHR$(106)
 4090 PRINT TAB(8,16);CHR$(151);CHR$(53);CHR$(32);CHR$(201);CHR$(32);CHR$(53);
CHR$(32);CHR$(207);CHR$(32);CHR$(53);CHR$(32);CHR$(32);CHR$(32);CHR$(32);CHR$
(32);CHR$(32);CHR$(32);CHR$(32);CHR$(234)
 4100 PRINT TAB(8,17);CHR$(151);CHR$(53);CHR$(32);CHR$(32);CHR$(32);CHR$(53);
CHR$(32);CHR$(32);CHR$(32);CHR$(53);CHR$(32);CHR$(32);CHR$(32);CHR$(32);CHR$
(32);CHR$(32);CHR$(32);CHR$(32);CHR$(106)
 4110 PRINT TAB(8,18);CHR$(151);CHR$(53);CHR$(32);CHR$(201);CHR$(32);CHR$
(53);CHR$(32);CHR$(201);CHR$(32);CHR$(53);CHR$(32);CHR$(32);CHR$(32);CHR$(32);
CHR$(32);CHR$(32);CHR$(32);CHR$(32);CHR$(234)
 4120 PRINT TAB(8,19);CHR$(151);CHR$(117);CHR$(240);CHR$(240);CHR$(240);CHR$
(117);CHR$(240);CHR$(240);CHR$(240);CHR$(117);CHR$(240);CHR$(240);CHR$(240);
CHR$(240);CHR$(240);CHR$(240);CHR$(240);CHR$(240);CHR$(250)
 4200 ENDPROC
 5000 REM APPEND THE INPUTS
 5010 REM ONE INPUT
 5020 PROCline(4,I$)
 5030 RETURN
 5100 REM TWO INPUTS
 5110 PROCline(3,"B")
 5120 PROCline(5,"A")
 5130 RETURN
 6000 DEFPROCline(K,G$)
 6010 PRINT TAB(0,K);G$;"( )";CHR$(151);CHR$(44);CHR$(44);CHR$(44);CHR$(44);
CHR$(44);CHR$(44);CHR$(44)
 6020 ENDPROC
 7000 DEF PROCshow
 7010 LET A%=?PRT AND 1
 7020 LET B%=(?PRT AND 2)DIV 2
 7030 IF status=2*B%+4*A% THEN ENDPROC
 7040 REM CHANGE SCREEN VALUES ETC.
 7050 LET status=2*B%+4*A%
 7060 IF N%=2 OR N%=3 THEN 7100:REM ONE INPUT
 7070 PRINT TAB(2,3);B%
 7080 PRINT TAB(2,5);A%
 7090 GOTO 7200
 7100 IF N%=2 THEN PRINT TAB(2,4);A%
 7110 IF N%=3 THEN PRINT TAB(2,4);B%
 7200 REM CALCULATE OUTPUT DATA
 7210 ON (N%+1) GOSUB 3000,3100,3200,3300,3400,3500,3600,3700,3800,3900
 7220 REM SEND OUTPUT TO USER PORT
 7230 ?PRT= 16*VO%
 7240 REM SEND LOGIC LEVEL TO SCREEN
 7250 PRINT TAB(31,4);VO%
 8000 REM HIGHLIGHT TRUTH LINE
 8010 PRINT TAB(3,line);"      "
 8020 PRINT TAB(28,line);"      "
 8030 LET line=12+2*B%+4*A%
 8040 PRINT TAB(3,line);"]]]]]"
```

```
 8050 PRINT TAB(28,line);"[[[[["
 8060 REM FILL IN TRUTH TABLE
 8070 IF VO% THEN PRINT TAB(20,line);"I" ELSE PRINT TAB(20,line);"O"
 8080 ENDPROC
 9000 DEF PROCwrong
 9010 PRINT TAB(0,8);"         WRONG                              "
 9020 PRINT TAB(0,10);"       TRY AGAIN                            "
 9030 PRINT TAB(0,12);"or press A for the answer."
 9040 LET attempt=TRUE
 9050 ENDPROC
10000 DEF PROCdogate
10010 LET A%=?PRT AND 1
10020 LET B%=(?PRT AND 2)DIV 2
10030 IF status=2*B%+4*A% THEN ENDPROC
10040 PRINT TAB(2,3);B%
10050PRINT TAB(2,5);A%
10060 REM CALCULATE OUTPUT DATA
10070 ON (N%+1) GOSUB 3000,3100,3200,3300,3400,3500,3600,3700,3800,3900
10080 REM SEND OUTPUT TO USER PORT
10090 ?PRT= 16*VO%
10100 REM SEND LOGIC LEVEL TO SCREEN
10110 PRINT TAB(31,4);VO%
10120 ENDPROC
```

LOGIC TUTOR - PROGRAM 2

```
LIST
    1 MODE 7
   10 REM BOOLEAN FUNCTIONS
   20 PRT=&FE60:REM USER PORT
   25 DDR=&FE62:REM DATA DIRECTION REGISTER
   30 DIM I%(4):REM NUMBER OF INPUTS PER GATE
   35 DIM T$(4,4):REM FUNCTION VARIABLES (INPUTS,OUTPUTS)
   40 DIM A%(4):REM INPUT DATA FROM USER PORT
   50 DIM VI%(4):REM VALUES FOR INPUT DATA
   60 DIM F%(4):REM MENU VALUE OF FUNCTION
   70 N=0:M=0:REM INPUT AND OUTPUT REFERENCE NUMBERS
   80 SR=&7C00:REM SCREEN VALUE
   90 ?DDR=240:REM BITS 0 TO 3 ARE INPUTS, BITS 4 TO 7 ARE OUTPUTS
  100 FOR M=1 TO 4:F%(M)=0:NEXT M
  110 CLS
  120 PRINT TAB(12,0);"BOOLEAN FUNCTIONS"
  121 PRINT TAB(0,2);"SELECT DESIRED FUNCTION BY ENTERING ONE"
  122 PRINT TAB(0,4);"OF THE FOLLOWING NUMBERS."
  123 PRINT TAB(6,6);"1      AND"
  124 PRINT TAB(6,8);"2      OR"
  125 PRINT TAB(6,10);"3      NOT"
  126 PRINT TAB(6,12);"4      EXCLUSIVE-OR"
  127 PRINT TAB(6,14);"5      EQUIVALENCE"
  128 PRINT TAB(6,16);"6      NAND"
  129 PRINT TAB(6,18);"7      NOR"
  130 PRINT TAB(0,20);"THEN PRESS RETURN."
  140 INPUT S$
  145 S%=VAL(S$)
  150 IF S%<1 OR S%>7 THEN 140
```

```
151 CLS:PRINT TAB(0,5);"YOUR SELECTION IS"
152 IF S%=1 THEN PRINT TAB(20,5);"AND"
153 IF S%=2 THEN PRINT TAB(20,5);"OR"
154 IF S%=3 THEN PRINT TAB(20,5);"NOT"
155 IF S%=4 THEN PRINT TAB(20,5);"EXCLUSIVE-OR"
156 IF S%=5 THEN PRINT TAB(20,5);"EQUIVALENCE"
157 IF S%=6 THEN PRINT TAB(20,5);"NAND"
158 IF S%=7 THEN PRINT TAB(20,5);"NOR"
160 PRINT TAB(0,8);"WHICH OUTPUT FOR THIS FUNCTION ?"
170 PRINT TAB(0,10);"ENTER ONE OF W, X, Y OR Z "
180 PRINT TAB(0,12);"AND THEN PRESS RETURN."
190 INPUT O$
200 IF O$<>"W" AND O$<>"X" AND O$<>"Y" AND O$<>"Z" THEN 190
210 IF O$="W" THEN M=4
220 IF O$="X" THEN M=3
230 IF O$="Y" THEN M=2
240 IF O$="Z" THEN M=1
245 F%(M)=S%
246 IF S%=4 OR S%=5 THEN 280
250 IF S%<>3 THEN 290
260 CLS:PRINT TAB(0,2);"THE 'NOT' FUNCTION HAS ONE INPUT."
270 I%(M)=1:GOTO 340
280 CLS:PRINT TAB(0,2);"THIS FUNCTION HAS TWO INPUTS."
285 I%(M)=2:GOTO 350
290 PRINT TAB(0,15);"HOW MANY INPUTS ?"
300 PRINT TAB(0,18);"ENTER 1, 2, 3 OR 4 AND THEN PRESS RETURN"
310 INPUT I$
320 I%(M)=VAL(I$)
330 IF I%(M)<1 OR I%(M)>4 THEN 310
340 IF I%(M)=1 THEN PRINT:PRINT;"WHICH INPUT ?":GOTO 360
345 CLS
350 PRINT TAB(0,4);"WHICH INPUTS ?"
360 PRINT:PRINT"ENTER A, B, C OR D FOR EACH REQUEST."
365 IF I%(M)=1 THEN 400
370PRINT:PRINT"IT IS POSSIBLE TO USE ONE INPUT MORE"
380PRINT:PRINT"THAN ONCE, PROVIDED YOU HAVE ASKED"
390PRINT:PRINT"FOR ENOUGH INPUTS."
400 FOR N=1 TO 4:T$(N,M)="":NEXT N
410 FOR N=1 TO I%(M)
420 INPUT I$
430 IF I$<>"A" AND I$<>"B" AND I$<>"C" AND I$<>"D" THEN 420
440 T$(N,M)=I$
450 NEXT N
460 REM **********************
470 REM DISPLAY FUNCTIONS AND TERMINALS
480 REM **********************
490 CLS
500 FOR M=1 TO 4
501 C=(M-1)*6
505 IF F%(M)=0 THEN 610
510 GOSUB 1000:REM DISPLAY FUNCTION
530 ON F%(M) GOSUB 1100,1200,1300,1400,1500,1600,1700
540 PRINT TAB(13,C+2);P$
550 PRINT TAB(31,C+2);"( )";CHR$(91-M)
590 REM DISPLAY INPUTS
600 ON I%(M) GOSUB 5000,5100,5200,5300
610 NEXT M
620 PRINT TAB(0,24);"PRESS 'F' FOR MORE FUNCTIONS,'E' TO END";
630 A$=INKEY$(0)
640 IF A$="F" THEN 110
```

```
650 IF A$="E" THEN END
660 REM GET DATA
670 FOR N=1 TO 4
680 A%(N)=0
690 IF ?PRT AND 2^(N-1) THEN A%(N)=1
700 NEXT N
710 REM
720
730 REM CHANGE INPUT VALUES ON SCREEN
740 FOR PN=0 TO 22
750 SC=SR+PN*40
760 J=?SC-64
770 IF J<1 OR J>4 THEN 790
780 ?(SC+2)=(A%(J)+48)
790 NEXT PN
800 REM CALCULATE OUTPUT DATA
810 FOR M=1 TO 4
820 IF F%(M)=0 THEN 980
830 FOR N=1 TO I%(M)
840 IF T$(N,M)="A" THEN VI%(N)=A%(1)
850 IF T$(N,M)="B" THEN VI%(N)=A%(2)
860 IF T$(N,M)="C" THEN VI%(N)=A%(3)
870 IF T$(N,M)="D" THEN VI%(N)=A%(4)
900 NEXT N
910 ON F%(M) GOSUB 3100,3200,3300,3400,3500,3600,3700
920 REM SEND OUTPUT TO USER PORT
930 H=(2^(8-M))
940 ?PRT=(?PRT AND (255-H))
950 K%=H*VO%
960 ?PRT=(?PRT OR K%)
970 IF ?(31615+240*M)<>32 THEN ?(31616+240*M)=(48+VO%)
980 NEXT M
990 GOTO 630
1000 REM BOX DISPLAY
1010 PRINT TAB(11,C);CHR$(151);CHR$(55);CHR$(96);CHR$(96);CHR$(96);CHR$(96);
CHR$(96);CHR$(96);CHR$(107);CHR$(135)
1020 PRINT TAB(11,C+1);CHR$(151);CHR$(53);"        ";CHR$(106);CHR$(135)
1030 PRINT TAB(11,C+2);CHR$(151);CHR$(53);"        ";CHR$(106);CHR$(44);CHR$
(44);CHR$(44);CHR$(44);CHR$(44);CHR$(44);CHR$(44);CHR$(44);CHR$(44);CHR$(44);;
CHR$(135)
1040PRINT TAB(11,C+3);CHR$(151);CHR$(53);"        ";CHR$(106);CHR$(135)
1050PRINT TAB(11,C+4);CHR$(151);CHR$(117);CHR$(112);CHR$(112);CHR$(112);CHR$
(112);CHR$(112);CHR$(112);CHR$(122);CHR$(135)
1060 RETURN
1100 P$="  AND":RETURN
1200 P$="  OR":RETURN
1300 P$="  NOT":RETURN
1400 P$="EX OR":RETURN
1500 P$="EQUIV":RETURN
1600 P$=" NAND":RETURN
1700 P$=" NOR":RETURN
3000 REM DETERMINE OUTPUTS FOR EACH FUNCTION
3100 REM AND FUNCTION
3110 VO%=1
3120 FOR N=1 TO I%(M)
3130 VO%=VO% AND VI%(N)
3140 NEXT N
3150 RETURN
3200 REM OR FUNCTION
3210 VO%=0
```

```
3220 FOR N=1 TO I%(M)
3230 VO%=VO% OR VI%(N)
3240 NEXT N
3250 RETURN
3300 REM NOT FUNCTION
3310 VO%=0
3320 IF VI%(1)=0 THEN VO%=1
3330 RETURN
3400 REM EXCLUSIVE-OR FUNCTION
3410 VO%=1
3420 IF VI%(1)=VI%(2) THEN VO%=0
3430 RETURN
3500 REM EQUIVALENCE FUNCTION
3510 VO%=0
3520 IF VI%(1)=VI%(2) THEN VO%=1
3530 RETURN
3600 REM NAND FUNCTION
3610 VO%=1
3620 FOR N=1 TO I%(M)
3630 VO%=VO% AND VI%(N)
3640 NEXT N
3650 IF VO%=0 THEN VO%=1:RETURN
3660 IF VO%=1 THEN VO%=0:RETURN
3700 REM NOR FUNCTION
3710 VO%=0
3720 FOR N=1 TO I%(M)
3730 VO%=VO% OR VI%(N)
3740 NEXT N
3750 IF VO%=0 THEN VO%=1:RETURN
3760 IF VO%=1 THEN VO%=0:RETURN
5000 REM APPEND THE INPUTS
5010 REM ONE INPUT
5020 PROCline(2,T$(1,M))
5030 RETURN
5100 REM TWO INPUTS
5110 PROCline(1,T$(1,M))
5120 PROCline(3,T$(2,M))
5130 RETURN
5200 REM THREE INPUTS
5210 PROCline(0,T$(1,M))
5220 PROCline(2,T$(2,M))
5230 PROCline(4,T$(3,M))
5240 RETURN
5300 REM FOUR INPUTS
5310 PROCline(0,T$(1,M))
5320 PROCline(1,T$(2,M))
5330 PROCline(3,T$(3,M))
5340 PROCline(4,T$(4,M))
5350 RETURN
6000 DEFPROCline(K,G$)
6010 PRINT TAB(0,K+C);G$;"( )";CHR$(151);CHR$(44);CHR$(44);CHR$(44);CHR$(44);CHR$(44);CHR$(44);CHR$(44)
6020 ENDPROC
```

LOGIC MAKER – PROGRAM 3

```
LIST
    1 MODE 7
   10 REM BOOLEAN FUNCTIONS
   20 PRT=&FE60:REM USER PORT
   25 DDR=&FE62:REM DATA DIRECTION REGISTER
   30 ?DDR=240:REM BITS 0 TO 3 AS INPUTS, 4 TO 7 AS OUTPUTS
   40 DD=31994:DC=32114:DB=32234:DA=32354
   50 DZ=32012:DY=32132:DX=32252:DW=32372
   60 REM DECLARE OUTPUTS
   70 Z=0:Y=0:X=0:W=0
  100CLS
  110 PRINT TAB(10,0);"BOOLEAN FUNCTIONS"
  120 PRINT TAB(0,3);"You may enter any desired function"
  130 PRINT TAB(0,5);"by quitting this program and changing"
  140 PRINT TAB(0,7);"lines 5010 to 5100 of this program."
  150 PRINT TAB(0,9);"If you do not change the function,"
  160 PRINT TAB(0,11);"then it is automatically chosen to be"
  170 PRINT TAB(0,13);"A  AND  B, which appears at output Z."
  180 PRINT TAB(0,21);"Press 'C' to observe the function."
  200 PRINT TAB(0,23);"Press 'E' to quit the program.";
  210 A$=GET$
  220 IF A$<>"E" AND A$<>"C" THEN 210
  230 IF A$="E" THEN 400
  240 REM DISPLAY FUNCTIONS
  250 CLS
  260 PRINT TAB(8,3);"INPUTS            OUTPUTS"
  270 PRINT TAB(8,6);"D( )              Z( )"
  280 PRINT TAB(8,9);"C( )              Y( )"
  290 PRINT TAB(8,12);"B( )              X( )"
  300 PRINT TAB(8,15);"A( )              W( )"
  320 PRINT TAB(0,23);"Press 'E' to quit the program.";
  330 IF A$<>"E" THEN 500
  400 IF A$="E" THEN CLS:PRINT TAB(0,8);"Type LIST 5000,5100  then press
 RETURN"
  410 PRINT TAB(0,10);"Enter any desired functions"
  420 PRINT TAB(0,12);"as proper BASIC statements, "
  430 PRINT TAB(0,14);"and then restart the program with RUN."
  440 STOP
  500 REM GET INPUTS FROM USER PORT
  505 A=0:B=0:C=0:D=0
  510 IF (?PRT AND 1) THEN A=1
  520 IF (?PRT AND 2) THEN B=1
  530 IF (?PRT AND 4) THEN C=1
  540 IF (?PRT AND 8) THEN D=1
  560 REM DISPLAY INPUTS
  570 ?DD=D+48
  580 ?DC=C+48
  590 ?DB=B+48
  600 ?DA=A+48
  610 REM CALCULATE FUNCTION
  620 GOSUB 5000
  700 REM CHANGE OUTPUTS
  710 IF (Z AND 1) THEN ?PRT=(?PRT OR 128):?DZ=49
  720 IF (NOT Z AND 1) THEN ?PRT=(?PRT AND 127):?DZ=48
  730 IF (Y AND 1) THEN ?PRT=(?PRT OR 64):?DY=49
  740 IF (NOT Y AND 1) THEN ?PRT=(?PRT AND 191):?DY=48
  750 IF (X AND 1) THEN ?PRT=(?PRT OR 32):?DX=49
  760 IF (NOT X AND 1) THEN ?PRT=(?PRT AND 223):?DX=48
```

```
 770 IF (W AND 1) THEN ?PRT=(?PRT OR 16):?DW=49
 780 IF (NOT W AND 1) THEN ?PRT=(?PRT AND 239):?DW=48
 790 A$=INKEY$(0)
 800 GOTO 330
5000 REM BOOLEAN FUNCTIONS
5010  Z= A AND B
6000 RETURN
```

6502 MICROPROCESSOR SIMULATION - PROGRAM 4

Execute PAGE = &1C00 before loading this program

```
  1 MODE4
 20 DIM stack(7),mem(256),prog$(25)
 30 GOSUB 10000
 40 LET exec=26
 50 ON ERROR LET exec=26:IN$="COMMAND":J$=IN$:GOTO 20000
100 GOSUB 30000:REM DRAW DIAGRAM
110 GOSUB 25000:REM INITIALISE REGISTERS
120 GOTO 26000:REM DISPLAY REGISTER CONTENTS
130 IF exec<26 THEN GOSUB21000:GOTO141
140  INPUT LINE IN$
141  IF LEFT$(IN$,1)=" " THEN IN$=RIGHT$(IN$,(LEN(IN$)-1)):GOTO 141
142 PRINT IN$
143 IF IN$="COMMAND" THEN 140
145 J$=IN$:REM INSTRUCTION RETAINED
146 IF J$="" THEN PRINT"          ":GOTO130
150 REM DETERMINE OPERATION
153 IF J$="NEW" THEN 11000:REM WRITE NEW PROGRAM
154 IF J$="PROG" THEN 15140:REM CONTINUE WITH SAME PROGRAM
155 IF J$="CALL" THEN 20000
160 operation$=LEFT$(IN$,3)
170 operand$=RIGHT$(IN$,(LEN(IN$)-3))
180 RESTORE
200  J=0: FOR JJ=1 TO 43
210    READ P$
220    IF operation$=P$ THEN J=JJ
230    NEXT JJ
240 REM OPERATION NOT FOUND
250  IF J=0 THEN  1910
280 REM OPERATION FOUND
300 DATA NOP,INX,DEX,INY,DEY
310 DATA RTS,CLC,SEC,TXA,TAX
320 DATA TYA,TAY,PHA,PLA,BRK
330 DATA BNE,BEQ,BMI,BPL,BCC
340 DATA BCS,JMP,JSR,ADC,AND
350 DATA CMP,EOR,LDA,ORA,SBC
360 DATA CPX,CPY,LDX,LDY,STA
370 DATA STX,STY,INC,DEC,ROL
380 DATA ROR,LSR,ASL
400 REM DETERMINE OPERAND
410 Ln=LEN(operand$)
420 FF=0:REM OFFSET FLAG
430 IN=0:REM INDIRECTION FLAG
440 BR=0:REM BRANCH FLAG
450 CM=0:REM COMMA FLAG
460 NUM=0:REM NUMBER IN OPERAND
```

```
 470 AF=0:REM ACCUMULATOR FLAG
 480 IM=0:REM IMMEDIATE FLAG
 490 OP=0:REM OPERAND FLAG
 495 SN=0 :REM RESET OFFSET TO POSITIVE
 500 K=0:REM COUNTER
 510K=K+1
 520 IF K>Ln THEN 2000:REM OPERAND FINISHED
 530B$=MID$(operand$,K,1)
 540REM B$ IS ONE CHARACTER IN THE OPERAND
 550IF B$=" " THEN 510:REM GET NEXT CHARACTER
 560 IF AF=1 THEN 1955:REM ERROR
 570OP=1:REM THERE IS AN OPERAND
 580IF ASC(B$)>47 AND ASC(B$)<58 THEN 1200:REM OPERAND IS A NUMBER
 590IF B$="-" OR B$="+" THEN 1300:REM OPERAND IS AN OFFSET
 600IF B$="#" THEN 1400:REM OPERAND IS IMMEDIATE DATA
 610IF B$="(" THEN 1500:REM OPEN BRACKETS
 620IF B$=")" THEN 1600:REM CLOSE BRACKETS
 630IF B$="A" THEN 1700:REM OPERAND IS ACCUMULATOR
 640IF B$="," THEN CM=1:GOTO 510:REM SET COMMA FLAG AND GET NEXT CHARACTER
 650IF (B$="X" OR B$="Y") AND CM=1 THEN 1800:REM INDEXED
 660IF (B$="X" OR B$="Y") AND CM=0 THEN 1970:REM ERROR IN INDEXED MODE
 670GOTO 1910:REM CHARACTER IS UNRECOGNISED
1200 REM NUMBER: ADDRESS OR DATA
1210NUM=NUM*10+VAL(B$)
1220IF NUM>255 AND J<>22 AND J<>23 THEN 1920:REM OPERAND TOO LARGE ERROR
1230GOTO 510:REM GET NEXT CHARACTER
1300REM OFFSET
1310IF J>21 THEN 1930:REM ERROR IN SIGN
1320IF B$="-" THEN SN=1:REM NEGATIVE OFFSET
1330GOTO 510:REM GET NEXT CHARACTER
1400REM IMMEDIATE DATA
1410IF J<24 OR J>34 THEN 1940:REM ERROR IN IMMEDIATE MODE
1420IM=1
1430GOTO 510:REM GET NEXT CHARACTER
1500REM OPEN BRACKETS
1510IF BR=1 THEN 1950:REM ERROR IN INDIRECTION
1520IN=1
1530BR=1
1540GOTO 510:REM GET NEXT CHARACTER
1600REM CLOSE BRACKET
1610IF BR=0 THEN 1950:REM ERROR IN INDIRECTION
1620BR=0
1630GOTO 510:REM GET NEXT CHARACTER
1700REM ACCUMULATOR
1710IF J<40 THEN 1960:REM ACCUMULATOR ERROR
1720AF=1
1730GOTO 510:REM GET NEXT CHARACTER
1800REM INDEXATION
1810IF J<24 THEN 1970:REM ERROR IN INDEXATION
1820IF B$="X" THEN1850
1825 IF IN=1 THEN 1840:REM INDIRECTION
1830NUM=NUM+Y
1832IF NUM>255 THEN NUM=NUM-256
1835 GOTO 510:REM GET NEXT CHARACTER
1840 IF BR=1 THEN 1950:REM ERROR IN INDIRECTION
1842NUM=mem(NUM)+Y
1843IF NUM>255 THEN NUM=NUM-256
1845 GOTO 510:REM GET NEXT CHARACTER
1850 REM X-INDEX
1855 IF IN=1 THEN 1870:REM INDIRECTION
```

```
1860NUM=NUM+X
1865GOTO 510:REM GET NEXT CHARACTER
1870 REM X-INDIRECTION
1875 IF BR=0 THEN 1970:REM OPERAND ERROR
1880NUM=NUM+X
1885IF NUM>255 THEN NUM=NUM-256
1890NUM=mem(NUM)
1895GOTO 510:REM GET NEXT CHARACTER
1900 REM ERROR IN INSTRUCTION
1910E=1:GOTO 1990
1920E=2:GOTO 1990
1930E=3:GOTO 1990
1940E=4:GOTO 1990
1950E=5:GOTO 1990
1955E=6:GOTO 1990
1960E=7:GOTO 1990
1965E=8:GOTO 1990
1970E=9:GOTO 1990
1975E=10:GOTO 1990
1980E=11:GOTO 1990
1985E=12:GOTO 1990
1986E=13:GOTO 1990
1987E=14
1990  PRINT"  ERROR ";E;
1992  VDU8:VDU8:VDU8:VDU8:VDU8:VDU8:VDU8:VDU8:VDU8
1993 LET exec=26
1995 GOTO 130:REM GET NEXT INSTRUCTION
2000 REM DETERMINE DATA
2010 IF J<16 THEN 3000:REM SINGLE BYTE INSTRUCTION
2020 IF AF=1 THEN 5500:REM ACCUMULATOR INSTRUCTION
2025 PC=PC+1
2030IF J<24 THEN 4000:REM BRANCH OR JUMP
2040REM ADDRESS MODE INSTRUCTION
2050IF IM=1 THEN data=NUM:GOTO 2100:REM IMMEDIATE DATA
2060 data=mem(NUM):REM GET DATA FROM MEMORY
2100REM EXUCUTION OF INSTRUCTION
2110 IF J=35 OR J=36 OR J=37 THEN 2800:REM STORE INSTRUCTION
2120 IF J=24 THEN 6000:REM ADC
2130 IF J=25 THEN 6100:REM AND
2140IF J=26 THEN 6200:REM CMP
2150IF J=27 THEN 6300:REM EOR
2160IF J=28 THEN 6400:REM LDA
2170IF J=29 THEN 6500:REM ORA
2180IF J=30 THEN 6600:REM SBC
2190IF J=31 THEN 6700:REM CPX
2200IF J=32 THEN 6800:REM CPY
2210IF J=33 THEN 6900:REM LDX
2220IF J=34 THEN 7000:REM LDY
2230IF J=38 THEN 7100:REM INC
2240IF J=39 THEN 7200:REM DEC
2250IF J=40 THEN 7300:REM ROL
2260 IF J=41 THEN 7500:REM ROR
2270IF J=42 THEN 7600:REM LSR
2280IF J=43 THEN 7700:REM ASL
2500REM DETERMINE STATUS
2510C=0
2520IF Acc>255 THEN Acc=Acc-256:C=1
2530TP=Acc
2540GOTO 2630
2600REM DETERMINE SIGN STATUS
```

```
2610C=1
2620IF TP<0 THENTP=TP+256:C=0
2630S=0
2640IF TP>127 THEN S=1
2650Z=0
2660IF TP=0 THEN Z=1
2670GOTO 26080
2680
2700REM DETERMINE STATUS AND STORE DATA
2710mem(NUM)=data
2720S=0
2730IF data>127 THEN S=1
2740Z=0
2750IF data=0 THEN Z=1
2760GOTO 26000:REM DISPLAY RESULTS
2790
2800REM STORE INSTRUCTION
2810IF J=35 THEN data=Acc
2820IF J=36 THEN data=X
2830IF J=37 THEN data=Y
2840mem(NUM)=data
2860GOTO 26000:REM DISPLAY RESULTS
2870
3000REM SINGLE BYTE  INSTRUCTION
3010 IF J=1 THEN 26340:REM NOP
3020IF J=2 THEN 3200:REM INX
3030 IF J=3 THEN 3250:REM DEX
3040IF J=4 THEN 3300:REM INY
3050IF J=5 THEN 3350:REM DEY
3060IF J=6 THEN 3400:REM RTS
3070IF J=7 THEN C=0: GOTO 26340:REM CLC
3080IF J=8 THEN C=1: GOTO 26340:REM SEC
3090IF J=9 THEN 3500:REM TXA
3100 IF J=10 THEN 3550:REM TAX
3110 IF J=11 THEN 3600:REM TYA
3120IF J=12 THEN 3650:REM TAY
3130IF J=13 THEN 3700:REM PHA
3140IF J=14 THEN 3750:REM PLA
3150REM BRK
3160 NUM=16000
3170GOTO4600:REM TREAT IT AS A JSR
3200REM INX
3210X=X+1
3220IF X=256 THEN X=0
3230TP=X
3240GOTO 2630
3250REM DEX
3260X=X-1
3270IF X<0 THEN X=255
3280TP=X
3290GOTO 2630
3300REM INY
3310Y=Y+1
3320IF Y=256 THEN Y=0
3330TP=Y
3340GOTO 2630
3350REM DEY
3360Y=Y-1
3370IF Y<0 THEN Y=255
3380TP=Y
```

```
3390GOTO 2630
3400REM RTS
3405IF SP<2 THEN 1986:REM RTS ERROR
3410 HI=256*stack(SP)
3415SP=SP-1
3430PC=stack(SP) + HI
3440SP=SP-1
3450 GOTO 26080
3460
3500REM TXA
3510Acc=X
3520TP=X
3530GOTO 2630
3540
3550REM TAX
3560X=Acc
3570TP=Acc
3580GOTO 2630
3590
3600REM TYA
3610Acc=Y
3620TP=Y
3630GOTO 2630
3640
3650REM TAY
3660Y=Acc
3670TP=Acc
3680GOTO 2630
3690
3700REM PHA
3710IF SP=7 THEN 1975:REM STACK OVERFLOW ERROR
3720SP=SP+1
3730stack(SP)=Acc
3740GOTO 26080
3750REM PLA
3760IF SP=0 THEN 1985:REM STACK UNDERFLOW ERROR
3770 Acc=stack(SP)
3780SP=SP-1
3790GOTO 2530
3900
4000REM BRANCH INSTRUCTION
4005 IF J<22 AND SN=0 AND NUM>127 THEN 1987
4006 IF J<22 AND NUM>128 THEN 1987
4010IM=0:OP=0
4020IF J=16 THEN 4100:REM BNE
4030IF J=17 THEN 4150:REM BEQ
4040IF J=18 THEN 4200:REM BMI
4050IF J=19 THEN 4250:REM BPL
4060IF J=20 THEN 4300:REM BCC
4070IF J=21 THEN 4350:REM BCS
4080IF J=22 THEN 4500:REM JMP
4090IF J=23 THEN 4600:REM JSR
4100 REM BNE
4110IF Z=0 THEN 4400:REM BRANCH SUCCEEDS
4120GOTO 4900:REM BRANCH FAILS
4130
4150REM BEQ
4160IF Z=1 THEN 4400:REM BRANCH SUCCEEDS
4170GOTO 4900:REM BRANCH FAILS
4180
```

```
4200REM BMI
4210IF S=1 THEN 4400:REM BRANCH SUCCEEDS
4220GOTO 4900:REM BRANCH FAILS
4230
4250REM BPL
4260IF S=0 THEN 4400:REM BRANCH SUCCEEDS
4270GOTO 4900:REM BRANCH FAILS
4280
4300REM BCC
4310IF C=0 THEN 4400:REM BRANCH SUCCEEDS
4320GOTO 4900:REM BRANCH FAILS
4330
4350REM BCS
4360IF C=1 THEN 4400:REM BRANCH SUCCEEDS
4370GOTO 4900:REM BRANCH FAILS
4380
4400REM BRANCH SUCCEEDS
4410IF SN=1 THEN PC=PC-NUM:REM BACKWARD BRANCH
4420IF SN=0 THEN PC=PC+NUM:REM FORWARD BRANCH
4430 IF PC<0 THEN PC=PC+65536
4431 IF PC>65535 THEN PC=PC-65536
4440GOTO 26080
4450
4500REM JMP
4510PC=NUM-1
4520 IF PC<0 THEN PC=PC+65536
4521 IF PC>65535 THEN PC=PC-65536
4530IM=1:OP=0
4540GOTO 26080
4600REM JSR
4603 PC=PC+1
4605 IF SP>5 THEN 1975:REM STACK OVERFLOW ERROR
4610SP=SP+1
4620stack(SP)=PC MOD 256
4630SP=SP+1
4640stack(SP)=(PC DIV 256)MOD 256
4650PC=NUM-1
4660 IF PC<0 THEN PC=PC+65536
4661 IF PC>65535 THEN PC=PC-65536
4680IM=1:OP=0
4690GOTO 26080
4700
4900REM BRANCH FAILS
4910 IF PC<0 THEN PC=PC+65536
4911 IF PC>65535 THEN PC=PC-65536
4920GOTO 26080
4930
5500REM OPERAND IS ACCUMULATOR
5510IF J=40 THEN 5600:REM ROL
5520IF J=41 THEN 5700:REM ROR
5530IF J=42 THEN 5800:REM LSR
5540IF J=43 THEN 5900:REM ASL
5550
5600REM ROL
5610Acc=Acc+Acc+C
5620C=0
5630IF Acc>255 THEN Acc=Acc-256:C=1
5640GOTO 2530
5650
5700REM ROR
```

```
5710AA=0
5720IF C=1 THEN AA=128
5730TP=Acc DIV 2
5740C=Acc-TP*2
5750Acc=TP+AA
5760GOTO 2530
5790
5800REM LSR
5810AA=0
5820TP=Acc DIV 2
5830C=Acc-TP*2
5840Acc=TP+AA
5850GOTO 2530
5860
5900REM ASL
5910Acc=Acc+Acc
5920C=0
5930 IF Acc>255 THEN Acc=Acc-256:C=1
5940 GOTO 2530
6000REM ADC
6010Acc=Acc+C+data
6020GOTO 2500:REM DETERMINE STATUS
6040
6100REM AND
6110Acc=Acc AND data
6120GOTO 2530:REM DETERMINE STATUS
6130
6200REM CMP
6210TP=Acc-data
6220GOTO 2600:REM DETERMINE STATUS
6230
6300REM EOR
6310Acc=(Acc AND (NOT data)) OR ((NOT Acc) AND data)
6320GOTO 2630:REM DETERMINE STATUS
6330
6400REM LDA
6410Acc=data
6420GOTO 2530:REM DETERMINE STATUS
6430
6500REM ORA
6510Acc=Acc OR data
6520GOTO 2530:REM DETERMINE STATUS
6530
6600REM SBC
6610CC=0
6620IF C=0 THEN CC=1
6630Acc=Acc-CC-data
6640TP=Acc
6650IF Acc<0 THEN Acc=Acc+256
6660GOTO 2600:REM DETERMINE STATUS
6670
6700 REM CPX
6710TP=X-data
6720GOTO 2600:REM DETERMINE STATUS
6730IF data = 256 THEN data=0
6740GOTO 2700
6750
6800REM CPY
6810TP=Y-data
6820GOTO 2600
```

```
6830
6900REM LDX
6910X=data
6920TP=X
6930GOTO 2630
6940
7000REM LDY
7010Y=data
7020TP=Y
7030GOTO 2630
7040
7100REM INC
7110data=data+1
7120TP=data
7130IF data=256 THEN data=0
7140GOTO 2700
7150
7200REM DEC
7210data=data-1
7220TP=data
7230IF data<0 THEN data=255
7240GOTO 2700
7250
7300REM ROL
7310data=data+data+C
7320C=0
7330IF data>255 THEN data=data-256:C=1
7340GOTO 2700
7350
7500REM ROR
7510AA=0
7520IF C=1 THEN AA=128
7530TP= data DIV 2
7540C=data-TP*2
7550data=TP+AA
7560GOTO 2700
7570
7600REM LSR
7610AA=0
7620TP= data DIV 2
7630C=data-TP*2
7640data=TP+AA
7650GOTO 2700
7660
7700REM ASL
7710data=data+data
7720C=0
7730IF data>255 THEN data=data-256:C=1
7740GOTO 2700
7750
8000 STOP
9000 END
10000 REM DEFINE GRAPHICS CHARACTERS
10010REM
10020REM
10030REM
10040REM
10050REM
10060VDU23,118,0,0,0,31,16,16,16,16
10070VDU23,119,0,0,0,240,16,16,16,16
```

```
10080VDU23,120,16,16,16,240,0,0,0,0
10090VDU23,121,16,16,16,31,0,0,0,0
10100VDU23,122,0,0,0,255,0,0,0,0
10110VDU23,123,16,16,16,16,16,16,16,16
10120VDU23,113,16,16,16,240,16,16,16,16
10130VDU23,125,16,16,16,31,16,16,16,16
10140VDU23,126,0,0,0,255,16,16,16,16
10150VDU23,117,16,16,16,255,0,0,0,0
10160 RETURN
11000 REM PRODUCE A DUMMY PROGRAM
11020 FOR YY=1 TO 25
11030 LET prog$(YY)=""
11040 NEXT YY
15000 REM WRITE A PROGRAM
15010 MODE 7
15020 PRINT TAB(2,0) "6502 MICROPROCESSOR SIMULATION"
15030PRINT TAB(0,2) "You are now in programming mode."
15040 PRINT:PRINT"To enter a program just type in the"
15050PRINT:PRINT"mnemonics in the same way as before."
15060 PRINT:PRINT"Each instruction must be given a"
15070 PRINT:PRINT"a memory location in correct order."
15085 PRINT:PRINT"The last line in the prooram MUST be"
15086 PRINT:PRINT".END. This is not part of the program."
15090 PRINT:PRINT"To execute your program, type CALL."
15100 PRINT:PRINT"Any programming errors may cause a"
15110 PRINT:PRINT"CRASH, leaving you in the command mode."
15120 PRINT TAB(0,24) "Press SPACE to begin programming.";
15130 IF GET$<>" " THEN 15130
15140 MODE 7
15145PRINT TAB(10)".begin"
15150 FOR YY= 1 TO 25
15160 IF prog$(YY)<>"" THEN PRINT 15999+YY;"    ";prog$(YY)
15170 NEXT YY
15175 PRINT TAB(10)".END"
15180 PRINT:PRINT"Enter new line number and instruction."
15184 PRINT:PRINT"The last program line must be .END"
15185 PRINT:PRINT"Type CALL to execute the program."
15186 PRINT:PRINT"Type COMMAND to return to command mode."
15190 PRINT
15200 INPUT LINE ZZ$
15210 IF LEFT$(ZZ$,1)=" " THEN ZZ$=RIGHT$(ZZ$,(LEN(ZZ$)-1)):GOTO 15210
15211 IF ZZ$="COMMAND" THEN LET exec=26:IN$=ZZ$: PC=15999:GOTO 20000
15214 IF ZZ$="CALL" THEN LET exec=0: PC=15999:GOTO 20000
15215 LET proglin$=""
15220 IF ASC(LEFT$(ZZ$,1))>47 AND ASC(LEFT$(ZZ$,1))<58 THEN proglin$=proglin$
+LEFT$(ZZ$,1):ZZ$=RIGHT$(ZZ$,(LEN(ZZ$)-1)):GOTO 15220
15225 LET QQ%=INT(VAL(proglin$)) - 15999
15226 IF QQ% <1 OR QQ%> 25 THEN 15140
15230 IF LEFT$(ZZ$,1)=" " THEN ZZ$=RIGHT$(ZZ$,(LEN(ZZ$)-1)):GOTO 15230
15240 LET prog$(QQ%)=ZZ$
15250 GOTO 15140
20000 REM SET UP FOR RUNNING PROGRAM
20010 LET PC=15999
20020 MODE 4
20030 GOSUB 30000
20040 GOTO 26000
21000 REM EXECUTE PROGRAM
21005 LET exec=PC-15999
21010 FOR time=1 TO 2000:NEXT time
21015 IN$=prog$(exec)
```

```
21020 IF IN$="" THEN IN$="COMMAND"
21030 RETURN
25000 REM INITIALISE REGISTERS
25010 Acc=0
25020X=0
25030Y=0
25040FOR N=1 TO 7:stack(N)=0:NEXT N
25050SP=0:REM STACK POINTER
25060S=0:Z=0:C=0:REM STATUS
25070PC=15999:REM PROGRAM COUNTER
25080J$=".begin":REM PREVIOUS INSTRUCTION
25090IN$="":REM CURRENT INSTRUCTION
25100 IM=0:Add=0:NUM=0:REM FOR ADDRESS REGISTER
25110data=0
25120 FOR N=0 TO 255:mem(N)=RND(255):NEXT N
25130 REM RANDOMISE MEMORY CONTENTS
25140RETURN
26000 REM DISPLAY REGISTER CONTENTS
26004 VDU26:REM ENABLE SCREEN POSITIONS
26010REM MEMORY
26020FOR N=1 TO 7
26050 PROCPUT(33,(2+3*N),mem(N))
26060NEXT N
26080VDU26:REM ENABLE SCREEN POSITIONS : JUMP POSITION FOR REGISTER REFRESH
26100 REM STACK POINTER
26110FOR N=0 TO 7
26120 PRINT TAB(24,(5+N));" "
26130NEXT N
26140 PRINT TAB(24,(5+SP));"<"
26200REM STACK
26210FOR N=1 TO 7
26220PROCPUT(20,4+N,stack(N))
26230 NEXT N
26300REM X-INDEX
26310PROCPUT(2,5,X)
26320REM Y-INDEX
26330PROCPUT(11,5,Y)
26340 VDU26:REM INCREASE PROGRAM COUNTER AND DISPLAY IT
26350PC=PC+1
26360IF PC>65535 THEN PC=0
26362 PRINT TAB(2,15);"      "
26364 PRINT TAB(2,15);PC
26370REM ACCUMULATOR
26375 IF IM=1 AND NUM<>0 THEN Add=0:REM NOT ADDRESSING MODE
26376 IF IM=0 THEN Add=NUM
26380PROCPUT(2,9,Acc)
26390REM ADDRESS REGISTER
26400PROCPUT(3,19,Add)
26410REM DATA REGISTER
26420PROCPUT(3,23,data)
26430REM STATUS
26440PRINT TAB(8,9);S
26450PRINT TAB(12,9);Z
26460PRINT TAB(16,9);C
26470REM SET & CLEAR INSTRUCTION WINDOW
26475 VDU28,11,15,22,14
26480CLS
26490REM DISPLAY LAST INSTRUCTION
26500PRINT J$
26510 GOTO 130:REM GET NEXT INSTRUCTION
```

```
26525
27000 DEF PROCPUT(Xpos,Ypos,nmbr)
27010REM DISPLAY nmbr AT LOCATION Xpos,Ypos WITH RIGHT JUSTIFICATION
27020
27030AV=nmbr DIV 100
27040resid=nmbr MOD 100
27050BV=resid DIV 10
27060CV=resid MOD 10
27065 n=0
27070IF AV<>0 THEN 27200
27075 n=n+1
27080IF BV<>0 THEN 27200
27085 n=n+1
27200 PRINT TAB(Xpos,Ypos);"   "
27210 PRINT TAB(Xpos+n,Ypos);nmbr
27300 ENDPROC
30000CLS
30001PRINT
30005PRINT"   MICROPROCESSOR              MEMORY"
30010PRINT"vzzzzzzzzzzzzzzzzzzzzzzzzw"
30020PRINT"{                  STACK {      DATA"
30030PRINT"{vzzzw    vzzzw    vzzzw {     1vzzzw"
30040PRINT"{{   {    {   {    {   { {  vzzzq   }zw"
30050PRINT"{yzzzx    yzzzx    {   { { A{   yzzzx {"
30060PRINT"{X-INDEX Y-INDEX   {   { { D{  2vzzzw {"
30070PRINT"{vzzzw vzw vzw vzw {   { { D}zzzq   }zq"
30080PRINT"{{   { { { { { { { {   { { R{   yzzzx {"
30090PRINT"{yzzzx yzx yzx yzx {   { { E{  3vzzzw {"
30100PRINT"{ACCUM  S   Z   C  {   { { S}zzzq   }zq"
30110PRINT"{      STATUS REG. yzzzx { S{   yzzzx {"
30120PRINT"{PROGRAM  vzzzzzzzzzzzzw {  {  4vzzzw {"
30130PRINT"{vzzzzzw  {            { { B}zzzq   }zq"
30140PRINT"{{     }>>q            { { U{   yzzzx {"
30150PRINT"{yzzzzzx  yzzzzzzzzzzzzx { S{  5vzzzw {"
30160PRINT"{COUNTER    INSTRUCTION  {  }zzzq   }zq"
30170PRINT"{vzzzzzzw    REGISTER    {  {   yzzzx {"
30180PRINT"{{      }zzzzzzzzzzzzzzzzzzzq  6vzzzw {"
30200PRINT"{yzzzzzzx                {  }zzzq   }zq"
30202PRINT"{ADDRESS REGISTER        {  {   yzzzx {"
30204PRINT"{vzzzzzzw                {  {  7vzzzw {"
30206PRINT"{{      }zzzzzzzzzzzzzzzzzw yzzzq   }zq"
30208PRINT"{yzzzzzzx                {{     yzzzx {"
30210PRINT"{DATA REGISTER           {{           {"
30212PRINT"yzzzzzzzzzzzzzzzzzzzzzzzzxyzzzzzzzzzzzx"
30214PRINT"                           DATA BUS"
30250 RETURN
```

STOPCLOCK - PROGRAM 5

```
LIST
   1 MODE 7
   2 HIMEM = &7000
   3 GOSUB 10000:REM FIRST LOAD DISPLAY ROUTINE
1000 REM CLOCK ROUTINE
1010 CSLO = 594           (Note: CSLO = 662 for OS 1.0 and above)
1020 CSHI = &7201
1030 SECLO = &7202
1040 SECHI = &7203
1050 MINLO = &7204
1060 MINHI = &7205
1070 status = &7206
1090 PRT =&FE60
1100 DDRB = &FE62
1150 keyboardflag = &FE4D
2010 FOR pass = 0 TO 2 STEP 2
2015 P%=&7500
2020 [OPT pass
2025 .timer LDA #13 [DISPLAY M
2026  STA dgtval
2027  LDA #4
2028  STA dest
2029  JSR display
2035  LDA #10 \DISPLAY DECIMAL POINT
2036  STA dgtval
2037  LDA #10
2038  STA dest
2039  JSR display
2045  LDA #12 \DISPLAY S
2046  STA dgtval
2047  LDA #14
2048  STA dest
2049  JSR display
2050  LDA #0
2060  STA CSLO
2070  STA CSHI
2080  STA SECLO
2090  STA SECHI
2100  STA MINLO
2110  STA MINHI
2120  STA DDRB
2125  JSR showtimes
2130  LDA PRT
2140  AND #3
2150  STA status
2160 .wait LDA PRT
2170  AND #3
2180  CMP status
2190  BEQ wait
2195  STA status
2200  LDA #0
2205  STA CSLO
2210 .loop LDA CSLO
2220  CMP #10
2230  BCC cont
2240  LDA #0
2250  STA CSLO
2260  INC CSHI
```

```
2270  LDA CSHI
2280  CMP #10
2290  BNE cont
2300  LDA #0
2310  STA CSHI
2320  INC SECLO
2330  LDA SECLO
2340  CMP #10
2350  BNE cont
2360  LDA #0
2370  STA SECLO
2380  INC SECHI
2390  LDA SECHI
2400  CMP #6
2410  BNE cont
2414  LDA #0
2416  STA SECHI
2420  INC MINLO
2430  LDA MINLO
2440  CMP #10
2450  BNE cont
2460  LDA #0
2470  STA MINLO
2480  INC MINHI
2500  CMP #10
2510  BNE cont
2520  LDA #0
2530  STA MINHI
2540 .cont LDA keyboardflag
2542  AND #1 \IS A KEY BEING PRESSED ?
2544  BNE kyprss
2546  JSR showtimes
2548 .kyprss LDA PRT
2570  AND #3
2580  CMP status
2590  BNE done
2600  JMP loop
2610 .done RTS
2620 .showtimes  LDA CSLO
2630  STA dgtval
2640  LDA #12
2650  STA dest
2660  JSR display
2720  LDA CSHI
2730  STA dgtval
2740  LDA #11
2750  STA dest
2760  JSR display
2820  LDA SECLO
2830  STA dgtval
2840  LDA #7
2850  STA dest
2860  JSR display
2920  LDA SECHI
2930  STA dgtval
2940  LDA #6
2950  STA dest
2960  JSR display
3020  LDA MINLO
3030  STA dgtval
```

```
3040  LDA #2
3050  STA dest
3060  JSR display
3120  LDA MINHI
3130  STA dgtval
3140  LDA #1
3150  STA dest
3160  JSR display
3170  RTS
3300 ]
3400 NEXT pass
5000 CLS
5010 PRINT TAB(6,4);CHR$(141);"DIGITAL STOPCLOCK"
5020 PRINT TAB(6,5);CHR$(141);"DIGITAL STOPCLOCK"
5030 PRINT TAB(0,10);"This program waits for the status"
5040 PRINT TAB(0,12);"of bit 0 or bit 1 of the User Port"
5050 PRINT TAB(0,14);"to change, and then starts timing."
5060 PRINT TAB(0,16);"The timing stops when a second change"
5070 PRINT TAB(0,18);"in the status of either bit occurs."
5080 PRINT TAB(0,20);"The elaspsed time is displayed"
5090 PRINT TAB(0,22);"in large digits."
5100 PRINT TAB(0,24);"Press SPACE to begin.     ";
5200 IF GET$<>" " THEN 5200
5250 CLS
5260 PRINT TAB(0,24);"Press SPACE to hold the display.";
5300 CALL timer
5350 *FX 15,0
5400 PRINT TAB(0,24);"Press SPACE to restart.            ";
5500 GOTO 5200
6000 STOP
10000REM LOADER FOR MACHINE CODE SUBROUTINE
10010REM 'LARGE DIGIT DISPLAY'
10200REM DIGITS TABLE
10210 FOR I=&7100 TO &716F
10220 READ X
10230 ?I=X
10240NEXT I
10250DATA 124,68,68,68,68,68,124,0:REM DIGIT 0
10260DATA 8,8,8,8,8,8,8,0:REM DIGIT 1
10270DATA 124,68,4,4,124,64,124,0:REM DIGIT 2
10280DATA 124,4,4,124,4,4,124,0:REM DIGIT 3
10290DATA 64,64,64,72,124,8,8,0:REM DIGIT 4
10300DATA 124,64,64,124,4,4,124,0:REM DIGIT 5
10310DATA 124,64,64,124,68,68,124,0:REM DIGIT 6
10320DATA 124,4,4,4,4,4,4,0:REM DIGIT 7
10330DATA 124,68,68,124,68,68,124,0:REM DIGIT 8
10340DATA 124,68,68,124,4,4,4,0:REM DIGIT 9
10350 DATA 0,0,0,0,0,0,16,0:REM DECIMAL POINT
10360 DATA 0,0,0,124,0,0,0,0:REM NEGATIVE SIGN
10370 DATA 0,0,60,32,60,4,60,0:REM LETTER S
10380 DATA 0,0,254,146,146,146,146,0:REM LETTER M
11000 REM  LARGE DIGIT DISPLAY
12000 REM MACHINE CODE ROUTINE
12001 dest=114
12002 dgtval=115
12003 screen = 112: REM AND 113
12004 bitcnt = 116
12005 temp = &7080:REM AND NEXT SEVEN BYTES
12006 bittbl=&7100
12008 FOR pass = 0 TO 2 STEP 2
```

```
12010 P%=&7000
12020 [OPT pass
12030 .display LDA dest \GET DESTINATION
12040  CMP #10 \BOTTOM ROW ?
12050  BPL bottom \YES
12060  CMP #5 \MIDDLE ROW ?
12070  BPL middle \YES
12080  ASL A \MUST BE TOP
12090  ASL A
12100  ASL A \MULTIPLY BY 8
12110  STA screen \MAKE NOTE OF POSITION
12120  LDA #&7C
12130  STA screen + 1
12140  BNE begin \UNCONDITIONAL BRANCH
12150
12160 .bottom SEC
12170  SBC #10
12180  ASL A
12190  ASL A
12200  ASL A
12210  ADC #128 \MOVE TO CORRECT PLACE
12220  STA screen \AND SAVE IT
12230  LDA #&7E
12240  STA screen + 1
12250  BNE begin \UNCONDITIONAL BRANCH
12260 .middle SEC
12270  SBC #5
12280  ASL A
12290  ASL A
12300  ASL A
12310  ADC #64 \MOVE TO CORRECT PLACE
12320  STA screen \AND SAVE IT
12330  LDA #&7D
12340  STA screen + 1
12350
12360          \GET BITS FOR DIGIT
12370 .begin LDX #0  \INITIALISE BYTE POINTER
12380  LDA dgtval \GET DIGIT CODE
12390  ASL A
12400  ASL A
12410  ASL A \MULTIPLY BY 8
12420  TAY \POINT TO TABLE
12430 .bytget LDA bittbl,Y \GET BYTE
12440  STA temp,X \KEEP IN TEMP STORE
12450  INY        \ADVANCE TABLE POINTER
12460  INX        \ADVANCE BYTE POINTER
12470  CPX #8     \8 BYTES COLLECTED ?
12480  BNE bytget
12490  LDY #223  \SET SCREEN POINTER TO -32
12500  LDX #255  \SET ROW POINTER TO -1
12510 .nxtrow INX \READY FOR NEXT ROW
12520  CPX #7 \ALL ROWS DONE ?
12530  BEQ finish
12540  LDA #8 \INITIALISE BIT COUNTER
12550  STA bitcnt
12560  CLC
12570  TYA      \GET SCREEN POINTER
12575  ADC #32 \ADVANCE TO NEXT ROW
12580  TAY      \RESTORE SCREEN POINTER
12590 .nxtbit INY \NEXT SCREEN POSITION
```

```
12600  ASL temp,X \SHIFT BIT INTO CARRY
12610  BCC empty \BIT IS ZERO
12620  LDA #127 \BIT IS ONE - SEND WHITE BLOCK
12630  BNE send \UNCONDITIONAL BRANCH
12640 .empty LDA #23 \SEND BLANK
12650 .send STA (screen),Y \SEND TO SCREEN
12660  DEC bitcnt \ALL BITS SENT ?
12670  BEQ nxtrow \YES DO NEXT ROW
12680  BNE nxtbit \NO SEND NEXT BIT
12690
12700  .finish RTS:]
12800 NEXT pass
13000 RETURN
```

REACTION TIMER - PROGRAM 6

```
LIST
  100 MODE 7
  110 DIM digit(5)
  200 REM INSTRUCTIONS
  210CLS
  220PRINT TAB(10,2) "REACTION TIMER"
  230PRINT TAB(10,4) "by R.A.Sparkes"
  235 GOSUB 10000:REM LOAD MACHINE CODE DISPLAY ROUTINE
  240 PRINT TAB(0,7) "This program measures reaction time."
  250PRINT TAB(0,9) "A few seconds after you press the"
  260PRINT TAB(0,11) "RETURN key, the screen will go blank."
  270PRINT TAB(0,13) "As soon as this happens, you must press"
  280PRINT TAB(0,15) "the SPACE bar. Your reaction time"
  290PRINT TAB(0,17) "will then be displayed."
  300PRINT TAB(0,22) "Press RETURN to begin."
  310IF GET$<>CHR$(13) THEN 310
  315PRINT TAB(0,22) "The screen will go blank very soon.     "
  320time=RND(500)+300
  330TIME=0
  340REPEAT
  350UNTIL TIME>time
  360 IF INKEY$(0)=" " THEN 600
  370TIME=0
  375 CLS
  380IF GET$<>" " THEN 380
  390number=TIME/100
  400pos=5
  410GOSUB 9000
  420GOSUB 9500
  430 PRINT TAB(0,1)"Press RETURN to start again"
  440 IF GET$<>CHR$(13) THEN 440
  450CLS
  460PRINT TAB(10,2) "REACTION TIMER"
  470PRINT TAB(10,4) "by R.A.Sparkes"
  480 GOTO 240
  600 REM CHEAT ROUTINE
  610 CLS
  620 PRINT TAB(0,10) "PLEASE WAIT UNTIL THE SCREEN GOES BLANK"
  630 PRINT TAB(0,22) "Press RETURN to begin again."
```

```
  640 IF GET$<>CHR$(13) THEN 640
  650 GOTO 450
 9000 REM DIGIT SEPARATION AND DISPLAY
 9005 loc=114:dgtval=115
 9010 decpt=0:sign=1
 9020IF number<0 THEN number=ABS(number):sign=-1
 9030IF number>=1 THEN number=number/10:decpt=decpt+1:GOTO 9030
 9040IF decpt>4 THEN 500:REM OUT OF RANGE
 9050FOR I=0 TO 3
 9060digit=INT(number*10)
 9070number=number*10-digit
 9080 IF I<decpt THEN digit(I)=digit
 9090IF I>=decpt THEN digit(I+1)=digit
 9100NEXT I
 9110digit(decpt)=10
 9120IF sign<0 THEN FOR I= 4 TO 1 STEP -1:digit(I)=digit(I-1):NEXT I:digit
(0)=11
 9200REM DIGIT DISPLAY ROUTINE
 9210sigfig=2:REM SET NUMBER OF SIG. FIGS.
 9220IF sign <0 THEN sigfig=sigfig+1
 9230FOR I=0 TO sigfig
 9240 ?loc=(I+pos):?dgtval=digit(I)
 9250CALL display
 9260NEXT I
 9270RETURN
 9500 REM DISPLAY 'S'
 9510 ?loc=9:?dgtval=12
 9520 CALL display
 9530 RETURN
10000REM LOADER FOR MACHINE CODE SUBROUTINE
10010REM 'LARGE DIGIT DISPLAY'
10020 display=28672
10030HIMEM=&7000
10035 loc=114:dgtval=115:display=28672
10040 FOR I=28672 TO 28781
10050READ X
10060?I=X
10070NEXT I
10080 DATA 165,114,201,10,16,15,201,5,16,27
10090DATA 10,10,10,133,112,169,124,133,113,208
10100DATA 28,56,233,10,10,10,10,105,128,133
10110DATA 112,169,126,133,113,208,14,56,233,5
10120DATA 10,10,10,105,64,133,112,169,125,133
10130 DATA 113,162,0,165,115,10,10,10,168,185
10140DATA 0,113,157,128,112,200,232,224,8,208
10150DATA 244,160,223,162,255,232,224,7,240,29
10160DATA 169,8,133,116,24,152,105,32,168,200
10170DATA 30,128,112,144,4,169,127,208,2,169
10180DATA 23,145,112,198,116,240,224,208,236,96
10200REM DIGITS TABLE
10210 FOR I=28928 TO 29031
10220 READ X
10230?I=X
10240NEXT I
10250DATA 124,68,68,68,68,68,124,0:REM DIGIT 0
10260DATA 8,8,8,8,8,8,8,0:REM DIGIT 1
10270DATA 124,68,4,4,124,64,124,0:REM DIGIT 2
10280DATA 124,4,4,124,4,4,124,0:REM DIGIT 3
10290DATA 64,64,64,72,124,8,8,0:REM DIGIT 4
10300DATA124,64,64,124,4,4,124,0:REM DIGIT 5
```

```
10310DATA 124,64,64,124,68,68,124,0:REM DIGIT 6
10320DATA 124,4,4,4,4,4,4,0:REM DIGIT 7
10330DATA 124,68,68,124,68,68,124,0:REM DIGIT 8
10340DATA 124,68,68,124,4,4,4,0:REM DIGIT 9
10350 DATA 0,0,0,0,0,0,16,0:REM DECIMAL POINT
10360 DATA 0,0,0,124,0,0,0,0:REM NEGATIVE SIGN
10370 DATA 0,0,60,32,60,4,60,0:REM LETTER S
10380 RETURN
```

FAST TIMER - PROGRAM 7

```
LIST
   10 HIMEM=&6000
   20 GOSUB 10000:REM LOAD MACHINE CODE ROUTINES
  100 MODE 7
  110 DIM digit(5)
  200 REM INSTRUCTIONS
  210CLS
  220PRINT TAB(12,2) "FAST TIMER"
  230PRINT TAB(10,4) "by R.A.Sparkes"
  240 PRINT TAB(0,7) "This program measures time intervals"
  250PRINT TAB(0,9) "between 0 and 600 milliseconds"
  260PRINT TAB(0,11) "in units of about 10 microseconds."
  270PRINT TAB(0,13) "The timing begins when any of the"
  280PRINT TAB(0,15) "User Port changes its status."
  290PRINT TAB(0,19) "Press RETURN when you are ready"
  300PRINT TAB(0,21) "to begin taking readings."
  310IF GET$<>CHR$(13) THEN 310
  320 CLS
  330PRINT TAB(10,2) "FAST TIMER"
  340PRINT TAB(0,5);"Ready for input changes."
  350 CALL timer
  360 IF ?errflag=0 THEN 400
  365 PRINT TAB(0,8) "Time interval exceeds 600 milliseconds."
  370 PRINT:PRINT"Press SPACE to begin again."
  380 REPEAT UNTIL GET$=" "
  385 CLS
  390 GOTO 200
  400 REM RETRIEVE RESULT
  405 LET number=(256*?&85+?&84)*0.0095
  410 CLS
  420 GOSUB 9000
  430 PRINT TAB(0,1)"Press RETURN to start again"
  440 IF GET$<>CHR$(13) THEN 440
  450 GOTO 320
 9000 REM DIGIT SEPARATION AND DISPLAY
 9005 loc=114:dgtval=115
 9010 decpt=0:sign=1
 9020IF number<0 THEN number=ABS(number):sign=-1
 9030IF number>=1 THEN number=number/10:decpt=decpt+1:GOTO 9030
 9050FOR I=0 TO 3
 9060digit=INT(number*10)
 9070number=number*10-digit
 9080 IF I<decpt THEN digit(I)=digit
 9090IF I>=decpt THEN digit(I+1)=digit
```

```
 9100NEXT I
 9110digit(decpt)=10
 9120IF sign<0 THEN FOR I= 4 TO 1 STEP -1:digit(I)=digit(I-1):NEXT I:
digit(0)=11
 9200REM DIGIT DISPLAY ROUTINE
 9210sigfig=4:REM SET NUMBER OF SIG. FIGS.
 9220IF sign <0 THEN sigfig=sigfig+1
 9230FOR I=0 TO sigfig
 9240 ?loc=(I+5):?dgtval=digit(I)
 9250CALL display
 9260NEXT I
 9400 REM DISPLAY 'M'
 9410 ?loc=13:?dgtval=13
 9420 CALL display
 9500 REM DISPLAY 'S'
 9510 ?loc=14:?dgtval=12
 9520 CALL display
 9530 RETURN
10000REM LOADER FOR MACHINE CODE SUBROUTINE
10010REM 'LARGE DIGIT DISPLAY'
10030 loc=114:dgtval=115:display=28672
10040 FOR I=28672 TO 28781
10050READ X
10060?I=X
10070NEXT I
10080 DATA 165,114,201,10,16,15,201,5,16,27
10090DATA 10,10,10,133,112,169,124,133,113,208
10100DATA 28,56,233,10,10,10,10,105,128,133
10110DATA 112,169,126,133,113,208,14,56,233,5
10120DATA 10,10,10,105,64,133,112,169,125,133
10130 DATA 113,162,0,165,115,10,10,10,168,185
10140DATA 0,113,157,128,112,200,232,224,8,208
10150DATA 244,160,223,162,255,232,224,7,240,29
10160DATA 169,8,133,116,24,152,105,32,168,200
10170DATA 30,128,112,144,4,169,127,208,2,169
10180DATA 23,145,112,198,116,240,224,208,236,96
10200REM DIGITS TABLE
10210 FOR I=28928 TO 29039
10220 READ X
10230?I=X
10240NEXT I
10250DATA 124,68,68,68,68,68,124,0:REM DIGIT 0
10260DATA 8,8,8,8,8,8,8,0:REM DIGIT 1
10270DATA 124,68,4,4,124,64,124,0:REM DIGIT 2
10280DATA 124,4,4,124,4,4,124,0:REM DIGIT 3
10290DATA 64,64,64,72,124,8,8,0:REM DIGIT 4
10300DATA124,64,64,124,4,4,124,0:REM DIGIT 5
10310DATA 124,64,64,124,68,68,124,0:REM DIGIT 6
10320DATA 124,4,4,4,4,4,4,0:REM DIGIT 7
10330DATA 124,68,68,124,68,68,124,0:REM DIGIT 8
10340DATA 124,68,68,124,4,4,4,0:REM DIGIT 9
10350 DATA 0,0,0,0,0,0,16,0:REM DECIMAL POINT
10360 DATA 0,0,0,124,0,0,0,0:REM NEGATIVE SIGN
10370 DATA 0,0,60,32,60,4,60,0:REM LETTER S
10380 DATA 0,0,127,73,73,73,73,0:REM LETTER M
11000 REM FAST TIMER ROUTINE
11010 LET status= &80
11014 ?65122=0:REM USER PORT AS INPUT
11015 LET PRT=65120:REM USER PORT
11020 LET errflag= &81
```

```
11030 FOR pass=0 TO 2 STEP 2
11040 P%=&6000
11050[OPT pass
11060 .timer   SEI
11070          LDA #0
11080          STA errflag
11090          TAX
11100          TAY             \INITIALIZE CLOCK
11110          LDA PRT
11120          STA status
11130 .wait    LDA PRT         \WAIT TILL STATUS CHANGES
11140          CMP status
11150          BEQ wait
11155          STA status      \KEEP NEW STATUS
11160 .loop    INX
11170          BNE delay
11180          INY
11190          BNE cont
11200          LDA #1
11210          STA errflag     \CLOCK OVERFLOW
11220          CLI
11230          RTS
11240 .delay   NOP             \COMPENSATORY DELAY
11250          NOP
11260 .cont    LDA PRT         \FINISHED?
11270          CMP status
11280          BEQ loop        \CARRY ON TIMING
11285          STY &85
11286          STX &84         \SAVE CLOCK READING
11290          CLI
11300          RTS
11310 ]
11320 NEXT pass
11330 RETURN
```

TIME, SPEED & ACCELERATION METER – PROGRAM 8

```
LIST
    1 MODE7
    2 HIMEM = &6000
    3 GOSUB 10000:REM FIRST LOAD DISPLAY ROUTINE
    4 GOSUB 15000:REM LOAD TIMING ROUTINE
    5 @%=00020306:REM FIXED FORMAT
    6 DIM A(4)
    7 DIM S(4)
    8 DIM T(4)
    9 DIM digit(4)
  100 REM TIME SPEED AND ACCELERATION METER
  110 CLS
  120 PRINT "  TIME, SPEED AND ACCELERATION METER"
  130 PRINT TAB(0,3);"For acceleration, press  A"
  140 PRINT TAB(0,5);"For speed, press  S"
  150  PRINT TAB(0,7);"For time intervals, press  T"
  160A$=GET$
  170 IF A$="A" THEN 5000
```

```
 180 IF A$="S" THEN 6000
 190 IF A$="T" THEN 7000
 200 GOTO 160:REM IGNORE OTHER KEYS
1000 END
5000 CLS
5010 PRINT TAB(3,1);"Measuring ACCELERATION"
5020 GOSUB 8000
5030 GOSUB 9000
5040  GOTO 5060
5050  PRINT TAB(0,1);"Ready to take reading number ";counter
5060?evntctr=4:REM FOUR EVENTS
5070 CALL timer
5080  GOSUB 14000:REM COLLECT RESULTS
5090 T2=T2 + (T1+T3)/2
5100 Q=0.04*((1/T3 - 1/T1)/T2):REM CALCULATE ACCELERATION
5110 A(counter) = Q:REM KEEP CURRENT MEASUREMENT
5120 GOSUB 13000:REM DISPLAY MEASUREMENT
5130 counter = counter + 1
5140 IF counter>maxcount THEN 7500:REM ALL READINGS TAKEN
5150  GOTO 5050:REM TAKE NEXT READING
6000 CLS
6010 PRINT TAB(5,1);"Measuring SPEED"
6020 GOSUB 8000
6030 GOSUB 9000
6040  GOTO 6060
6050  PRINT TAB(0,1);"Ready to take reading number ";counter
6060 ?evntctr=2:REM TWO EVENTS
6070 CALL timer
6080  GOSUB 14000:REM COLLECT RESULTS
6100 Q=0.04/T1:REM CALCULATE SPEED
6110 S(counter) = Q:REM KEEP CURRENT MEASUREMENT
6120 GOSUB 13000:REM DISPLAY MEASUREMENT
6130 counter = counter + 1
6140 IF counter>maxcount THEN 7500:REM ALL READINGS TAKEN
6150  GOTO 6050:REM TAKE NEXT READING
7000 CLS
7010 PRINT TAB(1,1);"Measuring TIME INTERVALS"
7020 GOSUB 8000
7030 GOSUB 9000
7040  GOTO 7060
7050  PRINT TAB(0,1);"Ready to take reading number ";counter
7060?evntctr=2:REM TWO EVENTS
7070 CALL timer
7080  GOSUB 14000:REM COLLECT RESULTS
7100 Q= T1
7110 T(counter) = Q:REM KEEP CURRENT MEASUREMENT
7120 GOSUB 13000:REM DISPLAY MEASUREMENT
7130 counter = counter + 1
7140 IF counter>maxcount THEN 7500:REM ALL READINGS TAKEN
7150  GOTO 7050:REM TAKE NEXT READING
7500 REM RESTART ROUTINE
7510 PRINT:PRINT"Press  R  to restart"
7520 PRINT:PRINT"Press  M to recall previous readings"
7530 C$=GET$
7540 IF C$="R" THEN 100
7550 IF C$="M" AND A$="A" THEN 9800:REM LIST ACCELERATION READINGS
7560 IF C$="M" AND A$="S" THEN 9700:REM LIST SPEED READINGS
7570 IF C$="M" AND A$="T" THEN 9600:REM LIST TIME INTERVAL READINGS
7580 GOTO 7530:REM IGNORE OTHER KEYS
8000 REM NUMBER OF DISPLAYED DIGITS
```

```
8010 PRINT:PRINT"Enter the number of digits to be"
8020PRINT:PRINT"displayed  (2 to 4)."
8030 E$=GET$
8040 maxdig=VAL(E$)
8050 IF maxdig<2 OR maxdig>4 THEN 8030
8060 RETURN
9000 REM SELECT NUMBER OF SUCCESSIVE READINGS
9010 PRINT:PRINT:PRINT"You may take 1, 2, 3 or 4 successive"
9020 PRINT:PRINT"readings which will be stored "
9030 PRINT:PRINT"as well as being displayed."
9040 PRINT:PRINT:PRINT"When you are ready to begin,"
9050 PRINT:PRINT"press one of these numbers."
9060 B$=GET$
9070 maxcount=VAL(B$)
9080 IF maxcount<1 OR maxcount>4 THEN 9060
9090 PRINT:PRINT:PRINT"OK. I am ready."
9100 counter=1:REM INITIALISE READINGS COUNTER
9110 RETURN
9500 REM LIST STORED READINGS
9600 REM TIME INTERVALS
9610 CLS
9620 FOR Z=1 TO maxcount
9630 PRINT TAB(0,Z*2);"TIME";Z;" = ";T(Z)
9640 NEXT Z
9650 PRINT:PRINT"Press  R  to restart."
9660 D$=GET$
9670 IF D$<>"R" THEN 9660
9680 GOTO 100
9700 REM SPEEDS
9710 CLS
9720 FOR Z=1 TO maxcount
9730 PRINT TAB(0,Z*2);"SPEED";Z;" = ";S(Z)
9740 NEXT Z
9750 PRINT:PRINT"Press  R  to restart."
9760 D$=GET$
9770 IF D$<>"R" THEN 9760
9780 GOTO 100
9800 REM ACCELERATIONS
9810 CLS
9820 FOR Z=1 TO maxcount
9830 PRINT TAB(0,Z*2);"ACCELERATION";Z;" = ";A(Z)
9840 NEXT Z
9850 PRINT:PRINT"Press  R  to restart."
9860 D$=GET$
9870 IF D$<>"R" THEN 9860
9880 GOTO 100
9991 FOR i=&6800 TO &6882
9992 PRINT;" ";?i;
9993 NEXT i
9994 STOP
10000REM LOADER FOR MACHINE CODE SUBROUTINE
10010REM 'LARGE DIGIT DISPLAY'
10200REM DIGITS TABLE
10210 FOR I=&7100 TO &716F
10220 READ X
10230 ?I=X
10240NEXT I
10250DATA 124,68,68,68,68,68,124,0:REM DIGIT 0
10260DATA 8,8,8,8,8,8,8,0:REM DIGIT 1
10270DATA 124,68,4,4,124,64,124,0:REM DIGIT 2
```

```
10280DATA 124,4,4,124,4,4,124,0:REM DIGIT 3
10290DATA 64,64,64,72,124,8,8,0:REM DIGIT 4
10300DATA 124,64,64,124,4,4,124,0:REM DIGIT 5
10310DATA 124,64,64,124,68,68,124,0:REM DIGIT 6
10320DATA 124,4,4,4,4,4,4,0:REM DIGIT 7
10330DATA 124,68,68,124,68,68,124,0:REM DIGIT 8
10340DATA 124,68,68,124,4,4,4,0:REM DIGIT 9
10350 DATA 0,0,0,0,0,0,16,0:REM DECIMAL POINT
10360 DATA 0,0,0,124,0,0,0,0:REM NEGATIVE SIGN
10370 DATA 0,0,60,32,60,4,60,0:REM LETTER S
10380 DATA 0,0,127,73,73,73,73,0:REM LETTER M
11000 REM  LARGE DIGIT DISPLAY
12000 REM MACHINE CODE ROUTINE
12001 dest=114
12002 dgtval=115
12003 screen = 112: REM AND 113
12004 bitcnt = 116
12005 temp = &7080:REM AND NEXT SEVEN BYTES
12006 bittbl=&7100
12008 FOR pass = 0 TO 2 STEP 2
12010 P%=&7000
12020 [OPT pass
12030 .display LDA dest \GET DESTINATION
12040  CMP #10 \BOTTOM ROW ?
12050  BPL bottom \YES
12060  CMP #5 \MIDDLE ROW ?
12070  BPL middle \YES
12080  ASL A \MUST BE TOP
12090  ASL A
12100  ASL A \MULTIPLY BY 8
12110  STA screen \MAKE NOTE OF POSITION
12120  LDA #&7C
12130  STA screen + 1
12140  BNE begin \UNCONDITIONAL BRANCH
12150
12160 .bottom SEC
12170  SBC #10
12180  ASL A
12190  ASL A
12200  ASL A
12210  ADC #128 \MOVE TO CORRECT PLACE
12220  STA screen \AND SAVE IT
12230  LDA #&7E
12240  STA screen + 1
12250  BNE begin \UNCONDITIONAL BRANCH
12260 .middle SEC
12270  SBC #5
12280  ASL A
12290  ASL A
12300  ASL A
12310  ADC #64 \MOVE TO CORRECT PLACE
12320  STA screen \AND SAVE IT
12330  LDA #&7D
12340  STA screen + 1
12350
12360         \GET BITS FOR DIGIT
12370 .begin LDX #0  \INITIALISE BYTE POINTER
12380  LDA dgtval \GET DIGIT CODE
12390  ASL A
12400  ASL A
```

```
12410  ASL A \MULTIPLY BY 8
12420  TAY \POINT TO TABLE
12430 .bytget LDA bittbl,Y \GET BYTE
12440  STA temp,X \KEEP IN TEMP STORE
12450  INY        \ADVANCE TABLE POINTER
12460  INX        \ADVANCE BYTE POINTER
12470  CPX #8     \8 BYTES COLLECTED ?
12480  BNE bytget
12490  LDY #223   \SET SCREEN POINTER TO -32
12500  LDX #255   \SET ROW POINTER TO -1
12510 .nxtrow INX \READY FOR NEXT ROW
12520  CPX #7 \ALL ROWS DONE ?
12530  BEQ finish
12540  LDA #8 \INITIALISE BIT COUNTER
12550  STA bitcnt
12560  CLC
12570  TYA      \GET SCREEN POINTER
12575  ADC #32 \ADVANCE TO NEXT ROW
12580  TAY      \RESTORE SCREEN POINTER
12590 .nxtbit INY \NEXT SCREEN POSITION
12600  ASL temp,X \SHIFT BIT INTO CARRY
12610  BCC empty \BIT IS ZERO
12620  LDA #255 \BIT IS ONE - SEND WHITE BLOCK
12630  BNE send \UNCONDITIONAL BRANCH
12640 .empty LDA #151 \SEND BLANK
12650 .send STA (screen),Y \SEND TO SCREEN
12660  DEC bitcnt \ALL BITS SENT ?
12670  BEQ nxtrow \YES DO NEXT ROW
12680  BNE nxtbit \NO SEND NEXT BIT
12690
12700  .finish RTS:]
12800 NEXT pass
12900 RETURN
13000 REM DIGIT SEPARATION AND DISPLAY
13010 CLS
13020 decpt=0
13030 sign=1
13040 IF Q<0 THEN Q=ABS(Q):sign=-1
13050 IF Q>=1 THEN Q=Q/10:decpt=decpt+1:GOTO 13050
13060 IF decpt>4 THEN PRINT:PRINT:PRINT:PRINT"OUT OF RANGE.":GOTO 7500
13070 FOR i= 0 TO 3
13080 digit=INT(Q*10)
13090 Q=Q*10-digit
13100 IF i<decpt THEN digit(i)=digit ELSE digit(i+1)=digit
13110 NEXT i
13120 digit(decpt)=10
13130 IF sign<0 THEN GOSUB 13500:REM INSERT NEGATIVE SIGN
13140 REM SEND DIGITS TO DISPLAY
13150 FOR n=0 TO maxdig
13160 ?dest=n+5
13170 ?dgtval=digit(n)
13180 CALL display
13190 NEXT n
13200 REM DISPLAY UNITS
13210 ?dest=13
13220 ?dgtval=12
13230 CALL display:REM DISPLAY 's'
13240 IF A$="T" THEN 13310
13250 ?dest=12
13260 ?dgtval=13
```

```
 13270 CALL display:REM DISPLAY 'm'
 13280 ?32453=135:?32415=135:REM ALPHANUMERICS
 13283 ?32454=141:?32416=141:REM DOUBLE EIGHT CHARACTERS
 13285 ?32455=61:REM DISPLAY NEGATIVE SIGN
 13290 IF A$="A" THEN ?32417=50:?32457=50 :REM DISPLAY '2'
 13300 IF A$="S" THEN ?32417=49:?32457=49:REM DISPLAY '1'
 13310 RETURN
 13500 REM  NEGATIVE SIGN
 13510 FOR i=4 TO 1 STEP -1
 13520 digit(i)=digit(i-1)
 13530 NEXT i
 13540 digit(0)=11:REM NEGATIVE SIGN
 13550 RETURN
 14000REM COLLECT TIME INTERVALS MEASURED BY TIMER ROUTINE
 14010 J1=65536:J2=256:J3=4.975E-5
 14020 ST=store +4
 14030 T1=(J1*?(ST+2) + J2*?(ST+1) + ?(ST))*J3
 14040 T2=(J1*?(ST+6) + J2*?(ST+5) + ?(ST+4))*J3
 14050 T3=(J1*?(ST+10) + J2*?(ST+9) + ?(ST+8))*J3
 14060 IF (ST=store+4) AND (T1+T2+T3=0) THEN ST=store+64:GOTO 14030
 14070 RETURN
 15000 REM ADVANCED TIMER
 15010 ptr = &6880:REM PTR1 IS &6880
 15020  REM PTR2 IS &68C0
 15030  store=&6800 :REM TO &687F
 15040 status = &6881
 15050 evntctr = &6882
 15060 clocklo = &70
 15070 clockmid = &71
 15080 clockhi = &72
 15090 PRT=&FE60
 15100 DDRB=&FE62
 15110 flag=&FE6D
 15120 T1LLO=&FE64
 15130 T1LHI=&FE65
 15140 ACR=&FE6B
 15150 ?ACR=64:REM  GENERATE CONTINUOUS TIMEOUTS ON TIMER 1
 15160 ?&FE6E=127:REM DISABLE ALL INTERRUPTS
 15170 ?T1LLO=48:?T1LHI=0:REM TIMEOUTS AT 50 MICROSECOND INTERVALS
APPROXIMATELY
 15200 keyboardflag=&FE4D
 16010 FOR pass = 0 TO 3 STEP 3
 16020 P%=&6000
 16030  [OPT pass
 16040 .timer SEI
 16050 CLD
 16060  LDX #127
 16070 LDA #0
 16080 STA clocklo
 16090 STA clockmid
 16100 STA clockhi
 16110.nxtclr STA store,X
 16120 DEX  \CLEAR STORES
 16130 BPL nxtclr
 16140 STA DDRB \USER PORT IS INPUTS
 16150 LDA #252 \SET POINTERS TO -4
 16160 STA ptr
 16170 STA ptr+64
 16180  LDA PRT  \GET CURRENT INPUT STATUS
 16190  AND #3 \MASK FOR BITS 0 AND 1
```

```
16200  STA status  \SAVE CURRENT STATUS
16210 .wait LDA PRT
16220 AND #3
16230 TAY
16240  CPY status  \SAME STATUS ?
16250  BEQ wait   \WAIT UNTIL IT CHANGES
16260  .query TYA \RETRIEVE INPUT
16270  EOR status \WHICH INPUT CHANGED
16280  STY status \KEEP NEW STATUS
16290  CMP #1     \INPUT 1 ?
16300  BEQ chan1  \YES
16310  CMP #2     \INPUT 2 ?
16320  BEQ chan2  \YES
16330  TYA        \BOTH CHANNELS
16340  EOR #2     \IGNORE CHAN2 THIS TIME
16350  STA status
16360 .chan1 LDX #0
16370  BEQ cont \UNCONDITIONAL BRANCH
16380 .chan2 LDX #64
16390 .cont LDA ptr,X \GET EVENT POINTER
16400  CLC
16410  ADC #4 \INCREASE BY 4
16420  STA ptr,X  \PUT IT BACK
16430  CLC
16440  TXA        \GET CHANNEL POINTER
16450  ADC ptr,X  \ADD EVENT POINTER
16460  TAX        \RESTORE TO X-INDEX
16470  LDA clocklo \STORE CURRENT CLOCK READING
16480  STA store,X
16490  LDA clockmid
16500  STA store+1,X
16510  LDA clockhi
16520  STA store+2,X
16530  DEC evntctr \ALL EVENTS FINISHED ?
16540  BEQ done
16550 LDA keyboardflag
16551 STA keyboardflag \CLEAR FLAGS
16560 .count CLC
16570 LDA clocklo \INCREMENT CLOCK
16580 ADC #1
16590 STA clocklo
16600 LDA clockmid
16610 ADC #0
16620 STA clockmid
16630 LDA clockhi
16640 ADC #0
16650 STA clockhi
16660 LDA keyboardflag
16665 AND #1
16668 BNE done  \KEY PRESSED  FINISH
16670 .timewait LDA flag
16672  AND #64  \TIMEOUT ?
16674  BEQ timewait
16675  STA flag \RESET TIMEOUT FLAG
16700  LDA PRT   \CHECK IF INPUT CHANGED
16710 AND #3
16720 TAY
16730 CMP status
16740 BEQ count \CONTINUE TIMING
16750 BNE query
```

```
16760 .done  LDX #120 \CONVERT STORES TO TIME INTERVALS
16770  .nxtstore SEC
16780 LDA store+4,X
16790 SBC store+0,X
16800 STA store+4,X
16810 LDA store+5,X
16820 SBC store+1,X
16830 STA store+5,X
16840 LDA store+6,X
16850 SBC store+2,X
16860 STA store+6,X
16870 DEX
16880 DEX
16890 DEX
16900 DEX
16910 BPL nxtstore
16920 CLI
16930 RTS:]
16940 NEXT pass
16950 RETURN
```

CONSERVATION OF MOMENTUM - PROGRAM 9

```
LIST
    1 MODE7
    2 HIMEM = &6000
    4 GOSUB 15000:REM LOAD TIMING ROUTINE
    5 @%=&00020206:REM FORMAT
    9 DIM digit(4)
  100 REM CONSERVATION OF MOMENTUM
  110 CLS
  120 PRINT"   CONSERVATION OF MOMENTUM"
  130 PRINT TAB(0,3);"This program measures the speeds of"
  140 PRINT TAB(0,5);"40-mm cards crossing photocells,"
  150  PRINT TAB(0,7);"which are connected to bits 0 and 1"
  160 PRINT TAB(0,9);"of the User Port."
  170 PRINT TAB(0,12);"Measurements via bit 0 are listed"
  180 PRINT TAB(0,14);"under CHANNEL 1."
  190 PRINT TAB(0,16);"Measurements via bit 1 are listed"
  200 PRINT TAB(0,18);"under CHANNEL 2."
  210 PRINT TAB(0,20);"The measurements are in chronological"
  220 PRINT TAB(0,22);"order within each channel."
  230PRINT TAB(25,24);"Press SPACE";
  240 REPEAT UNTIL GET$=" "
 6000 CLS
 6010 PRINT TAB(5,1);"Measuring SPEED"
 6060 ?evntctr=8:REM EIGHT EVENTS
 6070 CALL timer
 6080 CLS:PRINT TAB(5,0);"CONSERVATION OF MOMENTUM"
 6090 PRINT TAB(0,4);"Measurement          Speed"
 6095 PRINT:PRINT"CHANNEL 1"
 6100 FOR reading = 1 TO 4
 6110 LET value%=8*(reading-1)
 6120 LET tableposition=&6804+value%
 6130 LET timeinterval=(65536*?(tableposition+2)+256*?(tableposition+1)+?
(tableposition))*0.00005
```

```
 6140 IF timeinterval=0 THEN LET reading=4 : GOTO 6190
 6150 LET speed=40/timeinterval
 6180 PRINT:PRINT"Speed (";STR$(reading);") = ";speed;TAB(20);"mm/s"
 6190 NEXT reading
 6200 PRINT:PRINT"CHANNEL 2"
 6210 FOR reading = 1 TO 4
 6220 LET value%=8*(reading-1)
 6230 LET tableposition=&6844+value%
 6240 LET timeinterval=(65536*?(tableposition+2)+256*?(tableposition+1)+?
(tableposition))*0.00005
 6250 IF timeinterval=0 THEN LET reading=4 : GOTO 6300
 6260 LET speed=40/timeinterval
 6270 PRINT:PRINT"Speed (";STR$(reading);") = ";speed;TAB(20);"mm/s"
 6300 NEXT reading
 6400 PRINT TAB(0,24);"Press SPACE to repeat";
 6500 REPEAT UNTIL GET$=" "
 6600 GOTO 100
15000 REM ADVANCED TIMER
15010 ptr = &6880:REM PTR1 IS &6880
15020  REM PTR2 IS &68C0
15030  store=&6800 :REM TO &687F
15040 status = &6881
15050 evntctr = &6882
15060 clocklo = &70
15070 clockmid = &71
15080 clockhi = &72
15090 PRT=&FE60
15100 DDRB=&FE62
15110 flag=&FE6D
15120 T1LLO=&FE64
15130 T1LHI=&FE65
15140 ACR=&FE6B
15150 ?ACR=64:REM  GENERATE CONTINUOUS TIMEOUTS ON TIMER 1
15160 ?&FE6E=127:REM DISABLE ALL INTERRUPTS
15170 ?T1LLO=48:?T1LHI=0:REM TIMEOUTS AT 50 MICROSECOND INTERVALS
APPROXIMATELY
15200 keyboardflag=&FE4D
16010 FOR pass = 0 TO 2 STEP 2
16020 P%=&6000
16030  [OPT pass
16040 .timer SEI
16050 CLD
16060  LDX #127
16070 LDA #0
16080 STA clocklo
16090 STA clockmid
16100 STA clockhi
16110.nxtclr STA store,X
16120 DEX  \CLEAR STORES
16130 BPL nxtclr
16140 STA DDRB \USER PORT IS INPUTS
16150 LDA #252 \SET POINTERS TO -4
16160 STA ptr
16170 STA ptr+64
16180  LDA PRT  \GET CURRENT INPUT STATUS
16190  AND #3 \MASK FOR BITS 0 AND 1
16200  STA status  \SAVE CURRENT STATUS
16210 .wait LDA PRT
16220 AND #3
16230 TAY
```

```
16240  CPY status  \SAME STATUS ?
16250  BEQ wait   \WAIT UNTIL IT CHANGES
16260  .query TYA \RETRIEVE INPUT
16270  EOR status \WHICH INPUT CHANGED
16280  STY status \KEEP NEW STATUS
16290  CMP #1     \INPUT 1 ?
16300  BEQ chan1  \YES
16310  CMP #2     \INPUT 2 ?
16320  BEQ chan2  \YES
16330  TYA        \BOTH CHANNELS
16340  EOR #2     \IGNORE CHAN2 THIS TIME
16350  STA status
16360 .chan1 LDX #0
16370  BEQ cont \UNCONDITIONAL BRANCH
16380 .chan2 LDX #64
16390 .cont LDA ptr,X \GET EVENT POINTER
16400  CLC
16410  ADC #4 \INCREASE BY 4
16420  STA ptr,X  \PUT IT BACK
16430  CLC
16440  TXA        \GET CHANNEL POINTER
16450  ADC ptr,X  \ADD EVENT POINTER
16460  TAX        \RESTORE TO X-INDEX
16470  LDA clocklo \STORE CURRENT CLOCK READING
16480  STA store,X
16490  LDA clockmid
16500  STA store+1,X
16510  LDA clockhi
16520  STA store+2,X
16530  DEC evntctr \ALL EVENTS FINISHED ?
16540  BEQ done
16550 LDA keyboardflag
16551 STA keyboardflag \CLEAR FLAGS
16560 .count CLC
16570 LDA clocklo \INCREMENT CLOCK
16580 ADC #1
16590 STA clocklo
16600 LDA clockmid
16610 ADC #0
16620 STA clockmid
16630 LDA clockhi
16640 ADC #0
16650 STA clockhi
16660 LDA keyboardflag
16665 AND #1
16668 BNE done  \KEY PRESSED  FINISH
16670 .timewait LDA flag
16672  AND #64  \TIMEOUT ?
16674  BEQ timewait
16675  STA flag \RESET TIMEOUT FLAG
16700  LDA PRT   \CHECK IF INPUT CHANGED
16710 AND #3
16720 TAY
16730 CMP status
16740 BEQ count \CONTINUE TIMING
16750 BNE query
16760 .done  LDX #120 \CONVERT STORES TO TIME INTERVALS
16770  .nxtstore SEC
16780 LDA store+4,X
16790 SBC store+0,X
```

```
16800 STA store+4,X
16810 LDA store+5,X
16820 SBC store+1,X
16830 STA store+5,X
16840 LDA store+6,X
16850 SBC store+2,X
16860 STA store+6,X
16870 DEX
16880 DEX
16890 DEX
16900 DEX
16910 BPL nxtstore
16920 CLI
16930 RTS:]
16940 NEXT pass
16950 RETURN
```

SPEED-TIME PLOTTER - PROGRAM 10

```
LIST
    1 MODE7
    2 HIMEM = &4000
    4 GOSUB 15000:REM LOAD TIMING ROUTINE
    5 @%=&020209
    6 DIM timeinterval(32)
    7 DIM speed(32)
    8 DIM elapsedtime(32)
   10 ON ERROR GOTO 100
  100 REM SPEED-TIME PLOTTER
  110 MODE7
  120 PRINT "          SPEED-TIME PLOTTER"
  130 PRINT TAB(0,2);"This program measures the time taken"
  140 PRINT TAB(0,4);"for each 'tooth' of the following"
  150 PRINT TAB(0,6);"card to cross in front of a photocell"
  160 PRINT TAB(0,8);"connected to bit 0 of the User Port."
  170 LET B$=CHR$(32):LET A$=CHR$(255)
  175 PRINT:PRINT"    1cm    1cm    16 teeth in total"
  180 PRINT"    > <     > <"
  190 PRINT CHR$(151);B$;B$;A$;B$;A$;B$;A$;B$;A$;B$;A$;B$;A$;B$;A$;B$;A$;B$;
A$;B$;A$;B$;A$;B$;A$;B$;A$;B$;A$;B$;A$
  200 PRINTCHR$(151);B$;B$;A$;B$;A$;B$;A$;B$;A$;B$;A$;B$;A$;B$;A$;B$;A$;B$;
A$;B$;A$;B$;A$;B$;A$;B$;A$;B$;A$;B$;A$
  210 PRINTCHR$(151);B$;B$;A$;A$;A$;A$;A$;A$;A$;A$;A$;A$;A$;A$;A$;A$;A$;A$;
A$;A$;A$;A$;A$;A$;A$;A$;A$;A$;A$;A$;A$
  214 PRINTCHR$(147);B$;A$;A$;A$;A$;A$;A$;A$;A$;A$;A$;A$;A$;A$;A$;A$;A$;A$;
A$;A$;A$;A$;A$;A$;A$;A$;A$;A$;A$;A$;A$
  215 PRINTCHR$(147);B$;A$;A$;A$;A$;A$;A$;A$;A$;A$;A$;A$;" TROLLEY ";A$;A$;
A$;A$;A$;A$;A$;A$;A$;A$;A$;A$;A$
  216 PRINTCHR$(147);B$;A$;A$;A$;A$;A$;A$;A$;A$;A$;A$;A$;A$;A$;A$;A$;A$;A$;
A$;A$;A$;A$;A$;A$;A$;A$;A$;A$;A$;A$;A$;A$
  230 PRINT TAB(5,20);"Ready to take readings."
  240 PRINT TAB(5,22);"Release the trolley now."
  250 PRINT TAB(3,24);"Press ESCAPE if problems occur.";
 7010 REM Measuring TIME INTERVALS
 7060?evntctr=31:REM THIRTY-ONE EVENTS
```

```
 7070 CALL timer
 7080 GOSUB 14000:REM COLLECT RESULTS
 7100 REM DISPLAY SPEED-TIME GRAPH
 7110 MODE 4
 7120 MOVE50,0:DRAW 50,1023
 7130 MOVE0,50:DRAW 1279,50
 7140 PRINT TAB(12,0);"SPEED-TIME GRAPH"
 7150 PRINT TAB(5,1);"Press SPACE for DISTANCE-TIME GRAPH"
 7160 PRINT TAB(5,2);"Press R for new readings."
 7170 MOVE 50,50
 7180 FOR reading=1 TO 30
 7190 DRAW 50+elapsedtime(reading),50+speed(reading)
 7200 NEXT reading
 7250 *FX15,0
 7300 LET A$=INKEY$(255)
 7400 IF A$=" " THEN 8000
 7500 IF A$="R" THEN 100
 7600 GOTO 7300
 8000 CLS
 8010 REM DISPLAY DISTANCE-TIME GRAPH
 8020 MOVE50,0:DRAW 50,1023
 8030 MOVE0,50:DRAW 1279,50
 8040 PRINT TAB(10,0);"DISTANCE-TIME GRAPH"
 8050 PRINT TAB(5,1);"Press SPACE for SPEED-TIME GRAPH"
 8060 PRINT TAB(5,2);"Press R for new readings."
 8100 MOVE 50,50
 8180 FOR reading=1 TO 30
 8190 DRAW elapsedtime(reading)+50,reading*30+50
 8200 NEXT reading
 8250 *FX15,0
 8300 LET A$=INKEY$(255)
 8400 IF A$=" " THEN 7100
 8500 IF A$="R" THEN 100
 8600 GOTO 8300
14000REM COLLECT TIME INTERVALS MEASURED BY TIMER ROUTINE
14010 J1=65536:J2=256:J3=0.1
14020 FOR reading=1 TO 31
14030 LET timestore=store+reading*4
14035 LET intervalstore=128 + timestore
14040 LETtimeinterval(reading)=(J1*?(intervalstore+2) + J2*?(intervalstore+1)
+ ?(intervalstore))*J3
14045 IF timeinterval(reading)=0 THEN LET reading=31:GOTO 14060
14050 LET speed(reading)=10000/timeinterval(reading)
14056 LET elapsedtime(reading)=(J1*?(timestore+2) + J2*?(timestore+1) + ?
(timestore))*J3
14060 NEXT reading
14100 RETURN
15000 REM ADVANCED TIMER
15010 ptr = &4880:REM PTR1 IS &4880
15020 REM PTR2 IS &48C0
15030 store=&4800 :REM TO &487F
15040 status = &4881
15050 evntctr = &4882
15060 clocklo = &70
15070 clockmid = &71
15080 clockhi = &72
15090 PRT=&FE60
15100 DDRB=&FE62
15110 flag=&FE6D
15120 T1LLO=&FE64
```

```
15130 T1LHI=&FE65
15140 ACR=&FE6B
15150 ?ACR=64:REM  GENERATE CONTINUOUS TIMEOUTS ON TIMER 1
15160 ?&FE6E=127:REM DISABLE ALL INTERRUPTS
15170 ?T1LLO=48:?T1LHI=0:REM TIMEOUTS AT 50 MICROSECOND INTERVALS
APPROXIMATELY
15200 keyboardflag=&FE4D
16010 FOR pass = 0 TO 2 STEP 2
16020 P%=&4000
16030  [OPT pass
16040 .timer SEI
16050 CLD
16060  LDX #127
16070 LDA #0
16080 STA clocklo
16090 STA clockmid
16100 STA clockhi
16110.nxtclr STA store,X
16120 DEX  \CLEAR STORES
16130 BPL nxtclr
16140 STA DDRB \USER PORT IS INPUTS
16150 LDA #252 \SET POINTERS TO -4
16160 STA ptr
16170 STA ptr+64
16180  LDA PRT  \GET CURRENT INPUT STATUS
16190  AND #3 \MASK FOR BITS 0 AND 1
16200  STA status  \SAVE CURRENT STATUS
16210 .wait LDA PRT
16220 AND #3
16230 TAY
16240  CPY status  \SAME STATUS ?
16250  BEQ wait   \WAIT UNTIL IT CHANGES
16260  .query TYA \RETRIEVE INPUT
16270  EOR status \WHICH INPUT CHANGED
16280  STY status \KEEP NEW STATUS
16290  CMP #1     \INPUT 1 ?
16300  BEQ chan1  \YES
16310  CMP #2     \INPUT 2 ?
16320  BEQ chan2  \YES
16330  TYA        \BOTH CHANNELS
16340  EOR #2     \IGNORE CHAN2 THIS TIME
16350  STA status
16360 .chan1 LDX #0
16370  BEQ cont \UNCONDITIONAL BRANCH
16380 .chan2 LDX #64
16390 .cont LDA ptr,X \GET EVENT POINTER
16400  CLC
16410  ADC #4 \INCREASE BY 4
16420  STA ptr,X  \PUT IT BACK
16430  CLC
16440  TXA        \GET CHANNEL POINTER
16450  ADC ptr,X  \ADD EVENT POINTER
16460  TAX        \RESTORE TO X-INDEX
16470  LDA clocklo \STORE CURRENT CLOCK READING
16480  STA store,X
16490  LDA clockmid
16500  STA store+1,X
16510  LDA clockhi
16520  STA store+2,X
16530  DEC evntctr \ALL EVENTS FINISHED ?
```

```
16540  BEQ done
16550 LDA keyboardflag
16551 STA keyboardflag \CLEAR FLAGS
16560 .count CLC
16570 LDA clocklo \INCREMENT CLOCK
16580 ADC #1
16590 STA clocklo
16600 LDA clockmid
16610 ADC #0
16620 STA clockmid
16630 LDA clockhi
16640 ADC #0
16650 STA clockhi
16660 LDA keyboardflag
16665 AND #1
16668 BNE done  \KEY PRESSED  FINISH
16670 .timewait LDA flag
16672  AND #64  \TIMEOUT ?
16674  BEQ timewait
16675  STA flag \RESET TIMEOUT FLAG
16700  LDA PRT   \CHECK IF INPUT CHANGED
16710 AND #3
16720 TAY
16730 CMP status
16740 BEQ count \CONTINUE TIMING
16750 BNE query
16760 .done  LDX #120 \CONVERT STORES TO TIME INTERVALS
16770  .nxtstore SEC
16780 LDA store+4,X
16790 SBC store+0,X
16800 STA store+132,X
16810 LDA store+5,X
16820 SBC store+1,X
16830 STA store+133,X
16840 LDA store+6,X
16850 SBC store+2,X
16860 STA store+134,X
16870 DEX
16880 DEX
16890 DEX
16900 DEX
16910 BPL nxtstore
16920 CLI
16930 RTS:]
16940 NEXT pass
16950 RETURN
```

PULSE TIMER - PROGRAM 11

```
>LIST
    1 MODE 7
    2 HIMEM=&7000
  100 REM SIMPLE TIMER
  110 PRT=&FE60
```

```
120 DDRB=&FE62
130 T1LLO=&FE64
140 T1LHI=&FE65
150 T2LO=&FE68
160 T2HI=&FE69
170 SR=&FE6A
180 ACR=&FE6B
190 PCR=&FE6C
200 FLAG=&FE6D
210 IER=&FE6E
300
310 REM INITIALISE TIMER
320 ?IER=127:REM DISABLE ALL INTERRUPTS
330 ?ACR=224:REM SET UP PB6 TO COUNT PULSES AND PB7 AS FREE-RUNNING OUTPUT
340 ?PCR=0:REM TURN OFF LATCHES ETC.
350 ?DDRB=128:REM BIT 7 AS OUTPUT
360 ?T2LO=255
370 ?T2HI=255:REM INITIALISE COUNTER
380 ?FLAG=127:REM CLEAR ALL FLAGS
390
500 CLS
510 PRINT TAB(8,2);CHR$(141);"SIMPLE TIMER"
520 PRINT TAB(8,3);CHR$(141);"SIMPLE TIMER"
530 PRINT TAB(0,6);"When input X goes HIGH, 1 millisecond"
540 PRINT TAB(0,8);"pulses will be counted by Timer 2."
550 PRINT TAB(0,10);"This continues until input X goes LOW."
555 GOSUB 2000
560 PRINT TAB(0,20);"When you are ready for the timing"
570 PRINT TAB(0,22);"to start, press SPACE."
580 IF GET$<>" " THEN 580
590 PRINT TAB(0,24);"O.K. Waiting for POSITIVE pulse.";
600 REM START TIMER 1 TO PROVIDE 1 KHZ PULSES ON PB7
610 ?T1LLO=244
620 ?T1LHI=1
630 IF(?PRT AND 1)=0 THEN 630
640 PRINT TAB(0,24);"O.K.   Timing is under way.          ";
650 IF (?PRT AND 1) THEN 650
655 t=256*(255-?T2HI) + (255-?T2LO)
660 CLS
670 PRINT TAB(8,2);CHR$(141);"SIMPLE TIMER"
680 PRINT TAB(8,3);CHR$(141);"SIMPLE TIMER"
690 PRINT TAB(0,8);"The measured time interval is "
700 PRINT TAB(0,10);t;" milliseconds."
720 PRINT TAB(0,16);"Press SPACE for another measurement."
730  IF GET$<>" " THEN 730
740 GOTO 300
2000 REM DRAW DIAGRAM
2010 PRINT TAB(5,12);CHR$(151);CHR$(32);CHR$(32);CHR$(32);CHR$(32);CHR$(32);
CHR$(32);CHR$(112);CHR$(112);CHR$(112);CHR$(112);CHR$(112);CHR$(112);CHR$(112)
2020 PRINT TAB(0,13);"Input X    ";CHR$(151);CHR$(53);"      ";CHR$(106)
2030 PRINT TAB(0,14);"& PB0";CHR$(151);CHR$(79);CHR$(44);CHR$(44);CHR$(44);
CHR$(44);CHR$(44);CHR$(53);"NAND ";CHR$(106)
2040 PRINT TAB(5,15);CHR$(151);"      ";CHR$(53);"      ";;CHR$(106);CHR$(44)
;CHR$(44);CHR$(44);CHR$(44);CHR$(44);CHR$(79);CHR$(135);" TO PB6"
2050 PRINT TAB(1,16);"PB7 ";CHR$(151);CHR$(79);CHR$(44);CHR$(44);CHR$(44);
CHR$(44);CHR$(44);CHR$(53);"GATE ";CHR$(106)
2060 PRINT TAB(0,17);"1 ms pulses";CHR$(151);;CHR$(53);"      ";CHR$(106)
2070 PRINT TAB(11,18);CHR$(151);CHR$(96);CHR$(96);CHR$(96);CHR$(96);CHR$(96)
;CHR$(96);CHR$(96)
2100 RETURN
```

FREQUENCY METER - PROGRAM 12

```
LIST
    1 MODE 7
  100 REM FAST FREQUENCY METER
  110 PRT=&FE60
  120 DDRB=&FE62
  130 T1LLO=&FE64
  140 T1LHI=&FE65
  150 T2LO=&FE68
  160 T2HI=&FE69
  170 SR=&FE6A
  180 ACR=&FE6B
  190 PCR=&FE6C
  200 FLAG=&FE6D
  210 IER=&FE6E
  300
  310 REM INITIALISE TIMER
  320 ?IER=127:REM DISABLE ALL INTERRUPTS
  330 ?ACR=160:REM SET UP PB6 TO COUNT PULSES AND PB7 AS SINGLE PULSE OUTPUT
  340 ?PCR=0:REM TURN OFF LATCHES ETC.
  350 ?DDRB=128:REM BIT 7 AS OUTPUT
  360 ?T2LO=255
  370 ?T2HI=255:REM INITIALISE COUNTER
  380 ?FLAG=127:REM CLEAR ALL FLAGS
  390
  560 GOSUB 2000
  600 GOSUB 1000:REM OPEN GATE FOR 50 MILLISECONDS
  640 f=256*(255-?T2HI) + (255-?T2LO)
  650 freq = f * 20
  655 IF freq<2000 THEN GOTO 800:REM LOW FREQUENCY ROUTINE
  660 CLS
  670 PRINT TAB(8,2);CHR$(141);"FREQUENCY METER"
  680 PRINT TAB(8,3);CHR$(141);"FREQUENCY METER"
  690 PRINT TAB(0,8);"The measured frequency is "
  700 PRINT TAB(0,10);freq;" Hz"
  720 PRINT TAB(0,16);"Press SPACE for another measurement."
  730  IF GET$<>" " THEN 730
  740 GOTO 300
  800 REM LOW FREQUENCY ROUTINE
  810 ?ACR=32:REM DISABLE PB7 OUTPUT
  820 ?PRT=128:REM PB7 HIGH INITIALLY
  830 ?T2LO=255
  840 ?T2HI=255 :REM RELOAD COUNTER
  860 PRINT TAB(0,24);"O.K. Now taking measurement.";
  870 ?PRT=0:REM OPEN PB7 GATE
  880 FOR count = 1 TO 20:GOSUB 1000:NEXT count
  890 ?PRT=128:REM CLOSE PB7 GATE
  900 f=256*(255-?T2HI) + (255-?T2LO)
  910 freq = f
  920 GOTO 660
 1000 REM DELAY FOR 50 MILLISECONDS
 1010 ?T1LLO=79:?T1LHI=195:REM RESTART TIMER 1 AND RESET FLAG
 1020 IF (?FLAG AND 64) = 0 THEN 1020:REM WAIT FOR TIME-OUT ON TIMER 1
 1030 RETURN
 2000 REM DISPLAY DIAGRAM AND INSTRUCTIONS
 2010 CLS
 2020 PRINT TAB(8,1);CHR$(141);"FREQUENCY METER"
 2030 PRINT TAB(8,2);CHR$(141);"FREQUENCY METER"
 2040 PRINT TAB(0,4);"When started, the PB7 line goes LOW to"
```

```
 2050 PRINT TAB(0,6);"enable pulses to be counted."
 2060 PRINT TAB(0,8);"by Timer 2 via PB6."
 2070 PRINT TAB(0,10);"              ";CHR$(151);CHR$(112);CHR$(112);CHR$(112);
CHR$(112);CHR$(112);CHR$(112);CHR$(112)
 2080 PRINT TAB(0,11);"From PB7  ";CHR$(151);CHR$(53);" NOT ";CHR$(106)
 2090 PRINT TAB(0,12);"     ";CHR$(151);"O";CHR$(44);CHR$(44);CHR$(44);CHR$
(44);CHR$(44);CHR$(53);"      ";CHR$(106);CHR$(44);CHR$(44);CHR$(44);CHR$(44);
CHR$(52)
 2100 PRINT TAB(0,13);"              ";CHR$(151);CHR$(53);"GATE ";CHR$(106);
"    ";CHR$(53)
 2110 PRINT TAB(0,14);"              ";CHR$(151);CHR$(96)CHR$(96)CHR$(96)CHR$(96)
CHR$(96)CHR$(96)CHR$(96);"     ";CHR$(53);" ";CHR$(112);CHR$(112);CHR$(112);
CHR$(112);CHR$(112);CHR$(112);CHR$(112)
 2120 PRINT TAB(21,15);CHR$(151);CHR$(45);CHR$(44);CHR$(53);"NAND ";CHR$(106)
;CHR$(135);"  To PB 6"
 2130 PRINT TAB(5,16);"Unknown freq.      ";CHR$(151);CHR$(53);"      ";CHR$
(106);CHR$(44);CHR$(44);CHR$(44);CHR$(44);CHR$(79)
 2140 PRINT TAB(4,17);CHR$(151);CHR$(79);CHR$(44);CHR$(44);CHR$(44);CHR$(44);
CHR$(44);CHR$(44);CHR$(44);CHR$(44);CHR$(44);CHR$(44);CHR$(44);CHR$(44);CHR$
(44);CHR$(44);CHR$(44);CHR$(44);CHR$(44);CHR$(44);CHR$(53);"GATE ";CHR$(106)
 2150 PRINT TAB(23,18);CHR$(151);CHR$(96);CHR$(96);CHR$(96);CHR$(96);CHR$(96);
CHR$(96);CHR$(96)
 2160 PRINT TAB(0,20);"Press SPACE to take the measurement."
 2170 IF GET$<>" " THEN 2170
 2200 RETURN
```

PROGRAMMABLE OSCILLATOR - PROGRAM 13

```
LIST
    1 REM PROGRAMMABLE OSCILLATOR
    2 HIMEM = &4000
    3 MODE 4
   10 GOSUB 1000:REM LOAD MACHINE CODE ROUTINE
   20 CLS
   30 PRINT TAB(8,1);"PROGRAMMABLE OSCILLATOR"
   40 PRINT TAB(0,3);"This program allows you to select any"
   50 PRINT TAB(0,5);"waveform to be output through the DAC."
   60 PRINT TAB(0,7);"The frequency can also be selected"
   70 PRINT TAB(0,9);"up to a maximum of 200 Hz."
   80 PRINT TAB(0,11);"Enter the waveform equation like this:"
   90 PRINT TAB(0,13);"      function(T)       For example:"
   95 PRINT TAB(0,15);"SINE   128 + 120*SIN(T*PI/128)"
   96 PRINT TAB(0,17);"SQUARE   250 * INT(T/128) "
   97 PRINT TAB(0,19);"TRIANGULAR   ABS(128-T)"
  100 INPUT A$
  110 FOR T=0 TO 255
  120 V= EVAL(A$)
  125 IF V>255 THEN V=255
  126 IF V<0 THEN V=0
  130 ?(store + T) = INT(V)
  140 NEXT T
  150 PRINT TAB(0,21);"Enter the required frequency.";
  160 INPUT freq
  170 IF freq > 200 THEN PRINT TAB(0,24);"up to a maximum of 200 Hz.":GOTO 150
```

```
 180 reptn=1000000/(freq*256) - 9
 181 ?reptnhi=INT(reptn/256)
 182 ?reptnlo=reptn - 256*INT(reptn/256)
 190 PRINT TAB(0,24);"The waveform is now being output."
 200 PRINT TAB(0,26);"Press any key to stop."
 205 FOR T=1 TO 1000:NEXT T:REM DELAY TO ALLOW KEY TO BE RELEASED
 210 CALL output
 220 CLS
 230 PRINT TAB(0,3);"Do you wish to alter the waveform ?"
 240 PRINT TAB(0,5);"Press 'Y' for yes and 'N' for no."
 250 C$ = GET$:IF C$<>"Y" AND C$<>"N" THEN 250
 260 IF C$="Y" THEN GOTO 20 ELSE GOTO 150
1000 REM MACHINE CODE ROUTINE
1010 PRT = &FE60
1020 DDR = &FE62
1030 timerlo=&FE64
1040 timerhi=&FE65
1050 ACR = &FE6B
1060 PCR = &FE6C
1070 FLAG= &FE6D
1080 keyboardflag = &FE4D
1095 reptnlo = &4100
1096 reptnhi = &4101
1097 store = &4200
1099 FOR pass = 0 TO 2 STEP 2
1100 P% = &4000
1105
1110 [OPT pass
1120 .output SEI
1125  LDA #64
1130  STA ACR \ENABLE TIMER ONE CONTINUOUS INTERRUPTS
1154  LDA reptnlo
1156  STA timerlo
1160  LDA reptnhi
1170  STA timerhi \START COUNTDOWN
1173  LDA #64
1175  STA FLAG \RESET FLAG
1180  LDX #0
1200 .next LDA FLAG
1210  AND #64
1220  BEQ next
1225  STA FLAG \RESET FLAG
1230  LDA store,X
1235  STA PRT
1240  INX
1250  BNE next
1260  LDA keyboardflag
1270  AND #1
1280  BEQ next
1290  CLI:RTS:]
1300
1310 NEXT pass
1320 RETURN
2000 FOR I =&4200 TO &42FF
2010 PRINT ?I;
2020 NEXT I
```

CAPACITOR DISCHARGE - PROGRAM 14

```
LIST
 100 REM CAPACITOR DISCHARGE PLOT
 110 MODE1
 120 CLS
 123 VDU19,0,7,0,0,0
 124 VDU19,3,0,0,0,0
 130 CLG
 140 PRINT TAB(0,0) "       THE VOLTAGE ACROSS A CAPACITOR   "
 150 PRINT TAB(0,2) "        PRESS THE SPACE BAR TO BEGIN    "
 180 PRINT TAB(0,6) " 1.6-"
 185 PRINT TAB(0,9) " 1.4-"
 190 PRINT TAB(0,12) " 1.2-"
 195 PRINT TAB(0,15) " 1.0-"
 200 PRINT TAB(0,18) " 0.8-"
 205 PRINT TAB(0,21) " 0.6-"
 210 PRINT TAB(0,24) " 0.4-"
 220 PRINT TAB(0,27) " 0.2-"
 225 PRINT TAB(0,30) "   0-"
 250 MOVE 150,850
 260 DRAW 150,50
 270 DRAW 1200,50
 300 PRINT TAB(4,31) "0  2  3  4  5  6  7  8  9 10 11 12";
 310 PRINT TAB(38,29) "t"
 700 VDU30
 800 X$=GET$
 850 PRINT TAB(4,3) "V                                  "
 900 X=150
 950 PRINT TAB(0,0) "       THE VOLTAGE ACROSS A CAPACITOR   "
 960 PRINT TAB(0,2) "        PRESS THE SPACE BAR TO BEGIN     "
1000 REM MEASURE VOLTAGE AND CONVERT TO TRUE READING
1010 Y=(ADVAL(1)-672)/68 + 80
1020 PLOT69,X,Y
1025 REPEAT
1030 Y=(ADVAL(1)-672)/68 + 80
1040 PLOT5,X,Y
1050 X=X+1
1060 UNTIL X>1200
1065 SOUND1,-15,100,10
1070 PRINT TAB(0,0);"Press SPACE for another graph or      "
1080 PRINT TAB(0,2);"press RETURN to finish.               "
1090 LET S$=GET$
1100 IF S$=CHR$(13) THEN END
1110 IF S$=" " THEN 900
1120 GOTO 1090
```

FAST ANALOGUE CONVERTER - PROGRAM 15

```
>LIST
   10 REM CONFIGURE USER PORT
   20 BPRT=65120:REM USER PORT
   30 DDRB=65122:REM DATA DIRECTION REGISTER
   40 ACR=65131:REM AUXILIARY CONTROL REGISTER
   50 PCR=65132:REM PERIFERAL CONTROL REGISTER
```

```
  60 FLAG=65133:REM FLAG REGISTER
  70 IER=65134:REM INTERRUPT REGISTER
 100 REM ?DDRB=0:REM B-PORT IS INPUT
 110 ?ACR=2:REM ACR SET TO ENABLE B-PORT LATCH
 120 ?PCR=176:REM PCR SET TO LATCH ON LOW-HIGH TRANSITION
 125 REM PCR SET TO PROVIDE CB2 PULSE OUTPUT ON DATA WRITE
 130 ?FLAG=16:REM RESET CB1 FLAG
 140 ?IER=127:REM DISABLE VIA INTERRUPTS
 150 GOSUB 24000:REM COMPILE ASSEMBLY CODE
 500 REM INSTRUCTIONS
 510 MODE4
 520 CLS
 530 PRINT TAB(5,1);"FAST ANALOGUE CONVERTER"
 540 PRINT TAB(0,5);"This program collects 256 readings "
 550 PRINT TAB(0,7);"from the fast ADC connected"
 560 PRINT TAB(0,9);"to the User Port."
 570 PRINT TAB(0,11);"Choose the time interval between"
 580 PRINT TAB(0,13);"successive readings in microseconds."
 590 PRINT TAB(0,15);"(minimum 15, maximum 1280)"
 600 PRINT:INPUT interval
 610 IF interval<15 OR interval>1280 THEN 600
 620 ?delay=1+INT((interval-15)/5)
 630  PRINT TAB(0,20);"Enter the threshold voltage level"
 640 PRINT TAB(0,22);"(range 0 to 2.0 volts)"
 650 PRINT:INPUT startvolts
 660 ?threshold=startvolts*100
 661 PRINT TAB(0,28);"For a centre-zero graph press C"
 662 PRINT TAB(0,30);"For a bottom-zero graph press B"
 663 LET S$=INKEY$(255)
 664 IF S$="C" THEN 1000
 665 IF S$="B" THEN 2000
 666 GOTO 663
1000 REM CENTRE-ZERO GRAPH
1005 CLS
1006 PRINT TAB(5,0);"Ready to take readings             "
1007 CALL begin
1010 MOVE 100,0:DRAW 100,1000
1020 MOVE 0,500:DRAW 1200,500
1030 VDU5
1040 MOVE 0,1000:PRINT"2.0"
1050 MOVE 0,750:PRINT"1.0"
1060 MOVE 0,490:PRINT"0"
1070 MOVE 0,250:PRINT"-1"
1080 MOVE 0,32:PRINT"-2"
1090 MOVE 110,490:PRINT"0"
1100 FOR i=1 TO 5
1110 MOVE 102+200*i,490:PRINTSTR$(interval*.05*i)
1120 NEXT i
1130 MOVE 400,450:PRINT"time/milliseconds"
1140 VDU4
1150 GOTO 3000
2000 REM BOTTOM-ZERO GRAPH
2005 CLS
2006 PRINT TAB(5,0);"Ready to take readings             "
2007 CALL begin
2010 MOVE 100,0:DRAW 100,1000
2020 MOVE 0,80:DRAW 1200,80
2030 VDU5
2040 MOVE 0,900:PRINT"4.0"
2050 MOVE 0,700:PRINT"3.0"
```

```
 2060 MOVE 0,500:PRINT"2.0"
 2070 MOVE 0,300:PRINT"1.0"
 2080 MOVE 0,70:PRINT" 0"
 2090 MOVE 110,70:PRINT"0"
 2100 FOR i=1 TO 5
 2110 MOVE 102+200*i,70:PRINTSTR$(interval*.05*i)
 2120 NEXT i
 2130 MOVE 400,35:PRINT"time/milliseconds"
 2140 VDU4
 3000 N=4
 3010 FOR i=0 TO 255
 3020 PLOTN,100+i*4,?(i+&4100)*3.6+100
 3025 N=5
 3030 NEXT i
 3040 PRINT TAB(5,0);"S for same interval, N for new "
 3050 LET A$=INKEY$(255)
 3060 IF A$="N" THEN 500
 3070 IF A$="S" AND S$="C" THEN 1006
 3080 IF A$="S" AND S$="B" THEN 2006
 3090 GOTO 3050
24000 REM MACHINE CODE ROUTINE FOR FAST ADC
24010
24020 threshold=&70
24030 delay=&80
24040 store=&4100:REM AND NEXT 256 BYTES
24200 FOR pass=0 TO 3 STEP 3
24205 P%=&4000
24210 [OPT pass
24220 .begin  SEI
24230         LDY #0
24234 .wait   LDA BPRT \CLEAR LATCH
24235         STA BPRT \BEGIN NEXT CONVERSION
24236         NOP
24238         NOP
24240         NOP
24242         NOP
24244         NOP
24246         NOP
24248         LDA BPRT
24250         STA BPRT \BEGIN NEXT CONVERSION
24252         CMP threshold
24260         BCC wait  \WAIT FOR CHANGE
24320 .new    LDA BPRT
24340         STA BPRT \BEGIN NEXT CONVERSION
24350         STA store,Y
24360         LDX delay
24370 .pause  NOP \2 CYCLES
24374         LDA delay \DUMMY LOAD FOR 3 CYCLES
24376         DEX  \2CYCLES
24380         BNE pause \3 CYCLES
24390         INY
24400         BNE new
24410         CLI
24420         RTS
24430]
24440 NEXT pass
24500 RETURN
```

DIGITAL MULTIMETER - PROGRAM 16

```
LIST
 100 MODE 7
 110 DIM digit(5)
 200 REM INSTRUCTIONS
 210CLS
 220PRINT TAB(8,2) "DIGITAL MULTIMETER"
 230PRINT TAB(10,4) "by R.A.Sparkes"
 235 GOSUB 10000:REM LOAD MACHINE CODE DISPLAY ROUTINE
 240 PRINT TAB(0,7) "This program measures and displays"
 250PRINT TAB(0,9) "voltage input to analogue channel 1"
 260PRINT TAB(0,11) "current input to analogue channel 2"
 270PRINT TAB(0,13) "and their product, power"
 280PRINT TAB(0,15) "or their ratio, resistance."
 300PRINT TAB(0,22) "Press R for resistance or P for power."
 305 LET A$=GET$
 310IF A$<>"P" AND A$<>"R" THEN 305
 320 CLS
 330 FOR I=31777 TO 32737 STEP 40
 340 ?I=23
 350 NEXT I
 351 PRINT TAB(0,23)"Press R for resistance or P for power.";
 355 REM DISPLAY V
 360 PRINT TAB(34,0)"5   j"
 370 PRINT TAB(34,1)"5   j"
 380 PRINT TAB(34,2)"5   j"
 385 PRINT TAB(34,3)"5   j"
 390 PRINT TAB(34,4)"m   >"
 392 PRINT TAB(35,5)"m >"
 394 PRINT TAB(36,6)"m>"
 395 REM DISPLAY A
 400  PRINT TAB(36,8)">m"
 402 PRINT TAB(35,9)"> m"
 404 PRINT TAB(34,10)">   m"
 406 PRINT TAB(34,11)"5   j"
 408 PRINT TAB(34,12)"=,,,n"
 410 PRINT TAB(34,13)"5   j"
 412 PRINT TAB(34,14)"5   j"
 420 IF A$="R" THEN 700
 425 REM DISPLAY W
 430 PRINT TAB(34,16)"5   j"
 440 PRINT TAB(34,17)"5   j"
 450 PRINT TAB(34,18)"5   j"
 460 PRINT TAB(34,19)"5 j5 j"
 470 PRINT TAB(34,20)"5 j5 j"
 480 PRINT TAB(34,21)"5 j5 j"
 490 PRINT TAB(34,22)"m|>m|>"
 500 REM MEASURE VOLTAGE AND CURRENT
 510 voltage=(ADVAL(1) -600)/30000
 520 number=voltage
 530 pos=0
 540 GOSUB 9000
 550 current=(ADVAL(2)-600)/30000
 560 number=current
 570 pos=5
 580 GOSUB 9000
 590 number=current*voltage
 600 pos=10
 610 GOSUB 9000
```

```
 620 IF INKEY$(0)="R" THEN 700
 630 GOTO 500
 700 REM RESISTANCE
 710 REM DISPLAY OHMS
 720 PRINT TAB(34,16)" _<10 "
 730 PRINT TAB(34,17)" j  5 "
 740 PRINT TAB(34,18)" 7  k "
 750 PRINT TAB(34,19)" 5  j "
 760 PRINT TAB(34,20)" i  6 "
 770 PRINT TAB(34,21)"  5j  "
 780 PRINT TAB(34,22)",.!""-,"
 800 REM MEASURE VOLTAGE AND CURRENT
 810 voltage=(ADVAL(1) -600)/30000
 820 number=voltage
 830 pos=0
 840 GOSUB 9000
 850 current=(ADVAL(2)-600)/30000
 860 number=current
 870 pos=5
 880 GOSUB 9000
 890 number=voltage/current
 900 pos=10
 910 GOSUB 9000
 920 IF INKEY$(0)="P" THEN 425
 930 GOTO 800
 9000 REM DIGIT SEPARATION AND DISPLAY
 9005 loc=114:dgtval=115
 9010 decpt=0:sign=1
 9020IF number<0 THEN number=ABS(number):sign=-1
 9030IF number>=1 THEN number=number/10:decpt=decpt+1:GOTO 9030
 9040IF decpt>4 THEN 500:REM OUT OF RANGE
 9050FOR I=0 TO 3
 9060digit=INT(number*10)
 9070number=number*10-digit
 9080 IF I<decpt THEN digit(I)=digit
 9090IF I>=decpt THEN digit(I+1)=digit
 9100NEXT I
 9110digit(decpt)=10
 9120IF sign<0 THEN FOR I= 4 TO 1 STEP -1:digit(I)=digit(I-1):NEXT I:digit
(0)=11
 9200REM DIGIT DISPLAY ROUTINE
 9210sigfig=3:REM SET NUMBER OF SIG. FIGS.
 9220IF sign <0 THEN sigfig=sigfig+1
 9230FOR I=0 TO sigfig
 9240 ?loc=(I+pos):?dgtval=digit(I)
 9250CALL display
 9260NEXT I
 9270RETURN
10000REM LOADER FOR MACHINE CODE SUBROUTINE
10010REM 'LARGE DIGIT DISPLAY'
10020 display=28672
10030HIMEM=&7000
10035 loc=114:dgtval=115:display=28672
10040 FOR I=28672 TO 28781
10050READ X
10060?I=X
10070NEXT I
10080 DATA 165,114,201,10,16,15,201,5,16,27
10090DATA 10,10,10,133,112,169,124,133,113,208
10100DATA 28,56,233,10,10,10,10,105,128,133
```

```
10110DATA 112,169,126,133,113,208,14,56,233,5
10120DATA 10,10,10,105,64,133,112,169,125,133
10130 DATA 113,162,0,165,115,10,10,10,168,185
10140DATA 0,113,157,128,112,200,232,224,8,208
10150DATA 244,160,223,162,255,232,224,7,240,29
10160DATA 169,8,133,116,24,152,105,32,168,200
10170DATA 30,128,112,144,4,169,127,208,2,169
10180DATA 23,145,112,198,116,240,224,208,236,96
10200REM DIGITS TABLE
10210 FOR I=28928 TO 29031
10220 READ X
10230?I=X
10240NEXT I
10250DATA 124,68,68,68,68,68,124,0:REM DIGIT 0
10260DATA 8,8,8,8,8,8,8,0:REM DIGIT 1
10270DATA 124,68,4,4,124,64,124,0:REM DIGIT 2
10280DATA 124,4,4,124,4,4,124,0:REM DIGIT 3
10290DATA 64,64,64,72,124,8,8,0:REM DIGIT 4
10300DATA124,64,64,124,4,4,124,0:REM DIGIT 5
10310DATA 124,64,64,124,68,68,124,0:REM DIGIT 6
10320DATA 124,4,4,4,4,4,4,0:REM DIGIT 7
10330DATA 124,68,68,124,68,68,124,0:REM DIGIT 8
10340DATA 124,68,68,124,4,4,4,0:REM DIGIT 9
10350 DATA 0,0,0,0,0,0,16,0:REM DECIMAL POINT
10360 DATA 0,0,0,124,0,0,0,0:REM NEGATIVE SIGN
10370 DATA 0,0,60,32,60,4,60,0:REM LETTER S
10380 RETURN
```

CURRENT-VOLTAGE PLOTTER – PROGRAM 17

```
LIST
    1 MODE7
   10 PRINTTAB(8,1);"VOLTAGE-CURRENT PLOT"
   20 PRINT:PRINT:PRINT"This program produces a ramp voltage"
   30 PRINT:PRINT"from a digital-to-analogue converter"
   40 PRINT:PRINT"connected to the User Port."
   50 PRINT:PRINT"This can drive a current through a diode"
   60PRINT"or other device and this current can be"
   70PRINT:PRINT"measured at analogue channel 0 as the"
   80PRINT:PRINT"voltage across a small series resistor."
   90PRINTTAB(0,23);"Press SPACE to begin taking readings."
   95 REPEAT UNTIL GET$=" "
  100 REM VOLTAGE-CURRENT PLOT
  110 MODE1
  120 CLS
  123 VDU19,0,7,0,0,0
  124 VDU19,3,0,0,0,0
  130 CLG
  140 PRINT TAB(0,1) "         CURRENT-VOLTAGE PLOT"
  180 PRINT TAB(0,6) "  16-"
  185 PRINT TAB(0,9) "  14-"
  190 PRINT TAB(0,12) "  12-"
  195 PRINT TAB(0,15) "  10-"
  200 PRINT TAB(0,18) "   8-"
  205 PRINT TAB(0,21) "   6-"
```

```
 210 PRINT TAB(0,24) "   4-"
 220 PRINT TAB(0,27) "   2-"
 225 PRINT TAB(0,30) "   0-"
 250 MOVE 150,850
 260 DRAW 150,50
 270 DRAW 1200,50
 300 PRINT TAB(4,31) "0      1      2      3      4 volt ";
 320 PRINT TAB(2,3) "milli-":PRINT TAB(2,4);"amps"
 700 VDU30
 800 REM INITIALIZE VALUES
 810 LET n=4:REM PLOT FIRST POINT
 820 LET dac=&FE60:REM USER PORT ADDRESS
 830 ?&FE62=255:REM USER PORT SET FOR OUTPUT
 840 PRINT TAB(0,0);"                                        "
 845 PRINT TAB(0,2);"                                        "
 850 PRINT TAB(0,1) "       CURRENT-VOLTAGE PLOT"
 855 X=150
 860 REPEAT
 900 REM OUTPUT VOLTAGE
 910 LET volt%=(X-150)DIV4
 920 ?dac=volt%
1000 REM MEASURE VOLTAGE AND CONVERT TO CURRENT READING
1010 Y=(ADVAL(1)-672)/68 + 80
1020 PLOTn,X,Y
1030 LET n=5:REM DRAW FROM NOW ON
1050 X=X+4
1060 UNTIL X>1200
1065 SOUND1,-15,100,10
1070 PRINT TAB(0,0);"Press SPACE for another graph or       "
1075PRINTTAB(0,1);"                                      "
1080 PRINT TAB(0,2);"press RETURN to finish.                "
1090 LET S$=GET$
1100 IF S$=CHR$(13) THEN MODE 7:END
1110 IF S$=" " THEN 800
1120 GOTO 1090
```

FOUR-CHANNEL CHART RECORDER - PROGRAM 18

```
LIST
    1 HIMEM=&4000
    2 MODE 4
   10 REM CHART RECORDER
   20 REM BY R.A.SPARKES
   30 REM AFTER AN IDEA BY S. RUSHBROOK-WILLIAMS
   31 REM THIS PROGRAM DISPLAYS FOUR VOLTAGES
   32 REM MEASURED BY THE ANALOGUE PORT
   33 REM AND SCROLLS THEM ACROSS THE SCREEN
   34 REM CHANNEL 0 IS DISPLAYED AT THE BOTTOM
   35 REM AND CHANNEL 3 IS AT THE TOP
   50 GOSUB 10000
  100 CLS
  110 PRINT TAB(5,0);"FOUR-CHANNEL CHART RECORDER"
  120 PRINT TAB(0,2);"Press any key to finish"
  130 PRINT TAB(2,30);"Channel 0"
  140 PRINT TAB(2,22);"Channel 1"
```

```
  150 PRINT TAB(2,14);"Channel 2"
  160 PRINT TAB(2,6);"Channel 3"
  170 CALL chtrec
  180 PRINT TAB(0,0);"Press R to restart"
  190 REPEAT UNTIL GET$="R"
  200 GOTO 170
10000 REM MACHINE CODE ROUTINE FOR PLOTTING
10001 xpos=&4200
10002 ypos=&4300
10005 adval=655
10006 flag=&FE4D :REM KEYBOARD FLAG
10010 y=&70
10020 rowcnt=&71
10030 pointer=&72
10040 scrlo=&73
10050 scrhi=&74
10060 temp=&75
10070 FOR pass=0 TO 2 STEP 2
10075 P% = &4100
10080 [OPTpass
10090 .chtrec LDA #4
10100         STA pointer \POINTER TO ADC CHANNELS
10110 .nxadc  LDY pointer
10120         LDA adval,Y  \GET NEXT READING
10122         LSR A
10124         LSR A  \DIVIDE BY 4
10130         STA y
10131         LDA pointer
10132         SEC
10133         SBC #1
10134         ASL A
10135         ASL A
10136         ASL A
10137         ASL A
10138         ASL A
10139         ASL A  \MULT BY 64
10140         CLC
10142         ADC y
10144         EOR #255 \INVERT
10146         STA y  \KEEP VERTICAL POSITION
10150         LSR A
10160         LSR A
10170         LSR A
10190         STA scrlo
10210         CLC
10220         ADC #&58
10230         STA scrhi
10232         LDA #0
10240         LDX #6
10250 .next   ASL scrlo
10252         ROL A
10254         DEX
10256         BNE next
10270         ADC scrhi
10280         STA scrhi
10300
10320         LDA y
10330         AND #7
10380         CLC
10390         ADC scrlo
```

```
10400          STA scrlo
10410          LDY#0
10420          LDA #128
10430          ORA (scrlo),Y
10440          STA (scrlo),Y
10480          JSR scroll
10490          DEC pointer
10500          BNE nxadc
10510          LDA flag
10520          AND #1
10530          BEQ chtrec
10536
10540          RTS
10560
10600]
11000 P%=&4000
11010[OPT pass
11012 .scroll LDA #&58
11014          STA &4018
11016          LDA #&00
11018          STA &4017  \RESTORE SCREEN ADDRESS
11020          LDA #32  \ROW COUNT
11030          STA rowcnt
11040 .nxrow   LDY #40 \COLUMN COUNT
11050          CLC
11060          LDA #0
11070 .nxcol   ROR A
11080          LDX #8   \8 LINES PER COLUMN
11090 .nxlin   ROR &4040 \SELF MODIFYING ADDRESS
11100          ROR A
11110          INC &4017
11120          BNE cont
11130          INC &4018
11140 .cont    DEX
11150          BNE nxlin
11160          DEY
11170          BNE nxcol
11180          DEC rowcnt
11190          BNE nxrow
11200          RTS
11500]
12400 NEXT pass
12500 RETURN
```

MECHANICS DRILL - PROGRAM 19

```
LIST
   10 REM MECHANICS DRILL
   20 REM BY R.A.SPARKES
   30
   50 *FX11,0
   60 REM TURN OFF AUTO-REPEAT FACILITY
   70 ON ERROR GOTO 300
```

```
  100 MODE 7
  110 PRINT TAB(7,1);"MECHANICS DRILL"
  120 PRINT TAB(0,4);"This program tests your ability to "
  130 PRINT:PRINT"solve equations in mechanics."
  140PRINT:PRINT:PRINT"First I should like to know your name."
  150 PRINT:PRINT"Type your first name. If you make"
  160 PRINT:PRINT"a mistake, you can rub it out with"
  170 PRINT:PRINT"the DELETE key at the bottom-right."
  180 PRINT:PRINT"When you have typed your name correctly,"
  190PRINT"press the key marked RETURN, then"
  200 PRINT:PRINT"I will know that you have finished."
  210PRINT
  220 INPUT name$
  280
  290 REM WHAT SORT OF QUESTIONS
  300 MODE1
  310 PRINT TAB(7,0);"MECHANICS DRILL"
  320 PRINT:PRINT"You can choose questions for"
  330 PRINT:PRINT"three different equations, as follows:"
  340 VDU5:MOVE 200,700:PRINT"1.    s = ut +  at":MOVE 680,716:PRINT"1":MOVE
680,684:PRINT"2":MOVE 776,716::PRINT"2":VDU4
  350 VDU5:MOVE 200,600:PRINT"2.    v  = u  + 2as":MOVE 424,616:PRINT"2":
MOVE 584,616::PRINT"2":VDU4
  360 VDU5:MOVE 200,500:PRINT"3.    v = u + at":VDU4
  370 PRINT TAB(0,28);"Press one of these numbers to choose."
  380 LET N$=INKEY$(255)
  390 IF ASC(N$)<45 THEN N$=CHR$(ASC(N$)+16)
  400 IF N$<>"1" AND N$<>"2" AND N$<>"3" THEN 380
  410 ON VAL(N$) GOTO 1000,2000,3000
 1000 REM S = UT + AT^2/2
 1005 LET attempts=0
 1010 PROCgetnum
 1020 CLS
 1025 LET attempts=attempts+1
 1030 VDU5:MOVE 200,1000:PRINT"      s = ut +  at":MOVE 680,1016:PRINT"1":
MOVE 680,984:PRINT"2":MOVE 776,1016::PRINT"2":VDU4
 1040 PRINT TAB(0,4);"What is the value of s"
 1050PRINT:PRINT"if   u has the value ";v1;" m/s"
 1060PRINT:PRINT"     t has the value ";v2;" s"
 1070PRINT:PRINT"     a has the value ";v3:PRINT TAB(24,10);"m s    ?":PRINT
TAB(27,9);"-2"
 1075 IF attempts>3 THEN response$="Press SPACE BAR for a different
question":PRINT:PRINT:PRINT:PRINT"This seems to be too difficult.":PRINT:
PRINT"The correct answer is ";true;" m":correct=TRUE:GOTO 1130
 1080PRINT:PRINT:PRINT"Give your answer as a number of metres."
 1090 PRINT:PRINT:PRINT"Type this number now."
 1100 PRINT:PRINT"Then press the RETURN key.":PRINT
 1110 INPUT ans
 1120 true = v1*v2 + v3*v2*v2/2
 1125 IF ABS(ans - true)/true<0.01 THEN PROCcorrect ELSE PROCwrong
 1130 PRINT:PRINT response$
 1150 PRINT:PRINT"Press ESCAPE to choose a different"
 1160 PRINT:PRINT"equation."
 1170 LET A$=INKEY$(255)
 1180 IF A$<>" " THEN 1170
 1190 IF correct THEN 1000 ELSE 1020
 1200
 2000 REM V^2=U^2+2AS
 2005 LET attempts=0
 2010 PROCgetnum
```

```
 2020 CLS
 2025 LET attempts=attempts+1
 2030 VDU5:MOVE 200,1000:PRINT"      v  = u  + 2as":MOVE 424,1016:PRINT"2":
MOVE 580,1016::PRINT"2":VDU4
 2040 PRINT TAB(0,4);"What is the value of v"
 2050PRINT:PRINT"if   u has the value ";v1;" m/s"
 2060PRINT:PRINT"     s has the value ";v2;" m"
 2070PRINT:PRINT"     a has the value ";v3:PRINT TAB(24,10);"m s    ?":PRINT
TAB(27,9);"-2"
 2075 IF attempts>3 THEN response$="Press SPACE BAR for a different
question":PRINT:PRINT:PRINT:PRINT"This seems to be too difficult.":PRINT:
PRINT"The correct answer is ";true;" m/s":correct=TRUE:GOTO 2130
 2080PRINT:PRINT:PRINT"Give your answer as a number of m/s."
 2090 PRINT:PRINT:PRINT"Type this number now."
 2100 PRINT:PRINT"Then press the RETURN key.":PRINT
 2110 INPUT ans
 2120 true = SQR(v1*v1 + 2*v3*v2)
 2125 IF ABS(ans - true)/true<0.01 THEN PROCcorrect ELSE PROCwrong
 2130 PRINT:PRINT response$
 2150 PRINT:PRINT"Press ESCAPE to choose a different"
 2160 PRINT:PRINT"equation."
 2170 LET A$=INKEY$(255)
 2180 IF A$<>" " THEN 2170
 2190 IF correct THEN 2000 ELSE 2020
 2200
 3000 REM V = U + AT
 3005 LET attempts=0
 3010 PROCgetnum
 3020 CLS
 3025 LET attempts=attempts+1
 3030 VDU5:MOVE 200,1000:PRINT"      v  = u + at":VDU4
 3040 PRINT TAB(0,4);"What is the value of v"
 3050 PRINT:PRINT"if   u has the value ";v1;" m/s"
 3060 PRINT:PRINT"     t has the value ";v2;" s"
 3070 PRINT:PRINT"     a has the value ";v3:PRINT TAB(24,10);"m s    ?":
PRINT TAB(27,9);"-2"
 3075 IF attempts>3 THEN response$="Press SPACE BAR for a different
question":PRINT:PRINT:PRINT:PRINT"This seems to be too difficult.":PRINT:
PRINT"The correct answer is ";true;" m/s":correct=TRUE:GOTO 3130
 3080PRINT:PRINT:PRINT"Give your answer as a number of m/s."
 3090 PRINT:PRINT:PRINT"Type this number now."
 3100 PRINT:PRINT"Then press the RETURN key.":PRINT
 3110 INPUT ans
 3120 true = v1 + v3*v2
 3125 IF ABS(ans - true)/true<0.01 THEN PROCcorrect ELSE PROCwrong
 3130 PRINT:PRINT response$
 3150 PRINT:PRINT"Press ESCAPE to choose a different"
 3160 PRINT:PRINT"equation."
 3170 LET A$=INKEY$(255)
 3180 IF A$<>" " THEN 3170
 3190 IF correct THEN 3000 ELSE 3020
 3200
 4000 DEF PROCcorrect
 4010 PRINT:PRINT"WELL DONE, ";name$
 4020 LET response$="Press SPACE BAR for another question."
 4050 LET correct=TRUE
 4090 ENDPROC
 4100 DEF PROCwrong
 4110 PRINT:PRINT"This is not good enough."
 4120 LET response$="Press SPACE BAR to try again."
```

```
4150 LET correct=FALSE
4190 ENDPROC
4999 END
5000 DEF PROCgetnum
5010 REM RETURNS WITH THREE VARIABLES
5020 LET v1=RND(50)
5030 LET v2=RND(50)
5040 LET v3=RND(50)
5050 ENDPROC
```

INTEGRATED SCIENCE TEST - PROGRAM 20_

```
LIST
    1 REM INTEGRATED SCIENCE TEST
    5 ON ERROR GOTO 90
    6 *FX11,0
   10 REM INITIALISE VARIABLES
   20 LET max=5:REM 5 QUESTIONS IN TEST
   30 DIM score(max)
   35 DIM response$(max)
   40 DIM questions(max)
   50 LET totalscore=0
   60 PROCdefinegraphics
   70
   80 REM MAIN PROGRAM
   90 MODE7
  100 PROCinstructions
  110 PROCgetname
  115 MODE 4
  120 FOR n=1 TO max
  140 PROCaskquestion(n)
  150 LET totalscore=totalscore+score(n)
  160 NEXT n
  170 PROCscore
  180
  190 GOTO 50
  200 END
  300
  700
  800
 1000 REM ***     THE  QUESTIONS  ****
 2000
 3000 DEF PROCaskquestion(qnum)
 3020 ON qnum GOSUB 4000, 4500, 5000, 5500,6000
 3030 ENDPROC
 3500
 4000 REM *** QUESTION ONE ***
 4010 CLS:PRINT"Question 1"
 4020 LET attempts=0
 4025 RESTORE
 4030 FOR row = 1 TO 9
 4040 FOR column = 1 TO 16
 4050 READ char
 4060 PRINT TAB(10+column,row);CHR$(char)
 4070 NEXT column
```

```
4080 NEXT row
4090 PRINT TAB(0,11);"A bulb gives out light energy"
4100 PRINT TAB(0,13);"when it is switched on."
4110 PRINT TAB(0,15);"It also gives out another kind of"
4120 PRINT TAB(0,17);"energy. Which one ?"
4130 REPEAT
4140 PROCshowanswers
4150 LET attempts=attempts+1
4200 PROCgetletter
4210 IF letter$="a" OR letter$="A" THEN correct = TRUE ELSE correct = FALSE
4220 LET clue$="A bulb gives out light energy
AND heat energy."
4230 IF correct THEN PROCcorrect ELSE PROCwrong
4240 UNTIL next OR attempts=3
4250  IF attempts=1 THEN LET score(1)=1 ELSE LET score(1)=0
4260 RETURN
4300 DATA 236,241,241,241,241,241,241,233,241,241,241,241,241,241,241,238
4301 DATA 240,32,32,32,32,32,32,253,32,32,32,32,32,32,32,239
4302 DATA 243,255,255,255,249,32,32,253,32,32,32,32,32,32,32,239
4303 DATA 240,32,32,32,253,32,250,42,249,32,32,32,32,32,239
4304 DATA 240,32,32,32,253,32,32,32,32,32,32,32,32,32,32,239
4305 DATA 240,32,32,45,253,32,32,32,32,32,32,32,239,32,32,239
4306 DATA 240,32,32,32,253,32,247,255,255,255,247,32,239,32,32,239
4307 DATA 240,32,32,32,253,32,253,32,32,32,253,239,238,32,32,239
4308 DATA 241,241,241,241,241,241,241,241,241,241,241,241,241,241,241,241
4490
4500 REM *** QUESTION TWO ***
4510 CLS:PRINT"Question 2"
4520 LET attempts=0
4530 FOR row = 1 TO 9
4540 FOR column = 1 TO 16
4550 READ char
4560 PRINT TAB(10+column,row);CHR$(char)
4570 NEXT column
4580 NEXT row
4590 PRINT TAB(0,13);"What kind of energy is stored in food ?"
4600  REPEAT
4610 PROCshowanswers
4680 LET attempts=attempts+1
4690 PROCgetletter
4700 IF letter$="b" OR letter$="B" THEN correct = TRUE ELSE correct = FALSE
4710 LET clue$="Food is chemical energy,
 we turn it into heat and movement energy                    when we eat it.
"
4720 IF correct THEN PROCcorrect ELSE PROCwrong
4730 UNTIL next OR attempts=3
4740 IF attempts=1 THEN LET score(2)=1 ELSE LET score(2)=0
4750 RETURN
4800 DATA 240,32,32,32,239,32,32,32,32,32,32,32,32,32,32,32
4810 DATA 240,32,32,32,239,32,32,32,32,32,32,32,32,32,32,32
4820 DATA 240,32,32,32,239,32,32,32,32,32,32,32,32,32,32,32
4830 DATA 240,32,32,32,239,32,32,32,32,32,32,32,32,32,32,32
4840 DATA 232,232,232,232,232,32,32,32,32,32,32,32,32,32,32,32
4850 DATA 232,232,232,232,232,32,32,32,32,32,32,32,32,32,32,32
4860 DATA 232,232,232,232,232,32,32,32,32,32,32,32,32,32,32,32
4870 DATA 232,232,232,232,232,32,32,32,32,230,230,230,230,230,230,32
4880 DATA 232,232,232,232,232,32,32,32,231,230,230,230,230,230,230,231
4999
5000 REM *** QUESTION THREE ***
5010 CLS:PRINT"Question 3"
```

```
5015 REM DRAW ROAD
5020 FOR position = 0 TO 39
5030 PRINT TAB(position,10);CHR$(230)
5040 NEXT position
5090 REM DEFINE VAN
5100 LET line1$=CHR$(32)+CHR$(232)+CHR$(232)+CHR$(232)+CHR$(232)+CHR$(232)
+CHR$(232)+CHR$(111)+CHR$(32)
5110 LET line2$=CHR$(32)+CHR$(232)+CHR$(77)+CHR$(73)+CHR$(76)+CHR$(75)+CHR$
(232)+CHR$(232)+CHR$(233)
5120 LET line3$=CHR$(32)+CHR$(232)+CHR$(232)+CHR$(232)+CHR$(232)+CHR$(232)
+CHR$(232)+CHR$(232)+CHR$(232)
5130 LET line4$=CHR$(32)+CHR$(32)+CHR$(111)+CHR$(32)+CHR$(32)+CHR$(32)+CHR$
(32)+CHR$(111)
5140 LET back$=CHR$(8)+CHR$(8)+CHR$(8)+CHR$(8)+CHR$(8)+CHR$(8)+CHR$(8)+CHR$
(8)+CHR$(8)
5150 LET down$=CHR$(10)
5160 LET van$=line1$+back$+down$+line2$+back$+down$+line3$+back$+down$+
line4$
5170 REM MOVE VAN ALONG
5180 FOR position=0 TO 24
5190 PRINT TAB(position,6);van$
5200 NEXT position
5220 LET attempts=0
5230 PRINT TAB(0,12);"What kind of energy does the engine"
5240 PRINT TAB(0,14);"give to the van ?"
5250 REPEAT
5260 PROCshowanswers
5330 LET attempts=attempts+1
5340 PROCgetletter
5350 IF letter$="c" OR letter$="C" THEN correct = TRUE ELSE correct = FALSE
5360 LET clue$="The engine makes the van move along."
5370 IF correct THEN PROCcorrect ELSE PROCwrong
5380 UNTIL next OR attempts=3
5390 IF attempts=1 THEN LET score(3)=1 ELSE LET score(3)=0
5400 RETURN
5490
5500 REM *** QUESTION FOUR ***
5510 CLS:PRINT"Question 4"
5520 LET attempts=0
5530 LET B$=CHR$(32)
5540 LET W$=CHR$(232)
5550  PRINT TAB(15,4);W$;B$;W$;B$;W$;B$;W$;B$;W$;B$;W$
5560  PRINT TAB(15,5);W$;W$;W$;W$;W$;W$;W$;W$;W$;W$;W$
5570  PRINT TAB(15,6);W$;W$;W$;W$;W$;"A";W$;W$;W$;W$;W$
5580  PRINT TAB(15,7);W$;W$;"SPARKES";W$;W$
5590  PRINT TAB(15,8);W$;W$;"BATTERY";W$;W$
5600  PRINT TAB(15,9);W$;W$;W$;W$;W$;W$;W$;W$;W$;W$;W$
5700 PRINT TAB(0,11);"What sort of energy is stored"
5710 PRINT TAB(0,13);"in a battery ?"
5720 REPEAT
5730 PROCshowanswers
5800 LET attempts=attempts+1
5810 PROCgetletter
5820 IF letter$="b" OR letter$="B" THEN correct = TRUE ELSE correct = FALSE
5830 LET clue$="A battery stores its energy as chemical energy. This is turned
into electrical energy only if connected into a circuit."
5840 IF correct THEN PROCcorrect ELSE PROCwrong
5850 UNTIL next OR attempts=3
5870 IF attempts=1 THEN LET score(4)=1 ELSE LET score(4)=0
5900 RETURN
```

```
5950
6000 REM *** QUESTION FIVE ***
6010 CLS:PRINT"Question 5"
6020 REM DRAW PATH
6030 MOVE 0,945:DRAW 200,945:DRAW 505,635:DRAW 1279,635
6040 REM MAKE BALL MOVE ALONG
6050 VDU5:GCOL0,3
6055 FOR pos=0 TO 192 STEP 8:MOVE pos,976:PRINT"O";
6060 FOR T=1 TO 50:NEXT T
6070 VDU127:NEXT pos
6100 FOR pos= 200 TO 496 STEP 16:MOVE pos,1176-pos:PRINT"O";
6110 FOR T=1 TO 10000 STEP pos:NEXT T
6120 VDU127:NEXT pos
6130 VDU4
6140 FOR pos= 16 TO 39:PRINT TAB(pos,11);CHR$(79);
6150 FOR T=1 TO 50:NEXT T
6160 PRINT CHR$(127);:NEXT pos
6200 LET attempts=0
6210 PRINT TAB(0,15);"What kind of energy is the ball LOSING ?"
6220 REPEAT
6230 PROCshowanswers
6240 LET attempts=attempts+1
6250 PROCgetletter
6260 IF letter$="d" OR letter$="D" THEN correct = TRUE ELSE correct = FALSE
6270 LET clue$="The ball is losing potential and
gaining movement energy."
6280 IF correct THEN PROCcorrect ELSE PROCwrong
6290 UNTIL next OR attempts=3
6300 IF attempts=1 THEN LET score(5)=1 ELSE LET score(5)=0
6310 RETURN
6400
6500 REM ************************
6600
6700 REM          PROCEDURES
6800
6900 REM ************************
7000
8000 DEF PROCinstructions
8010 CLS:PRINT TAB(5,1);"HOW TO RUN THIS PROGRAM"
8020 PRINT TAB(0,3);"You will be asked to answer some"
8030 PRINT:PRINT"integrated science questions."
8040 PRINT:PRINT"After each question there are five"
8050 PRINT:PRINT"possible answers, A, B, C, D and E."
8060 PRINT:PRINT"Choose the best of these answers and"
8070 PRINT:PRINT"press  ONE  of these letters."
8080 PRINT:PRINT"Sometimes you will be asked to press"
8090 PRINT:PRINT"the SPACE BAR to go on to the next page."
8100 PRINT:PRINT:PRINT"Press the SPACE BAR now."
8110 PROCwait(" ")
8120 ENDPROC
8400
8500 DEF PROCgetname
8510 CLS:PRINT TAB(0,5);"First I want to know your name."
8520 PRINT:PRINT"Type your first name. If you make"
8530 PRINT:PRINT"mistake, you can rub it out with the"
8540 PRINT:PRINT"DELETE key (the bottom row of keys,"
8550 PRINT:PRINT"on the right side)."
8560 PRINT:PRINT"When you have typed your name correctly,"
8570 PRINT"press the RETURN key (on the right)."
8580 PRINT:INPUT name$
```

```
 8590 ENDPROC
 8600
10000 DEF PROCwait(a$)
10010 *FX15,0
10020 IF INKEY$(255)<>a$ THEN 10020
10030 ENDPROC
11000 DEF PROCgetletter
11010 letter$=""
11020 REPEAT
11030 *FX15,1
11040 LET letter$=GET$
11050 UNTIL letter$="A" OR  letter$="B" OR letter$="C" OR letter$="D" OR
letter$="E" OR letter$="a" OR letter$="b" OR letter$="c" OR letter$="d"
OR letter$="e"
11060 IF attempts=1 THEN LET response$(qnum)=letter$
11070 ENDPROC
13000 DEF PROCcorrect
13010 PROCclearlines(20,30)
13070 PRINT TAB(0,20);"Well done, ";name$
13080 PRINT TAB(0,24);clue$
13090 PRINT TAB(0,30);"Press SPACE for the next question."
13100 PROCwait(" ")
13110 LET next=TRUE
13120 ENDPROC
14000 DEF PROCwrong
14010 PROCclearlines(20,30)
14070 PRINT TAB(0,20);"Sorry, ";name$
14080 PRINT TAB(0,22);"that is not right."
14090 PRINT TAB(0,24);clue$
14100 PRINT TAB(0,30);"Press SPACE to try again."
14110 PROCwait(" ")
14120 LET next=FALSE
14130 ENDPROC
15000 DEF PROCclearlines(begin,end)
15010 FOR i= begin TO end
15020 PRINT TAB(0,i);"                                        "
15030 NEXT i
15040 ENDPROC
16000 DEF PROCshowanswers
16010 PROCclearlines(20,30)
16020 PRINT TAB(0,20);"A        Heat energy"
16030 PRINT TAB(0,22);"B        Chemical energy"
16040 PRINT TAB(0,24);"C        Movement energy"
16050 PRINT TAB(0,26);"D        Potential energy"
16060 PRINT TAB(0,28);"E        Electrical energy"
16070 PRINT TAB(0,30);"Press ONE of the letters A, B, C, D or E";
16080 ENDPROC
20000 DEF PROCdefinegraphics
20010 REM LINE GRAPHICS
20020 VDU23,255,0,0,0,255,255,0,0,0
20030 VDU23,253,16,16,16,16,16,16,16,16
20070 VDU23,250,0,0,0,31,31,16,16,16
20080 VDU23,249,0,0,0,240,240,16,16,16
20090 VDU23,248,16,16,16,255,255,0,0,0
20100 VDU23,247,0,0,0,255,255,16,16,16
20120 VDU23,245,16,16,16,31,31,16,16,16
20130 VDU23,244,128,128,128,255,255,128,128,128
20160 VDU23,243,128,128,128,255,255,128,128,128
20170 VDU23,240,128,128,128,128,128,128,128,128
20175 VDU23,241,255,0,0,0,0,0,0,0
```

```
20180 VDU23,239,1,1,1,1,1,1,1,1
20190 VDU23,238,255,1,1,1,1,1,1,1
20210 VDU23,236,255,128,128,128,128,128,128,128
20220 VDU23,235,128,128,128,128,128,128,128,255
20230 VDU23,234,0,0,0,0,0,0,0,255
20240 VDU23,233,255,16,16,16,16,16,16,16
20250 VDU23,232,255,255,255,255,255,255,255,255
20260 VDU23,231,0,0,0,0,0,255,255,255
20270 VDU23,230,85,170,85,170,85,170,85,170
20300 ENDPROC
24000
25000 DEF PROCscore
25010 CLS
25020 PRINT TAB(5,0);name$;"'S SCORE"
25030 PRINT TAB(0,4);"You scored  ";totalscore;" first-time"
25040 PRINT TAB(0,6);"correct answers out of ";max;" questions."
25050 PRINT TAB(0,9);"Question         first answer"
25060 FOR n= 1 TO max
25070 PRINT TAB(4,n*2+9);n;TAB(22);response$(n);"   ";
25080 IF score(n)=1 THEN PRINT"correct" ELSE PRINT"wrong"
25090 NEXT n
25100 PRINT TAB(0,29);"Press RETURN to repeat the test."
25110 PRINT TAB(0,31);"Press F to finish. ";
25120 LET G$=GET$
25130 IF G$=CHR$(13) THEN ENDPROC
25140 IF G$="F" OR G$="f" THEN CLS:END
25150 GOTO 25120
```

```
    RADIOACTIVE DECAY - PROGRAM 21
LIST
    1 MODE 1
    5 DIM nucleus(40,10)
   10 ON ERROR CLS:GOTO 20
   15 VDU23;8202;0;0;0
   20 REM SET UP MOLECULES
   30 FOR Y=0 TO 9
   40 FOR X=0 TO 39
   50 PRINT TAB(X,Y);CHR$(79)
   55 LET  nucleus(X,Y)=1
   60 NEXT X
   70 NEXT Y
   80 MOVE 50,0:DRAW 50,700
   90 MOVE 0,32:DRAW 1279,32
  100 PRINT TAB(12,10);"RANDOM DECAY PLOT"
  105 PRINT TAB(0,11);"400"
  110 PRINT TAB(0,16);"300"
  120 PRINT TAB(0,21);"200"
  130 PRINT TAB(0,26);"100"
  135 PRINT TAB(0,30);"0"
  140 VDU5:FOR X%=0 TO 30 STEP 5:MOVE X%*40-240,31:PRINT X%:NEXT X%:VDU4
  150 LET count=400
  160 LET x=50
  170 PLOT69,x,32+count*1.55
  180 REPEAT
  220 REM ALLOW NUCLEI TO DECAY AT RANDOM
```

```
  230 LET xpos=RND(40)-1
  240 LET ypos=RND(10)-1
  250 IF nucleus(xpos,ypos)=1 THEN PROCdonuc
  300 LET x=x+1
  310 PLOT69,x,32+count*1.55
  320 UNTIL x>1250
  330 PRINT TAB(0,0);"PLOT FINISHED
    "
  340 PRINT"Press ESCAPE
  350 GOTO 350
20000 DEF PROCdonuc
20010 LET nucleus(xpos,ypos)=0
20020 *FX21,4
20030SOUND0,-15,4,1
20040PRINT TAB(xpos,ypos);CHR$(42)
20050LET count=count-1
20060 ENDPROC
```

SUM OF TWO DICE - PROGRAM 22

```
LIST
 100 REM SUM OF TWO DICE
 110 MODE4
 120 CLS
 130 CLG
 140 PRINT TAB(10,2) "THE SUM OF TWO DICE"
 150 DIM S(12)
 160 PRINT TAB(4,4) "TOTAL NUMBER OF THROWS = "
 180 PRINT TAB(0,6) " 160-"
 190 PRINT TAB(0,12) " 120-"
 200 PRINT TAB(0,18) "  80-"
 210 PRINT TAB(0,24) "  40-"
 220 PRINT TAB(0,30) "   0-"
 250 MOVE 150,850
 260 DRAW 150,50
 270 DRAW 1200,50
 300 PRINT TAB(4,31) "0  2  3  4  5  6  7  8  9 10 11 12";
1000 total=0
1010 FOR I= 2 TO 12:S(I)=0:NEXT I
1015
1020 REM SHAKE THE DICE AND ADD THEM UP
1021 REM AND DETERMINE WHICH VALUE
1022
1030 REPEAT
1040 dice1=RND(6)
1050 dice2=RND(6)
1060 sum=dice1+dice2
1080 FOR I=2 TO 12
1090 IF sum =I THEN S(I)=S(I)+1:PROCplot(I,S(I))
1100 NEXT I
1110 total=total+1
1120 PRINT TAB(29,4);total
1130 UNTIL total=1000
1140 END
3000 DEF PROCplot(H,V)
```

```
3005 LOCAL X,Y
3010 X=H*96+32
3020 Y=V*5+50
3030 PLOT4,X,Y
3040 PLOT4,X+32,Y
3050 PLOT85,X,Y+5
3060 PLOT85,X+32,Y+5
3070 ENDPROC
```

STANDING WAVES - PROGRAM 23

```
LIST
    1 HIMEM=&4000
    2 MODE4
   10 REM BASIC WAVE ROUTINE
   20 REM TO DEMONSTRATE THE PRINCIPLES INVOLVED
   30 REM BY R.A.SPARKES
   50 CLS
   60 PRINT TAB(0,10);"Please wait while tables are constructed"
   70 GOSUB 10000 :REM MACHINE CODE ROUTINES AND TABLE COMPILATION
  100 REM OBTAIN VALUES
  110 CLS
  130 PRINT
  140 INPUT "Wave 1: number of waves ? (1 to 8) " W1
  150 ?wvln1=W1
  160 PRINT
  170 INPUT "Wave 2: number of waves ? (1 to 8) " W2
  180 ?wvln2=W2
  190 PRINT
  200 INPUT "Amplitude of wave 1 (0 to 9) " A1
  210 ?amp1=A1+&45
  220 PRINT
  230 INPUT "Amplitude of wave 2 (0 to 9) " A2
  240 ?amp2=A2+&45
  245 PRINT
  250 INPUT "Speed (range 1 to 6) " S
  260 REM SPEED DEPENDS UPON WAVELENGTH
  290 LET S=S*W1
  300 ?speed=S
 1000 CLS
 2000 CALL begin
 3000 GOTO 100
10000 REM MACHINE CODE ROUTINE FOR PLOTTING
10001 opos1=&4200
10002 opos2=&4300
10003 opos3=&4400
10004 sintbl=&84:?sintbl=0
10005 tblhi=&85
10006 REM tblhi IS ALTERED FROM WITHIN THE
10007 REM ROUTINE TO POINT TO ONE OF SIX
10008 REM DIFFERENT SINE TABLES,
10009 REM EACH WITH A DIFFERENT AMPLITUDE
10010 y=&70
10020 x=&71
10030 Xval=&72
```

```
10040 scrlo=&73
10050 scrhi=&74
10060 temp=&75
10061 amp1=&76
10062 amp2=&77
10063 wvln1=&78
10064 wvln2=&79
10065 speed=&7A
10066 time=&7B
10067 mult1=&7C
10068 mult2=&7D
10069 flag=&FE4D
10070 FOR pass=0 TO 2 STEP 2
10075 P% = &4000
10080 [OPTpass
10090 .find   STX Xval
10095         LDA y
10150         LSR A
10160         LSR A
10170         LSR A
10190         STA scrlo
10210         CLC
10220         ADC #&58
10230         STA scrhi
10232         LDA #0
10240         LDX #6
10250 .next   ASL scrlo
10252         ROL A
10254         DEX
10256         BNE next
10270         ADC scrhi
10280         STA scrhi
10300
10320         LDA y
10330         AND #7
10333         STA temp
10380
10400         LDA x
10410         AND #&F8
10420         ADC temp
10425         ADC scrlo
10430         STA scrlo
10440         LDA scrhi
10450         ADC #0
10460         STA scrhi
10470         LDY#0
10480         LDA x
10490         AND #7
10500         TAX
10505         SEC
10512         LDA #0
10515 .shift  ROR A
10516         DEX
10520         BPL shift
10530         STA temp
10535         LDX Xval
10536
10540         RTS
10560
12000    \WAVE MOTION
```

```
12010          NOP
12020 .begin   NOP
12030 .nxwave  LDX #0
12060 .nxpos   LDA opos1,X \GET OLD POSITION FOR WAVE 1
12070          STA y
12075          STX x
12080          JSR find
12090          EOR #255 \INVERT DOT
12100          AND (scrlo),Y
12120          STA (scrlo),Y \ERASE OLD POSITION
12130
12140          LDA wvln1   \WAVELENGTH OF WAVE 1
12150          STA mult1
12170          STX mult2
12180          JSR mult  \GET KX
12190          CLC
12200          ADC time  \ KX-WT
12210          TAY       \KEEP RESULT
12220          LDA amp1  \GET WAVE 1 AMPLITUDE
12230          STA tblhi
12240          LDA (sintbl),Y \GET SINE
12270          CLC
12280          ADC #38   \ADD OFFSET FOR WAVE 1
12290          STA opos1,X \KEEP NEW POSITION
12300          STA y
12310          JSR find
12320          ORA (scrlo),Y
12330          STA (scrlo),Y \PLOT NEW WAVE
12350         \REPEAT FOR WAVE 2
12400          LDA opos2,X \GET OLD POSITION FOR WAVE 2
12410          STA y
12420          STX x
12430          JSR find
12440          EOR #255 \INVERT DOT
12450          AND (scrlo),Y
12460          STA (scrlo),Y \ERASE OLD POSITION
12470
12480          LDA wvln2   \WAVELENGTH OF WAVE 2
12490          STA mult1
12500          STX mult2
12510          JSR mult  \GET KX
12520          SEC
12530          SBC time  \BACKWARDS TRAVEL
12540          TAY       \KEEP RESULT
12550          LDA amp2
12560          STA tblhi
12570          LDA (sintbl),Y \GET SINE
12600          CLC
12610          ADC #110 \ADD OFFSET FOR WAVE 2
12620          STA opos2,X \KEEP NEW POSITION
12630          STA y
12640          JSR find
12650          ORA (scrlo),Y
12660          STA (scrlo),Y \PLOT NEW WAVE
12670          LDA opos3,X \GET OLD POSITION FOR WAVESUM
12680          STA y
12690          STX x
12692          JSR find
12694          EOR #255 \INVERT DOT
12696          AND (scrlo),Y
```

```
12698             STA (scrlo),Y \ERASE OLD POSITION
12700
12710             CLC    \SUM OF WAVES
12720             LDA opos2,X
12730             ADC opos1,X
12734             ADC #36
12735             STA opos3,X
12740             STA y
12750             STX x
12760             JSR find
12770             ORA (scrlo),Y
12780             STA (scrlo),Y \PLOT NEW WAVESUM
12800
12810            \DO NEXT POSITION
12820             INX
12830             INX
12840             BEQ endlin
12850             JMP nxpos
12860 .endlin     LDA time
12870             SEC
12880             SBC speed \ -WT
12890             STA time
12900
12910             \KEYBOARD CHECK
12920             LDA flag
12930             AND #1
12940             BNE finish
12945             JMP nxwave
12950 .finish     CLI
12960             RTS
13000
13010             \MULTIPLICATION ROUTINE
13020             \RESULT IN ACCUMULATOR
13030 .mult       LDA #0 \PRODUCT
13050             LDY #8 \8 BITS
13060 .nxmult     ASL  A
13070             ASL mult1
13080             BCC cont
13085             CLC
13090             ADC mult2
13100 .cont       DEY
13110             BNE nxmult
13111  STA &80
13120             RTS
13130]
13140 NEXT pass
14000
20000 REM SET UP SINE TABLE
20010 REM CONTAINS 256 DATA ITEMS
20020 FOR I= 0 TO 256
20024 LET angle = I*PI/128
20025 LET val=SIN(angle)
20030 ?(&4500+I)=0
20031 ?(&4600+I)=INT(4*val)
20032 ?(&4700+I)=INT(8*val)
20033 ?(&4800+I)=INT(12*val)
20034 ?(&4900+I)=INT(16*val)
20035 ?(&4A00+I)=INT(20*val)
20036 ?(&4B00+I)=INT(24*val)
20037 ?(&4C00+I)=INT(28*val)
```

```
20038 ?(&4D00+I)=INT(32*val)
20039 ?(&4E00+I)=INT(36*val)
20050 REM CLEAR OLD POSITIONS
20060 ?(&4200+I)=0
20070 ?(&4300+I)=0
20080 ?(&4400+I)=0
20090 NEXT I
25000 RETURN
```

SUPERPOSITION OF WAVES - PROGRAM 24

```
LIST
    1 HIMEM=&4000
    2 MODE 4
   10 REM WAVE SUPERPOSITION
   20 REM BY R.A.SPARKES
   50 GOSUB 10000
  100 CLS
  110PRINT:PRINT
  120 INPUT "Frequency of first wave (0 to 12) " f1
  130 PRINT
  140 INPUT "Frequency of second wave (0 to 12) " f2
  150 PRINT
  160 INPUT "Amplitude of first wave (0 to 10) " a1
  170 PRINT
  180 INPUT "Amplitude of second wave (0 to 10) " a2
  190 PRINT
  200 INPUT "Phase angle between the waves (degrees) " ph
  210 CLS
  219 PRINT"Press SPACE to stop"
  220 LET a=0
  225 REPEAT
  230 LET y1=850 + 15*a1*SIN(RAD(a*f1))
  240 LET y2=600 + 15*a2*SIN(RAD(a*f2 + ph))
  250 LET ysum=y1+y2-1150
  260 PLOT69,0,y1
  270 PLOT69,0,y2
  280 PLOT69,0,ysum
  290 CALL scroll
  300 LET a=a+1
  310 UNTIL INKEY$(0)<>""
  320 GOTO 100
10000 REM MACHINE CODE ROUTINE FOR PLOTTING
10020 rowcnt=&71
10070 FOR pass=0 TO 2 STEP 2
11000 P%=&4000
11010[OPT pass
11012 .scroll LDA #&58
11014         STA &4018
11016         LDA #&00
11018         STA &4017  \RESTORE SCREEN ADDRESS
11020         LDA #32  \ROW COUNT
11030         STA rowcnt
11040 .nxrow  LDY #40 \COLUMN COUNT
11050         CLC
```

```
11060         LDA #0
11070 .nxcol  ROR A
11080         LDX #8   \8 LINES PER COLUMN
11090 .nxlin  ROR &4040 \SELF MODIFYING ADDRESS
11100         ROR A
11110         INC &4017
11120         BNE cont
11130         INC &4018
11140 .cont   DEX
11150         BNE nxlin
11160         DEY
11170         BNE nxcol
11180         DEC rowcnt
11190         BNE nxrow
11200         RTS
11500]
12400 NEXT pass
12500 RETURN
```

WAVE REFELECTION - PROGRAM 25

```
LIST
 100 MODE4
 105 HIMEM =&3FFF
 110 GOSUB 10000
 111 CLS
 112 REM CLEAR KEYBOARD BUFFER
 113 *FX21,0
 114 PRINT:PRINT"You are asked to enter the angle"
 115PRINT:PRINT"at which the mirror is inclined"
 116PRINT:PRINT"to the horizontal."
 117PRINT:PRINT"Angles between 0 and 60 degrees are best"
 118PRINT"and 90 degrees causes a program crash !"
 119PRINT:PRINT:INPUT "ANGLE (IN DEGREES)  " angle
 120 M=TAN(RAD(angle))
 125 FM=(1+M*M)
 130 PRINT:PRINT:PRINT"Please wait while the appropriate tables"
 140PRINT:PRINT"are constructed."
 150 M=TAN(RAD(angle))
 160 FM=(1+M*M)
 170 YPOSLO%=0:REM Y POSITION LOW
 180 YPOSHI%=0:REM Y POSITION HIGH
 190 XPOSLO%=0:REM X POSITION LOW
 200 XPOSHI%=0:REM X POSITION HIGH
 210 YINITLO%=0:REM INITIAL Y SPEED LOW
 220 YINITHI%=1:REM INITIAL Y SPEED HIGH
 230 XINITLO%=0:REM INITIAL X SPEED LOW >
 240 XINITHI%=0:REM INITIAL X SPEED HIGH
 250 YSPEED=(M*M-1)/FM
 260 IF YSPEED<0 THEN YSPEED=YSPEED+256
 270 YFINLO%=(256*YSPEED) MOD 256:REM FINAL Y SPEED LOW
 280 YFINHI%=YSPEED:REM FINAL Y SPEED HIGH
 290 XSPEED=2*M/FM
 300 XFINLO%=(256*XSPEED) MOD 256:REM FINAL X SPEED LOW
 310 XFINHI%=XSPEED:REM FINAL X SPEED HIGH
1000
```

```
1200 REM PUT DATA INTO DATA STORES
1210 FOR I=0 TO 255
1220 ?(I+&4000)=(I MOD 6)*24:REM Y POSITION HIGH
1230 ?(I+&4100)=YPOSLO%
1240 ?(I+&4200)=I:REM X POSITION HIGH
1250 ?(I+&4300)=XPOSLO%
1260 ?(I+&4400)=YINITHI%
1270 ?(I+&4500)=YINITLO%
1280 ?(I+&4600)=XINITHI%
1290 ?(I+&4700)=XINITLO%
1300 ?(I+&4800)=YFINHI%
1310 ?(I+&4900)=YFINLO%
1320 ?(I+&4A00)=XFINHI%
1330 ?(I+&4B00)=XFINLO%
1340 NEXT I
1400 PRINT:PRINT:PRINT"Press the SPACE bar to stop the motion."
1410 PRINT:PRINT"Press B to begin."
1450 REPEAT UNTIL GET$="B"
1500
1600 REM DRAW MIRROR
1800 CLS
1810 FX=500*COS(RAD(angle))
1820 FY=500*SIN(RAD(angle))
1830 FOR Y=500 TO 505
1840 MOVE 200,Y
1850 PLOT5,200+FX,Y-FY
1860 NEXT Y
1870
1880 REM MOVE WAVE
1900 FOR pos=1 TO 240
2000 CALL wave
2100 NEXT pos
2200 GOTO 111
3000 END
10000 REM MACHINE CODE ROUTINE FOR PLOTTING
10005 DIM PROG 600
10010y=&70
10020 x=&71
10030 Xval=&72
10040scrlo=&73
10050scrhi=&74
10060temp=&75
10065 keyboardflag=&FE4D
10070 FOR pass =0 TO 1
10075 P% = PROG
10080[OPT0
10090 .find STX Xval
10095 LDA y
10150LSR A
10160LSR A
10170LSR A
10190STA scrlo
10210CLC
10220ADC #&58
10230 STA scrhi
10232LDA #0
10234STA temp
10240LDX #6
10250 .next ASL scrlo
10252 ROL temp
```

```
10254DEX
10256BNE next
10260 LDA scrhi
10270 ADC temp
10280 STA scrhi
10300
10325 LDA y
10330AND #7
10335 ADC scrlo
10340STA scrlo
10350LDA scrhi
10360ADC #0
10370STA scrhi
10380
10400 LDA x
10410AND #&F8
10420ADC scrlo
10430STA scrlo
10440 LDA scrhi
10450ADC #0
10460STA scrhi
10470 LDY#0
10480LDA x
10490 AND #7
10500 TAX
10505 SEC
10510INX
10512 LDA #0
10515 .shift ROR A
10516 DEX
10520 BNE shift
10535 LDX Xval
10540 RTS
10560
11000 .wave LDX #0
11010 .wait LDA keyboardflag
11011       AND #1
11012       BNE wait
11020 .rpt LDA &4000,X
11021 STA y
11022 LDA &4200,X
11023 STA x
11028JSR find
11029 EOR #255
11030AND (scrlo),Y
11031 STA (scrlo),Y
11032
11033 .nxtry CLC
11034LDA &4100,X
11035ADC &4500,X
11036STA &4100,X
11037LDA &4000,X
11038ADC &4400,X
11040STA y
11060
11070CLC
11075LDA &4300,X
11080ADC &4700,X
11085STA &4300,X
11090LDA &4200,X
```

```
11095ADC &4600,X
11110STA x
11120 JSR find
11130AND (scrlo),Y
11131 BEQ empty
11132 INC y
11133 JSR find
11134AND (scrlo),Y
11135BEQ empty
11136
11137LDA &4B00,X
11138STA &4700,X
11139LDA &4A00,X
11140STA &4600,X
11141LDA &4900,X
11142STA &4500,X
11143LDA &4800,X
11144STA &4400,X
11147 JMP nxtry
11148 .empty LDA y
11149 CMP #254
11150 BCS done
11151 STA &4000,X
11152 LDA x
11153 CMP #254
11154 BCS done
11155 STA &4200,X
11160 JSR find
11162 ORA (scrlo),Y
11163 STA (scrlo),Y
11230 .done INX
11240 BNE rpt
11250 RTS:]
11255 NEXT pass
11260 RETURN
```

MOLECULAR MOTION – PROGRAM 26

```
LIST
    1 HIMEM=&4000
   10 REM MULTI-MOLECULAR MOTION
   20 REM BY R.A.SPARKES
   30 GOSUB 10000
  100 REM BEGIN
  110 PROCmols
  154 *FX15,0
  155 PRINT TAB(0,0);"Press S to keep the same number of       "
  156 PRINT"molecules, or press N to change it."
  157 LET n$=GET$
  159 IF n$="n" OR n$="N" THEN 100
  160 PROCclear
  161 PRINT TAB(0,0);"Temperature ? (range 1 to 8) ?":PRINT:INPUT "     " S%
  165 IF S%<1 OR S%>8 THEN 160
  166 PROCclear
  167 PRINTTAB(0,0);"Press SPACE to change values"
```

```
  170 ?count=9-S%:?tptr=?count
  200 CALL mols
  204 IF ?flag=1 THEN ?flag=0:SOUND0,-15,4,1
  205 IF INKEY$(1)=" " THEN 154
  210 GOTO 200
  999 END
 4000 DEF PROCclear
 4020 FOR row=0 TO 6
 4030 PRINTTAB(0,row);"                                        "
 4040 NEXT row
 4050 ENDPROC
 5000 DEF PROCwalls
 5010 REM DRAW WALLS
 5020REM LEFT SIDE IS GRAPHICS WHITE CHARACTER (151)
 5030 REM LEFT WALL IS CHARACTER 234
 5040 REM RIGHT WALL IS CHARACTER 181
 5050 FOR I=32064 TO 32803 STEP 40
 5060 ?I=151:?(I+1)=234:?(I+39)=181
 5070 NEXT I
 5080
 5090 REM TOP SIDE IS CHARACTER 240
 5100 REM BOTTOM SIDE IS CHARACTER 163
 5110 FOR I=32065 TO 32103
 5120 ?I=240
 5130 ?(I+640)=163
 5140 NEXT
 5150 ENDPROC
 6000 DEF PROCmols
 6001 CLS
 6002 PROCwalls
 6005 PRINT TAB(0,0);"Number of molecules ? (1 to 255) ":PRINT:INPUT max%
 6006 ?max=max%
 6010 REM RANDOMLY ASSIGN MOLECULES TO POSITIONS AND DIRECTIONS
 6015 FOR molecule =1 TO max%
 6020 LET position%=RND(600)+32103
 6030 IF ?position%<>32 THEN 6020:REM REJECT IF MOLECULE IS IN END WALL OR
ON TOP OF ANOTHER MOLECULE
 6040 ?position%=79
 6050 ?(poslo+molecule)=position%MOD256
 6060 ?(poshi+molecule)=position%DIV256
 6070
 6080 REM CHOOSE RANDOM POSITIONS
 6090
 6100 LET number%=RND(8)
 6110 IF number%=1 THEN direction%=1:REM EAST
 6120 IF number%=2 THEN direction%=41:REM SOUTH-EAST
 6130 IF number%=3 THEN direction%=40:REM SOUTH
 6140 IF number%=4 THEN direction%=39:REM SOUTH-WEST
 6150 IF number%=5 THEN direction%=255:REM WEST
 6160 IF number%=6 THEN direction%=215:REM NORTH-WEST
 6170 IF number%=7 THEN direction%=216:REM NORTH
 6180 IF number%=8 THEN direction%=217:REM NORTH-EAST
 6190 ?(dr+molecule)=direction%
 6200 NEXT molecule
 6300 ENDPROC
10000 REM MOLECULE ASSEMBLY ROUTINE
10010
10020 oposlo=&70
10030 oposhi=&71
10040 nposlo=&72
```

```
10050 nposhi=&73
10060 tptr=&74
10070 drtn=&75
10080 count=&76
10090 max=&77
10100 flag=&79
10110 ?flag=0
10190 REM TABLE OF POSITIONS
10200 poslo=&4200
10210 poshi=&4300
10220 dr=&4400
11000 FOR pass = 0 TO 2 STEP 2
11010 P%=&4000
11020[OPT pass
11030       \SINGLE MOLECULE ROUTINE
11040
11050 .onemol  CLC
11110          LDA oposlo  \GET OLD POSITION
11120          ADC drtn    \COMPUTE NEW POSITION
11130          STA nposlo  \KEEP NEW POSITION
11140          LDA drtn    \IS DIRECTION NEGATIVE
11150          BMI negdr   \YES DO SUBTRACTION
11160          LDA oposhi   \NO- ADD DIRECTION
11170          ADC #0
11180          STA nposhi  \KEEP NEW POSITION
11190          BNE cont
11200.negdr    LDA oposhi
11210          SBC #0
11220          STA nposhi  \KEEP NEW POSITION
11230.cont     LDA (nposlo),Y \LOOK AT NEW SCREEN POSITION
11240          CMP #32        \IS IT EMPTY ?
11250          BEQ relay
11260          CMP #79     \ANOTHER MOLECULE ?
11265          BNE trywall
11270 .relay   JMP empty   \IGNORE IT
11280 .trywall CMP #240    \TOP WALL ?
11290          BEQ top     \YES- REFLECT
11300          CMP #234    \LEFT ?
11310          BEQ left    \YES- REFLECT
11320          CMP #181    \RIGHT ?
11330          BEQ right   \YES- REFLECT
11340          \IT MUST BE THE BOTTOM
11460          \DO NORMAL REFLECTION FROM BOTTOM
11470           LDA drtn
11480           CMP #39    \SOUTH-WEST?
11490           BEQ sw     \YES
11500           CMP #40    \SOUTH ?
11510           BEQ s      \YES
11520           \MUST BE SOUTH-EAST
11530           LDA #217   \GO NORTH-EAST
11540           STA drtn
11550           JMP exit
11560 .sw       LDA #215   \GO NORTH-WEST
11570           STA drtn
11580           BNE exit
11590.s         LDA #216   \GO NORTH
11600           STA drtn
11610           BNE exit
11620.top       \DO NORMAL REFLECTION FROM TOP
11630           LDA drtn
```

```
11640          CMP #215   \NORTH-WEST ?
11650          BEQ nw     \YES
11660          CMP #216    \NORTH ?
11670          BEQ n      \YES
11680          \MUST BE NORTH-EAST
11690          LDA #41    \GO SOUTH-EAST
11700          STA drtn
11710          BNE exit
11720.nw       LDA #39    \GO SOUTH-WEST
11730          STA drtn
11740          BNE exit
11750.n        LDA #40    \GO SOUTH
11760          STA drtn
11770          BNE exit
11780.left     \DO NORMAL REFLECTION FROM LEFT SIDE
11782         \MAKE SOUND
11784         LDA #1
11786         STA flag
11790          LDA drtn
11800          CMP #215   \NORTH-WEST ?
11810          BEQ lnw     \YES
11820          CMP #255    \WEST ?
11830          BEQ lw     \YES
11840          \MUST BE SOUTH-WEST
11850          LDA #41  \GO SOUTH-EAST
11860          STA drtn
11870          BNE exit
11880.lnw      LDA #217   \GO NORTH-EAST
11890          STA drtn
11900          BNE exit
11910.lw       LDA #1     \GO EAST
11920          STA drtn
11930          BNE exit
11940.right    \DO NORMAL REFLECTION FROM RIGHT SIDE
11950          LDA drtn
11960          CMP #217   \NORTH-EAST ?
11970          BEQ rne    \YES
11980          CMP #1     \EAST ?
11990          BEQ re     \YES
12000          \MUST BE SOUTH-EAST
12010          LDA #39  \GO SOUTH-WEST
12020          STA drtn
12030          BNE exit
12040.rne      LDA #215   \GO NORTH-WEST
12050          STA drtn
12060          BNE exit
12070.re       LDA #255   \GO WEST
12080          STA drtn
12090          BNE exit
12100         \ANOTHER MOLECULE - IGNORE IT
12170.empty   LDA #32   \RUB OUT OLD MOLECULE
12180         STA (oposlo),Y
12190         LDA #79    \GET MOLECULE CHARACTER
12200         STA (nposlo),Y
12210         LDA nposlo
12220         STA oposlo
12230         LDA nposhi  \SAVE NEW POSITIONS
12240         STA oposhi
12250 .exit   RTS
13000
```

```
13010 .mols     NOP
13020           DEC count  \IS COUNT AT ZERO ?
13030           BEQ domol \YES CARRY ON
13040           RTS       \NO  RETURN TO BASIC
13060 .domol    LDA tptr    \ BEGIN
13070           STA count
13080           LDY #0      \INITIALIZE POINTER
13090           LDX max     \GET NUMBER OF MOLECULES
13100 .nxmol    LDA poslo,X
13110           STA oposlo
13120           LDA poshi,X
13130           STA oposhi   \POSITION OF NEXT MOLECULE
13140           LDA dr,X
13150           STA drtn     \DIRECTION OF NEXT MOLECULE
13160           JSR onemol   \MOVE THIS MOLECULE
13170           LDA drtn
13180           STA dr,X     \RETAIN NEW DIRECTION
13190           LDA oposlo
13200           STA poslo,X
13210           LDA oposhi
13220           STA poshi,X  \RETAIN NEW POSITION
13230           DEX          \NEXT MOLECULE
13240           BNE nxmol
13260           RTS
15000 ]
16000 NEXT pass
17000 RETURN
```

SMOKE PARTICLE BROWNIAN MOTION - PROGRAM 27

```
LIST
    1 HIMEM=&4000
    2 MODE 4
    3 VDU23;8202;0;0;0
   10 REM BROWNIAN MOTION
   20 REM BY R.A.SPARKES
   30 REM AFTER AN IDEA BY W.JEFFRIES
  100 CLS
  110 PRINT TAB(4,10);"Setting up data, please wait."
  120 GOSUB 10000
  130 GOSUB 5000
  140 CLS
  150 LET word1$="  SMOKE  "
  160 LET word2$="PARTICLES"
  170 FOR n = 1 TO 9
  175 LET vertpos= 5+n*2
  180 PRINT TAB(33,vertpos);MID$(word1$,n,1);"  ";MID$(word2$,n,1)
  190 NEXT n
  200 CALL brown
  210 END
 5000 REM SET UP INITIAL POSITIONS
 5010 FOR I=0 TO 255
 5020 ?(xpos+I)=RND(256)-1
 5030 ?(ypos+I)=RND(256)-1
 5040 NEXT I
 5050 RETURN
```

```
10000 REM MACHINE CODE ROUTINE FOR PLOTTING
10001 xpos=&4200
10002 ypos=&4300
10010 y=&70
10020 x=&71
10030 Xval=&72
10040 scrlo=&73
10050 scrhi=&74
10060 temp=&75
10064 ?&FE6B=64 :REM ACR TO GIVE CONTINUOUS CLOCK
10065 ?&FE64=255:REM TIMER1 LO
10066 ?&FE65=255:REM START CLOCK
10067 clock=&FE64
10069 flag=&FE4D
10070 FOR pass=0 TO 2 STEP 2
10075 P% = &4000
10080 [OPTpass
10090 .find   STX Xval
10095         LDA y
10150         LSR A
10160         LSR A
10170         LSR A
10190         STA scrlo
10210         CLC
10220         ADC #&58
10230         STA scrhi
10232         LDA #0
10240         LDX #6
10250 .next   ASL scrlo
10252         ROL A
10254         DEX
10256         BNE next
10270         ADC scrhi
10280         STA scrhi
10300
10320         LDA y
10330         AND #7
10333         STA temp
10380
10400         LDA x
10410         AND #&F8
10420         ADC temp
10425         ADC scrlo
10430         STA scrlo
10440         LDA scrhi
10450         ADC #0
10460         STA scrhi
10470         LDY#0
10480         LDA x
10490         AND #7
10500         TAX
10505         SEC
10512         LDA #0
10515 .shift  ROR A
10516         DEX
10520         BPL shift
10530         STA temp
10535         LDX Xval
10536
10540         RTS
```

```
10560
12000
12010 .brown  LDX #0   \256 SMOKE PARTICLES
12020 .nxsmk  LDA ypos,X \GET OLD POSITION
12030          STA y
12035          LDA xpos,X \GET OLD POSITION
12040          STA x
12050          JSR find
12060          EOR #255
12070         AND (scrlo),Y
12080         STA (scrlo),Y
12090
12100         LDA clock
12110         AND #3
12115         ORA #1
12120         CLC
12130         ADC #254
12140         CLC
12150         ADC x
12160         STA x
12165          STA xpos,X
12170         LDA clock
12180         AND #3
12185         ORA #1
12190         CLC
12200         ADC #254
12210         CLC
12220         ADC y
12230         STA y
12240          STA ypos,X
12250          JSR find
12260          ORA (scrlo),Y
12270          STA (scrlo),Y
12280          INX
12290          BNE nxsmk
12300          LDA flag
12310          AND #1
12320          BEQ brown
12330          RTS
12360]
12400 NEXT pass
12500 RETURN
```

GRAVITY – PROGRAM 28

```
LIST
    1 MODE 7
    2 @%=&020209
    5 LET acceleration = -10
   10 CLS
   20 PRINT TAB(8,0);"VERTICAL HEIGHT"
   30 PRINT:PRINT:PRINT"This program prints the vertical height"
   40 PRINT:PRINT"reached by an object thrown vertically"
   50 PRINT:PRINT"upwards against gravity."
   60 PRINT:PRINT:INPUT"Initial speed (range 0 to 200)   " initspeed
```

```
 70 CLS
 80 PRINT TAB(8,0);"VERTICAL HEIGHT"
 90 PRINT:PRINT"Acceleration Speed    Height    Time"
100 FOR time = 0 TO 20
110 LET height=initspeed*time+0.5*acceleration*time*time
120 LET speed=initspeed+acceleration*time
130 PRINTacceleration,speed,height,time
140 NEXT time
```

LCR RESONANCE - PROGRAM 29

```
 LIST
  100 MODE1
  110 GCOL0,3
  120 MOVE 0,50
  130 DRAW 1279,50
  140 MOVE 50,0
  150 DRAW 50,1023
  155PRINT TAB(0,0);"
                                                        "
  160 PRINT TAB(0,0);"Inductance (mH) ";:INPUT L:PRINT TAB(22,0);"Resistance
";:INPUT R:PRINT TAB(0,2);"Capacitance (microfarad) ";:INPUT C
  170 PRINT TAB(0,14);"V"
  180 PRINT TAB(20,31);"frequency";
  190 IF R=0 THEN R=0.001
  200 LET E=50
  210 MOVE 50,50
  220 FOR frequency=1 TO 1279 STEP 5
  240 LET XL=frequency*L/1000:XC=1000000/(frequency*C)
  250 LET X=XL-XC
  260 LET Z=SQR(R*R+X*X)
  270 LET I=E/Z
  280 LET VC=I*XC
  290 DRAW frequency+50,VC+50
  300 NEXT frequency
  310 GOTO 155
```

PROJECTILES - PROGRAM 30

```
LIST
    1 MODE 4
    2 REM PROJECTILE MOTION
    3 REM BY R.A.SPARKES
    5 REM INITIAL VALUES
    6 speed=30
    7 angle=45
    8 g=10
    9 dragcoeff = 0
   10 CLS : PRINT TAB(9,1);"PROJECTILE MOTION"
   20 PRINT:PRINT:PRINT"The motion of a projectile depends upon"
```

```
  30 PRINT:PRINT"a)  the initial speed,"
  40 PRINT:PRINT"b)  the angle to the horizontal,"
  50 PRINT:PRINT"c)  the amount of friction."
  60 PRINT:PRINT"d)  the acceleration due to gravity."
  70 PRINT TAB(0,30);"Press SPACE to continue."
  80 REPEAT UNTIL GET$=" "
1000 REM SHOW CURRENT VALUES
1005 CLS
1010 PRINT:PRINT"A. initial speed               = ";speed
1020 PRINT:PRINT"B. angle of projection         = ";angle
1030 PRINT:PRINT"C. coefficient of friction     = ";dragcoeff
1040 PRINT:PRINT"D. acceleration due to gravity = ";g
1050 PRINT:PRINT:PRINT"Choose which quantity you want"
1053 PRINT:PRINT"to change by pressing A, B, C OR D"
1055 PRINT:PRINT"or press RETURN to confirm these values."
1058 *FX15,0
1060 LET S$=GET$
1070 IF S$<>"A" AND S$<>"B" AND S$<>"C" AND S$<>"D" AND S$<>CHR$(13)
THEN 1060
1080 IF S$="A" THEN 1500
1090 IF S$="B" THEN 1600
1100 IF S$="C" THEN 1700
1110 IF S$="D" THEN 1800
1120 REM VALUES ACCEPTED: CHOOSE WHICH VARIABLE
1130 PRINT:PRINT"Choose which variable you want"
1140 PRINT:PRINT"to investigate by pressing A, B, C OR D"
1145 *FX15,0
1150 LET x$=GET$
1160 IF x$<>"A" AND x$<>"B" AND x$<>"C" AND x$<>"D" THEN 1150
1165 CLS
1170 IF x$="A" THEN 2000
1180 IF x$="B" THEN 2100
1190 IF x$="C" THEN 2200
1200 IF x$="D" THEN 2300
1230
1500 PRINT:PRINT"Enter new initial speed (range 1 to 100)"
1510 INPUT speed
1520 GOTO 1000
1600 PRINT:PRINT"Enter new angle of projection in degrees"
1610 PRINT"range 10 to 80.  ";:INPUT angle
1620 GOTO 1000
1700 PRINT:PRINT"Enter new drag coefficient (0 to 10)    "
1710 INPUT dragcoeff
1720 GOTO 1000
1800 PRINT:PRINT"Enter new acceleration due to gravity  "
1810 PRINT:PRINT"range 0 to 20.  ";:INPUT g
1820 GOTO 1000
2000 REM SPEED
2010 PROCthrow
2020 IF Z$=CHR$(13) THEN 1000
2030 PRINT TAB(0,0);"Enter new initial speed (range 1 to 100)"
2040 INPUT speed
2050 GOTO 2000
2100 REM ANGLE
2110 PROCthrow
2120 IF Z$=CHR$(13) THEN 1000
2130 PRINT TAB(0,0);"Enter new angle of projection in degrees"
2140 PRINT"range 10 to 80.  ";
2150 INPUT angle
2160 GOTO 2100
```

```
2200 REM FRICTIONAL DRAG
2210 PROCthrow
2220 IF Z$=CHR$(13) THEN 1000
2230 PRINT TAB(0,0);"Enter new drag coefficient (0 to 10)    "
2240 INPUT dragcoeff
2250 GOTO 2200
2300 REM ACCELERATION DUE TO GRAVITY
2310 PROCthrow
2320 IF Z$=CHR$(13) THEN 1000
2330 PRINT TAB(0,0);"Enter new acceleration due to gravity   "
2340 PRINT:PRINT"range 0 to 20.  ";
2350 INPUT g
2360 GOTO 2300
4230 PRINT:PRINT "Enter the drag coefficient (0 to 10)"
5000 DEF PROCthrow
5020 LET timeinc=1
5030 REM AXES
5040 VDU29,0;300;
5050 MOVE 0,0
5060 DRAW 1279,0
5070 REM INITIAL POSITIONS
5080 LET X=0:Y=0:MOVE X,Y
5090 LET VX=speed*COS(RAD(angle))
5100 LET VY=speed*SIN(RAD(angle))
5110 LET acc=-g/10:LET drag=dragcoeff/100
5120 REPEAT
5130 REM MOTION IN X-DIRECTION
5140 LET VX=VX-drag*VX*timeinc
5150 LET X=X+VX*timeinc
5160 REM MOTION IN Y-DIRECTION
5170 LET AY=acc - drag*VY*timeinc
5180 LET VY=VY+AY*timeinc
5190 LET Y=Y+VY*timeinc
5200 REM PLOT NEW POSITIONS
5210 DRAW X,Y
5220 UNTIL X>1279 OR Y<-300
5230 PRINT TAB(0,0);"Press SPACE to change the same variable"
5240 PRINT TAB(0,2);"Press RETURN to change another variable"
5250 LET Z$=GET$
5260 IF Z$<>CHR$(13) AND Z$<>" " THEN 5250
5270 PRINT TAB(0,0);"
                                                         "
5280 ENDPROC
```

NEWTON – PROGRAM 31

```
LIST
 100 MODE1
 104 *FX11,0
 105 ON ERROR GOTO 100
 110 PRINT TAB(12,0);"SATELLITE MOTION"
 120 PRINT:PRINT"The aim of this program is"
 130 PRINT:PRINT"to set a rocket in orbit around"
 140 PRINT:PRINT"the moon from a space station,"
```

```
150 PRINT:PRINT"which is orbiting the earth."
160 PRINT:PRINT"You must choose the initial speed and"
170 PRINT:PRINT"direction for the rocket."
180PRINT
185 PRINT:PRINT"Crashing on the surface of the moon"
186 PRINT:PRINT"or losing your rocket in outer space"
187 PRINT:PRINT"causes a restart."
188 PRINT:PRINT"If you achieve an orbit or wish"
189 PRINT:PRINT"to restart the program, press ESCAPE."
190 PRINT:PRINT:PRINT:PRINT"Press B to begin."
195 A$=INKEY$(255)
200 IF A$<>"B" AND A$<>"b" THEN 195
210 REM DRAW EARTH-MOON SYSTEM
215 CLS
220 PROCcircle(33,600,500)
230 PRINT TAB(0,31);"Space station     o";
240 PRINT TAB(0,0);"SPEED (0 TO 10) ";:INPUT speed
250 PRINT TAB(0,1);"ANGLE (-90 TO +90) ";:INPUT angle
260 REM CALCULATE CURRENT POSITION AND SPEED
270 LET x=592:LET y=32
280 LET xvelocity=speed*SIN(RAD(angle))/4
290 LET yvelocity=speed*COS(RAD(angle))/4
300 MOVE x,y
310 LET crash=FALSE
350 REPEAT
400 REM MAIN CALCULATION
410 REM THE MOON IS AT 600,500
420 REM FIRST CALCULATE THE DISTANCE FROM THE CENTRE OF THE MOON
430 LET xdisplacement=x-600
440 LET ydisplacement=y-500
450 LET parameter=xdisplacement^2 + ydisplacement^2
455 LETdistance=SQR(parameter^3)
460 IF parameter<1200 THEN crash=TRUE
465 REM COMPUTE NEW SPEED
470 LET xvelocity=xvelocity-1000*xdisplacement/distance
480 LET yvelocity=yvelocity-1000*ydisplacement/distance
490 REM COMPUTE NEW POSITIONS
500 LET x=x + xvelocity
510 LET y=y + yvelocity
520 DRAW x,y
530 UNTIL x>1300 OR x<0 OR y>1100 OR y<0 OR crash
540 PRINT TAB(0,0);"
 "
550 GOTO 240
900 END
1000 DEF PROCcircle(radius,xcentre,ycentre)
1007 MOVE xcentre,ycentre
1010 FOR angle=0 TO 360 STEP 10
1020 LET x=xcentre + radius*COS(RAD(angle))
1030 LET y=ycentre + radius*SIN(RAD(angle))
1040 MOVE xcentre,ycentre
1050 PLOT85,x,y
1060 NEXT  angle
1070 ENDPROC
```

RUTHERFORD - PROGRAM 32

```
LIST
 100 MODE1
 105 ON ERROR GOTO 100
 110 PRINT TAB(5,0);"ALPHA PARTICLE SCATTERING"
 115PRINT:PRINT
 120 PRINT:PRINT"The aim of this program is"
 130 PRINT:PRINT"to fire alpha particles at random"
 140 PRINT:PRINT"at a nucleus of gold."
 145PRINT:PRINT
 150 PRINT:PRINT"The alpha particles are deflected by"
 155 PRINT:PRINT"the nucleus and there is a chance"
 160 PRINT:PRINT"that some will achieve a direct hit."
 165PRINT:PRINT
 170 PRINT:PRINT"Press SPACE to fire the particles."
 185 PRINT:PRINT"and see if you get the same result as"
 186 PRINT:PRINT"Rutherford, Geiger and Marsden."
 195 A$=INKEY$(255)
 200 IF A$<>" "THEN 195
 210 REM DRAW GOLD NUCLEUS
 215 CLS
 220 PROCcircle(10,600,500)
 230 PROCelectrons
 235 VDU23;8202;0;0;0
 240 PRINT TAB(0,0);"Press ESCAPE to restart.
 250 REM CALCULATE CURRENT POSITION AND SPEED
 270 LET x=0:LET y=RND(800)+100
 280 LET xvelocity=100
 290 LET yvelocity=0
 300 MOVE x,y
 310 LET crash=FALSE
 350 REPEAT
 400 REM MAIN CALCULATION
 410 REM THE NUCLEUS IS AT 600,500
 420 REM FIRST CALCULATE THE DISTANCE FROM THE CENTRE OF THE NUCLEUS
 430 LET xdisplacement=x-600
 440 LET ydisplacement=y-500
 450 LET parameter=xdisplacement^2 + ydisplacement^2
 455 LETdistance=SQR(parameter^3)
 460 IF parameter<120 THEN crash=TRUE
 465 REM COMPUTE NEW SPEED
 470 LET xvelocity=xvelocity+50000*xdisplacement/distance
 480 LET yvelocity=yvelocity+50000*ydisplacement/distance
 490 REM COMPUTE NEW POSITIONS
 500 LET x=x + xvelocity
 510 LET y=y + yvelocity
 520 DRAW x,y
 530 UNTIL x>1300 OR x<0 OR y>1100 OR y<0 OR crash
 550 GOTO 250
 900 END
1000 DEF PROCcircle(radius,xcentre,ycentre)
1005 GCOL0,2
1007 MOVE xcentre,ycentre
1010 FOR angle=0 TO 360 STEP 10
1020 LET x=xcentre + radius*COS(RAD(angle))
1030 LET y=ycentre + radius*SIN(RAD(angle))
1040 MOVE xcentre,ycentre
1050 PLOT85,x,y
1060 NEXT  angle
```

```
1065 GCOLO,3
1070 ENDPROC
1100 DEF PROCelectrons
1105 *FX9,2
1106 *FX10,2
1110 VDU19,1,12,0,0,0
1115 GCOLO,1
1120 FOR n=1 TO 79
1130 LET xval=RND(1000)+100
1140 LET yval=RND(1000)
1150 PLOT69,xval,yval
1160 NEXT n
1170 GCOLO,3
1180 ENDPROC
```

MASTERMIND - PROGRAM 33

```
LIST
   10 REM  MASTERMIND
   20 MODE 7
   30 DIM A(4),B(4),C(4)
   40 DIM R(25),S(25),T(25),Z(25)
   50 CLS
   60 PRINT TAB(15,10);"MASTERMIND"
   70 PRINT TAB(12,13);"BY  R.A.SPARKES"
   80PRINT:PRINT:PRINT
   90 PRINT TAB(0,20);"IF YOU WOULD LIKE TO PLAY,    PRESS Y"
  100 IF GET$<>"Y" THEN 100
  110 CLS:PRINT:PRINT
  120 PRINT"THIS GAME LETS YOU GUESS THE FOUR DIGITS"
  130 PRINT"WHICH I SHALL CHOOSE AT RANDOM."
  140PRINT
  150 PRINT"IT WORKS LIKE THIS."
  160PRINT
  170 PRINT"I PICK THE SEQUENCE OF DIGITS 1 2 3 4."
  180PRINT
  190 PRINT"YOU GUESS THIS SEQUENCE TO BE 4 2 6 3."
  200PRINT
  210 PRINT"YOU SCORE 1  BULL , BECAUSE 2 IS CORRECT"
  220 PRINT"AND IT IS IN THE CORRECT POSITION."
  230PRINT
  240 PRINT"YOU SCORE 2  COWS , BECAUSE 4 AND 3 ARE"
  250PRINT
  260 PRINT"CORRECT BUT IN THE WRONG POSITIONS."
  270PRINT
  280 PRINT"YOU CAN THEN GUESS AGAIN."
  290PRINT
  300 PRINT "PRESS 'SPACE' FOR A GAME."
  310 IF GET$<>" " THEN 310
  320 Z=1
  330 CLS
  340 PRINT"FIRST CHOOSE THE LEVEL OF DIFFICULTY."
  350PRINT:PRINT
  360 PRINT"THIS IS THE NUMBER OF DIFFERENT KINDS"
  370PRINT
  380 PRINT"OF DIGIT, I MAY CHOOSE FROM."
```

```
390PRINT
400 PRINT"PICK ONE FROM THE FOLLOWING LIST:"
410PRINT
420 PRINT"LEVEL 4 (DIGITS 1,2,3 OR 4)"
430 PRINT"LEVEL 5 (DIGITS 1,2,3,4 OR 5)"
440 PRINT"LEVEL 6 (DIGITS 1 TO 6)"
450 PRINT"LEVEL 7 (DIGITS 1 TO 7)"
460 PRINT"LEVEL 8 (DIGITS 1 TO 8)"
470 PRINT"LEVEL 9 (DIGITS 1 TO 9)"
480 PRINT TAB(0,17);"PRESS ONE OF THE KEYS 4 TO 9 TO CHOOSE."
490 K=VAL(GET$)
500 IF K>9 OR K<4 THEN PRINT TAB(0,23);"PRESS ONE OF THE KEYS 4 TO 9 ONLY.
":GOTO 490
510CLS
520 PRINT  :PRINT
530 FOR N=1 TO 4
540 A(N)=RND(K)
550 NEXT N
560 PRINT"NOW MAKE YOUR GUESS"
570PRINT
580 PRINT "TYPE OUT YOUR NEXT FOUR DIGITS "
590PRINT
600 PRINT"TYPE 0000 TO BE TOLD THE HIDDEN NUMBER."
610 FORI=1TO4
620 *FX15,0
630 B$=GET$
640 IF B$=CHR$(127) THEN I=I-1:PRINT TAB(5+2*I,20);" ":GOTO 620
650 B(I)=VAL(B$)
660 IF B(I)>K THEN PRINT TAB(0,22);"THAT VALUE IS NOT IN THE RANGE YOU
CHOSE":GOTO 620
670 PRINT TAB(0,22);"                                              "
680 PRINT TAB(5+2*I,20);B(I)
690 NEXT
700 IFB(1)=0ANDB(2)=0ANDB(3)=0ANDB(4)=0THEN 1140
710 R(Z)=1000*B(1)+100*B(2)+10*B(3)+B(4)
720 Y=0:X=0
730 FOR N=1 TO 4:C(N)=A(N):NEXT
740 FORN=1TO4
750 IFC(N)<>B(N)THEN770
760 X=X+1:C(N)=99:B(N)=100
770 NEXT N
780 FOR N=1 TO 4:FORM=1TO4
790 IF C(N)<>B(M) THEN 810
800 Y=Y+1:C(N)=99:B(M)=100
810 NEXT M:NEXT N
820CLS
830 PRINT"GUESS        BULLS        COWS       GUESS NO."
840 S(Z)=X:T(Z)=Y
850 FOR L=1 TO Z:PRINT;R(L);SPC(9);S(L);SPC(9);T(L);SPC(9);L:NEXT L
860 IF X=4 THEN 890
870 Z=Z+1:IFZ>16THEN940
880 GOTO 580
890 PRINT"WELL DONE, YOU HAVE GUESSED CORRECTLY"
900 PRINT"YOU TOOK ONLY  ";Z;"  GUESSES "
910 PRINT"IF YOU WANT TO TRY AGAIN, PRESS Y"
920 IF GET$<>"Y" THEN STOP
930 GOTO320
940 CLS:PRINT:PRINT"YOU DON'T SEEM TO KNOW HOW TO PLAY."
950PRINT
960 PRINT"YOU SHOULD NOT JUST MAKE WILD GUESSES."
```

```
 970PRINT
 980 PRINT"USE THE INFORMATION ABOUT BULLS AND COWS"
 990 PRINT"TO HELP YOU."
1000PRINT
1010 PRINT:PRINT"MAKE ONLY ONE CHANGE TO YOUR "
1020 PRINT:PRINT"GUESS EACH TIME, THEN YOU CAN SEE"
1030 PRINT:PRINT"IF THAT CHANGE HAS GIVEN AN EXTRA BULL"
1040 PRINT:PRINT"OR COW (OR ONE LESS)."
1050PRINT:PRINT"HAVE ANOTHER TRY AT A DIFFERENT"
1060PRINT:PRINT"SET OF DIGITS. PRESS Y"
1070 IF GET$<>"Y" THEN 1070
1080 GOTO 320
1140 REM GIVE ANSWER
1150 CLS
1160 PRINT:PRINT:PRINT"MY NUMBER IS ";A(1);A(2);A(3);A(4)
1170PRINT:PRINT"DO YOU SEE WHERE YOUR DIFFICULTY IS ?"
1180PRINT:PRINT"HAVE ANOTHER TRY AT A DIFFERENT"
1190PRINT:PRINT"SET OF DIGITS. PRESS Y"
1200 IF GET$<>"Y" THEN 1200
1210 GOTO 320
```

ELEMENTS - PROGRAM 34

```
LIST
    1 REM          ELEMENTS
    2 REM BY R.A.Sparkes
    3 MODE 7
    4 CLS
   10 *FX11,0
   20 PROCelements
   30 DIM p$(15), D$(15)
   50 PRINT TAB(10,1);CHR$(141);"ELEMENTS"
   51 PRINT TAB(10,2);CHR$(141);"ELEMENTS"
   52 PRINT:PRINT"ELEMENTS is a simple guessing game."
   53 PRINT:PRINT"You type in the missing letters"
   54 PRINT:PRINT"one at a time. Each correct letter"
   55 PRINT:PRINT"takes you nearer to guessing the whole"
   56 PRINT:PRINT"element. You are only allowed eight"
   57 PRINT:PRINT"incorrect guesses, after which you"
   58 PRINT:PRINT"will be told the correct answer."
   59 PRINT:PRINT"Press ESCAPE at any time during this"
   60 PRINT:PRINT"program, if you wish to finish."
   61 PRINT:PRINT"Press the SPACE BAR to continue."
   62 *FX15,0
   63 IF INKEY$(255)<>" "THEN 63
   64 CLS
   65 PRINT TAB(0,11);CHR$(141);"Type your name."
   66 PRINT TAB(0,12);CHR$(141);"Type your name."
   70 PRINT TAB(0,14);CHR$(141);"Then press the RETURN key"
   75 PRINT TAB(0,15) CHR$(141) "Then press the RETURN key"
   80 PRINT TAB(0,17)
   90 INPUT A$
  100 REM set up word
  110 PROCgetelement
  120 LET wordlength=LEN(word$)
```

```
130 FOR i = 1 TO wordlength
140 LET p$(i) = MID$(word$,i,1)
150 LET D$(i) = "-"
160 NEXT i
170 LET guess=0
180 CLS:PRINT TAB(10,11);
190 REM PRINT OUT LETTER POSITIONS
200 FOR n=1 TO wordlength
210 PRINT D$(n);
220 NEXT n
250 REM ASK QUESTION
260 PRINT TAB(0,1);CHR$(141);A$;","
270 PRINT TAB(0,2);CHR$(141);A$;","
300 PRINT TAB(0,4);CHR$(141);"Guess a letter."
310 PRINT TAB(0,5);CHR$(141);"Guess a letter."
330 LET letter$=GET$
333 IF ASC(letter$)>96 THEN letter$=CHR$(ASC(letter$) - 32)
340 IF ASC(letter$)<65 OR ASC(letter$)>90 THEN GOTO 330
360 LET flag = 0
370 FOR i= 1 TO wordlength
380 IF letter$<> p$(i) THEN GOTO 400
390 LET flag = 1
395 LET D$(i)=letter$
400 NEXT i
410 REM CONSTRUCT WORD SO FAR
415 LET guess$=""
420 FOR i= 1 TO wordlength
430 LET guess$=guess$ + D$(i)
440 NEXT i
500 PRINT TAB(0,11);CHR$(141); "The word is    ";guess$
510 PRINT TAB(0,12);CHR$(141); "The word is    ";guess$
520 IF flag = 0 THEN PRINT TAB(0,15) "Your letter is not in my word."
530 IF flag = 0 THEN PRINT TAB(0,17) "Try again."
540  IF flag = 1 THEN PRINT TAB(0,15) "                              "
545  IF flag = 1 THEN PRINT TAB(0,17) "          "
546 IF flag=0 THEN PROCno
550 IF guess$=word$ THEN GOTO 800
555 IF flag=0 THEN guess = guess +1
560 IF guess >8 THEN GOTO 880
580 IF flag=1 THEN PROCyes
590 GOTO 300
800 REM SUCCESSFUL
801 SOUND1,-15,97,10
802 SOUND1,-15,105,10
803 SOUND1,-15,89,10
804 SOUND1,-15,41,10
805 SOUND1,-15,69,20
806 PRINT TAB(0,1);CHR$(141);"Well done  ";A$
810 PRINT TAB(0,2);CHR$(141);"Well done  ";A$
815 PRINT TAB(0,4);CHR$(141);"The hidden element is"
816 PRINT TAB(0,5);CHR$(141);"The hidden element is"
818 PRINT TAB(0,8);CHR$(141);word$;"                "
819 PRINT TAB(0,9);CHR$(141);word$;"                "
820 PRINT TAB(0,20);"Press SPACE for another word"
830 PRINT TAB(0,15) "                  "
840 PRINT TAB(0,17) "          "
850 IF INKEY$(0)<>" " THEN GOTO 850
860 GOTO 100
880 REM TOO  MANY  GUESSES
900 PRINT TAB(0,1);CHR$(141);"No.  ";A$;",  the hidden element"
```

```
  905 PRINT TAB(0,2);CHR$(141);"No.  ";A$;",  the hidden element"
  910 PRINT TAB(0,4);CHR$(141);"   is   ";word$;"              "
  915 PRINT TAB(0,5);CHR$(141);"   is   ";word$;"            "
  916 PRINT TAB(0,15) "                                   "
  917 PRINT TAB(0,17) "               "
  920 PRINT TAB(0,8);"Press SPACE for another word"
  940 IF INKEY$(0)<>" " THEN GOTO 940
  950 GOTO 100
15000 DEF PROCelements
15010 DATA ACTINIUM,ALUMINIUM,AMERICIUM,ANTIMONY,ARGON
15020 DATA ARSENIC,ASTATINE,BARIUM,BERKELIUM,BERYLLIUM
15030 DATA BISMUTH,BORON,BROMINE,CADMIUM,CAESIUM
15040 DATA CALCIUM,CALIFORNIUM,CARBON,CERIUM,CHLORINE
15050 DATA CHROMIUM,COBALT,COPPER,CURIUM,DYSPROSIUM
15060 DATA EINSTEINIUM,ERBIUM,EUROPIUM,FERMIUM,FLUORINE
15070 DATA FRANCIUM,GADOLINIUM,GALLIUM,GERMANIUM,GOLD
15080 DATA HAFNIUM,HELIUM,HOLMIUM,HYDROGEN,INDIUM
15090 DATA IODINE,IRIDIUM,IRON,KRYPTON,LANTHANUM
15100 DATA LAWRENCIUM,LEAD,LITHIUM,LUTETIUM,MANGESIUM
15110 DATA MANGANESE,MENDELEVIUM,MERCURY,MOLYBDENUM,NEODYMIUM
15120 DATA NEON,NEPTUNIUM,NICKEL,NIOBIUM,NITROGEN
15130 DATA NOBELIUM,OSMIUM,OXYGEN,PALLADIUM,PHOSPHORUS
15140 DATA PLATINUM,PLUTONIUM,POLONIUM,POTASSIUM,PRASEODYMIUM
15150 DATA PROMETHIUM,PROTACTINIUM,RADIUM,RADON,RHENIUM
15160 DATA RHODIUM,RUBIDIUM,RUTHENIUM,SAMARIUM,SCANDIUM
15170 DATA SELENIUM,SILICON,SILVER,SODIUM,STRONTIUM
15180 DATA SULPHUR,TANTALUM,TECHNETIUM,TELLURIUM,TERBIUM
15190 DATA THALLIUM,THORIUM,THULIUM,TIN,TITANIUM
15200 DATA TUNGSTEN,URANIUM,VANADIUM,XENON,YTTERBIUM
15210 DATA YTTRIUM,ZINC,ZIRCONIUM
15220
15230 RESTORE 15010
15240 DIM element$(103)
15250 FOR n=1 TO 103
15260 READ element$(n)
15270 NEXT n
15280 ENDPROC
15290
15300 DEF PROCgetelement
15310 REPEAT
15320 R=RND(103)
15330 UNTIL element$(R)<>""
15340 LET word$=element$(R)
15350 LET element$(R)=""
15360 ENDPROC
20000 DEF PROCyes
20040 REM SUCCESSFUL NOISE
20050 SOUND1,-15,53,5
20060 SOUND1,-15,69,5
20070 SOUND1,-15,81,5
20100 ENDPROC
21000 DEF PROCno
21040 REM RASPBERRY
21050 SOUND0,-15,6,20
21100 ENDPROC
```

PILES - PROGRAM 35

```
LIST
    1REM  PILES
    2REM created by R.A.Sparkes
    3REM after an idea by A.Wiltshire
    4 MODE 7
    8 *FX11,0
    9 DIM brick(20),wall(4,4)
   10 CLS:PRINT TAB(4,2) CHR$(141);"Please type in your name."
   11 PRINT TAB(4,3) CHR$(141);"Please type in your name."
   12 PRINT TAB(4,6) CHR$(141);"Then press the RETURN key."
   13 PRINT TAB(4,7) CHR$(141);"Then press the RETURN key."
   14 PRINT TAB(10,10)
   15 INPUT A$
   20 REM TURN CURSOR OFF
   30 VDU23,1,0;0;0;0;
   50 REM SET UP TWENTY BRICKS IN WALL
   51 REM  TEN YELLOW, TEN BLUE
   54 LET yellow=0:LET blue =0:LET I = 0
   55 REPEAT
   56 LET brick(I)=RND(2)+146
   58 IF brick(I)=148 THEN LET blue=blue+1
   60 IF brick(I)=147 THEN LET yellow=yellow + 1
   65 LET I = I + 1
   70 UNTIL blue=10 OR yellow=10
   80 FOR Z=I TO 19
   90 LET brick(Z)=147+((yellow=10)AND1)
  100 NEXT Z
  110 CLS
  120 PRINT TAB(1,17) CHR$(141);"1       2       3       4       5"
  130 PRINT TAB(1,18) CHR$(141);"1       2       3       4       5"
  140 FOR I = 0 TO 19
  150 PROCblock(brick(I),(I DIV 4), (I MOD 4))
  160 LET wall((I DIV 4), (I MOD 4)) = brick(I)
  170 NEXT I
  180 FOR I=0 TO 4:LET wall(I,4)=0:NEXT I
  200 REM FIND WHICH BRICK TO MOVE
  205 FOR T=1 TO 2000:NEXT T
  210 PRINT TAB(3,21) CHR$(141);"Move      ?                            "
  220 PRINT TAB(3,22) CHR$(141);"Move      ?                            "
  230 LET N$=GET$
  240 LET N%=VAL(N$)
  250 IF N%<1 OR N%>5 THEN GOTO 230
  255 LET source=N% - 1
  260 PRINT TAB(14,21);N%;"     to     ?"
  270 PRINT TAB(14,22);N%;"     to     ?"
  280 LET N$=GET$
  290 LET N%=VAL(N$)
  300  PRINT TAB(27,21);N%
  310  PRINT TAB(27,22);N%
  320 destination= N% - 1
  400 REM CHECK ON VALIDITY OF MOVE
  405 REM DOES SOURCE BLOCK EXIST ?
  410 LET topsource=5:LET endcondition = FALSE
  420 REPEAT
  430 LET topsource=topsource-1
  440 LET allgone = (topsource=-1)
  445 IF allgone THEN SOUND0,-15,4,10 ELSE  endcondition = (wall(source,
topsource)<>0)
```

```
 450 UNTIL endcondition OR allgone
 460 IF allgone THEN PRINT TAB(3,21) CHR$(141);"         Not possible
 470 IF allgone THEN PRINT TAB(3,22) CHR$(141);"         Not possible
 480 IF topsource=-1 THEN GOTO 200
 500 REM DOES DESTINATION BLOCK EXIST ?
 510 IF wall(destination,4)=0 THEN GOTO 600
 515 SOUND0,-15,4,10
 520 PRINT TAB(3,21) CHR$(141);"        Not possible                    "
 530 PRINT TAB(3,22) CHR$(141);"        Not possible                    "
 540 GOTO 200
 600 REM ERASE SOURCE BLOCK
 605 SOUND0,-15,1,10
 610 LET brick = wall(source,topsource)
 620 LET wall(source,topsource)=0
 630 PROCblock(152,source,topsource)
 640 REM FIND TOP POSITION OF NEW BRICK
 650 LET topdest=-1
 660 REPEAT
 670 LET topdest=topdest + 1
 680 UNTIL (wall(destination,topdest)=0)
 700 REM PLACE BRICK IN NEW POSITION
 710 LET wall(destination,topdest)=brick
 720 PROCblock(brick,destination,topdest)
 790 finished = TRUE
 800 FOR position=0 TO 4
 810 FOR height= 0 TO 4
 820 IF wall(position,height)<>wall(position,0) THEN finished = FALSE
 840 NEXT height
 850 NEXT position
 900IF NOT finished THEN GOTO 210
 910 PRINT TAB(3,21) CHR$(141);"     Well done ";A$;"                        "
 920 PRINT TAB(3,22) CHR$(141);"     Well done ";A$;"                        "
 930 ENVELOPE 1,8,1,-1,1,1,1,1,121,-10,-5,-2,120,120
 940 SOUND 1,1,100,500
 941 SOUND 2,1,80,500
 950 PRINT TAB(0,24) "Press SPACE for a new game";
 960 IF INKEY$(0)<>" " THEN GOTO 960
 970 GOTO 50
1000 REM DEFINE BLOCK-MAKING ROUTINE
1001
1010 DEF PROCblock(colour,position,height)
1020 LET X=position*8
1030 LET Y=15 - height*3
1040 PRINT TAB(X,Y) CHR$(colour);CHR$(255);CHR$(124);CHR$(124);CHR$(255)
1050 PRINT TAB(X,Y-1) CHR$(colour);CHR$(255);CHR$(32);CHR$(32);CHR$(255)
1060 PRINT TAB(X,Y-2) CHR$(colour);CHR$(124);CHR$(124);CHR$(124);CHR$(124)
1070 ENDPROC
```

MACHINE CODE SCREEN TRANSFER - PROGRAM 36

```
LIST
    1 MODE 4
    2 HIMEM=&2F00
    3 GOSUB 30000
  100 REM MAIN PROGRAM
  110 REM etc.
 1000 REM EXAMPLE
 1500 CLS
 1600 PRINT:PRINT"It's much quicker with machine code."
 2000 !dest=&6C00:!source=&3000:?pages=20:CALL swap
 3000FOR T=1 TO 1000:NEXT T
 4000 !dest=&6C00:!source=&4400:?pages=20:CALL swap
 5000 GOTO 3000
30000 REM FLASH ROUTINE IN MODE 4
30010 REM EXCHANGES A SELECTED PART OF THE SCREEN
30020 REM WITH BYTES STORED IN MEMORY
30030
30040  pages =&71
30050  dest=&80:REM LOW/HIGH BYTES OF  SCREEN INTERIM ADDRESS
30070  source=&84:REM LOW/HIGH BYTES OF  STORE INTERIM ADDRESS
30090  temp=&70 :REM TEMPORARY STORE
30100  FOR pass = 0 TO 2 STEP 2
30110  P%=&2F00:REM STARTING ADDRESS FOR SWAP ROUTINE
30120  [OPT pass
30130  .swap   LDX pages      \SET COUNTER TO NUMBER OF PAGES
30140  .nxpage LDY #0
30150  .nxtpos LDA (source),Y \GET BYTE
30160          STA temp    !  \SAVE IN TEMPORARY STORE
30170          LDA (dest),Y \GET CURRENT SCREEN BYTE
30180          STA (source),Y \KEEP IN STORE
30190          LDA temp        \RETRIEVE SOURCE BYTE
30200          STA (dest),Y \SEND TO SCREEN
30210          INY             \END OF PAGE?
30220          BNE nxtpos      \NO DO NEXT BYTE
30230          INC (dest+1) \MOVE TO NEXT PAGE
30240          INC (source+1)
30250          DEX             \ALL PAGES DONE?
30260          BNE nxpage      \NO DO NEXT PAGE
30270          RTS
30280  ]
30290  NEXT pass
30300 REM CONSTRUCT GRAPHICS AND STORE IN MEMORY
30310 PROCyes
30320 !dest=&6C00:!source=&4400:?pages=20:CALL swap
30330 PROCno
30340 !dest=&6C00:!source=&3000:?pages=20:CALL swap
30350 RETURN
31000 DEF PROCyes
31010 CLS:PRINT:PRINT"Constructing responses in BASIC, please wait."
31015 REM Y
31020 MOVE 100,500:DRAW 225,250
31030 PLOT85,150,500
31040 PLOT85,275,250
31050 MOVE 400,500
31060 MOVE350,500
31070 PLOT85,275,250
31075 PLOT85,225,250
31080 MOVE 225,30
```

```
31090 PLOT85,275,250
31100 PLOT85,275,30
31110 REM E
31120 MOVE 500,30:MOVE  500,500
31130 PLOT85,550,30
31140 PLOT85,550,500
31150 MOVE 700,30:MOVE 550,30
31160 PLOT85,700,80
31170 MOVE 550,80
31180 PLOT85,550,30
31190 MOVE 550,250:MOVE 550,300
31200 PLOT85,660,250
31210 PLOT85,660,300
31220 MOVE 550,450:MOVE 550,500
31230 PLOT85,700,450
31240 PLOT85,700,500
31250 REM S
31260 FOR a=200 TO 450 STEP 10
31270 MOVE 930+90*COS(RAD(a)),152+90*SIN(RAD(a))
31280 MOVE 930+130*COS(RAD(a)),152+130*SIN(RAD(a))
31290 PLOT85,930+90*COS(RAD(a+10)),152+90*SIN(RAD(a+10))
31300 PLOT85,930+130*COS(RAD(a+10)),152+130*SIN(RAD(a+10))
31310 NEXT a
31460 FOR a=270 TO 20 STEP -10
31470 MOVE 930+90*COS(RAD(a)),370+90*SIN(RAD(a))
31480 MOVE 930+130*COS(RAD(a)),370+130*SIN(RAD(a))
31490 PLOT85,930+90*COS(RAD(a-10)),370+90*SIN(RAD(a-10))
31500 PLOT85,930+130*COS(RAD(a-10)),370+130*SIN(RAD(a-10))
31510 NEXT a
31520 ENDPROC
31600 DEF PROCno
31610 CLS:PRINT:PRINT"Constructing responses in BASIC, please wait."
31615 REM N
31620 MOVE 200,30:MOVE 250,30
31630 PLOT85,200,500
31640 PLOT85,250,500
31650 PLOT85,450,30
31660 PLOT85,500,30
31670 PLOT85,450,500
31680 PLOT85,500,500
31700 REM O
31710 FOR a=0 TO 360 STEP 10
31720 MOVE 770+110*COS(RAD(a)),265+195*SIN(RAD(a))
31730 MOVE 770+150*COS(RAD(a)),265+235*SIN(RAD(a))
31740 PLOT85,770+110*COS(RAD(a+10)),265+195*SIN(RAD(a+10))
31750 PLOT85,770+150*COS(RAD(a+10)),265+235*SIN(RAD(a+10))
31760 NEXT a
31770 ENDPROC
```

DISASSEMBLER - PROGRAM 37

```
LIST
 100 MODE7
 110 DIM O$(255)
 120 DIM N(255)
 130 DIM M(255)
 140 DIM bit(3)
 200 FOR I=0 TO 255
 210 READ O$(I)
 220 READ N(I)
 230 READ M(I)
 240 NEXT I
 250 DATA BRK,1,1,ORA,2,9,???,1,1,???,1,1
 260 DATA ???,1,1,ORA,2,3,ASL,2,3,???,1,1
 270 DATA PHP,1,1,ORA,2,2,ASL,1,12,???,1,1
 280 DATA ???,1,1,ORA,3,4,ASL,3,4,???,1,1
 290 DATA BPL,2,13,ORA,2,10,???,1,1,???,1,1
 300 DATA ???,1,1,ORA,2,5,ASL,2,5,???,1,1
 310 DATA CLC,1,1,ORA,3,8,???,1,1,???,1,1
 320 DATA ???,1,1,ORA,3,6,ASL,3,6,???,1,1
 340 DATA JSR,3,4,AND,2,9,???,1,1,???,1,1
 350 DATA BIT,2,3,AND,2,3,ROL,2,3,???,1,1
 360 DATA PLP,1,1,AND,2,2,ROL,1,12,???,1,1
 370 DATA BIT,3,4,AND,3,4,ROL,3,4,???,1,1
 380 DATA BMI,2,13,AND,2,10,???,1,1,???,1,1
 390  DATA ???,1,1,AND,2,5,ROL,2,5,???,1,1
 400 DATA SEC,1,1,AND,3,8,???,1,1,???,1,1
 410 DATA ???,1,1,AND,3,6,ROL,3,6,???,1,1
 420 DATA RTI,1,1,EOR,2,9,???,1,1,???,1,1
 430 DATA ???,1,1,EOR,2,3,LSR,2,3,???,1,1
 440 DATA PHA,1,1,EOR,2,2,LSR,1,12,???,1,1
 450 DATA JMP,3,4,EOR,3,4,LSR,3,4,???,1,1
 460 DATA BVC,2,13,EOR,2,10,???,1,1,???,1,1
 470 DATA ???,1,1,EOR,2,5,LSR,2,5,???,1,1
 480 DATA CLI,1,1,EOR,3,8,???,1,1,???,1,1
 490 DATA ???,1,1,EOR,3,6,LSR,3,6,???,1,1
 500 DATA RTS,1,1,ADC,2,9,???,1,1,???,1,1
 510 DATA ???,1,1,ADC,2,3,ROR,2,3,???,1,1
 520 DATA PLA,1,1,ADC,2,2,ROR,1,12,???,1,1
 530 DATA JMP,3,11,ADC,3,4,ROR,3,4,???,1,1
 540 DATA BVS,2,13,ADC,2,10,???,1,1,???,1,1
 550 DATA ???,1,1,ADC,2,5,ROR,2,5,???,1,1
 560 DATA SEI,1,1,ADC,3,8,???,1,1,???,1,1
 570 DATA ???,1,1,ADC,3,6,ROR,3,6,???,1,1
 580 DATA ???,1,1,STA,2,9,???,1,1,???,1,1
 590 DATA STY,2,3,STA,2,3,STX,2,3,???,1,1
 600 DATA DEY,1,1,???,1,1,TXA,1,1,???,1,1
 610 DATA STY,3,4,STA,3,4,STX,3,4,???,1,1
 620 DATA BCC,2,13,STA,2,10,???,1,1,???,1,1
 630 DATA STY,2,5,STA,2,5,STX,2,7,???,1,1
 640 DATA TYA,1,1,STA,3,8,TXS,1,1,???,1,1
 650 DATA ???,1,1,STA,3,6,???,1,1,???,1,1
 660 DATA LDY,2,2,LDA,2,9,LDX,2,2,???,1,1
 670 DATA LDY,2,3,LDA,2,3,LDX,2,3,???,1,1
 680 DATA TAY,1,1,LDA,2,2,TAX,1,1,???,1,1
 690 DATA LDY,3,4,LDA,3,4,LDX,3,4,???,1,1
 700 DATA BCS,2,13,LDA,2,10,???,1,1,???,1,1
 710 DATA LDY,2,5,LDA,2,5,LDX,2,5,???,1,1
 720 DATA CLV,1,1,LDA,3,8,TSX,1,1,???,1,1
```

```
 730 DATA LDY,3,6,LDA,3,6,LDX,3,8,???,1,1
 740 DATA CPY,2,2,CMP,2,9,???,1,1,???,1,1
 750 DATA CPY,2,3,CMP,2,3,DEC,2,3,???,1,1
 760 DATA INY,1,1,CMP,2,2,DEX,1,1,???,1,1
 770 DATA CPY,3,4,CMP,3,4,DEC,3,4,???,1,1
 780 DATA BNE,2,13,CMP,2,10,???,1,1,???,1,1
 790 DATA ???,1,1,CMP,2,5,DEC,2,5,???,1,1
 800 DATA CLD,1,1,CMP,3,8,???,1,1,???,1,1
 810 DATA ???,1,1,CMP,3,6,DEC,3,6,???,1,1
 820 DATA CPX,2,2,SBC,2,9,???,1,1,???,1,1
 830 DATA CPX,2,3,SBC,2,3,INC,2,3,???,1,1
 840 DATA INX,1,1,SBC,2,2,NOP,1,1,???,1,1
 850 DATA CPX,3,4,SBC,3,4,INC,3,4,???,1,1
 860  DATA BEQ,2,13,SBC,2,10,???,1,1,???,1,1
 870 DATA ???,1,1,SBC,2,5,INC,2,5,???,1,1
 880 DATA SED,1,1,SBC,3,8,???,1,1,???,1,1
 890 DATA ???,1,1,SBC,3,6,INC,3,6,???,1,1
 900
 910
1000 CLS
1010PRINT TAB(5,1) "DISASSEMBLER"
1020 PRINT TAB(0,3) "Enter the starting address."
1030 PRINT TAB(0,5) "If this is in hexadecimal, your number"
1035 PRINT TAB(0,7) "must be in the range 0 to FFFF"
1036 PRINT TAB(0,9) "and should begin with &"
1040 PRINT TAB(0,11)"Enter a decimal address directly."
1050 line=1
1060 PRINT TAB(1,14);:INPUT A$
1070 IF LEFT$(A$,1)="&" THEN PROChex ELSE address=VAL(A$)
1080 REM ADDRESS IS IN VARIABLE address
1200
3000 REM CHECK ADDRESS IN RANGE
3050 IF address<0 OR address>65535 THEN PRINT TAB(10,19) "OUT OF RANGE: TRY
AGAIN.":GOTO 1010
3060 IF address<>INT(address) THEN PRINT TAB(10,19) "WHOLE NUMBERS ONLY:
TRY AGAIN.":GOTO 1010
3070 REM LIST ASSEMBLY CODE
3080 CLS:PRINT
3090 FOR J=1 TO 20
3100 opcode=?(address)
3110 operation$=O$(opcode)
3120 numofbytes=N(opcode)
3130 type=M(opcode)
3210 ON type GOSUB 4010,4020,4030,4040,4050,4060,4070,4080,4090,4100,4110,
4120,4130
3400 code3$="": IF numofbytes>2 THEN PROCdechex(?(address+2)):code3$=hexval$
3410 code2$="": IF numofbytes>1 THEN PROCdechex(?(address+1)):code2$=hexval$
3420 PROCdechex(?(address)):code1$=hexval$
3510 PROCdechex(address)
3520 PRINT "&"+hexval$,code1$;" ";code2$;" ";code3$,operation$;" ";operand$
3570 address=address+numofbytes
3600
3800 NEXT J
3810 PRINT TAB(0,22);"Press SPACE for more, A for new address";
3820 X$=GET$
3830 IF X$=" " THEN 3070
3840 IF X$="A" THEN 1000
3850 GOTO 3820
4000 REM DETERMINE TYPE OF OPERATION
4010 REM SINGLE BYTE INSTRUCTION
```

```
 4011 operand$=""
 4012 RETURN
 4020 REM IMMEDIATE DATA
 4021 operand$="#"+STR$(?(address+1))
 4022 RETURN
 4030 REM ZERO PAGE ADDRESS
 4031 PROCdechex(?(address+1))
 4032 operand$="&"+hexval$
 4033 RETURN
 4040 REM ABSOLUTE ADDRESS
 4041 PROCdechex(?(address+1)+256*?(address+2))
 4042 operand$="&"+hexval$
 4043 RETURN
 4050 REM ZERO PAGE, X-INDEXED
 4051 PROCdechex(?(address+1))
 4052 operand$="&"+hexval$+",X"
 4053 RETURN
 4060 REM ABSOLUTE, X-INDEXED
 4061 PROCdechex(?(address+1)+256*?(address+2))
 4062 operand$="&"+hexval$+",X"
 4063 RETURN
 4070 REM ZERO PAGE, Y-INDEXED
 4071 PROCdechex(?(address+1))
 4072 operand$="&"+hexval$+",Y"
 4073 RETURN
 4080 REM ABSOLUTE, Y-INDEXED
 4081 PROCdechex(?(address+1)+256*?(address+2))
 4082 operand$="&"+hexval$+",Y"
 4083 RETURN
 4090 REM INDIRECT, X-INDEXED
 4091 PROCdechex(?(address+1))
 4092 operand$="(&"+hexval$+",X)"
 4093 RETURN
 4100 REM INDIRECT, Y-INDEXED
 4101 PROCdechex(?(address+1))
 4102 operand$="(&"+hexval$+"),Y"
 4103 RETURN
 4110 REM INDIRECT
 4111 PROCdechex(?(address+1)+256*?(address+2))
 4112 operand$="(&"+hexval$+")"
 4113 RETURN
 4120 REM ACCUMULATOR
 4121 operand$="A"
 4122 RETURN
 4130 REM BRANCH OFFSET
 4131 offset=?(address+1)
 4132 IF offset>127 THEN offset=offset-256
 4133 branchaddress=address+2+offset
 4134 PROCdechex(branchaddress)
 4135 operand$="&"+hexval$
 4136 RETURN
 5000 DEF PROCprinthex
 5010 PRINT TAB(0,20) "The hex. equivalent of this is  &";hexval$
 5020 ENDPROC
 9000 DEF PROChex
 9010 A$=RIGHT$(A$,(LEN(A$)-1))
 9030 PROChexdec(A$)
 9040 address=decval
 9050 ENDPROC
10000 DEF PROCdechex(add)
```

```
10005 REM PROCEDURE RETURNS WITH HEXADECIMAL VALUE IN hexval$
10010 bit(3)=INT(add/4096)
10020 add=add-bit(3)*4096
10030 bit(2)=INT(add/256)
10040 add=add-bit(2)*256
10050 bit(1)=INT(add/16)
10060 bit(0)=add-bit(1)*16
10070 add$=""
10075 IF bit(2)=0 AND bit(3)=0 THEN nibs=1 ELSE nibs=3
10080 FOR I= nibs TO 0 STEP -1
10090 IF bit(I)>9 THEN hex$=CHR$(55+bit(I)) ELSE hex$=STR$(bit(I))
10100 add$=add$ + hex$
10110 NEXT I
10120 hexval$=add$
10130 ENDPROC
11000 DEF PROChexdec(address$)
11005 REM PROCEDURE RETURNS WITH DECIMAL VALUE IN decval
11010 add$=RIGHT$("0000"+address$,4)
11020 decval=0
11030 FOR I=1 TO 4
11040 A$=MID$(add$,I,1)
11050 IF A$>="A" AND A$<="F" THEN bitval =ASC(A$)-55
11060 IF A$>="0" AND A$<="9" THEN bitval=VAL(A$)
11070 decval=decval*16+bitval
11080 NEXT I
11090 ENDPROC
```

Index